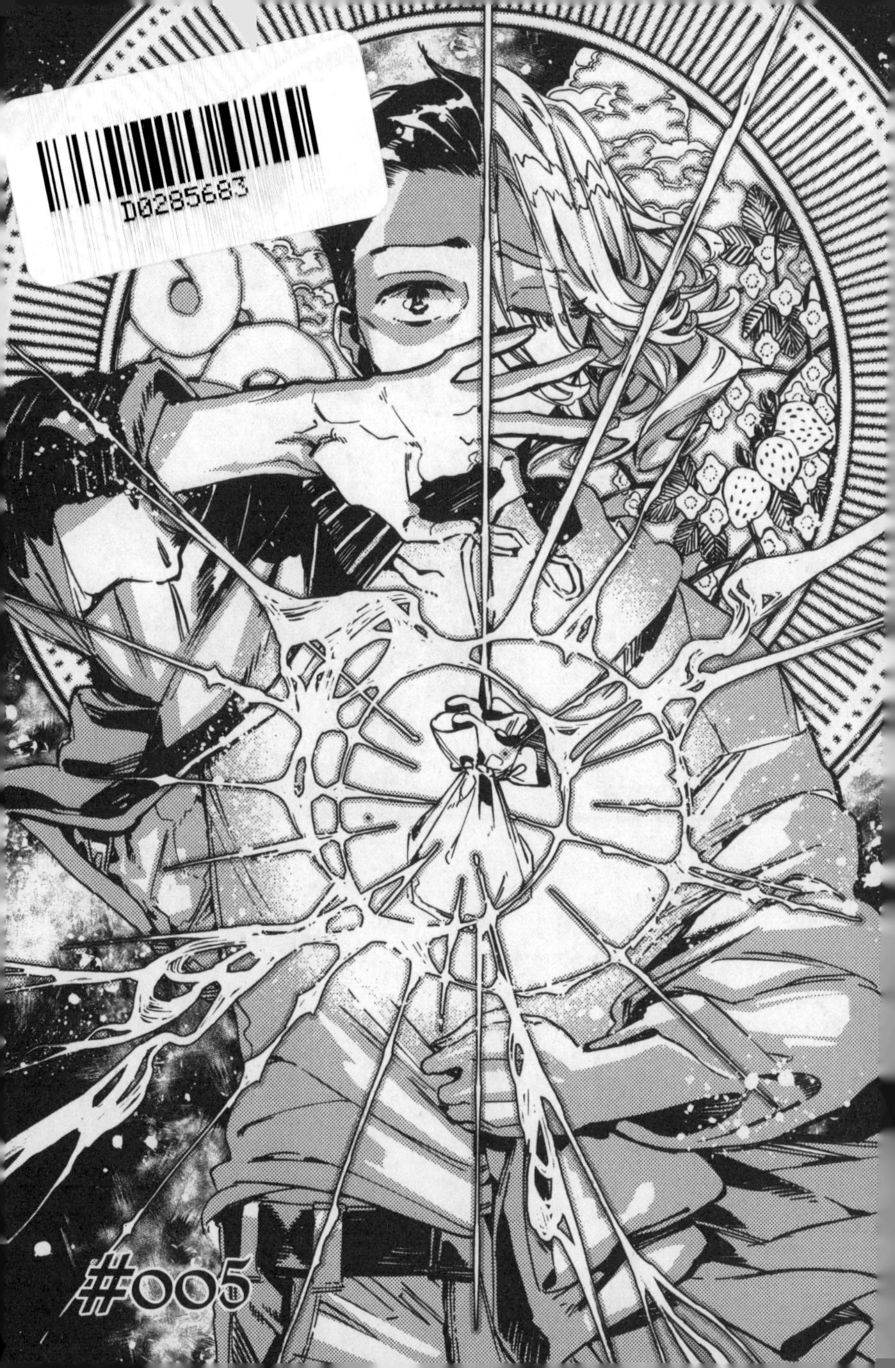
#005

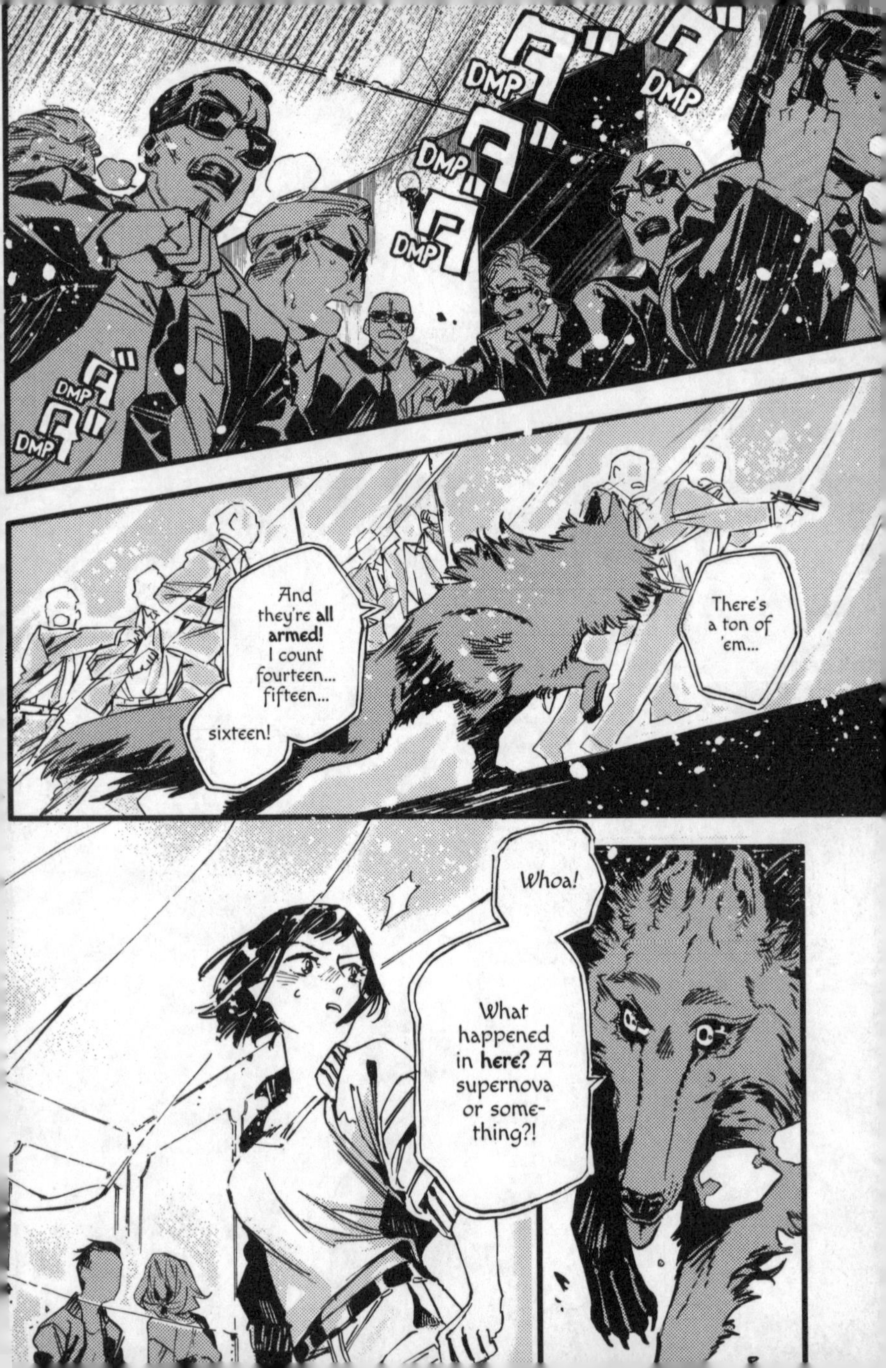
DMP
DMP
DMP
DMP
DMP
DMP
There's a ton of 'em...
And they're **all armed!** I count fourteen... fifteen...
sixteen!
Whoa!
What happened in **here?** A supernova or some-thing?!

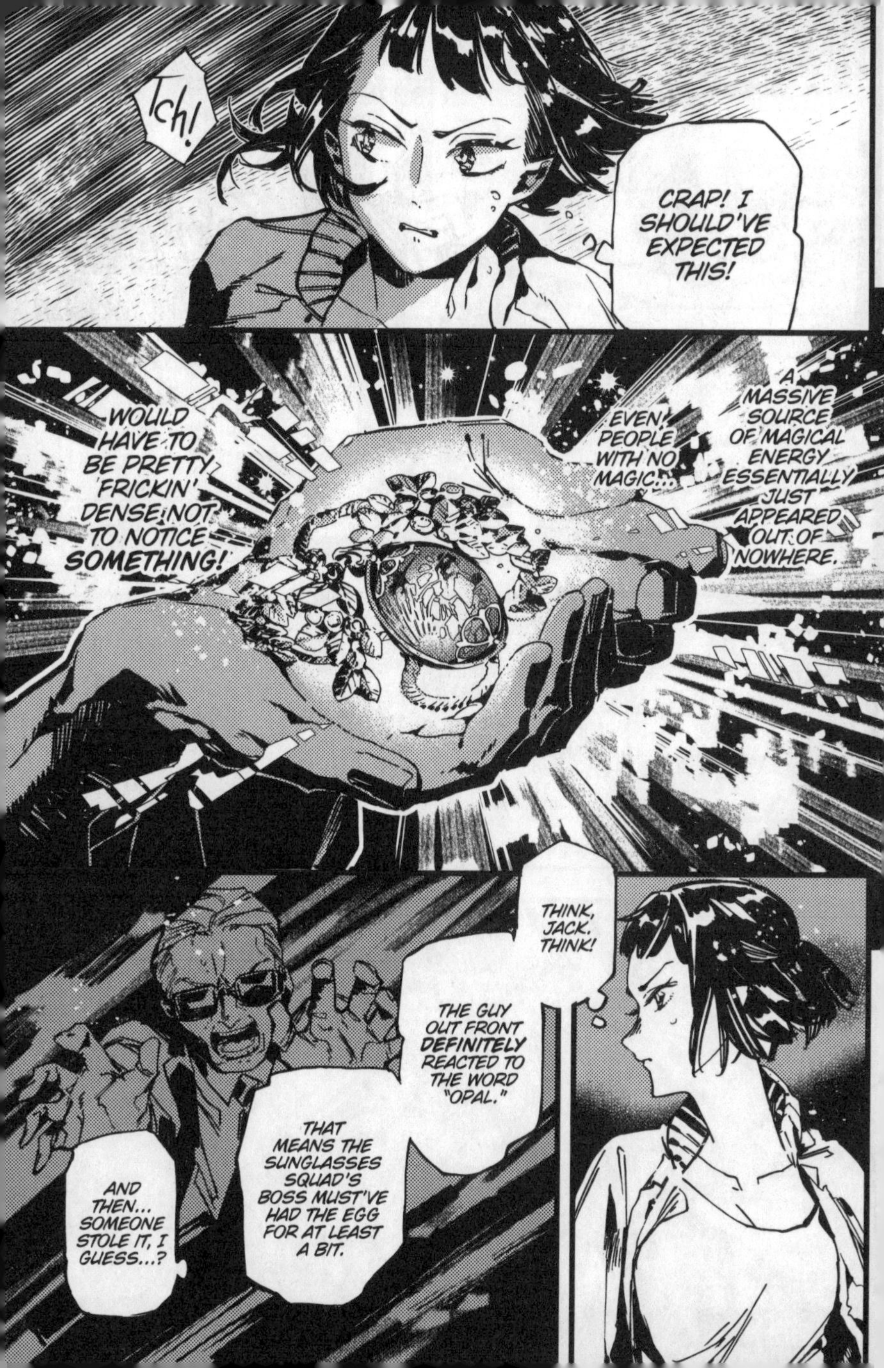
Tch!
CRAP! I SHOULD'VE EXPECTED THIS!
A MASSIVE SOURCE OF MAGICAL ENERGY ESSENTIALLY JUST APPEARED OUT OF NOWHERE.
EVEN PEOPLE WITH NO MAGIC...
WOULD HAVE TO BE PRETTY 'FRICKIN' DENSE NOT TO NOTICE SOMETHING!
THINK, JACK. THINK!
THE GUY OUT FRONT DEFINITELY REACTED TO THE WORD "OPAL."
THAT MEANS THE SUNGLASSES SQUAD'S BOSS MUST'VE HAD THE EGG FOR AT LEAST A BIT.
AND THEN... SOMEONE STOLE IT, I GUESS...?

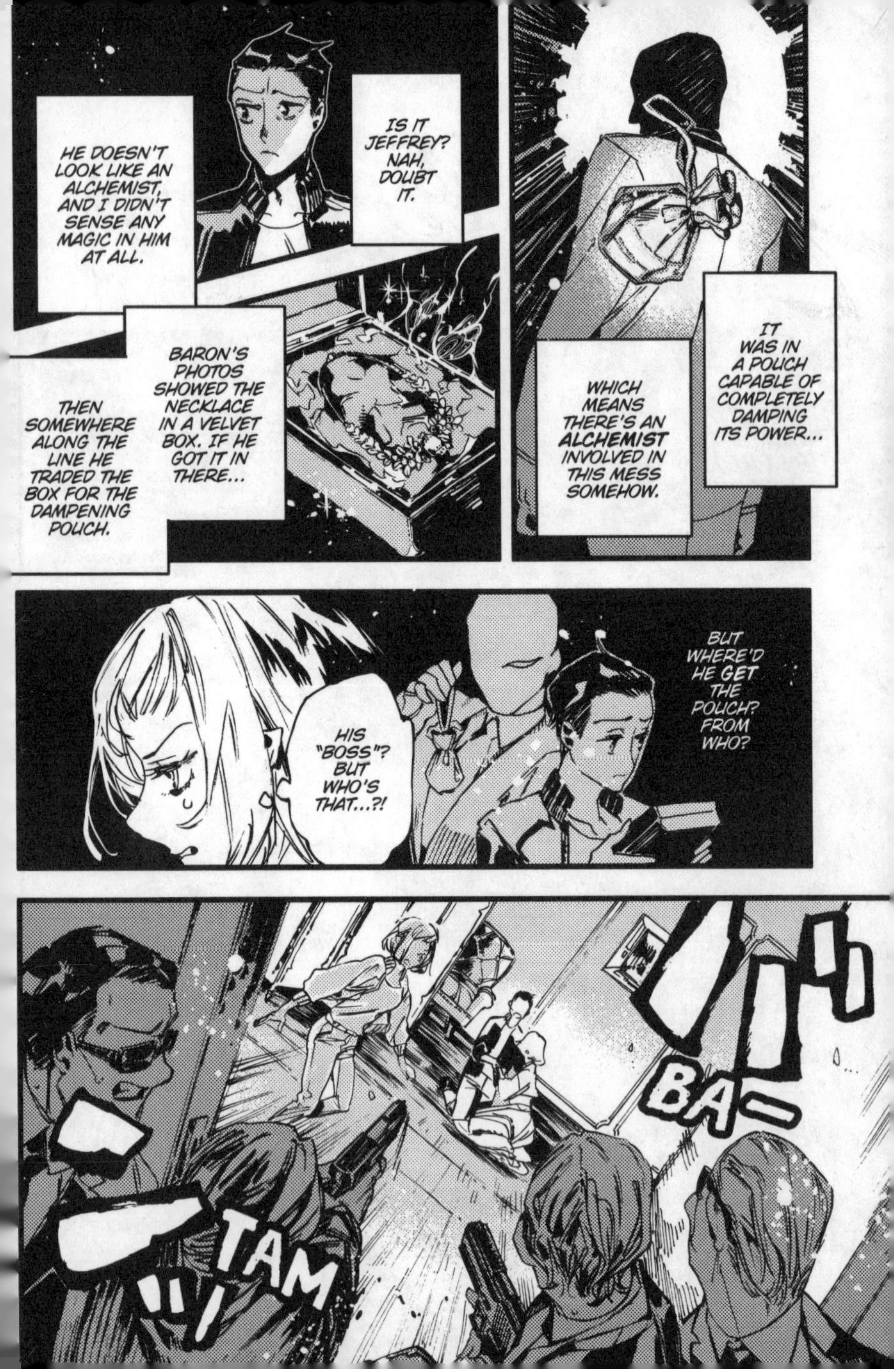
IT WAS IN A POUCH CAPABLE OF COMPLETELY DAMPING ITS POWER...
WHICH MEANS THERE'S AN ALCHEMIST INVOLVED IN THIS MESS SOMEHOW.
IS IT JEFFREY? NAH, DOUBT IT.
HE DOESN'T LOOK LIKE AN ALCHEMIST, AND I DIDN'T SENSE ANY MAGIC IN HIM AT ALL.
BARON'S PHOTOS SHOWED THE NECKLACE IN A VELVET BOX. IF HE GOT IT IN THERE...
THEN SOMEWHERE ALONG THE LINE HE TRADED THE BOX FOR THE DAMPENING POUCH.
BUT WHERE'D HE GET THE POUCH? FROM WHO?
HIS "BOSS"? BUT WHO'S THAT...?!
BA-
TAM !!

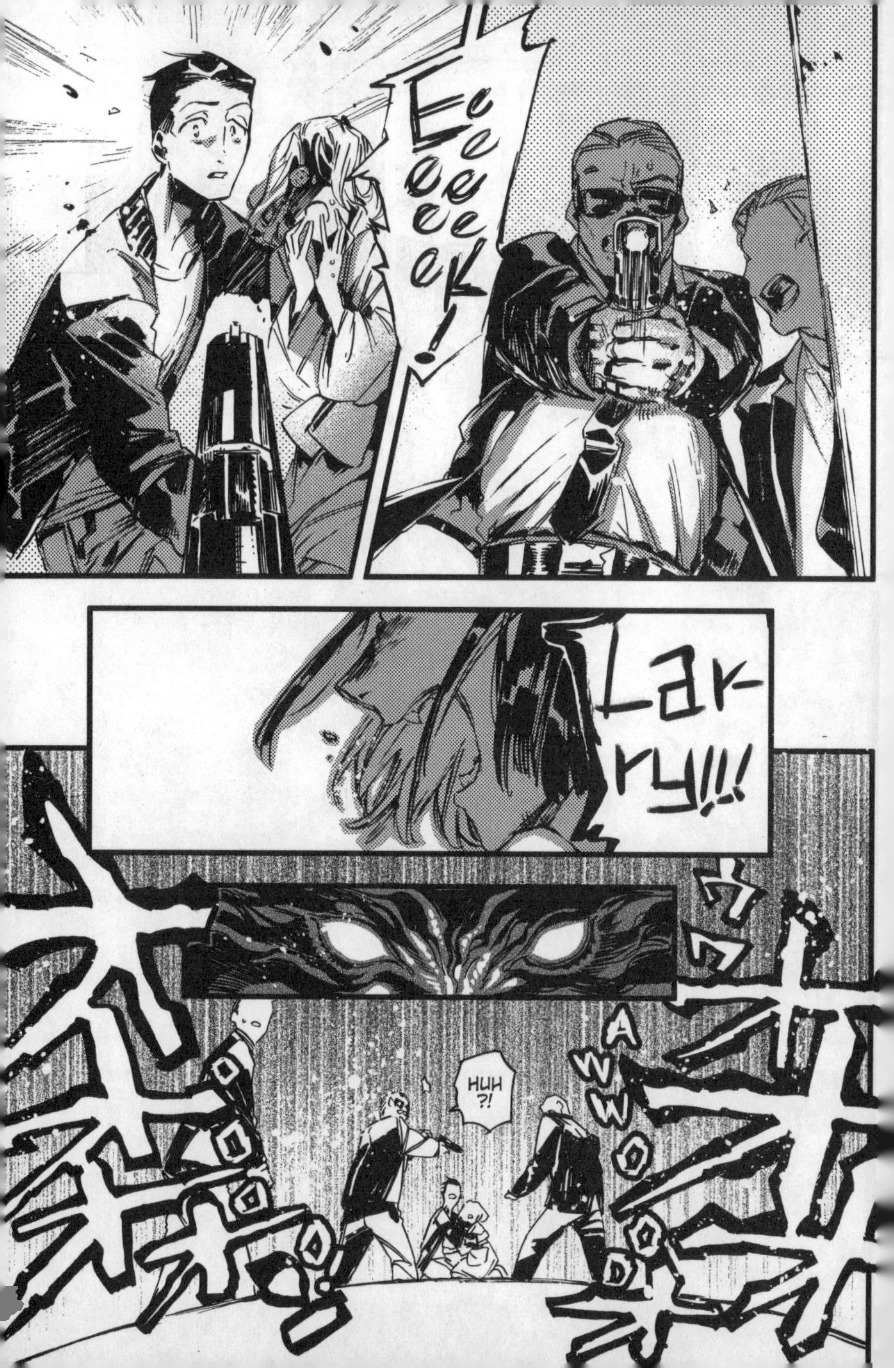
Eeeeeeeek!
Larry!!!
HUH ?!
AWWOOOD

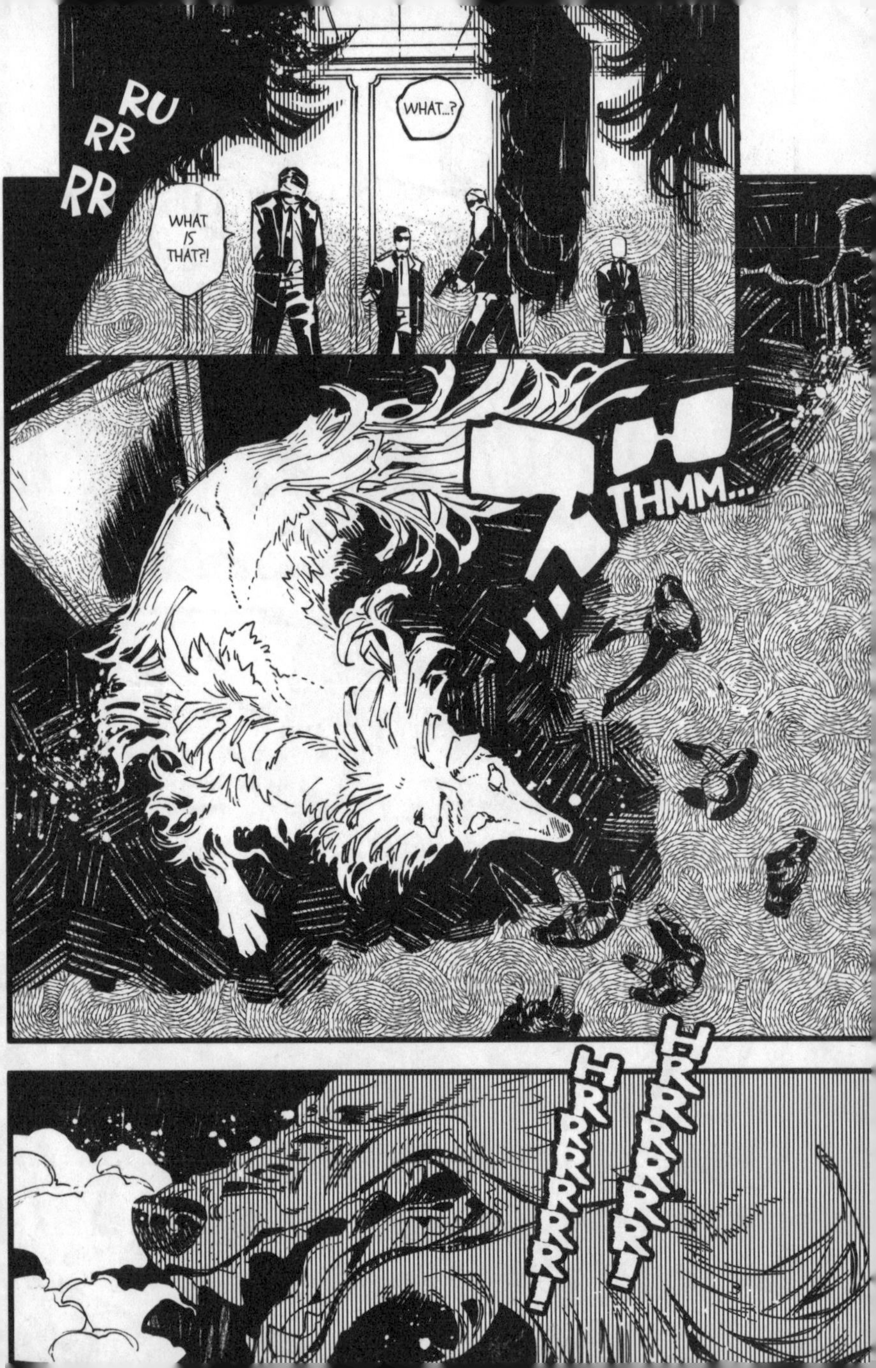
WHAT...?
RU RR RR
WHAT IS THAT?!
THMM...
HRRRRRRI!
HRRRRRRI!

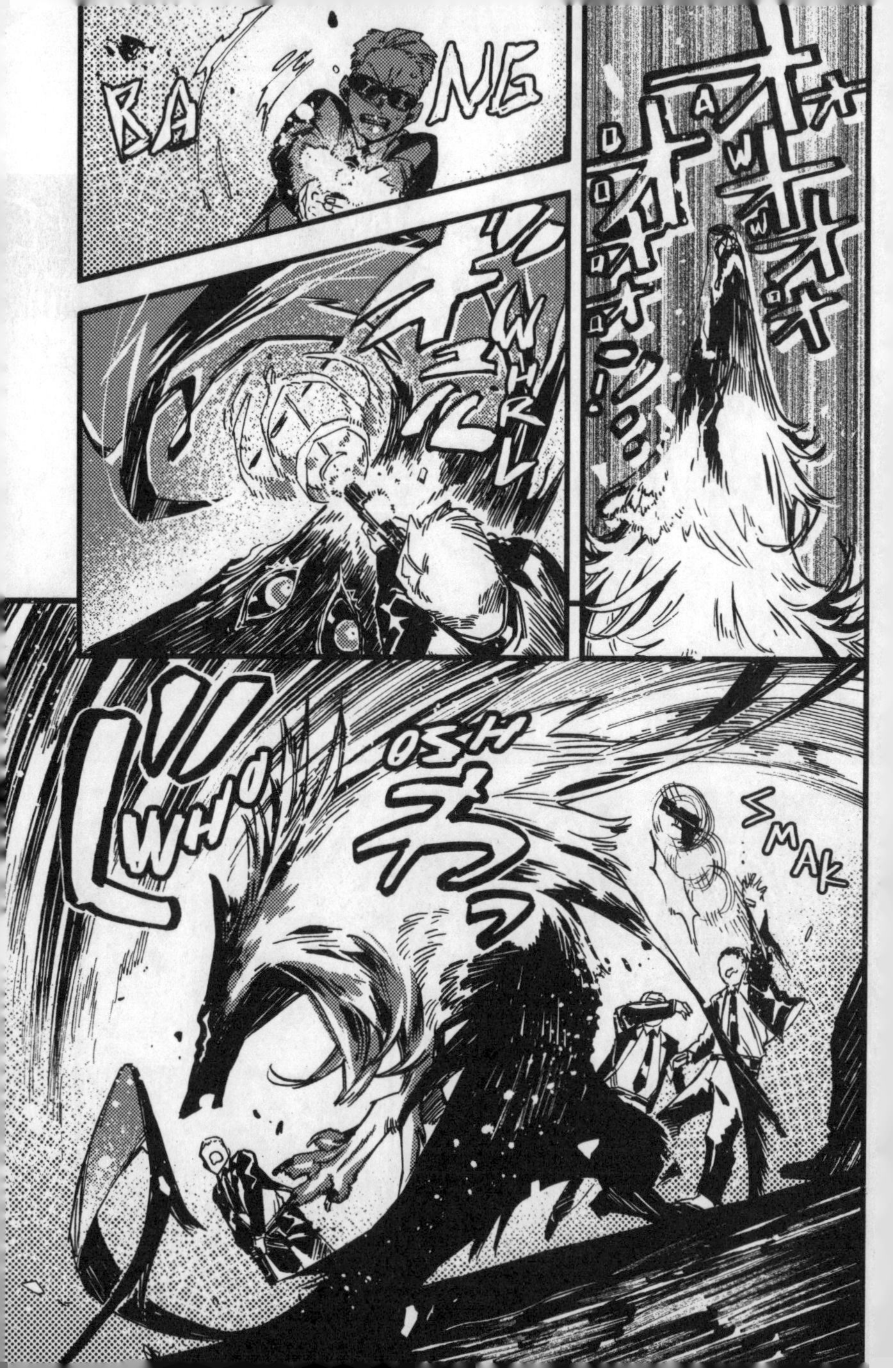
AWWOOOOO
BANG
WHRL
SMAK
WHOOSH

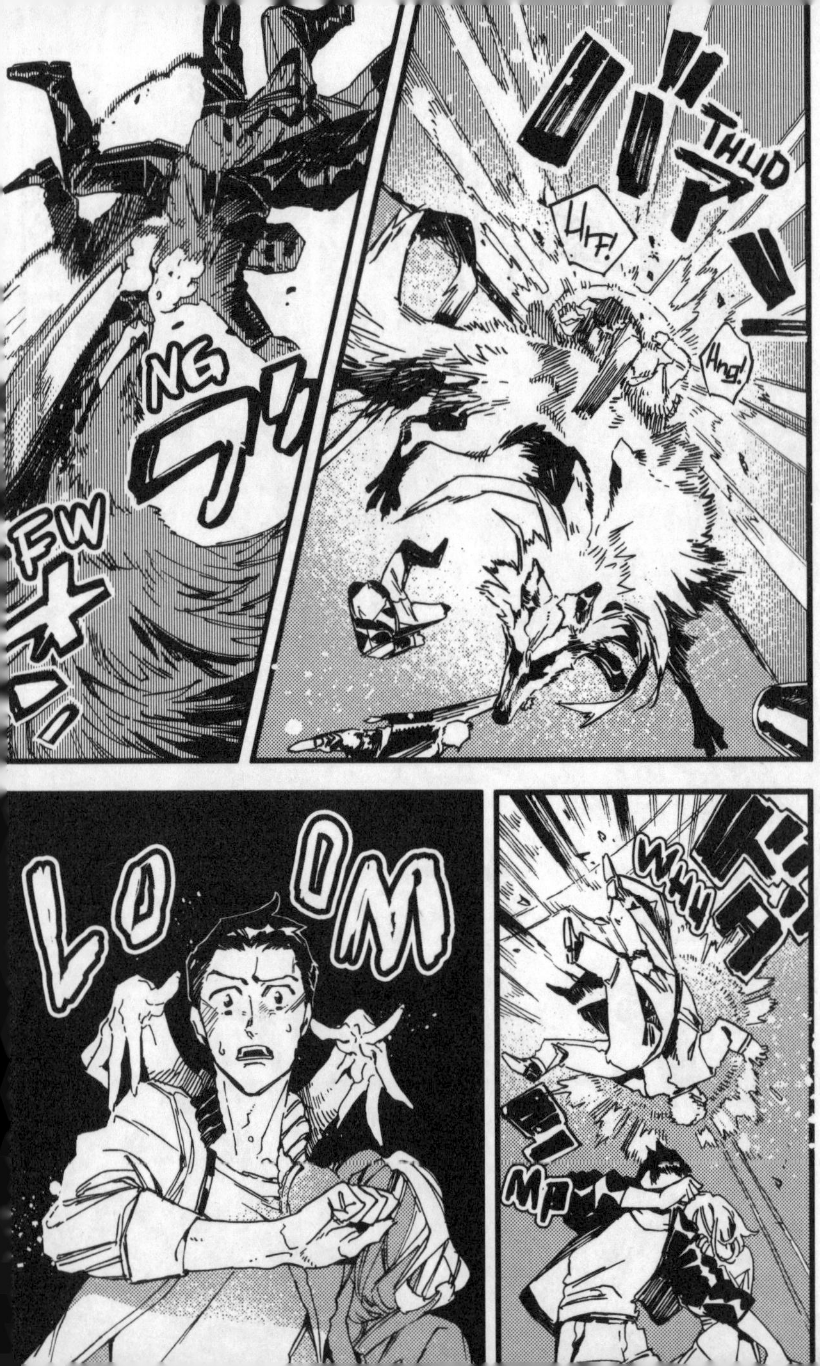
THUD
Urf!
Hng!
NG
FW
Whu
Mp
LOOM

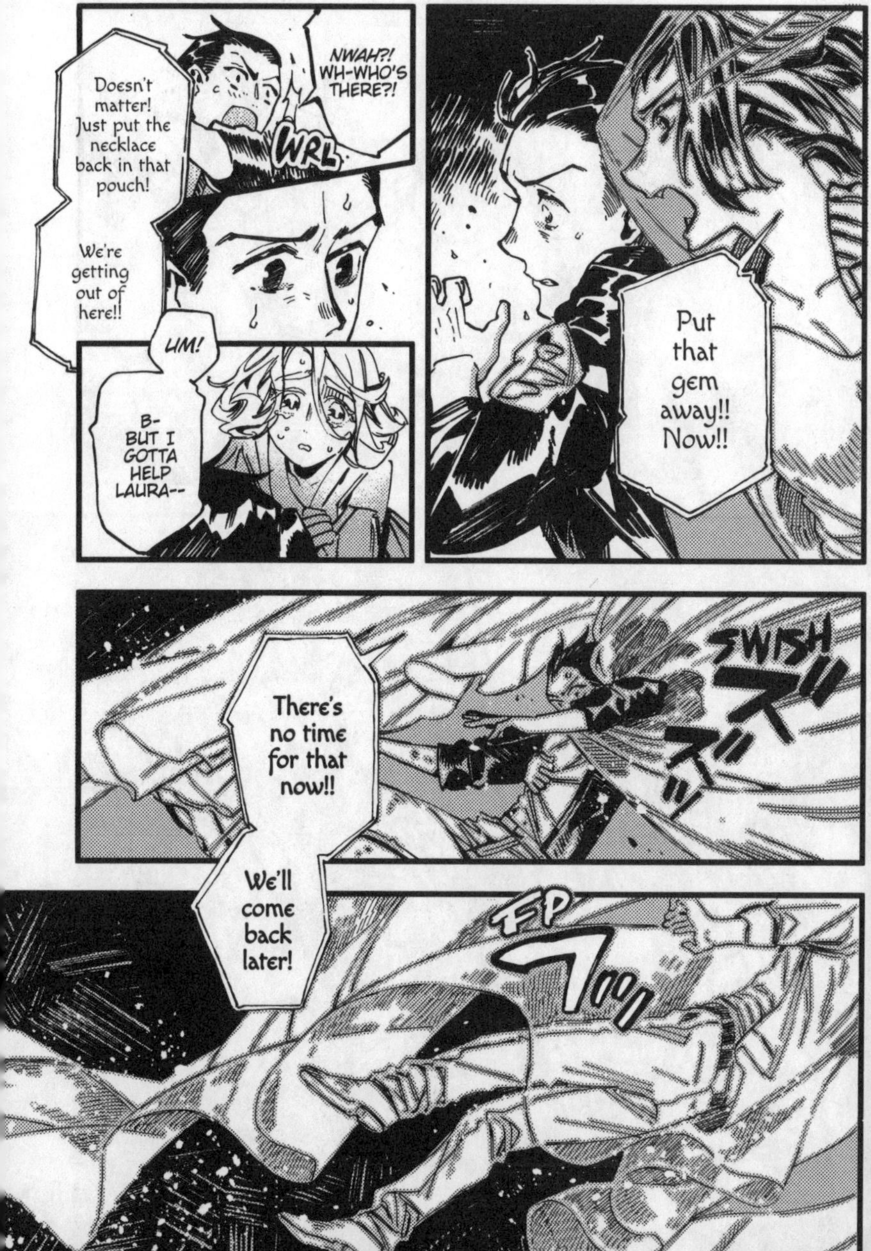

Put that gem away!! Now!!
NWAH?! WH-WHO'S THERE?!
Doesn't matter! Just put the necklace back in that pouch!
WRL
We're getting out of here!!
UM!
B- BUT I GOTTA HELP LAURA--
SWISH
There's no time for that now!!
We'll come back later!
FP

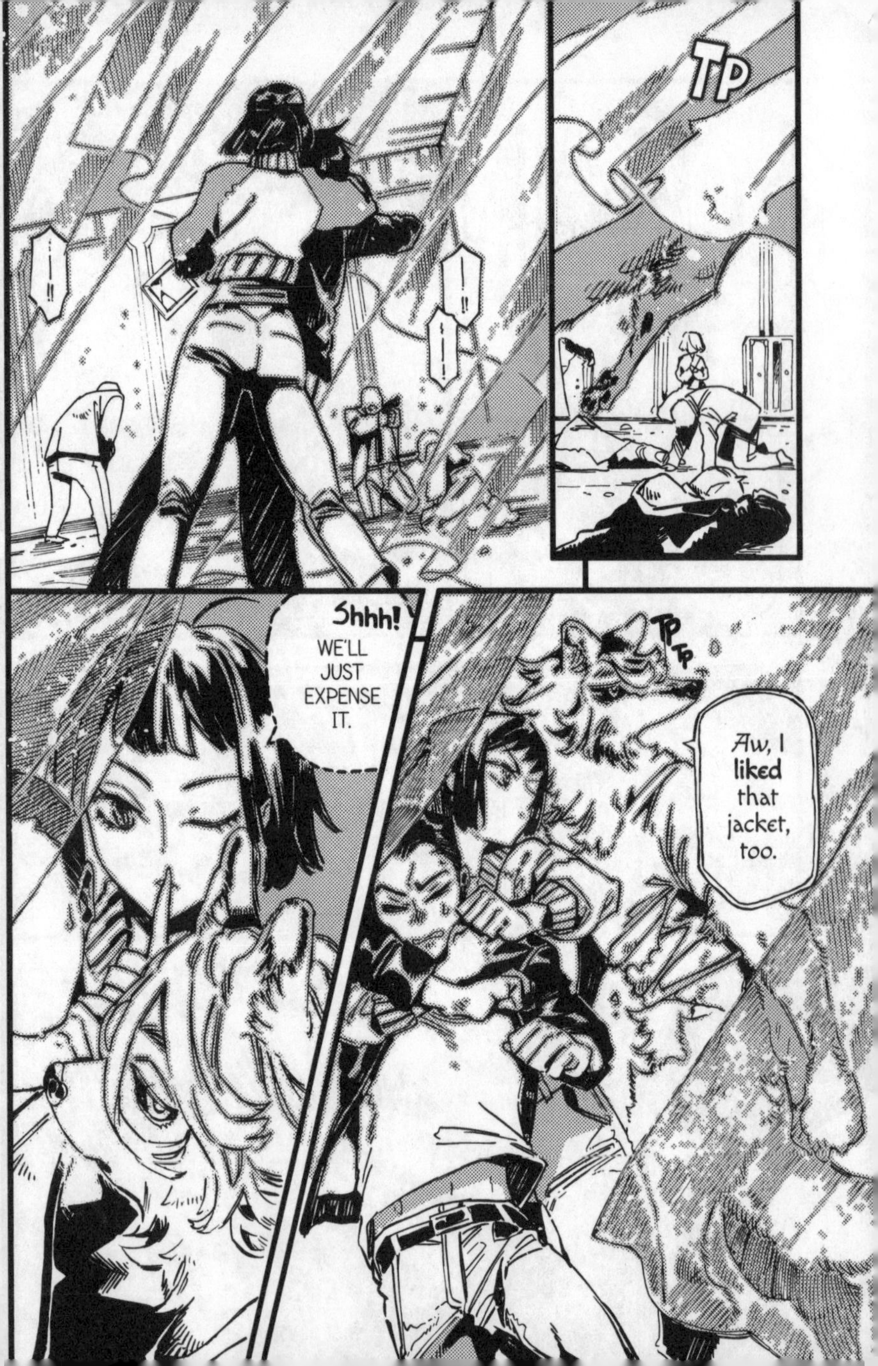
TP
!!
!!
!!
TP TP
Aw, I liked that jacket, too.
Shhh!
WE'LL JUST EXPENSE IT.

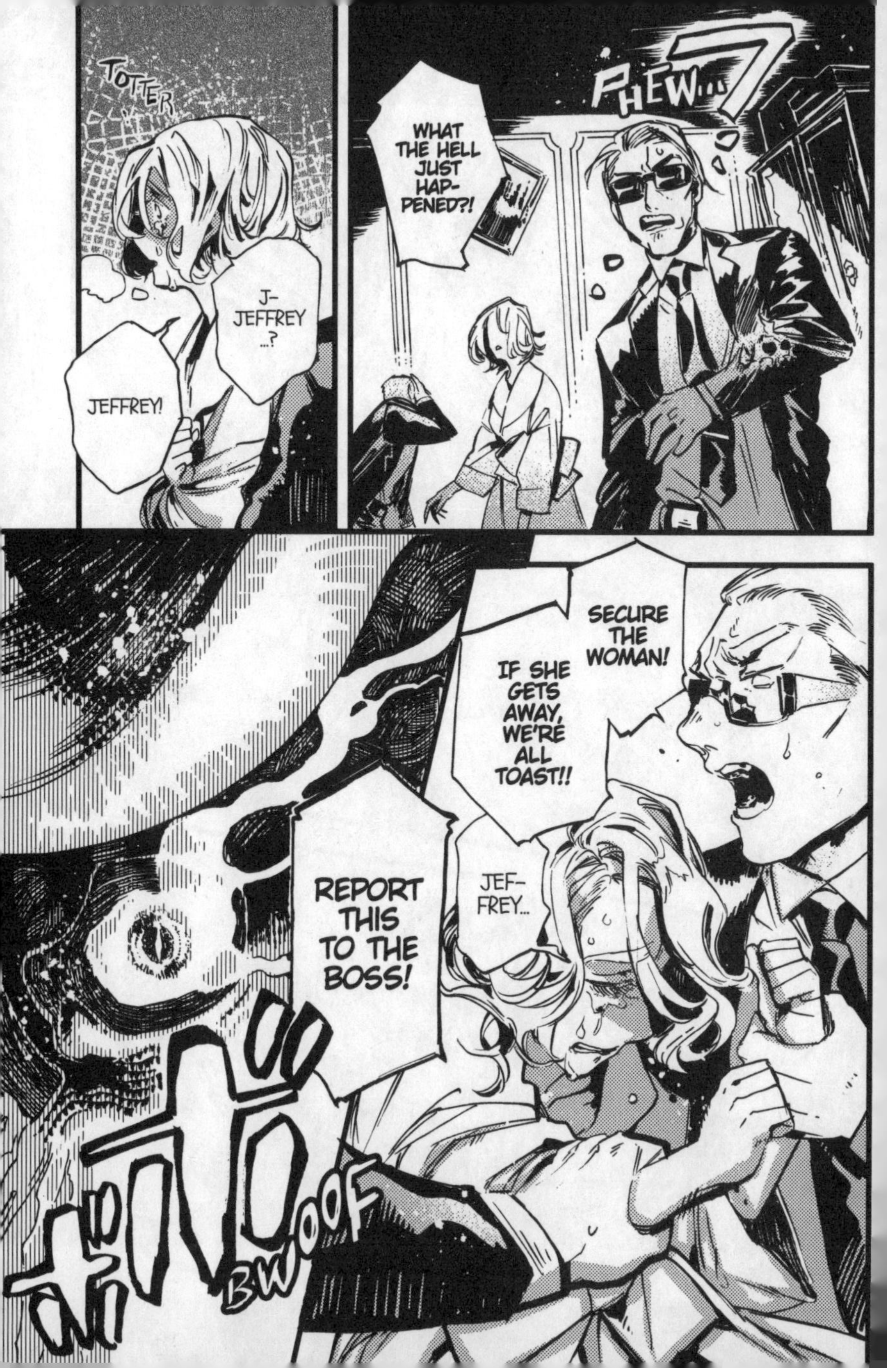
PHEW...
WHAT THE HELL JUST HAP-PENED?!
TOTTER
J-JEFFREY ...?
JEFFREY!
SECURE THE WOMAN!
IF SHE GETS AWAY, WE'RE ALL TOAST!!
JEF-FREY...
REPORT THIS TO THE BOSS!
BWOOF

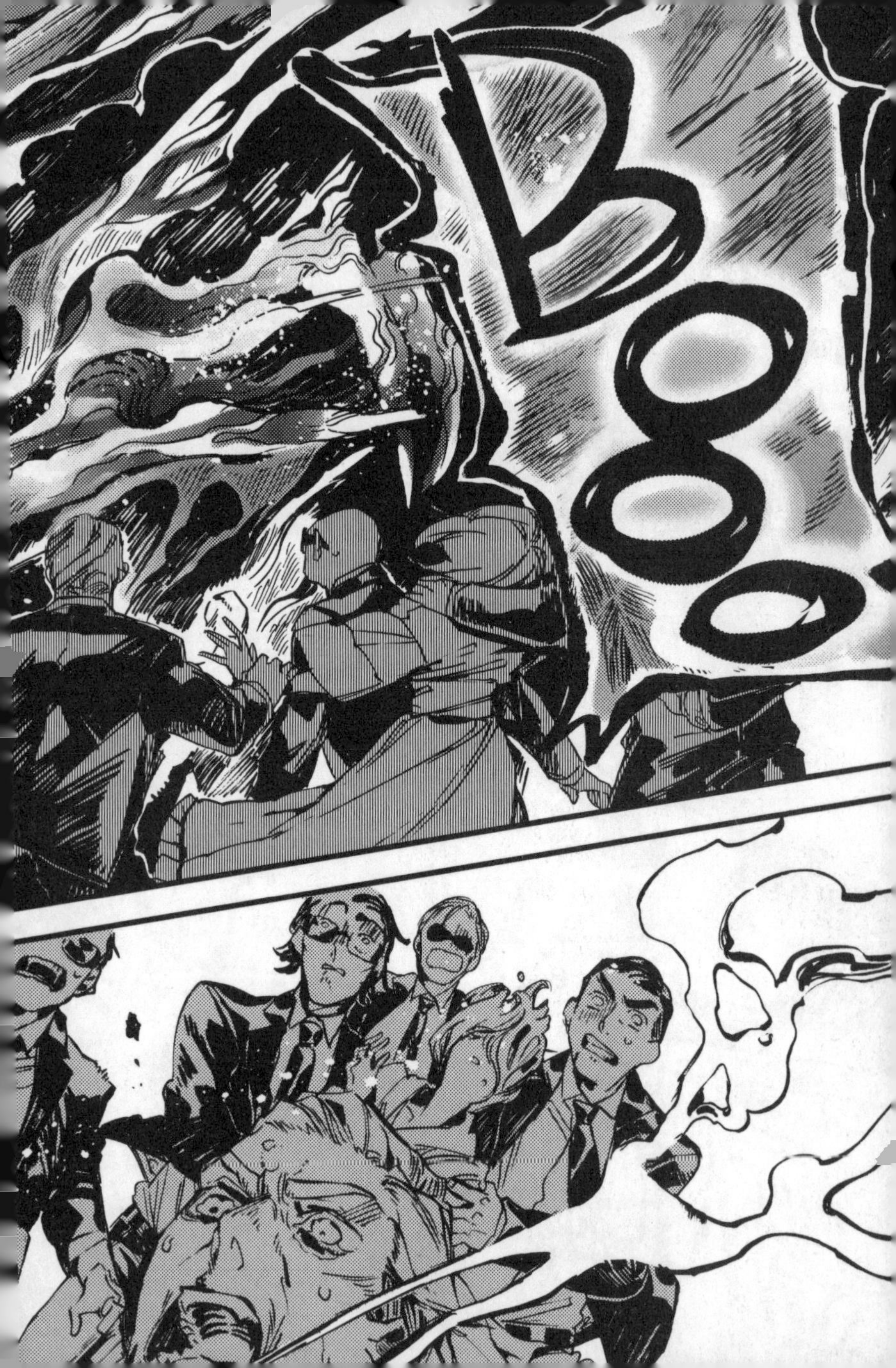
BOOO

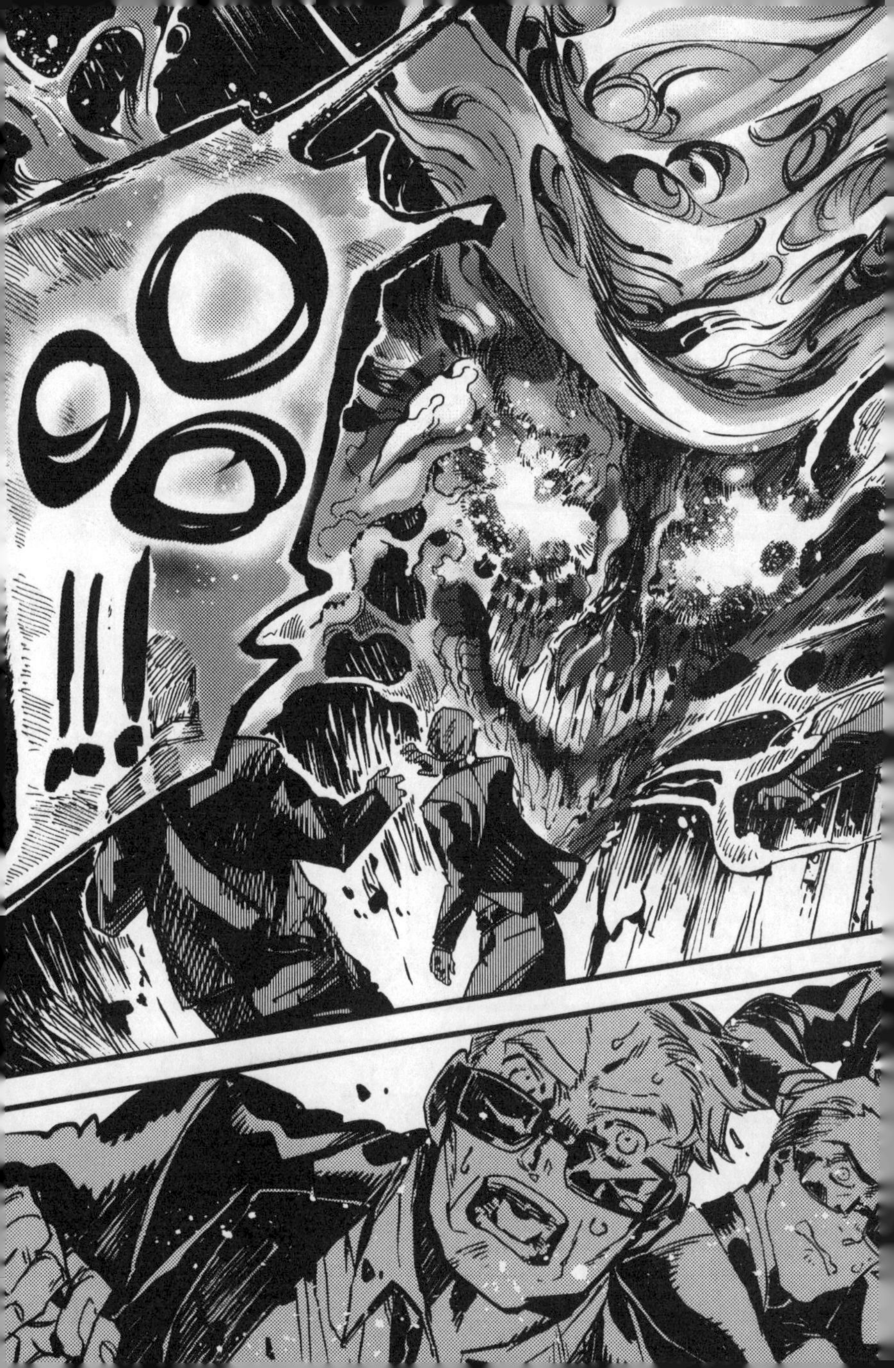
OOO!!!

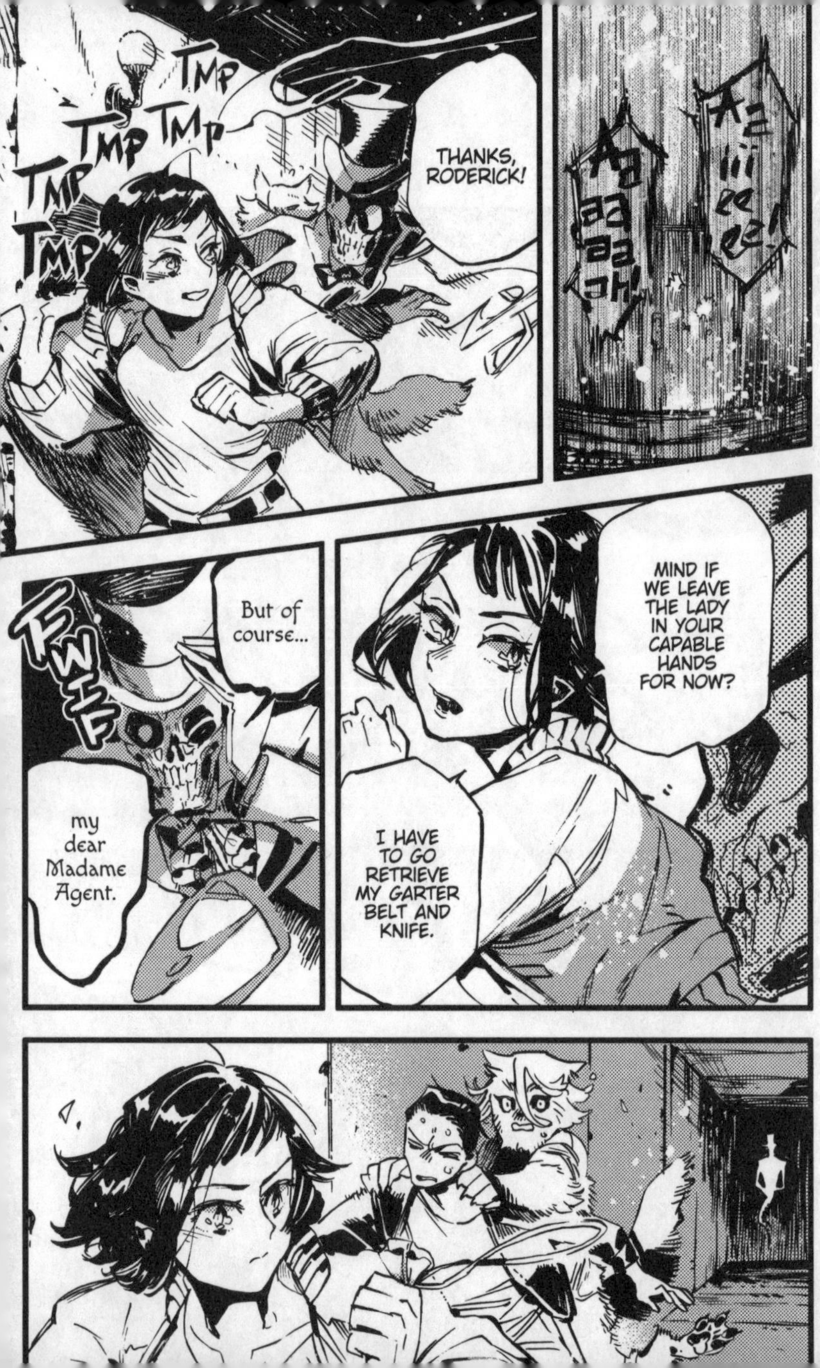
Aziiieeee!
Aaaaaaaah!
TMP TMP TMP TMP TMP TMP
THANKS, RODERICK!
MIND IF WE LEAVE THE LADY IN YOUR CAPABLE HANDS FOR NOW?
I HAVE TO GO RETRIEVE MY GARTER BELT AND KNIFE.
FWIF
But of course...
my dear Madame Agent.

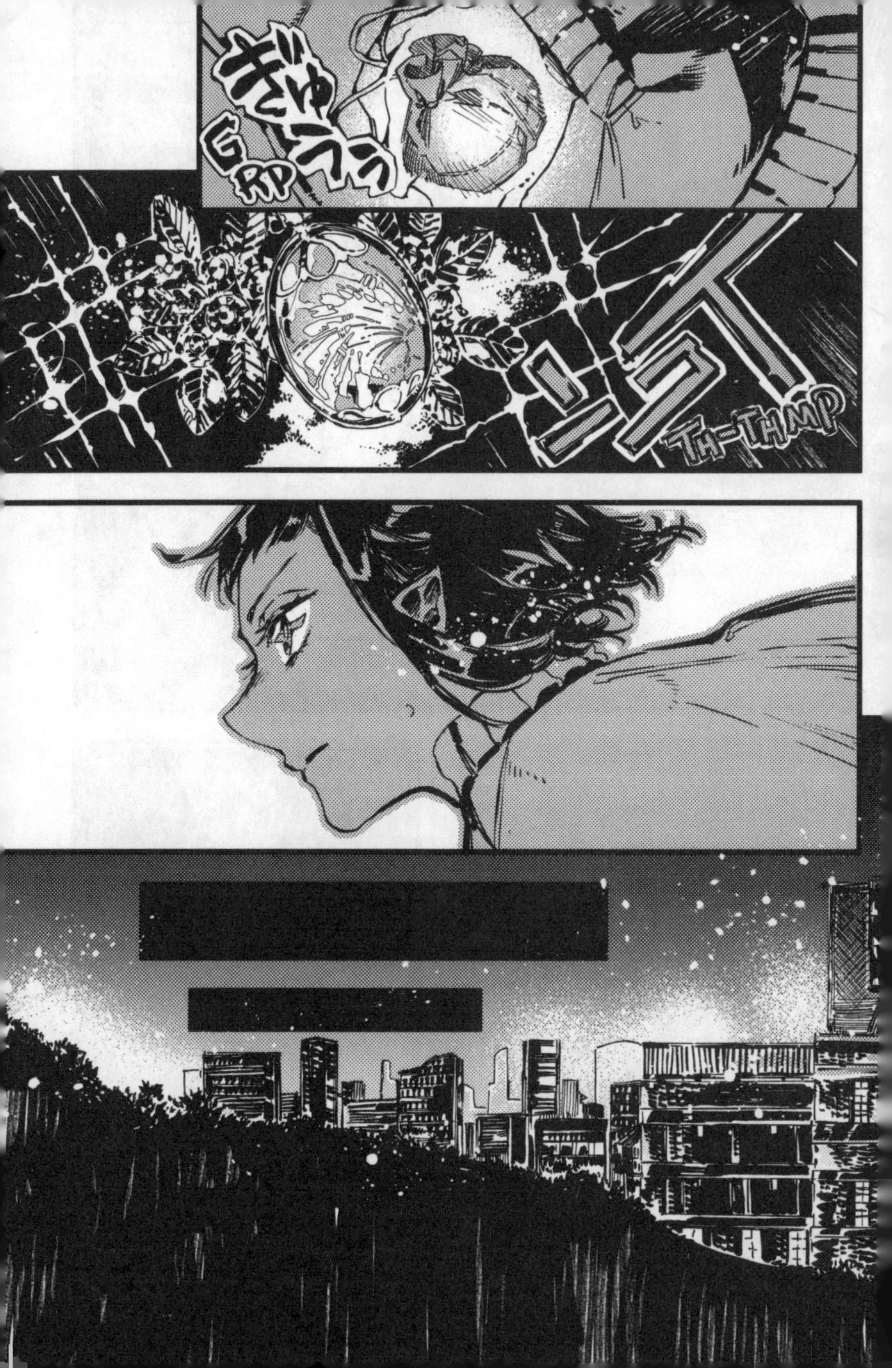
ぎゅうう
GRP
トンッ
TH-THMP
[redacted]
[redacted]

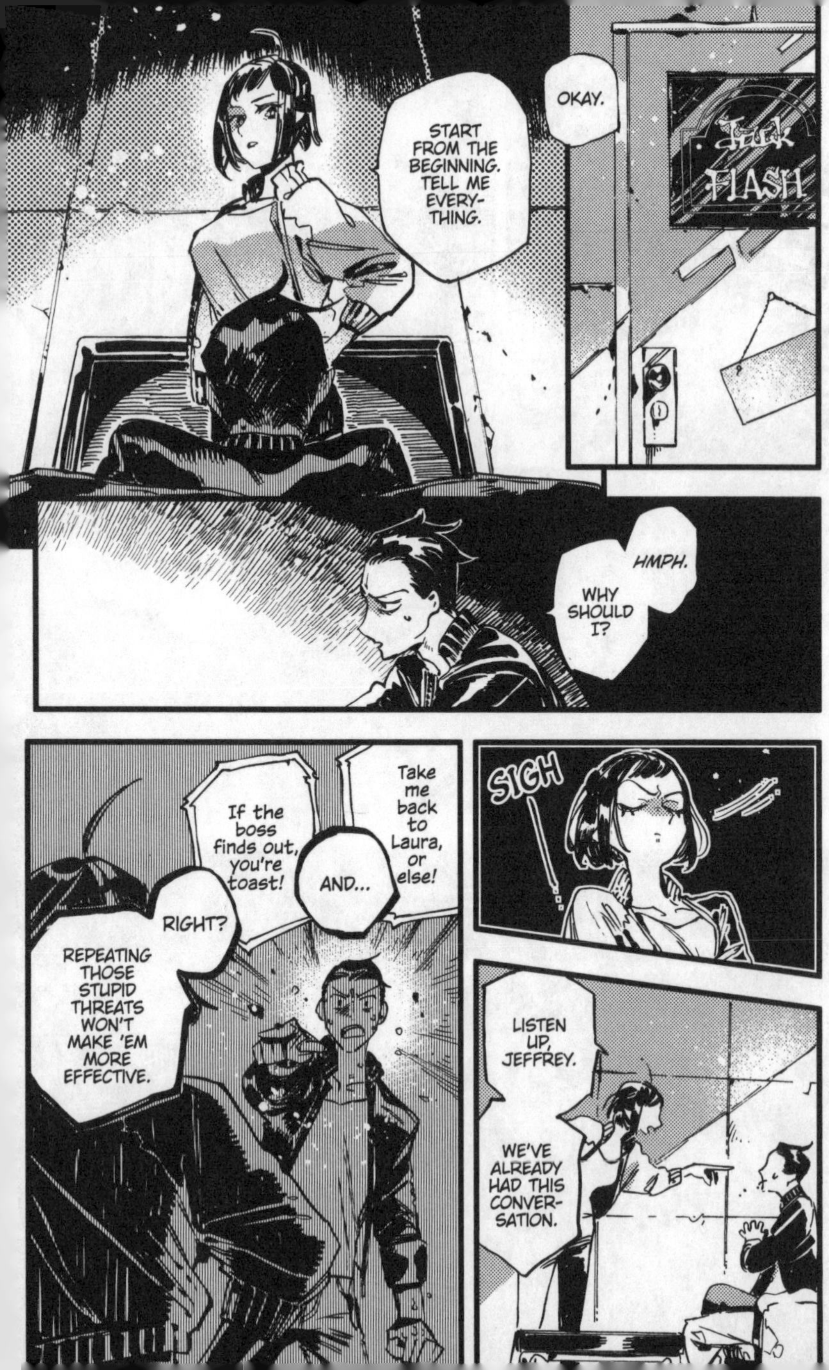
Jack
FLASH
OKAY.
START FROM THE BEGINNING. TELL ME EVERYTHING.
HMPH.
WHY SHOULD I?
SIGH
LISTEN UP, JEFFREY.
WE'VE ALREADY HAD THIS CONVERSATION.
Take me back to Laura, or else!
If the boss finds out, you're toast!
AND...
RIGHT?
REPEATING THOSE STUPID THREATS WON'T MAKE 'EM MORE EFFECTIVE.

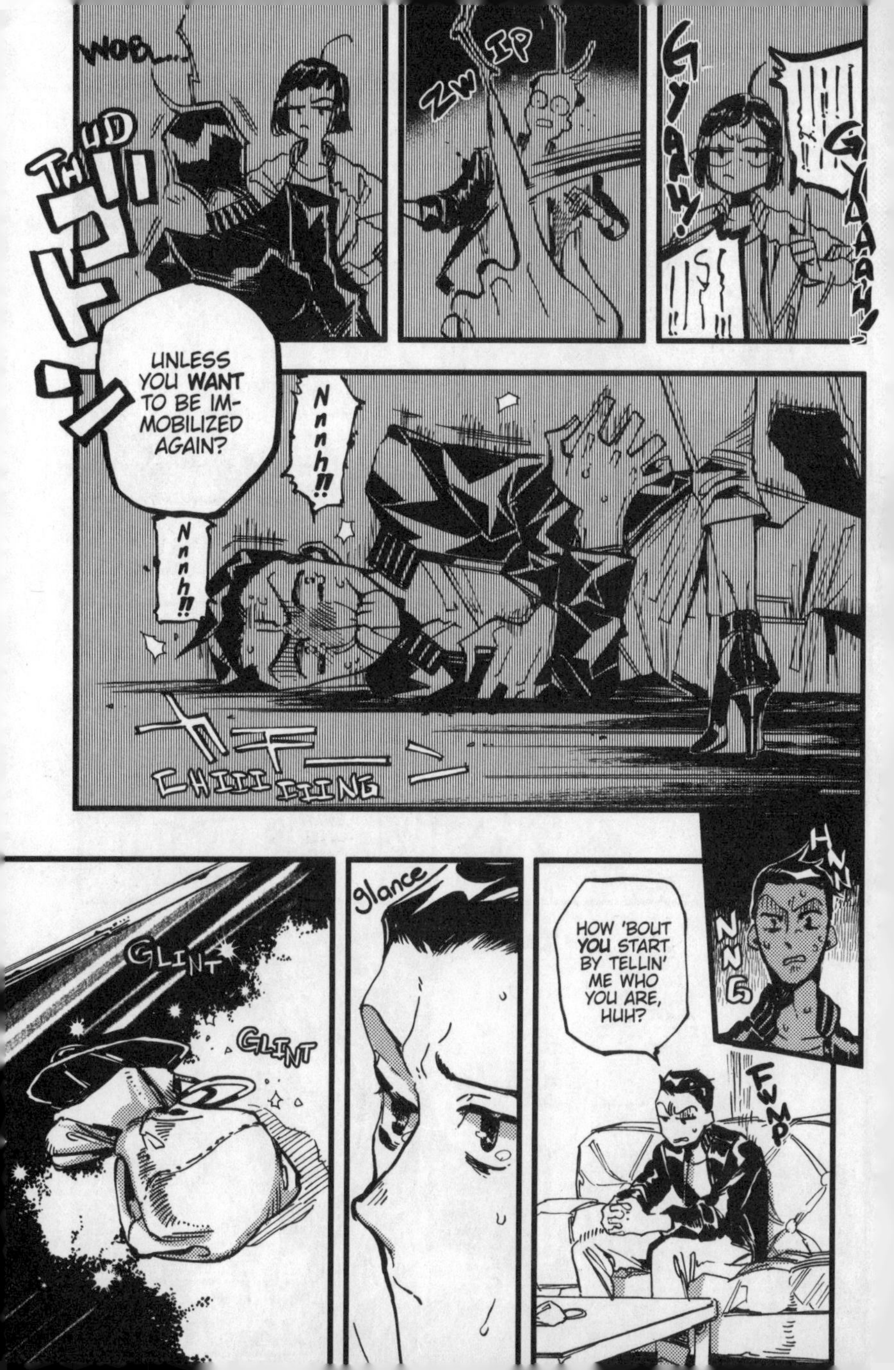
GYAAAAAH!
GYAAH!
ZWIP
WOB...
THUD
UNLESS YOU WANT TO BE IMMOBILIZED AGAIN?
Nnnh!!
Nnnh!!
CHIIIIIIING
HNNNG
HOW 'BOUT YOU START BY TELLIN' ME WHO YOU ARE, HUH?
FWMP
glance
GLINT
GLINT

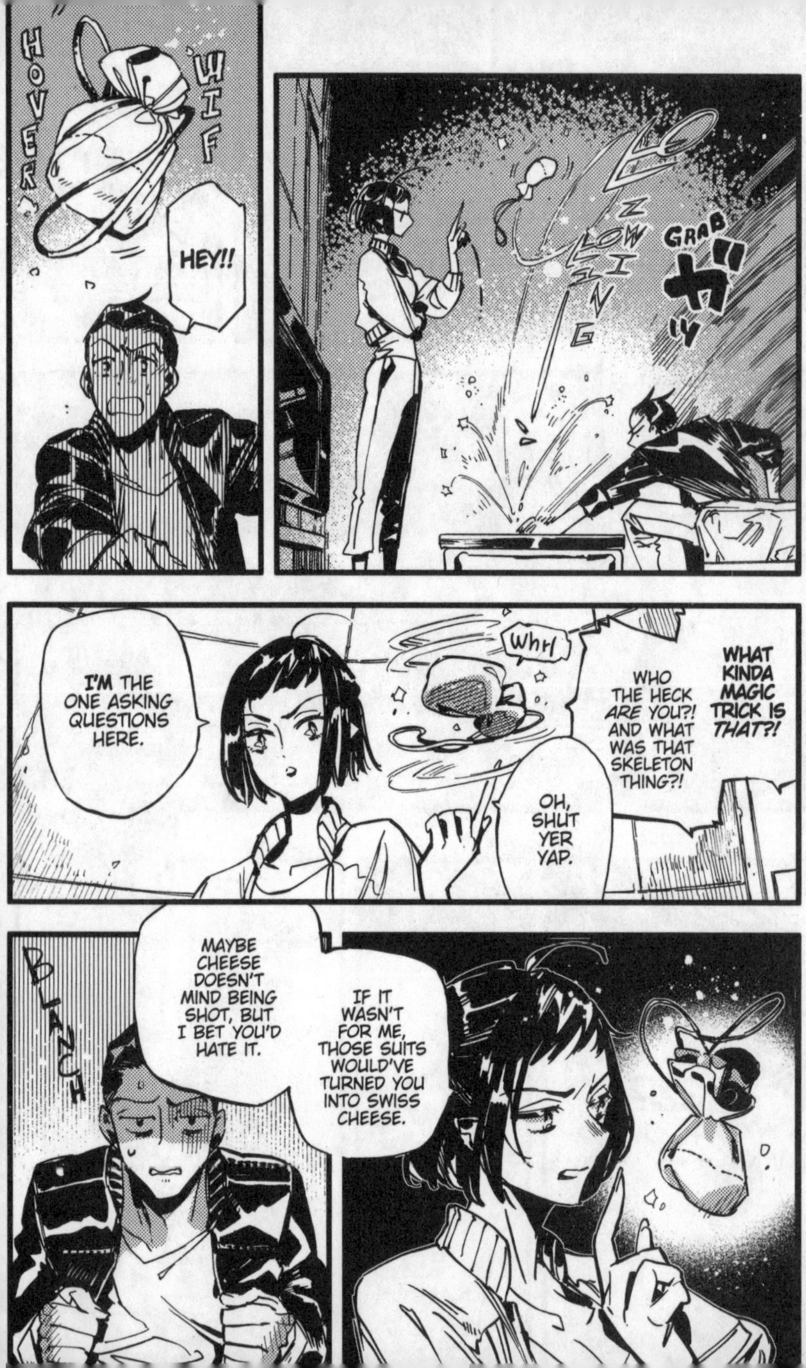
GRAB
ZOWING
HOVER
WHIF
HEY!!
WHAT KINDA MAGIC TRICK IS *THAT?!*
WHO THE HECK *ARE* YOU?! AND WHAT WAS THAT SKELETON THING?!
OH, SHUT YER YAP.
Whrl
I'M THE ONE ASKING QUESTIONS HERE.
IF IT WASN'T FOR ME, THOSE SUITS WOULD'VE TURNED YOU INTO SWISS CHEESE.
MAYBE CHEESE DOESN'T MIND BEING SHOT, BUT I BET YOU'D HATE IT.
BLANCH

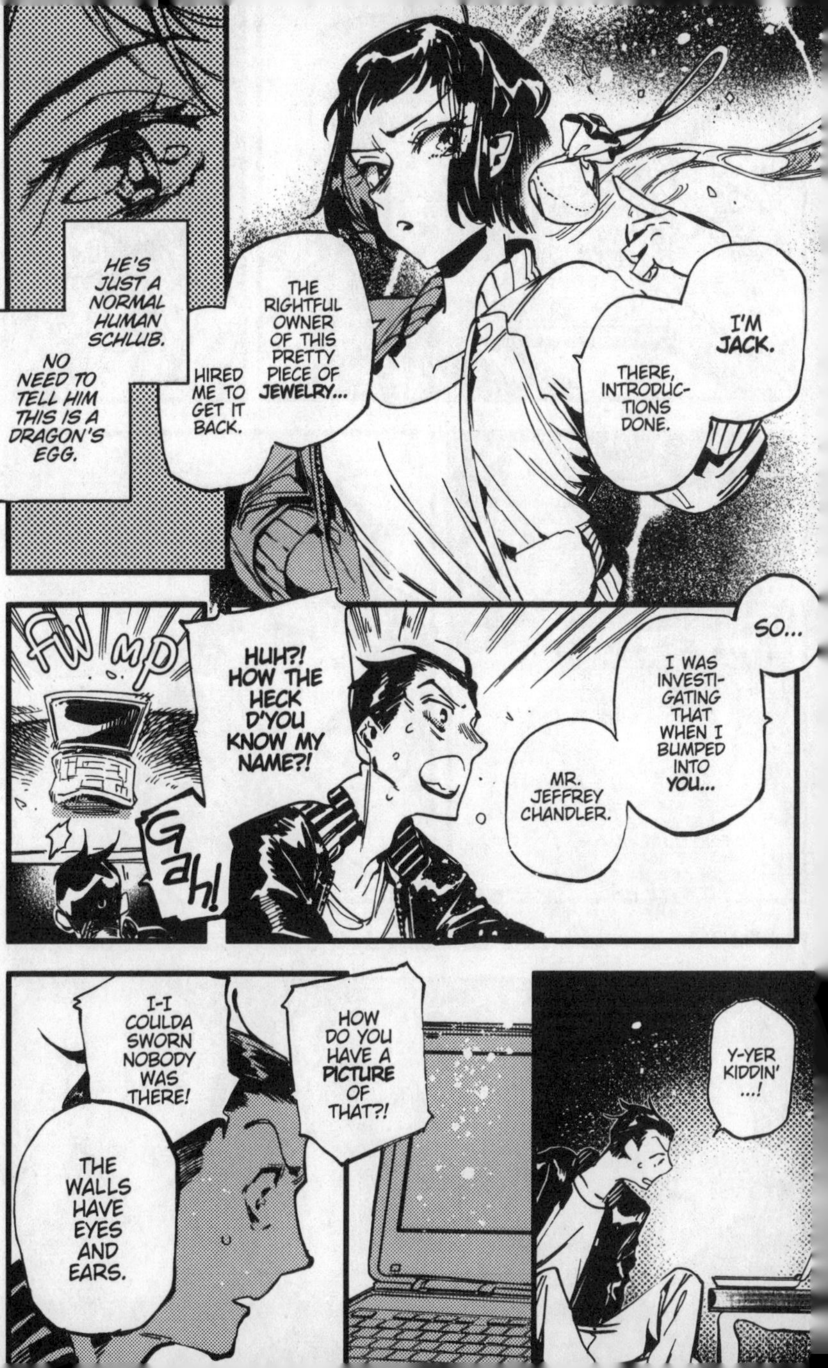
I'M JACK.
THERE, INTRODUCTIONS DONE.
THE RIGHTFUL OWNER OF THIS PRETTY PIECE OF JEWELRY...
HIRED ME TO GET IT BACK.
HE'S JUST A NORMAL HUMAN SCHLUB.
NO NEED TO TELL HIM THIS IS A DRAGON'S EGG.
SO...
I WAS INVESTIGATING THAT WHEN I BUMPED INTO YOU...
MR. JEFFREY CHANDLER.
HUH?! HOW THE HECK D'YOU KNOW MY NAME?!
FWMP
GAH!
Y-YER KIDDIN' ...!
HOW DO YOU HAVE A PICTURE OF THAT?!
I-I COULDA SWORN NOBODY WAS THERE!
THE WALLS HAVE EYES AND EARS.

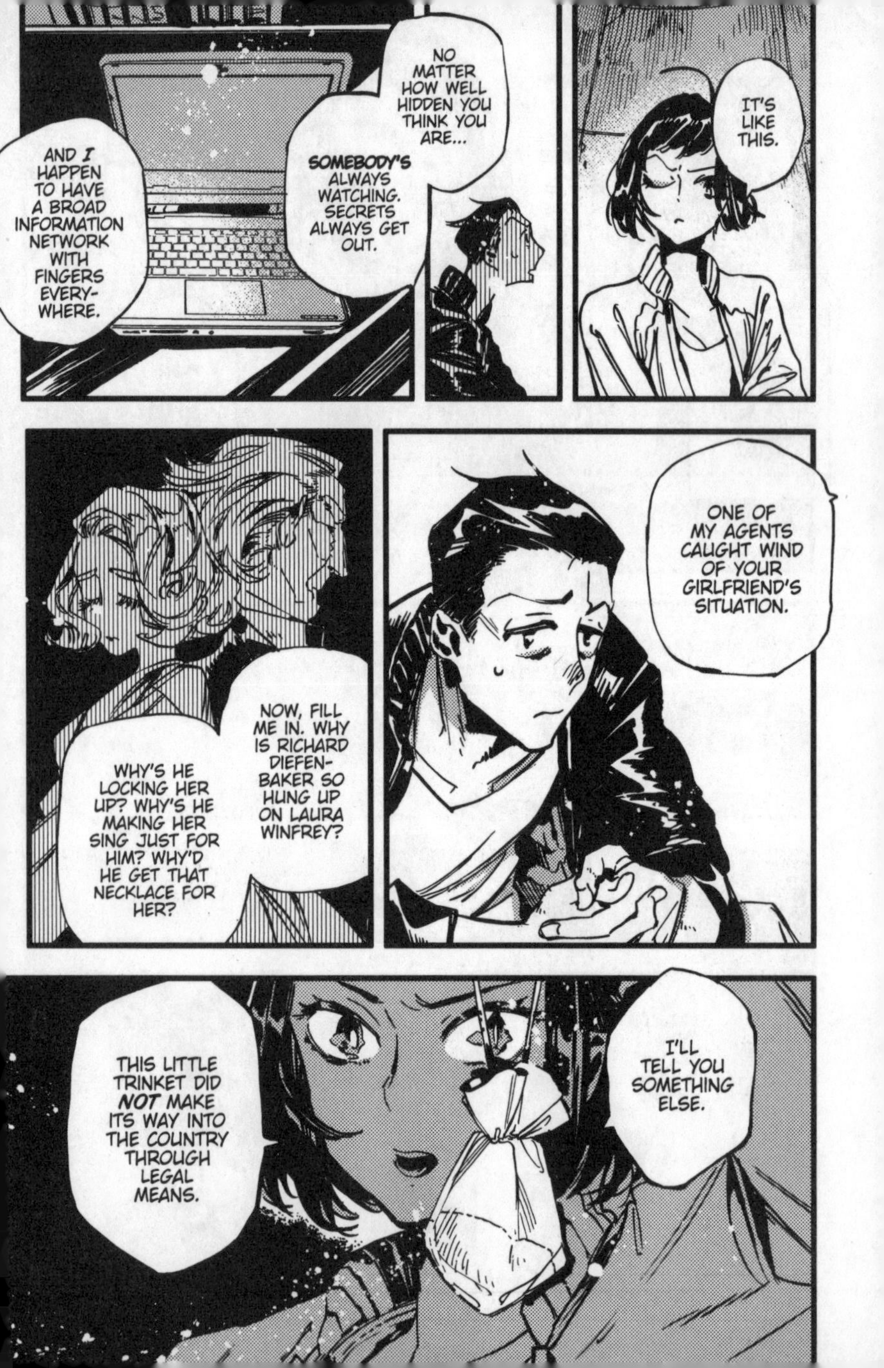

IT'S LIKE THIS.
NO MATTER HOW WELL HIDDEN YOU THINK YOU ARE...
SOMEBODY'S ALWAYS WATCHING. SECRETS ALWAYS GET OUT.
AND *I* HAPPEN TO HAVE A BROAD INFORMATION NETWORK WITH FINGERS EVERY-WHERE.
ONE OF MY AGENTS CAUGHT WIND OF YOUR GIRLFRIEND'S SITUATION.
NOW, FILL ME IN. WHY IS RICHARD DIEFEN-BAKER SO HUNG UP ON LAURA WINFREY?
WHY'S HE LOCKING HER UP? WHY'S HE MAKING HER SING JUST FOR HIM? WHY'D HE GET THAT NECKLACE FOR HER?
I'LL TELL YOU SOMETHING ELSE.
THIS LITTLE TRINKET DID ***NOT*** MAKE ITS WAY INTO THE COUNTRY THROUGH LEGAL MEANS.

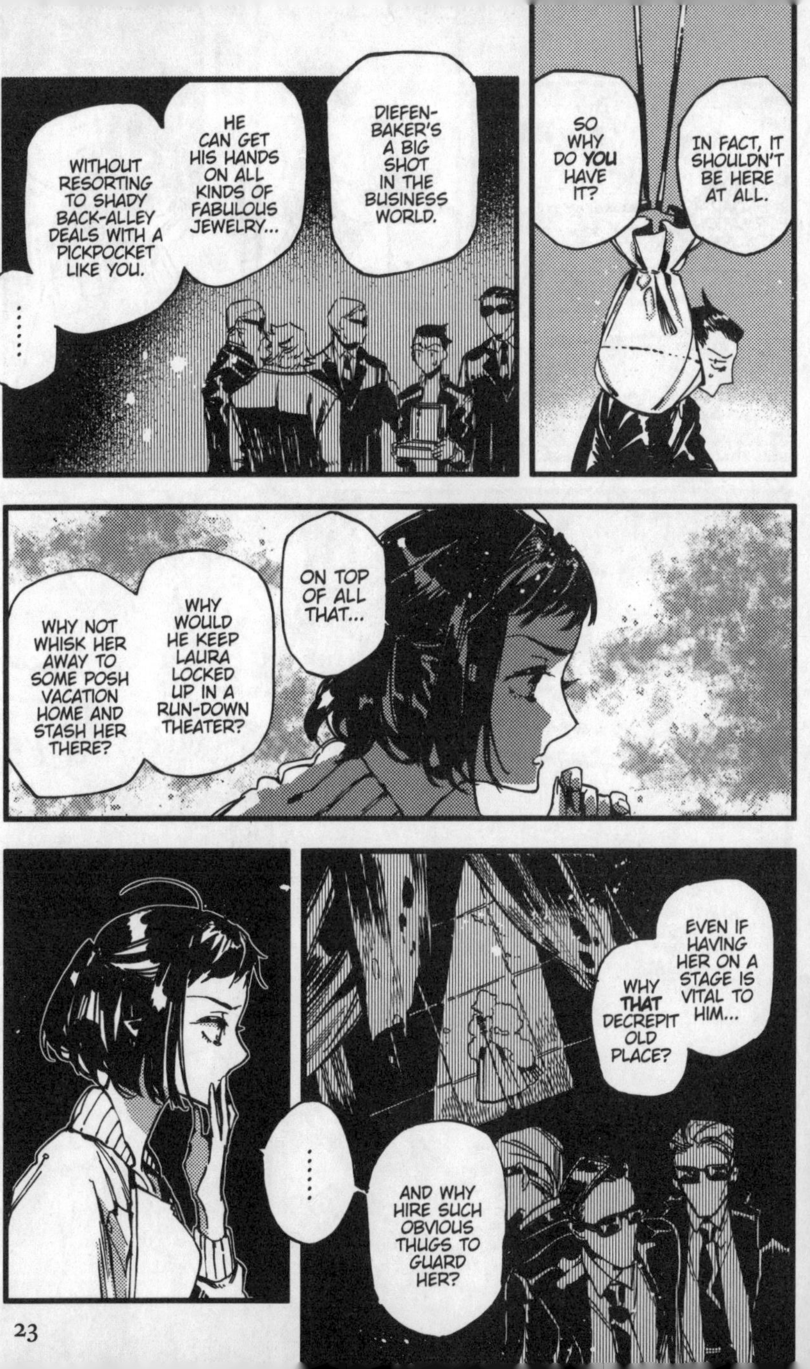
IN FACT, IT SHOULDN'T BE HERE AT ALL.
SO WHY DO **YOU** HAVE IT?
DIEFEN-BAKER'S A BIG SHOT IN THE BUSINESS WORLD.
HE CAN GET HIS HANDS ON ALL KINDS OF FABULOUS JEWELRY...
WITHOUT RESORTING TO SHADY BACK-ALLEY DEALS WITH A PICKPOCKET LIKE YOU.
......
ON TOP OF ALL THAT...
WHY WOULD HE KEEP LAURA LOCKED UP IN A RUN-DOWN THEATER?
WHY NOT WHISK HER AWAY TO SOME POSH VACATION HOME AND STASH HER THERE?
EVEN IF HAVING HER ON A STAGE IS VITAL TO HIM...
WHY **THAT** DECREPIT OLD PLACE?
AND WHY HIRE SUCH OBVIOUS THUGS TO GUARD HER?
......

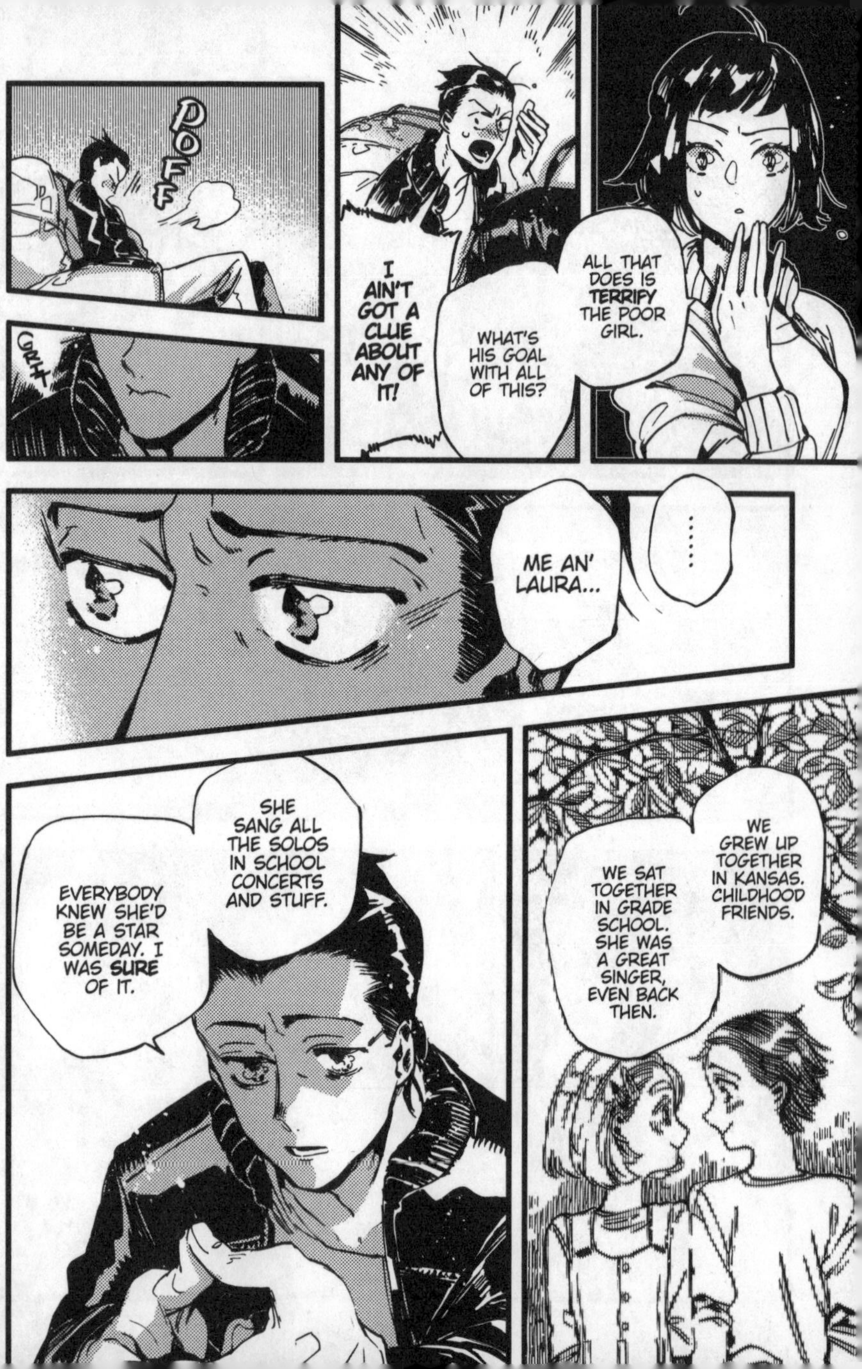
ALL THAT DOES IS **TERRIFY** THE POOR GIRL.
WHAT'S HIS GOAL WITH ALL OF THIS?
I AIN'T GOT A CLUE ABOUT ANY OF IT!
POFF
GRIT
......
ME AN' LAURA...
WE GREW UP TOGETHER IN KANSAS. CHILDHOOD FRIENDS.
WE SAT TOGETHER IN GRADE SCHOOL. SHE WAS A GREAT SINGER, EVEN BACK THEN.
SHE SANG ALL THE SOLOS IN SCHOOL CONCERTS AND STUFF.
EVERYBODY KNEW SHE'D BE A STAR SOMEDAY. I WAS **SURE** OF IT.

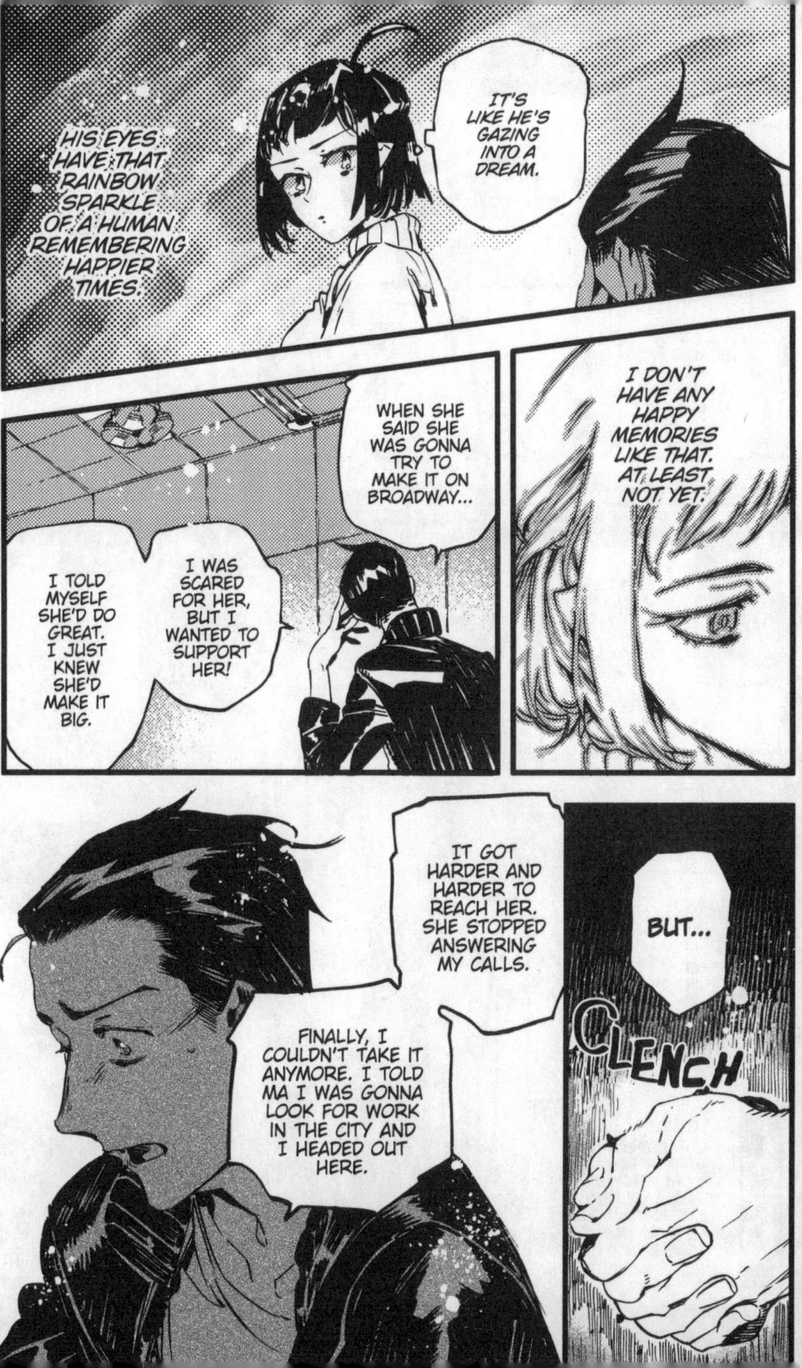
IT'S LIKE HE'S GAZING INTO A DREAM.
HIS EYES HAVE THAT RAINBOW SPARKLE OF A HUMAN REMEMBERING HAPPIER TIMES.
I DON'T HAVE ANY HAPPY MEMORIES LIKE THAT. AT LEAST NOT YET.
WHEN SHE SAID SHE WAS GONNA TRY TO MAKE IT ON BROADWAY...
I WAS SCARED FOR HER, BUT I WANTED TO SUPPORT HER!
I TOLD MYSELF SHE'D DO GREAT. I JUST KNEW SHE'D MAKE IT BIG.
BUT...
CLENCH
IT GOT HARDER AND HARDER TO REACH HER. SHE STOPPED ANSWERING MY CALLS.
FINALLY, I COULDN'T TAKE IT ANYMORE. I TOLD MA I WAS GONNA LOOK FOR WORK IN THE CITY AND I HEADED OUT HERE.

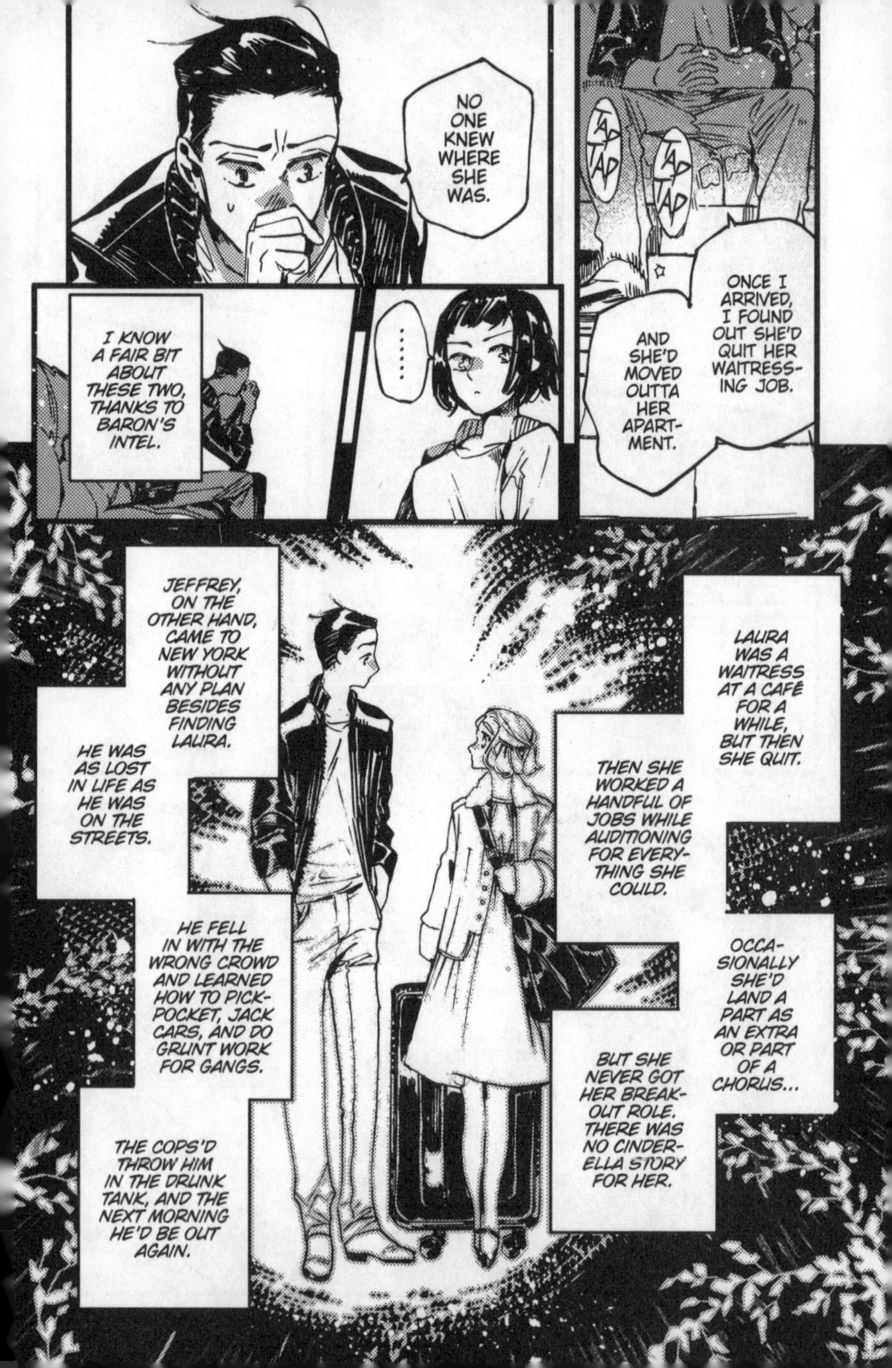
TAP TAP
TAP TAP
ONCE I ARRIVED, I FOUND OUT SHE'D QUIT HER WAITRESSING JOB.
AND SHE'D MOVED OUTTA HER APARTMENT.
NO ONE KNEW WHERE SHE WAS.
......
I KNOW A FAIR BIT ABOUT THESE TWO, THANKS TO BARON'S INTEL.
LAURA WAS A WAITRESS AT A CAFÉ FOR A WHILE, BUT THEN SHE QUIT.
THEN SHE WORKED A HANDFUL OF JOBS WHILE AUDITIONING FOR EVERYTHING SHE COULD.
OCCASIONALLY SHE'D LAND A PART AS AN EXTRA OR PART OF A CHORUS...
BUT SHE NEVER GOT HER BREAKOUT ROLE. THERE WAS NO CINDERELLA STORY FOR HER.
JEFFREY, ON THE OTHER HAND, CAME TO NEW YORK WITHOUT ANY PLAN BESIDES FINDING LAURA.
HE WAS AS LOST IN LIFE AS HE WAS ON THE STREETS.
HE FELL IN WITH THE WRONG CROWD AND LEARNED HOW TO PICKPOCKET, JACK CARS, AND DO GRUNT WORK FOR GANGS.
THE COPS'D THROW HIM IN THE DRUNK TANK, AND THE NEXT MORNING HE'D BE OUT AGAIN.

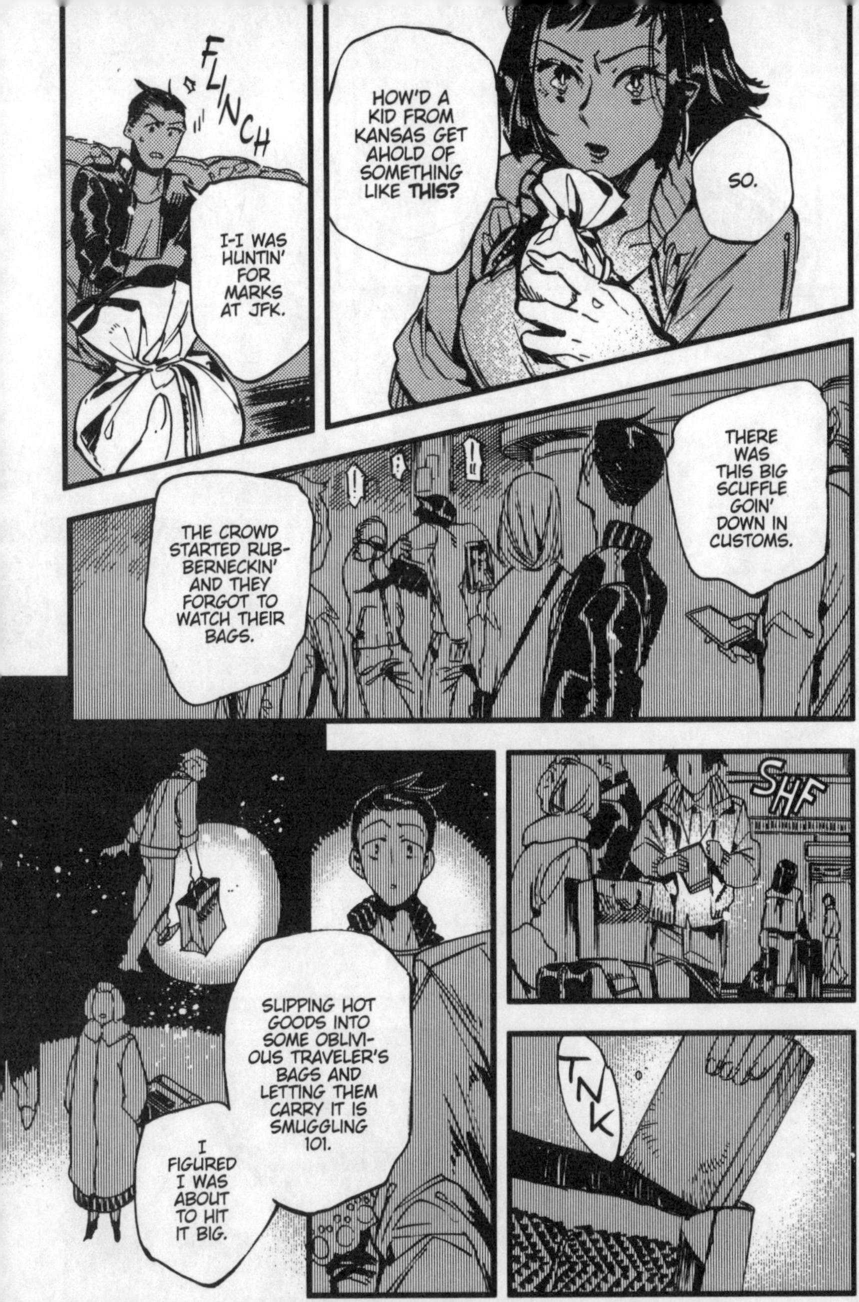
SO.
HOW'D A KID FROM KANSAS GET AHOLD OF SOMETHING LIKE THIS?
FLINCH
I-I WAS HUNTIN' FOR MARKS AT JFK.
THERE WAS THIS BIG SCUFFLE GOIN' DOWN IN CUSTOMS.
THE CROWD STARTED RUB-BERNECKIN' AND THEY FORGOT TO WATCH THEIR BAGS.
SHF
TNK
SLIPPING HOT GOODS INTO SOME OBLIVI-OUS TRAVELER'S BAGS AND LETTING THEM CARRY IT IS SMUGGLING 101.
I FIGURED I WAS ABOUT TO HIT IT BIG.

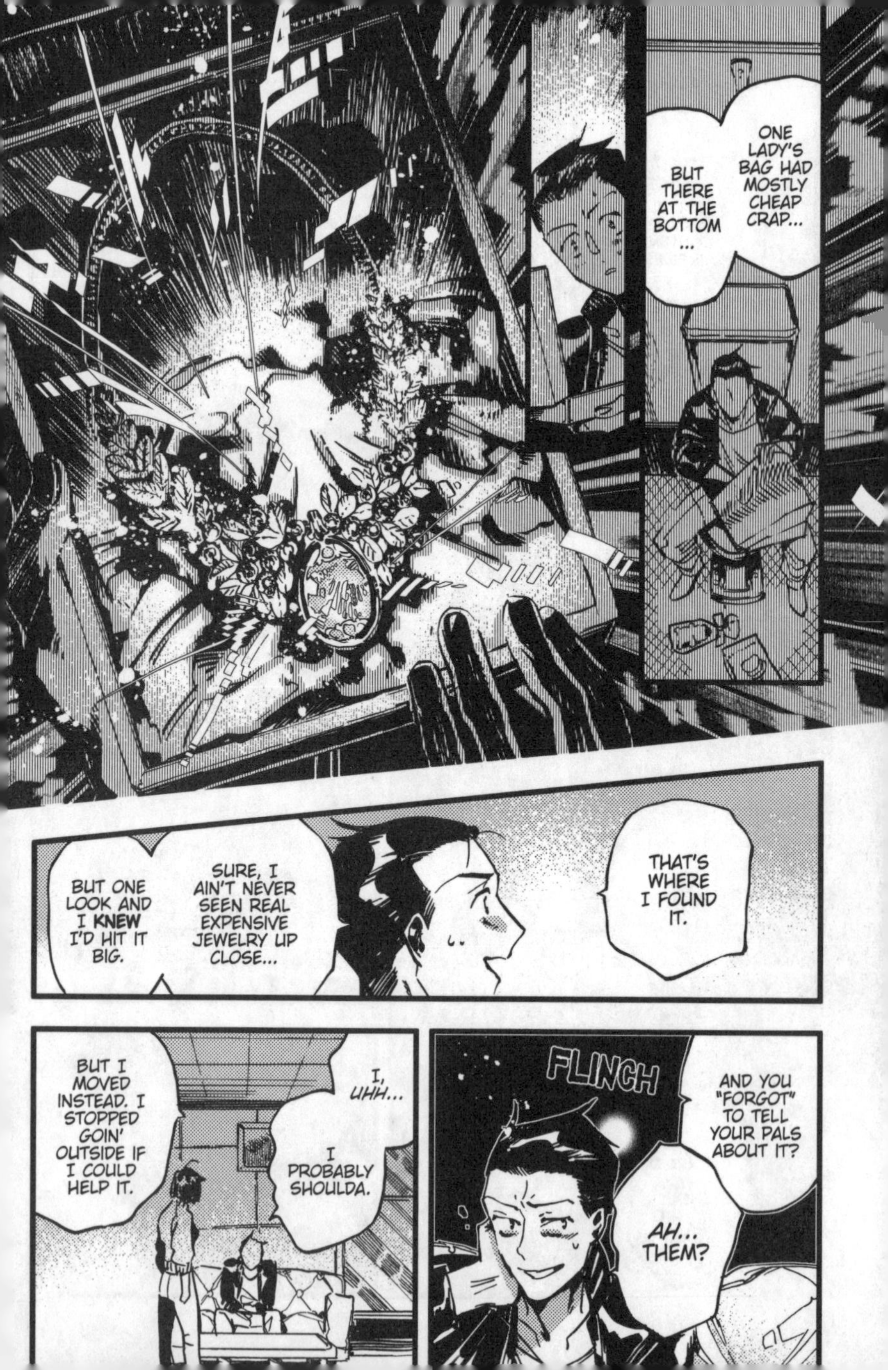
ONE LADY'S BAG HAD MOSTLY CHEAP CRAP...
BUT THERE AT THE BOTTOM ...
THAT'S WHERE I FOUND IT.
SURE, I AIN'T NEVER SEEN REAL EXPENSIVE JEWELRY UP CLOSE...
BUT ONE LOOK AND I **KNEW** I'D HIT IT BIG.
FLINCH
AND YOU "FORGOT" TO TELL YOUR PALS ABOUT IT?
AH... THEM?
I, *UHH...*
I PROBABLY SHOULDA.
BUT I MOVED INSTEAD. I STOPPED GOIN' OUTSIDE IF I COULD HELP IT.

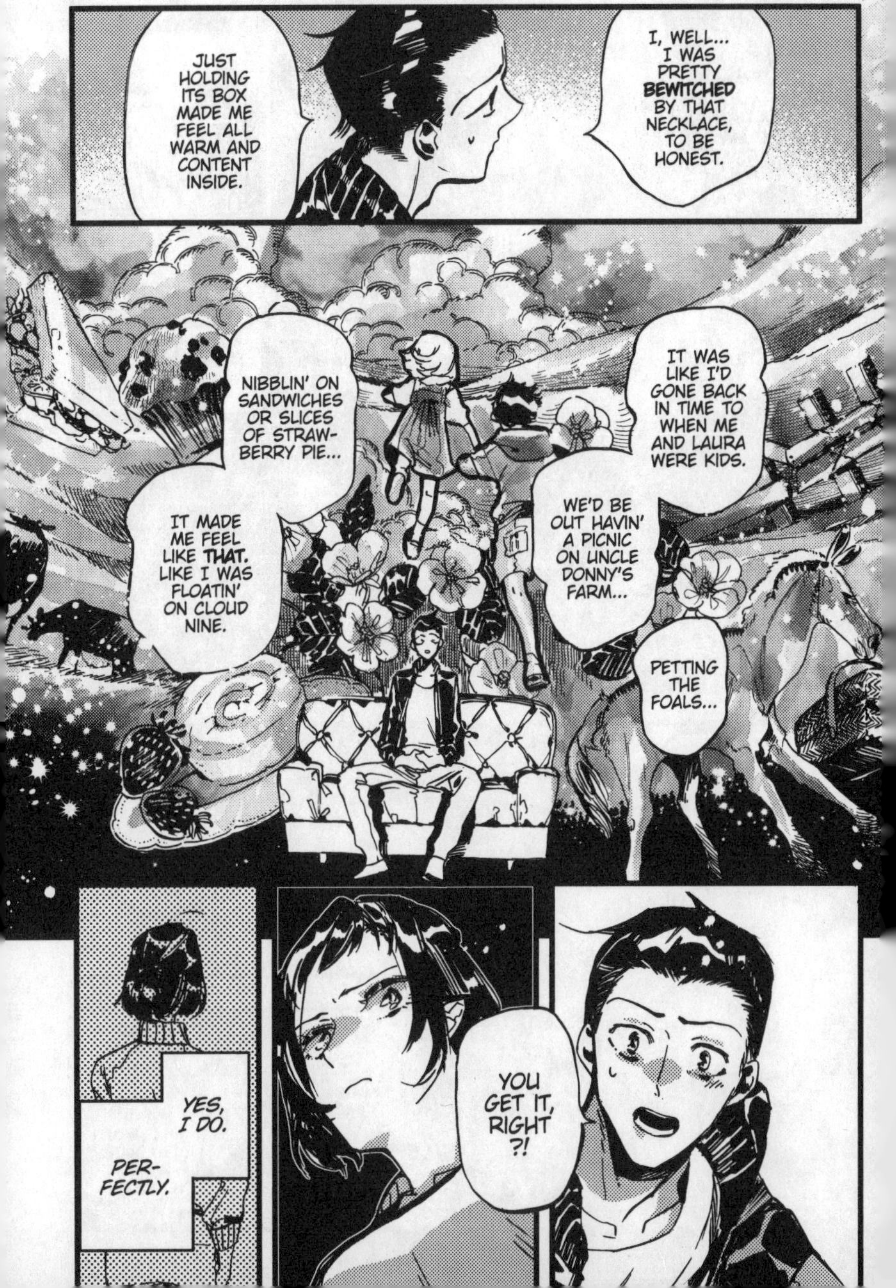
I, WELL... I WAS PRETTY **BEWITCHED** BY THAT NECKLACE, TO BE HONEST.
JUST HOLDING ITS BOX MADE ME FEEL ALL WARM AND CONTENT INSIDE.
IT WAS LIKE I'D GONE BACK IN TIME TO WHEN ME AND LAURA WERE KIDS.
WE'D BE OUT HAVIN' A PICNIC ON UNCLE DONNY'S FARM...
PETTING THE FOALS...
NIBBLIN' ON SANDWICHES OR SLICES OF STRAW-BERRY PIE...
IT MADE ME FEEL LIKE **THAT.** LIKE I WAS FLOATIN' ON CLOUD NINE.
YOU GET IT, RIGHT ?!
YES, I DO.
PER-FECTLY.

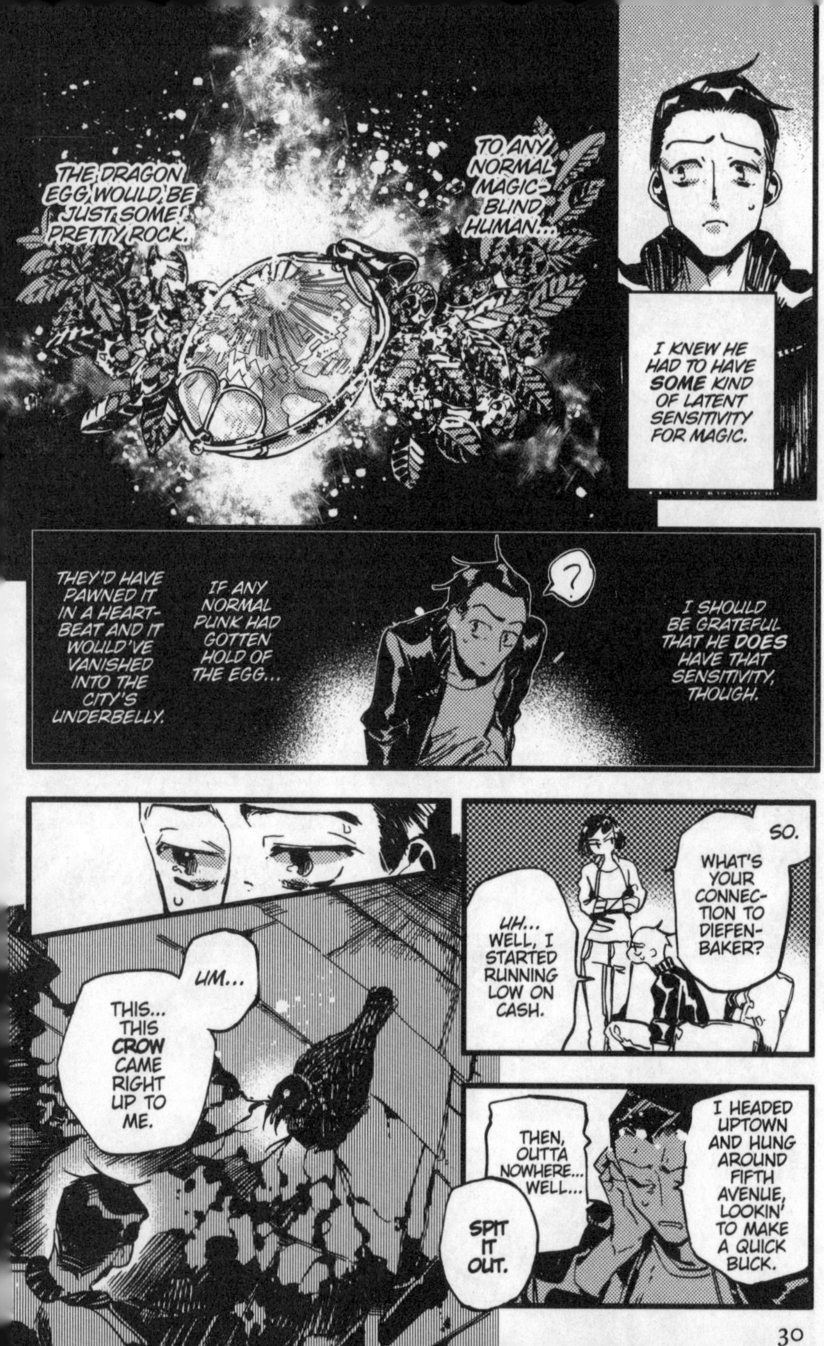
I KNEW HE HAD TO HAVE SOME KIND OF LATENT SENSITIVITY FOR MAGIC.
TO ANY NORMAL MAGIC-BLIND HUMAN...
THE DRAGON EGG WOULD BE JUST SOME PRETTY ROCK.
I SHOULD BE GRATEFUL THAT HE DOES HAVE THAT SENSITIVITY, THOUGH.
?
IF ANY NORMAL PUNK HAD GOTTEN HOLD OF THE EGG...
THEY'D HAVE PAWNED IT IN A HEART-BEAT AND IT WOULD'VE VANISHED INTO THE CITY'S UNDERBELLY.
SO.
WHAT'S YOUR CONNECTION TO DIEFEN-BAKER?
UH... WELL, I STARTED RUNNING LOW ON CASH.
I HEADED UPTOWN AND HUNG AROUND FIFTH AVENUE, LOOKIN' TO MAKE A QUICK BUCK.
THEN, OUTTA NOWHERE... WELL...
SPIT IT OUT.
UM...
THIS... THIS CROW CAME RIGHT UP TO ME.

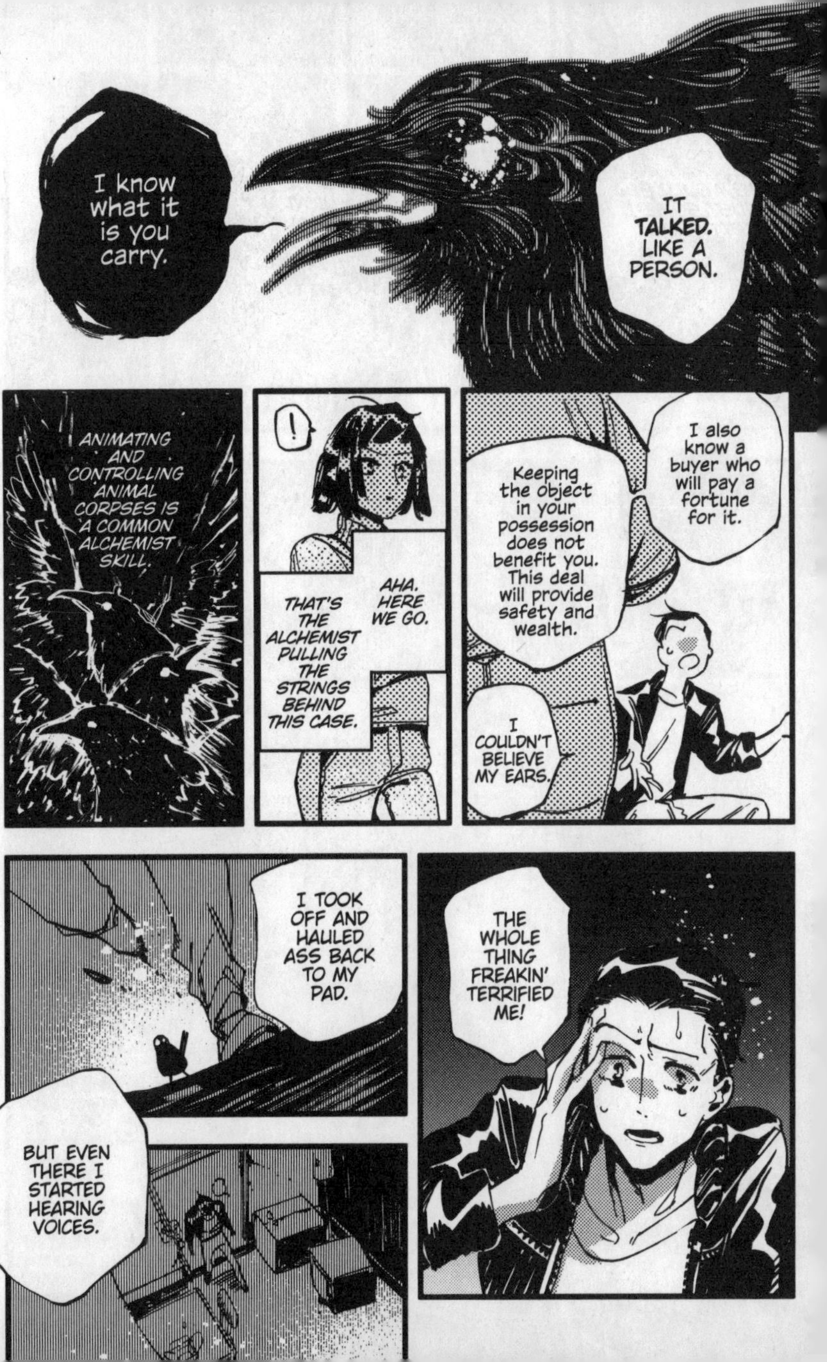
I know what it is you carry.
IT TALKED. LIKE A PERSON.
I also know a buyer who will pay a fortune for it.
Keeping the object in your possession does not benefit you. This deal will provide safety and wealth.
I COULDN'T BELIEVE MY EARS.
!
AHA. HERE WE GO.
THAT'S THE ALCHEMIST PULLING THE STRINGS BEHIND THIS CASE.
ANIMATING AND CONTROLLING ANIMAL CORPSES IS A COMMON ALCHEMIST SKILL.
THE WHOLE THING FREAKIN' TERRIFIED ME!
I TOOK OFF AND HAULED ASS BACK TO MY PAD.
BUT EVEN THERE I STARTED HEARING VOICES.

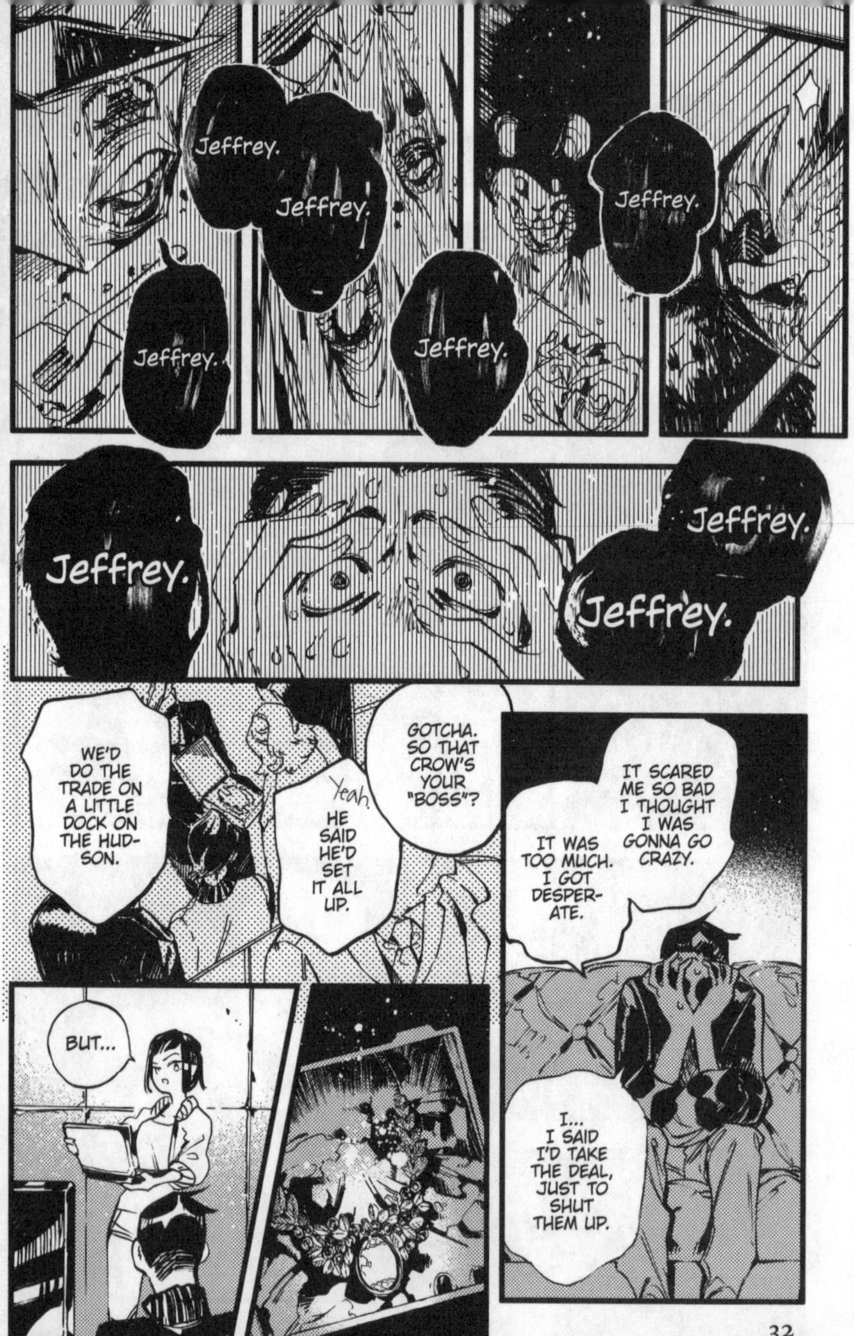

Jeffrey.
Jeffrey.
Jeffrey.
Jeffrey.
Jeffrey.
Jeffrey.
Jeffrey.
Jeffrey.
IT SCARED ME SO BAD I THOUGHT I WAS GONNA GO CRAZY.
IT WAS TOO MUCH. I GOT DESPERATE.
I... I SAID I'D TAKE THE DEAL, JUST TO SHUT THEM UP.
GOTCHA. SO THAT CROW'S YOUR "BOSS"?
Yeah.
HE SAID HE'D SET IT ALL UP.
WE'D DO THE TRADE ON A LITTLE DOCK ON THE HUD-SON.
BUT...

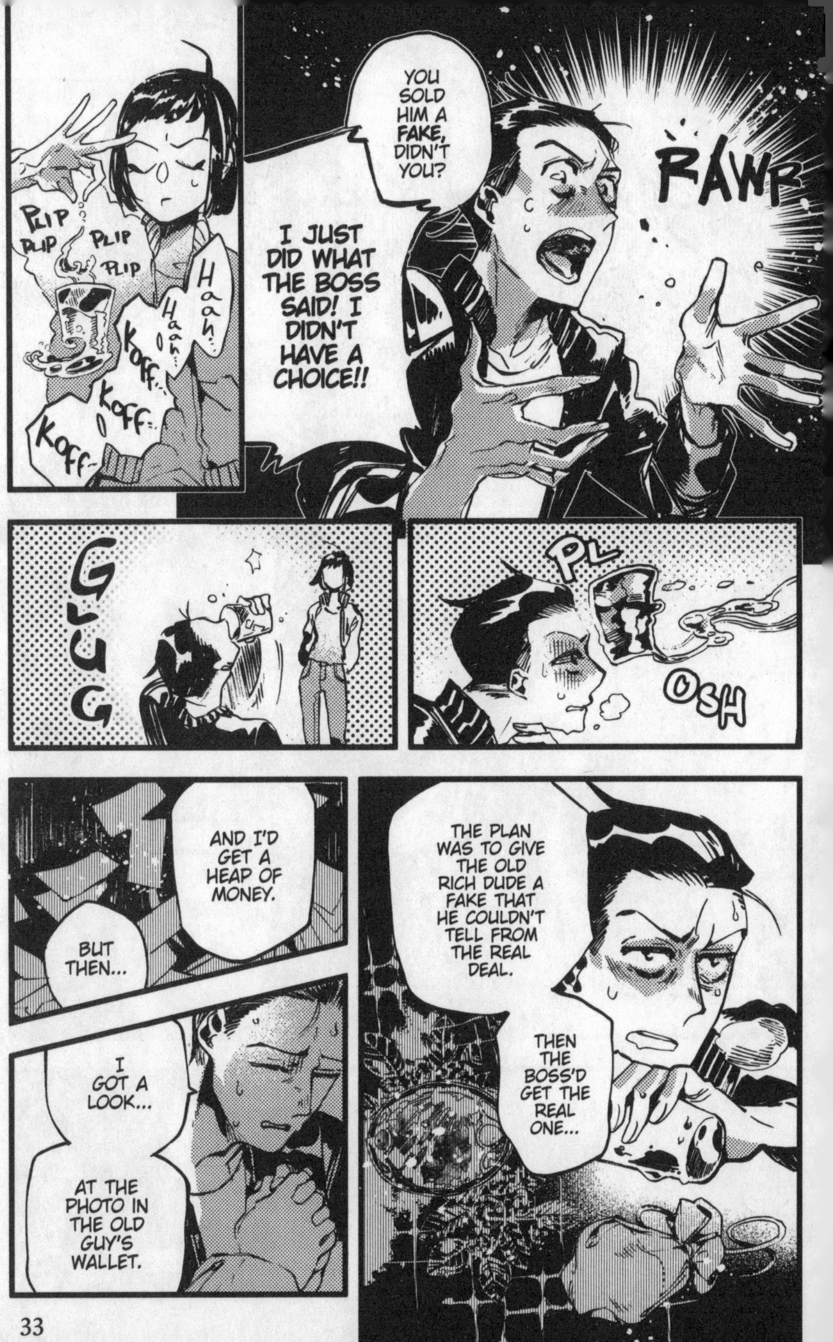
YOU SOLD HIM A FAKE, DIDN'T YOU?
RAWR
I JUST DID WHAT THE BOSS SAID! I DIDN'T HAVE A CHOICE!!
PLIP PLIP PLIP PLIP
Haan...
Haan...
KOFF...
KOFF...
KOFF...
PL OSH
GLUG
THE PLAN WAS TO GIVE THE OLD RICH DUDE A FAKE THAT HE COULDN'T TELL FROM THE REAL DEAL.
THEN THE BOSS'D GET THE REAL ONE...
AND I'D GET A HEAP OF MONEY.
BUT THEN...
I GOT A LOOK...
AT THE PHOTO IN THE OLD GUY'S WALLET.

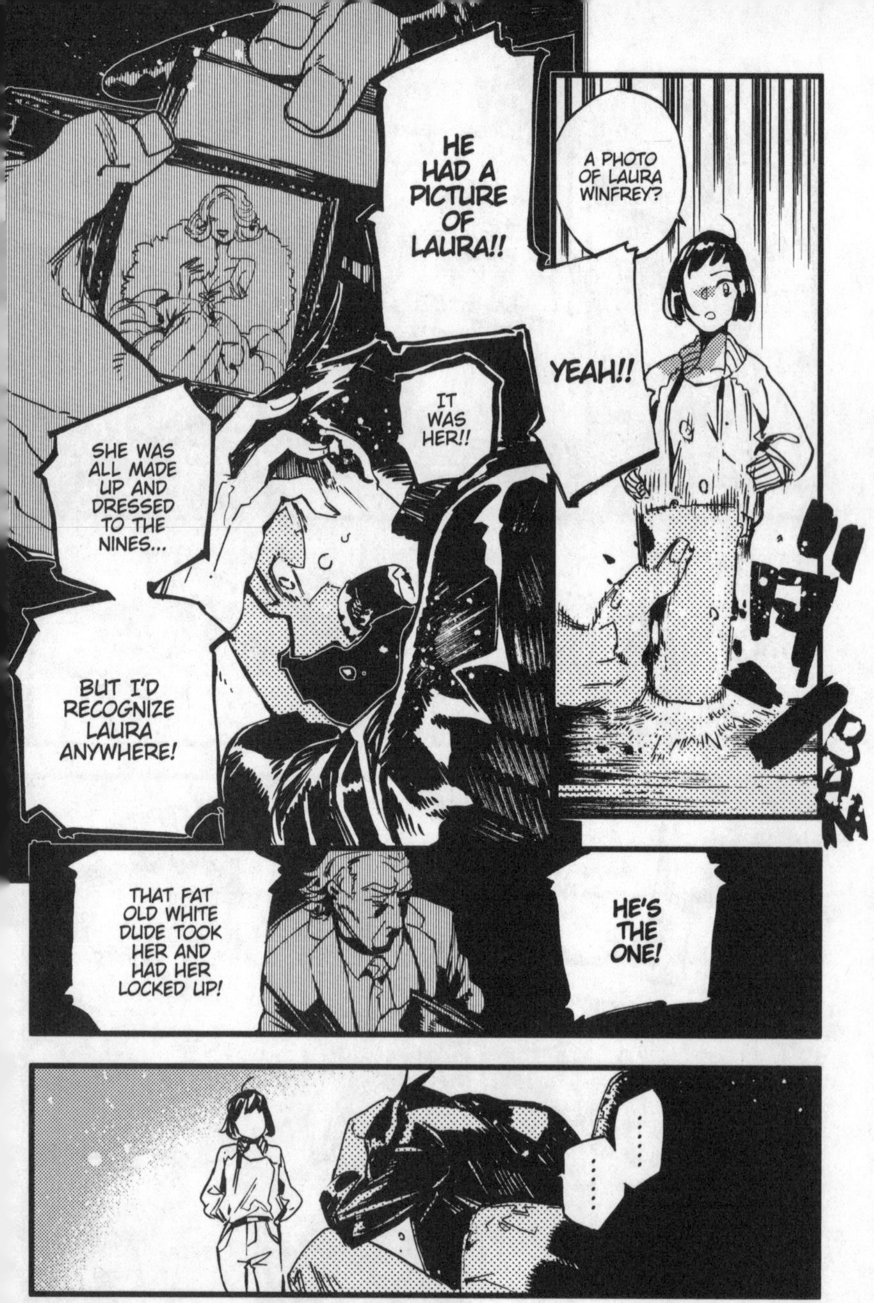
A PHOTO OF LAURA WINFREY?
YEAH!!
HE HAD A PICTURE OF LAURA!!
IT WAS HER!!
SHE WAS ALL MADE UP AND DRESSED TO THE NINES...
BUT I'D RECOGNIZE LAURA ANYWHERE!
HE'S THE ONE!
THAT FAT OLD WHITE DUDE TOOK HER AND HAD HER LOCKED UP!
......

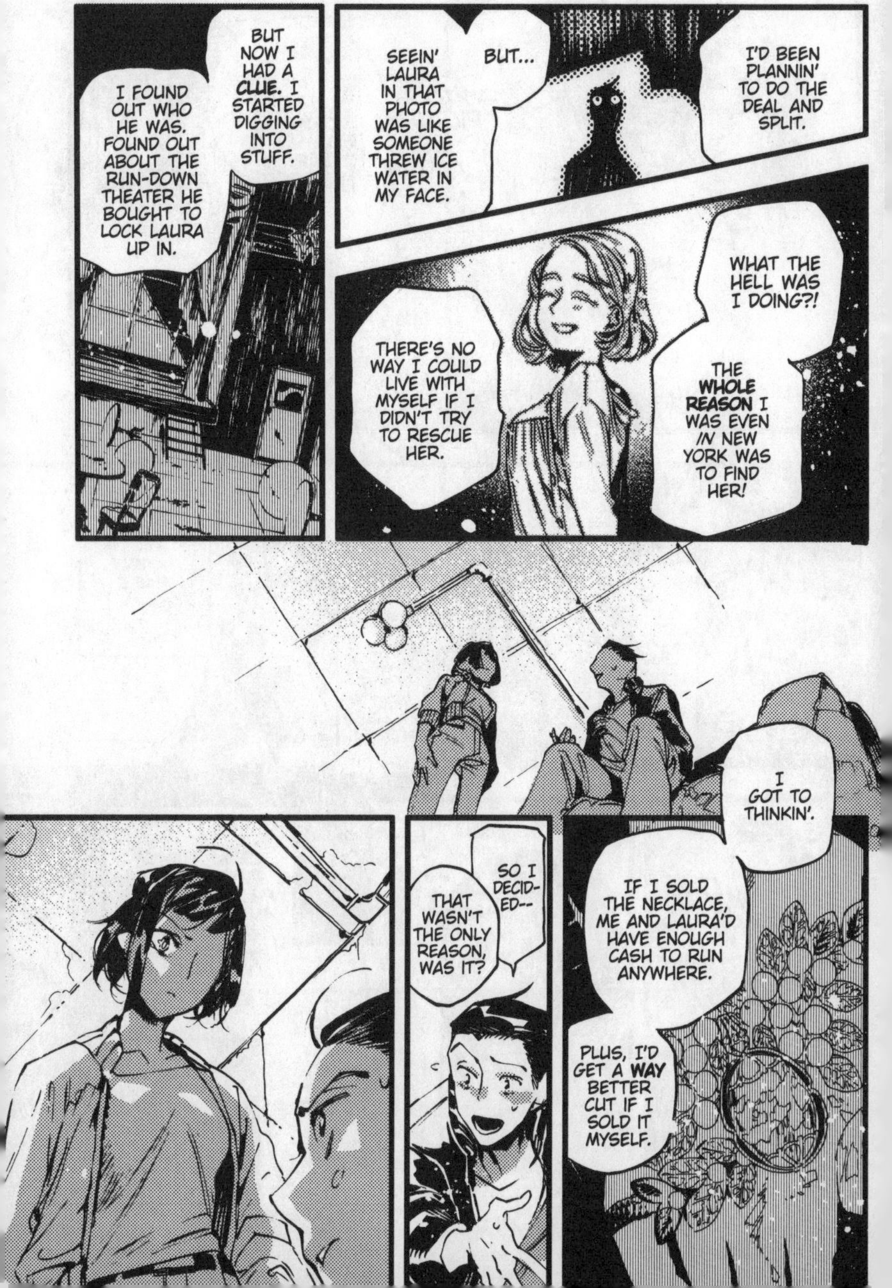

I'D BEEN PLANNIN' TO DO THE DEAL AND SPLIT.
BUT...
SEEIN' LAURA IN THAT PHOTO WAS LIKE SOMEONE THREW ICE WATER IN MY FACE.
WHAT THE HELL WAS I DOING?!
THE **WHOLE REASON** I WAS EVEN *IN* NEW YORK WAS TO FIND HER!
THERE'S NO WAY I COULD LIVE WITH MYSELF IF I DIDN'T TRY TO RESCUE HER.
BUT NOW I HAD A **CLUE.** I STARTED DIGGING INTO STUFF.
I FOUND OUT WHO HE WAS. FOUND OUT ABOUT THE RUN-DOWN THEATER HE BOUGHT TO LOCK LAURA UP IN.
I GOT TO THINKIN'.
IF I SOLD THE NECKLACE, ME AND LAURA'D HAVE ENOUGH CASH TO RUN ANYWHERE.
PLUS, I'D GET A **WAY** BETTER CUT IF I SOLD IT MYSELF.
SO I DECID-ED--
THAT WASN'T THE ONLY REASON, WAS IT?

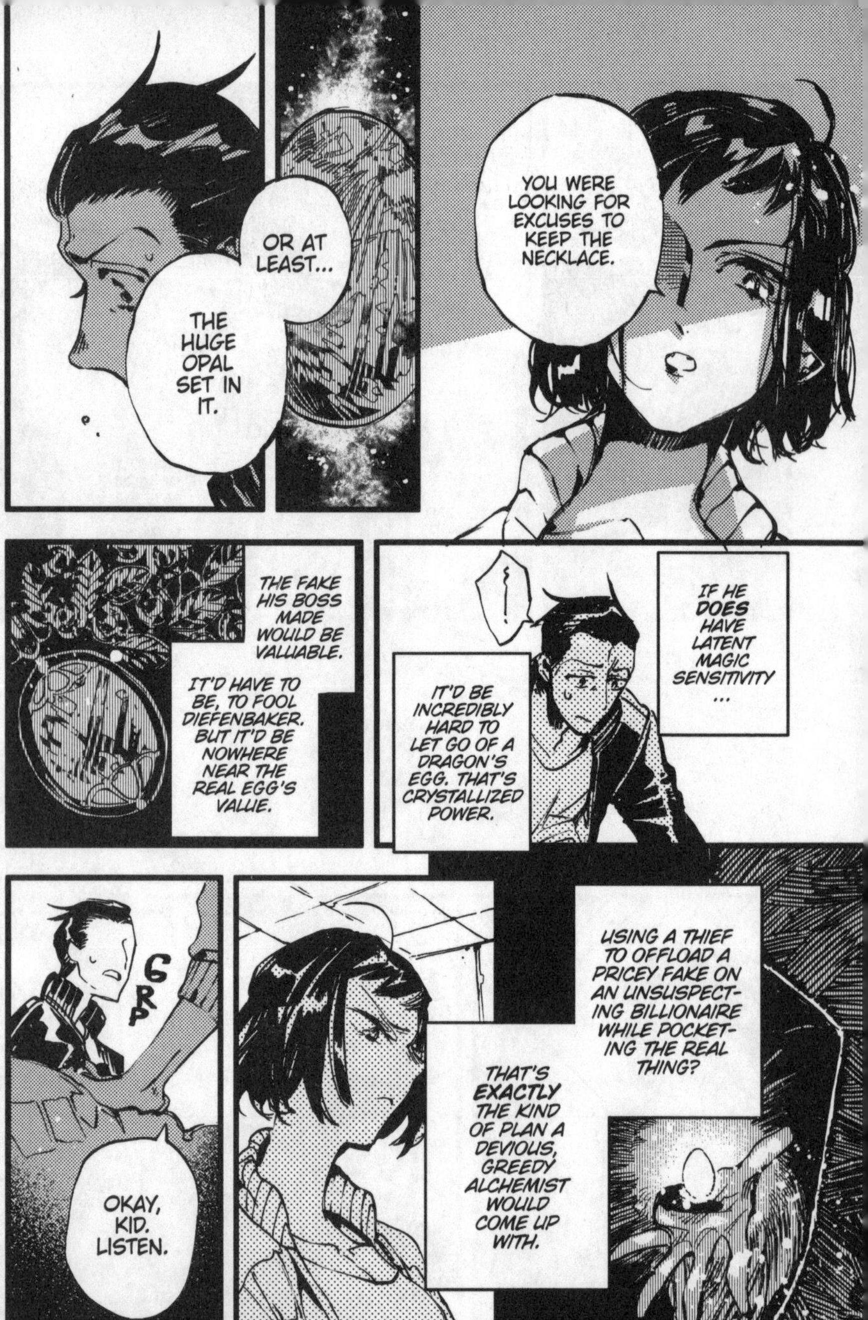
YOU WERE LOOKING FOR EXCUSES TO KEEP THE NECKLACE.
OR AT LEAST...
THE HUGE OPAL SET IN IT.
!
IF HE DOES HAVE LATENT MAGIC SENSITIVITY ...
IT'D BE INCREDIBLY HARD TO LET GO OF A DRAGON'S EGG. THAT'S CRYSTALLIZED POWER.
THE FAKE HIS BOSS MADE WOULD BE VALUABLE.
IT'D HAVE TO BE, TO FOOL DIEFENBAKER. BUT IT'D BE NOWHERE NEAR THE REAL EGG'S VALUE.
USING A THIEF TO OFFLOAD A PRICEY FAKE ON AN UNSUSPECTING BILLIONAIRE WHILE POCKETING THE REAL THING?
THAT'S EXACTLY THE KIND OF PLAN A DEVIOUS, GREEDY ALCHEMIST WOULD COME UP WITH.
GRP
OKAY, KID. LISTEN.

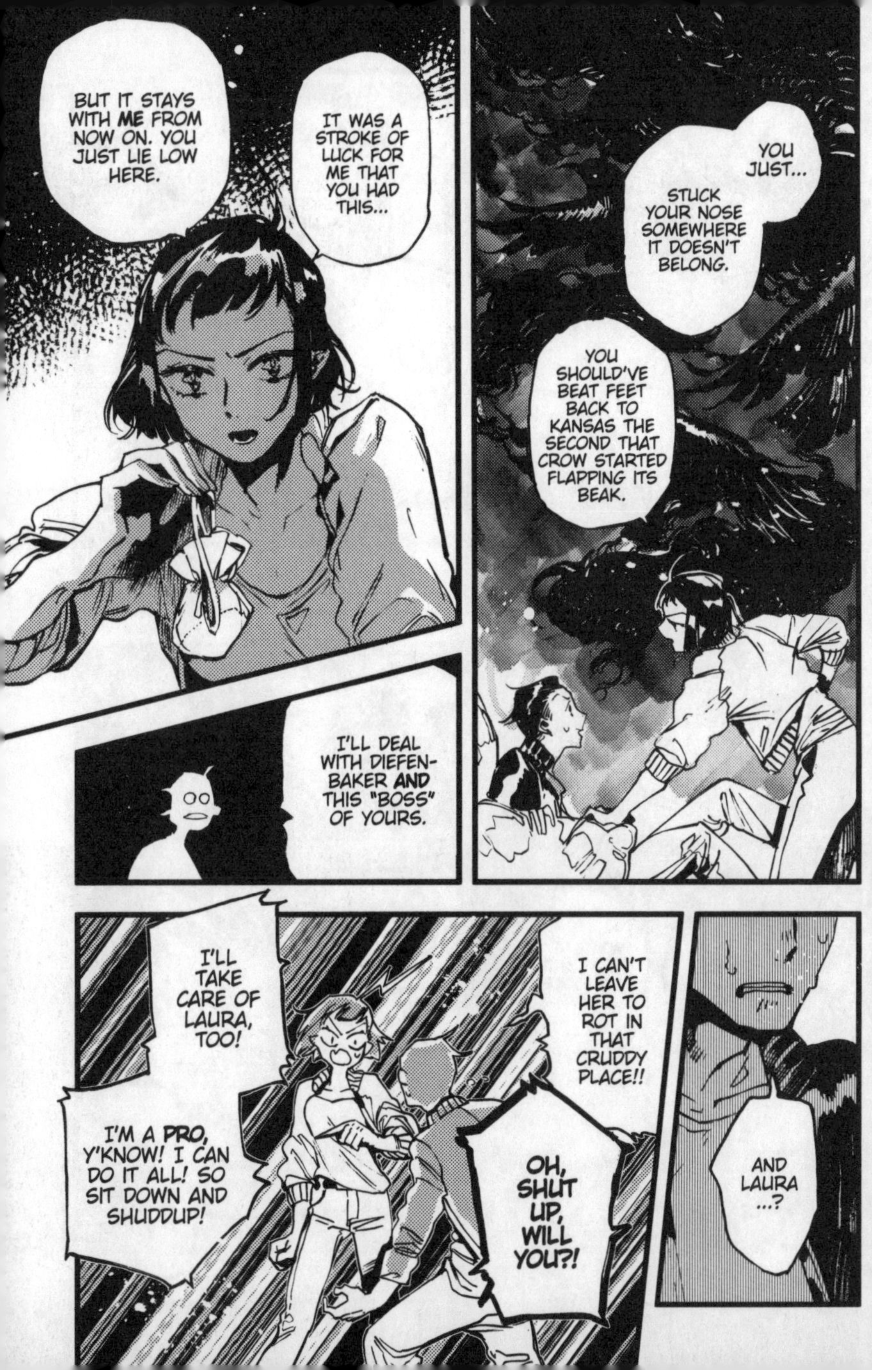
YOU JUST...
STUCK YOUR NOSE SOMEWHERE IT DOESN'T BELONG.
YOU SHOULD'VE BEAT FEET BACK TO KANSAS THE SECOND THAT CROW STARTED FLAPPING ITS BEAK.
IT WAS A STROKE OF LUCK FOR ME THAT YOU HAD THIS...
BUT IT STAYS WITH ME FROM NOW ON. YOU JUST LIE LOW HERE.
I'LL DEAL WITH DIEFEN-BAKER AND THIS "BOSS" OF YOURS.
AND LAURA ...?
I CAN'T LEAVE HER TO ROT IN THAT CRUDDY PLACE!!
I'LL TAKE CARE OF LAURA, TOO!
OH, SHUT UP, WILL YOU?!
I'M A PRO, Y'KNOW! I CAN DO IT ALL! SO SIT DOWN AND SHUDDUP!

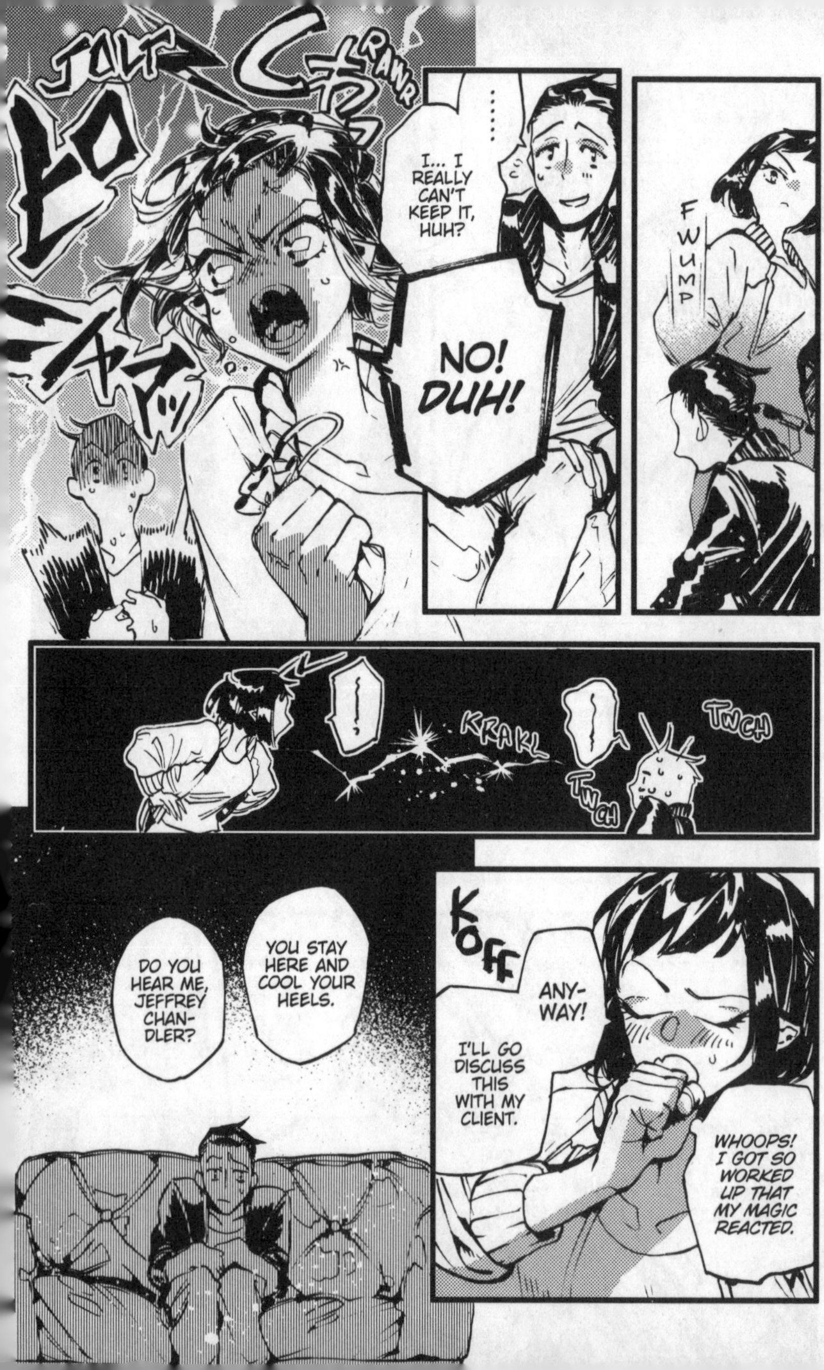

FWUMP
......
I... I REALLY CAN'T KEEP IT, HUH?
RAWR
JOLT
NO! DUH!
TWCH
TWCH
KRAKL
!
KOFF
ANY-WAY!
I'LL GO DISCUSS THIS WITH MY CLIENT.
WHOOPS! I GOT SO WORKED UP THAT MY MAGIC REACTED.
YOU STAY HERE AND COOL YOUR HEELS.
DO YOU HEAR ME, JEFFREY CHANDLER?

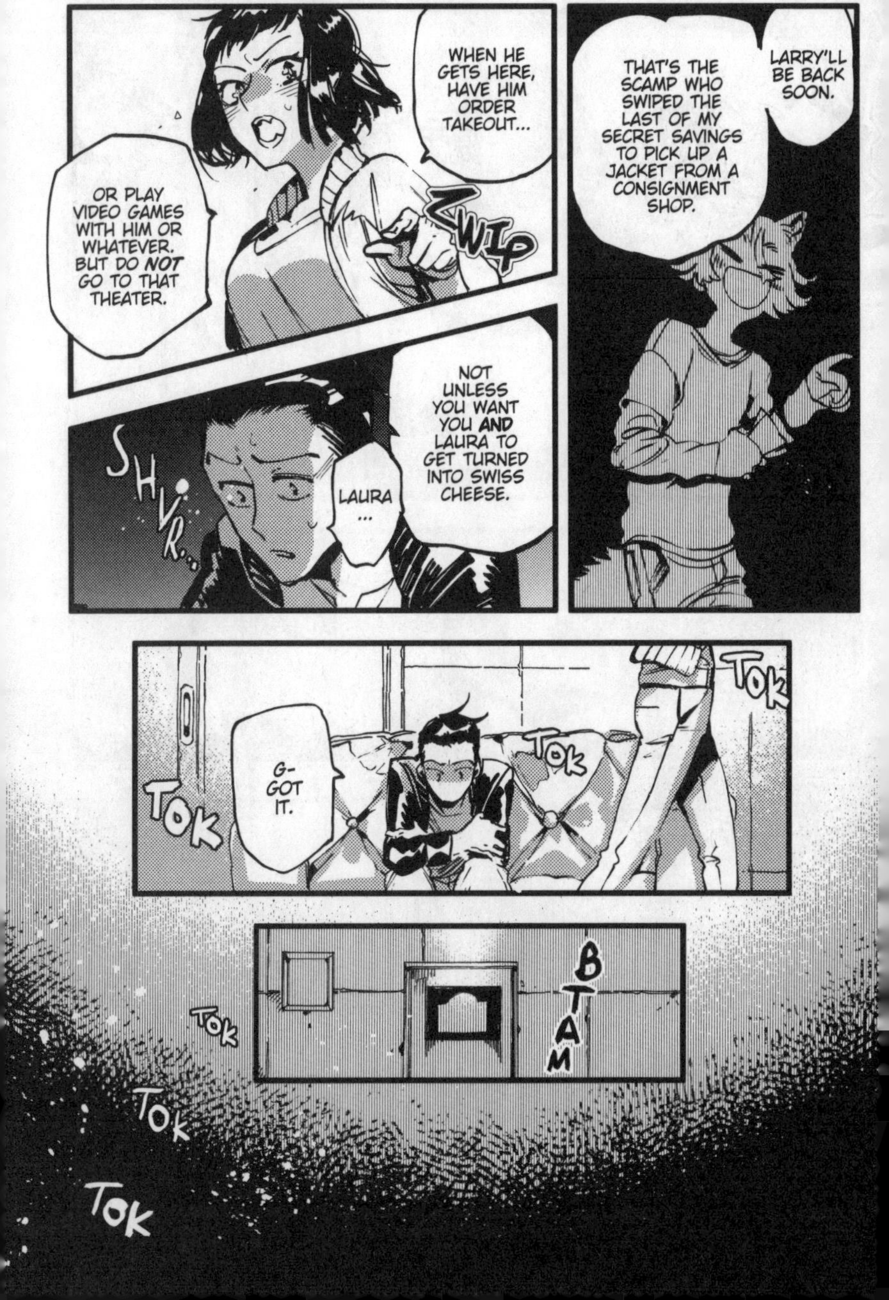
LARRY'LL BE BACK SOON.
THAT'S THE SCAMP WHO SWIPED THE LAST OF MY SECRET SAVINGS TO PICK UP A JACKET FROM A CONSIGNMENT SHOP.
WHEN HE GETS HERE, HAVE HIM ORDER TAKEOUT...
ZWIP
OR PLAY VIDEO GAMES WITH HIM OR WHATEVER. BUT DO NOT GO TO THAT THEATER.
NOT UNLESS YOU WANT YOU AND LAURA TO GET TURNED INTO SWISS CHEESE.
LAURA ...
SHVR...
TOK
TOK
G-GOT IT.
TOK
BTAM
TOK
TOK
TOK

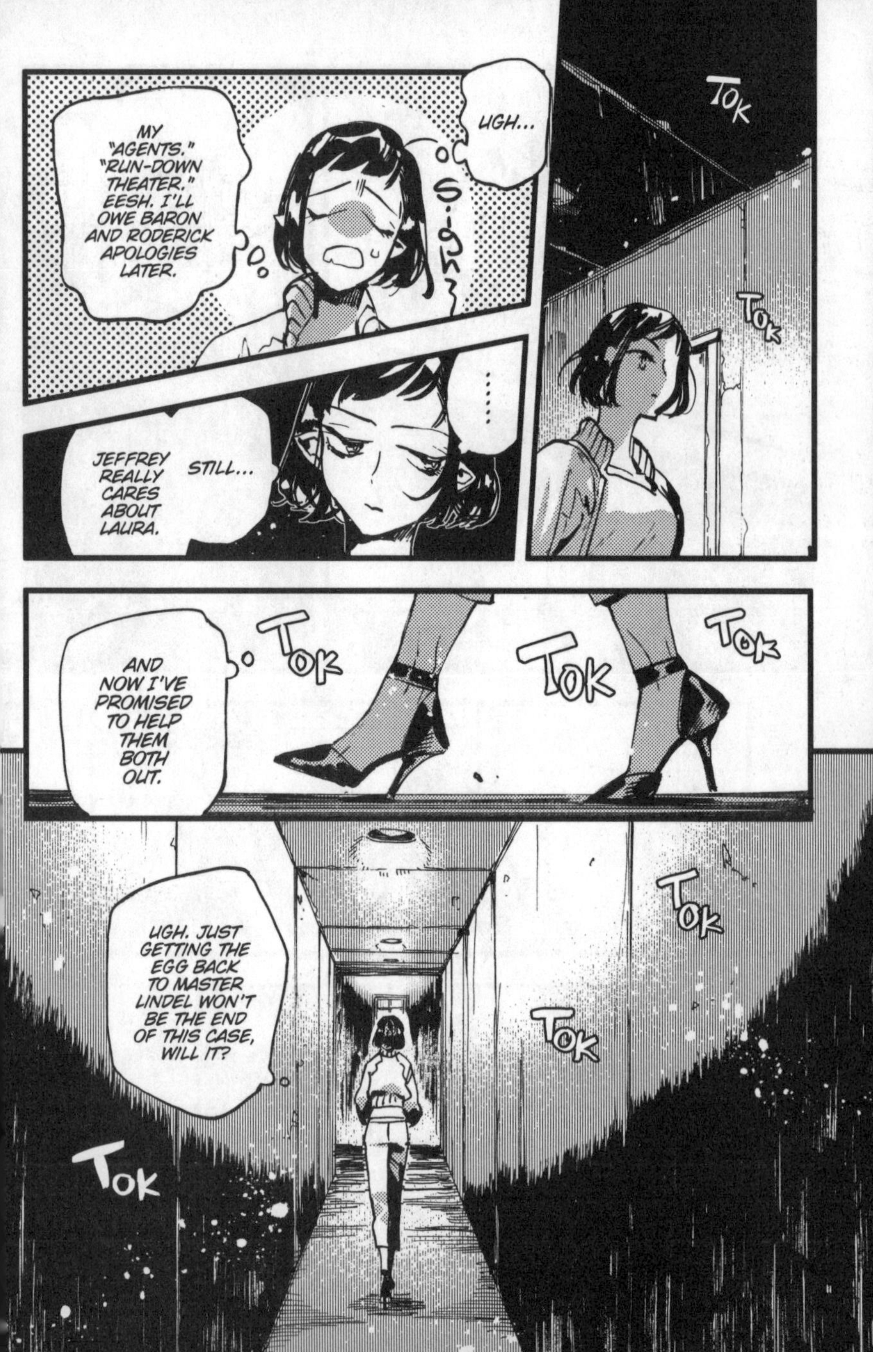
TOK
TOK
UGH...
Sigh
MY "AGENTS." "RUN-DOWN THEATER." EESH. I'LL OWE BARON AND RODERICK APOLOGIES LATER.
......
STILL...
JEFFREY REALLY CARES ABOUT LAURA.
TOK
TOK
TOK
AND NOW I'VE PROMISED TO HELP THEM BOTH OUT.
TOK
TOK
UGH. JUST GETTING THE EGG BACK TO MASTER LINDEL WON'T BE THE END OF THIS CASE, WILL IT?
TOK

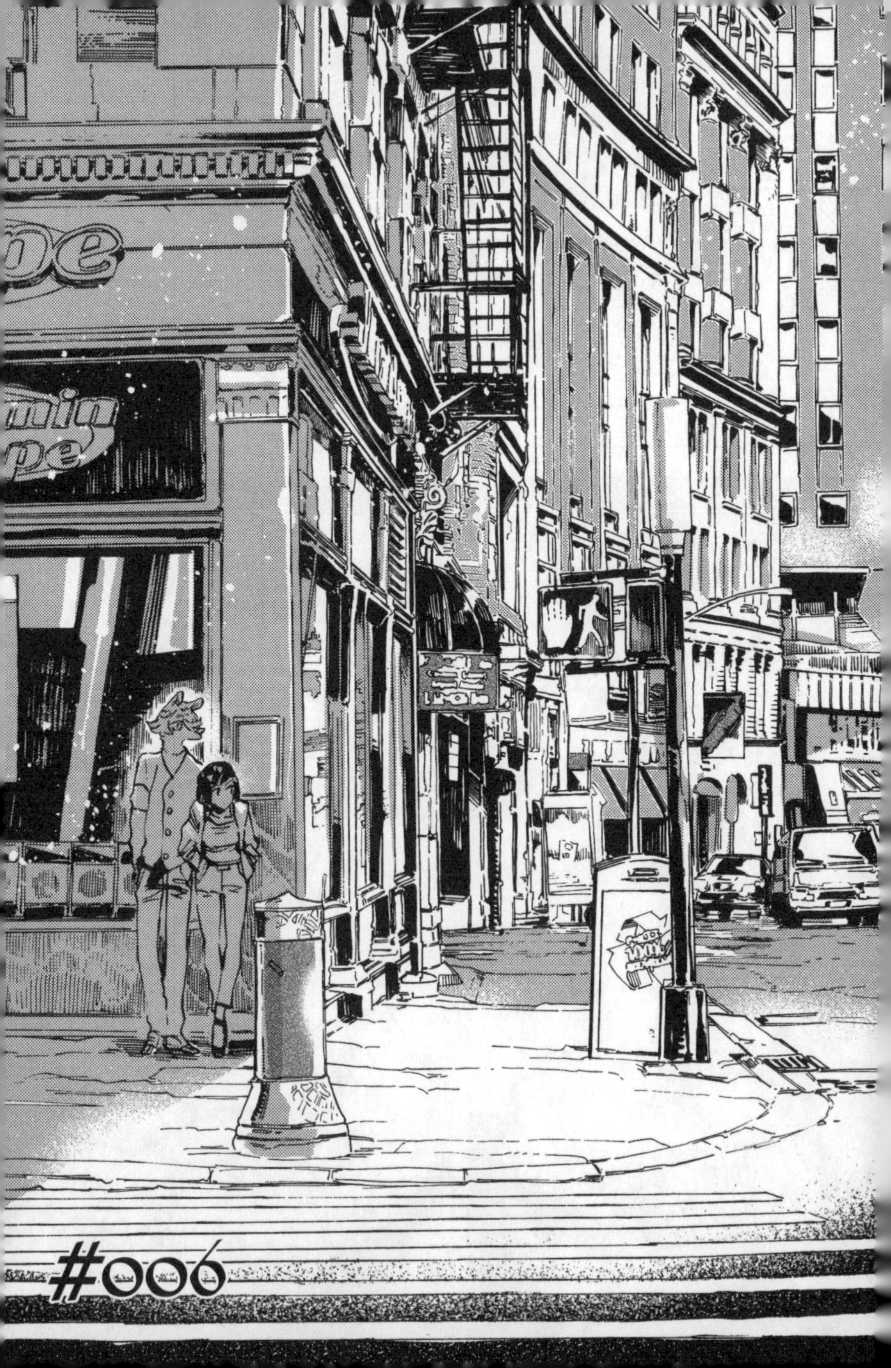
#006

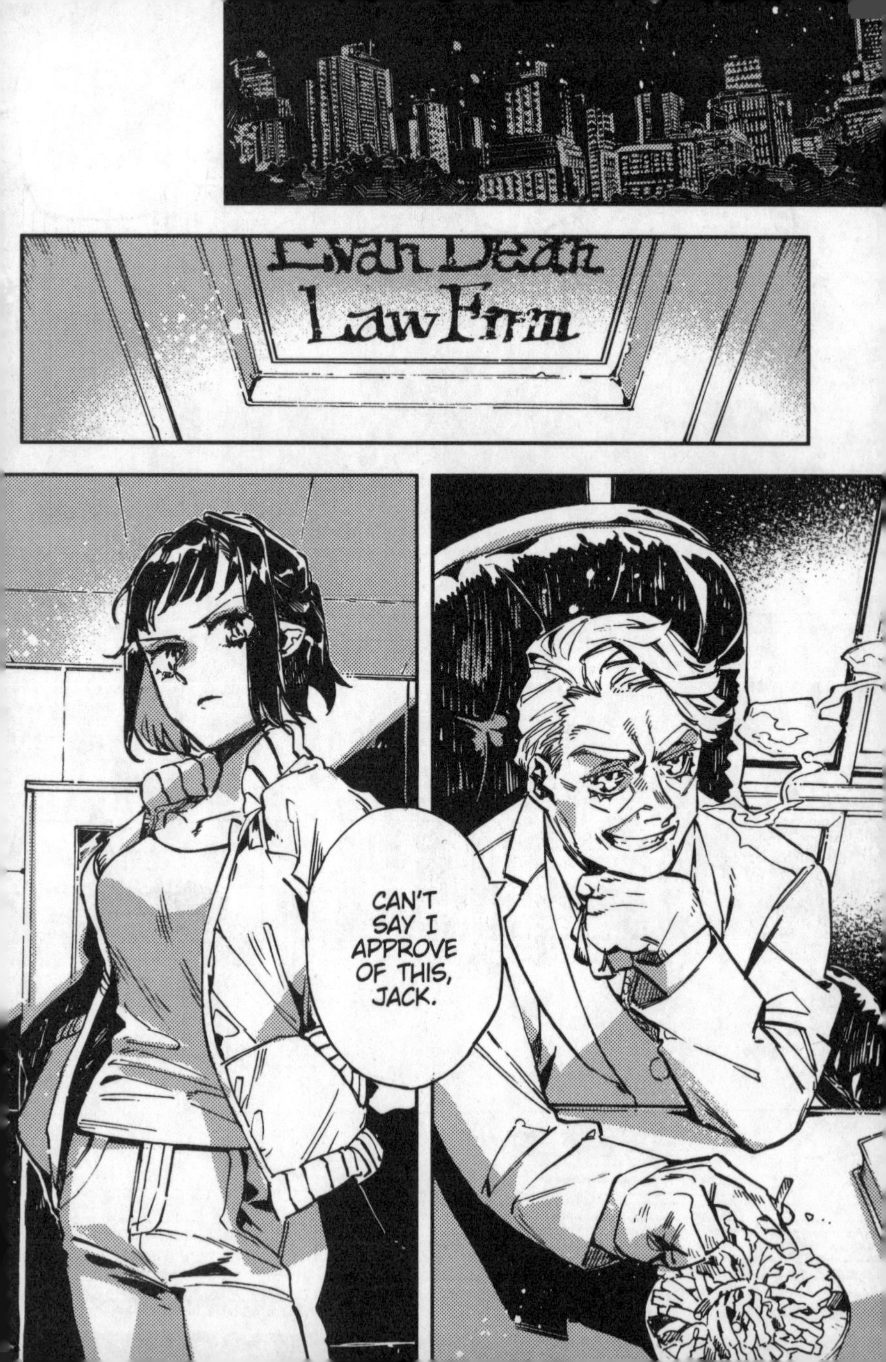
Law Firm
CAN'T SAY I APPROVE OF THIS, JACK.

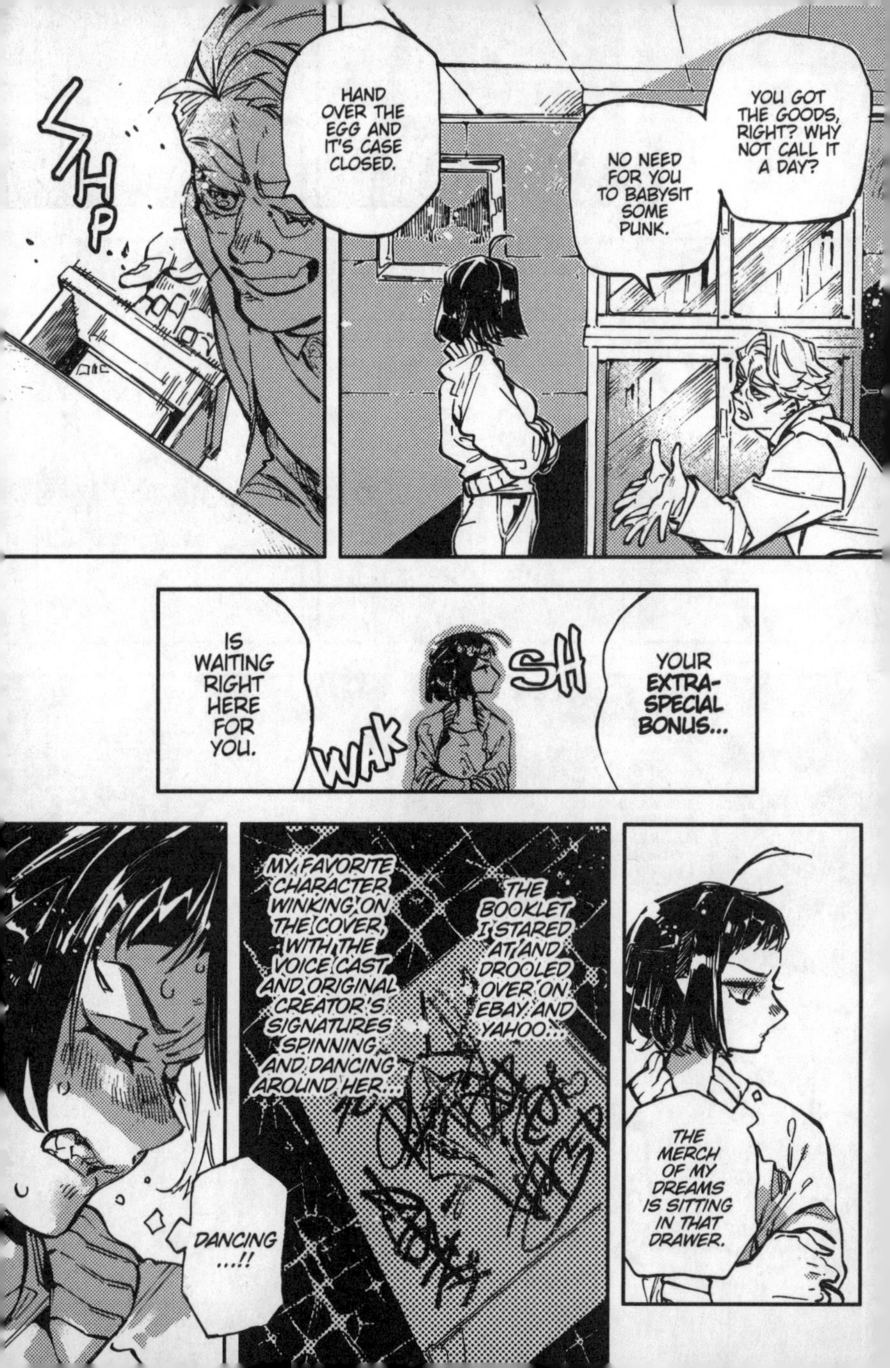
YOU GOT THE GOODS, RIGHT? WHY NOT CALL IT A DAY?
NO NEED FOR YOU TO BABYSIT SOME PUNK.
HAND OVER THE EGG AND IT'S CASE CLOSED.
SHP
YOUR EXTRA-SPECIAL BONUS...
SH
WAK
IS WAITING RIGHT HERE FOR YOU.
THE MERCH OF MY DREAMS IS SITTING IN THAT DRAWER.
THE BOOKLET I STARED AT AND DROOLED OVER ON EBAY AND YAHOO...
MY FAVORITE CHARACTER WINKING ON THE COVER, WITH THE VOICE CAST AND ORIGINAL CREATOR'S SIGNATURES SPINNING AND DANCING AROUND HER...
DANCING ...!!

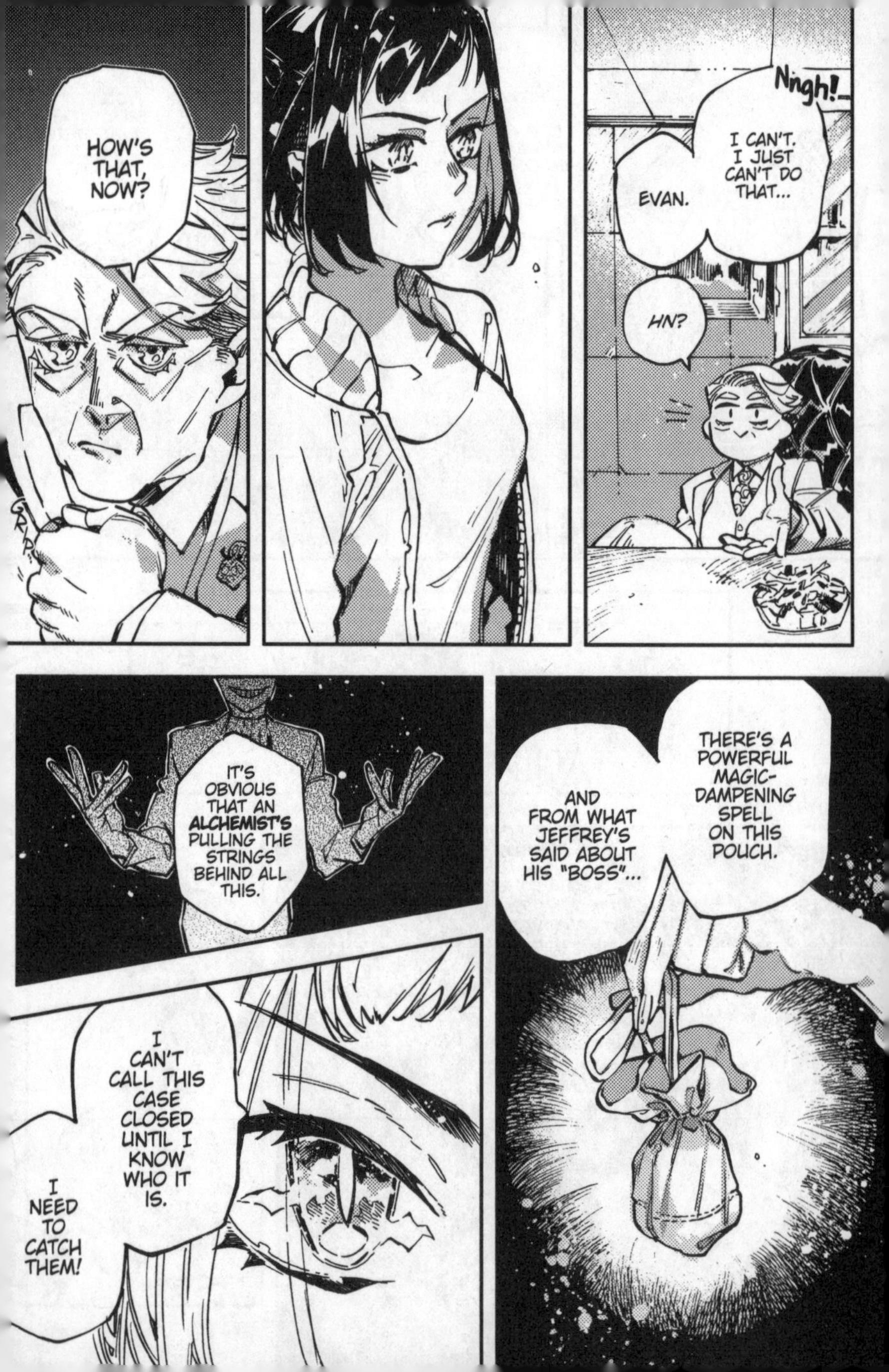
Ningh!
I CAN'T. I JUST CAN'T DO THAT...
EVAN.
HN?
HOW'S THAT, NOW?
GRIP
THERE'S A POWERFUL MAGIC-DAMPENING SPELL ON THIS POUCH.
AND FROM WHAT JEFFREY'S SAID ABOUT HIS "BOSS"...
IT'S OBVIOUS THAT AN **ALCHEMIST'S** PULLING THE STRINGS BEHIND ALL THIS.
I CAN'T CALL THIS CASE CLOSED UNTIL I KNOW WHO IT IS.
I NEED TO CATCH THEM!

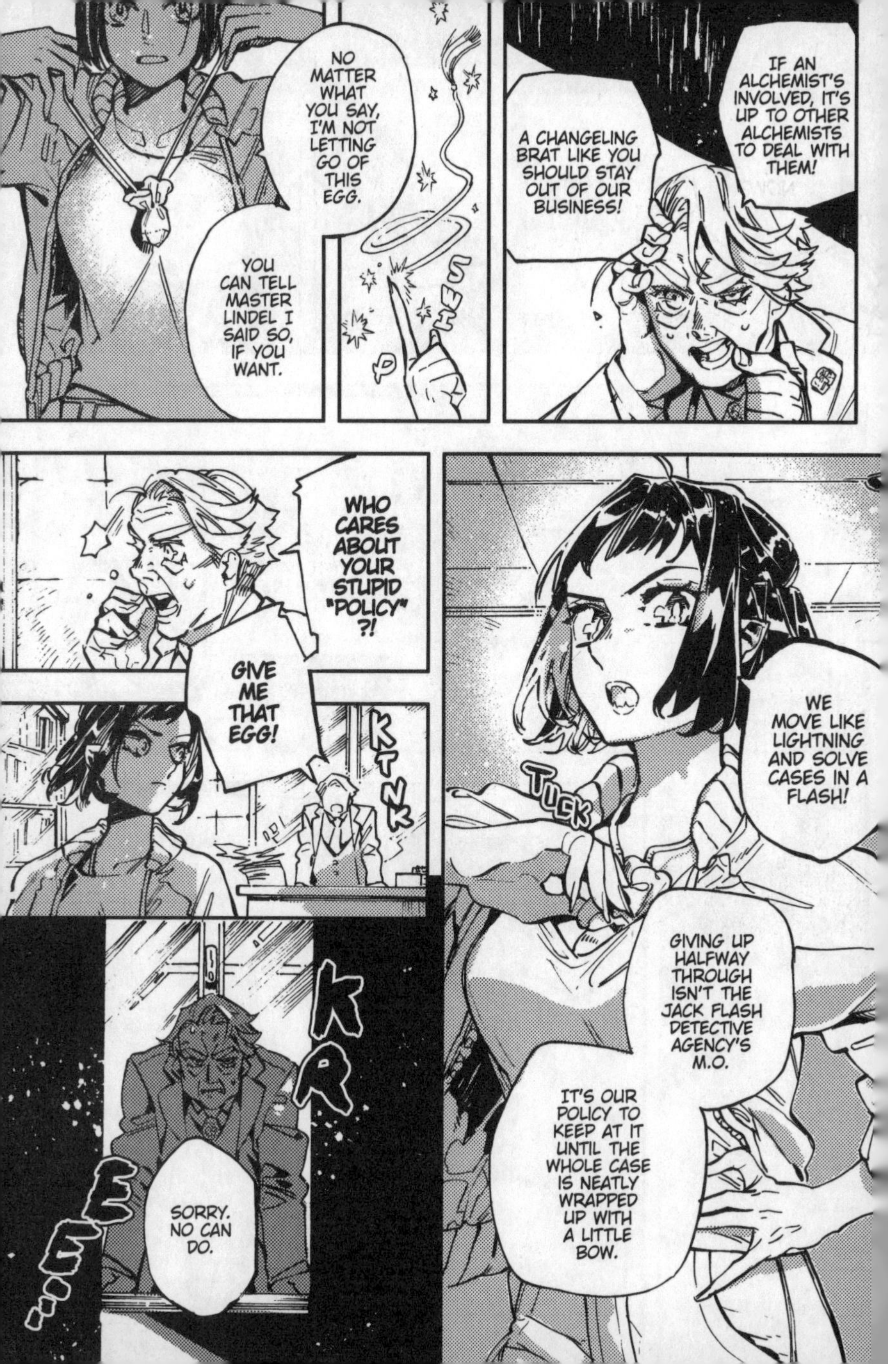
IF AN ALCHEMIST'S INVOLVED, IT'S UP TO OTHER ALCHEMISTS TO DEAL WITH THEM!
A CHANGELING BRAT LIKE YOU SHOULD STAY OUT OF OUR BUSINESS!
SWIP
NO MATTER WHAT YOU SAY, I'M NOT LETTING GO OF THIS EGG.
YOU CAN TELL MASTER LINDEL I SAID SO, IF YOU WANT.
WE MOVE LIKE LIGHTNING AND SOLVE CASES IN A FLASH!
TUCK
GIVING UP HALFWAY THROUGH ISN'T THE JACK FLASH DETECTIVE AGENCY'S M.O.
IT'S OUR POLICY TO KEEP AT IT UNTIL THE WHOLE CASE IS NEATLY WRAPPED UP WITH A LITTLE BOW.
WHO CARES ABOUT YOUR STUPID "POLICY"?!
GIVE ME THAT EGG!
KTNK
SORRY. NO CAN DO.
KREEE...

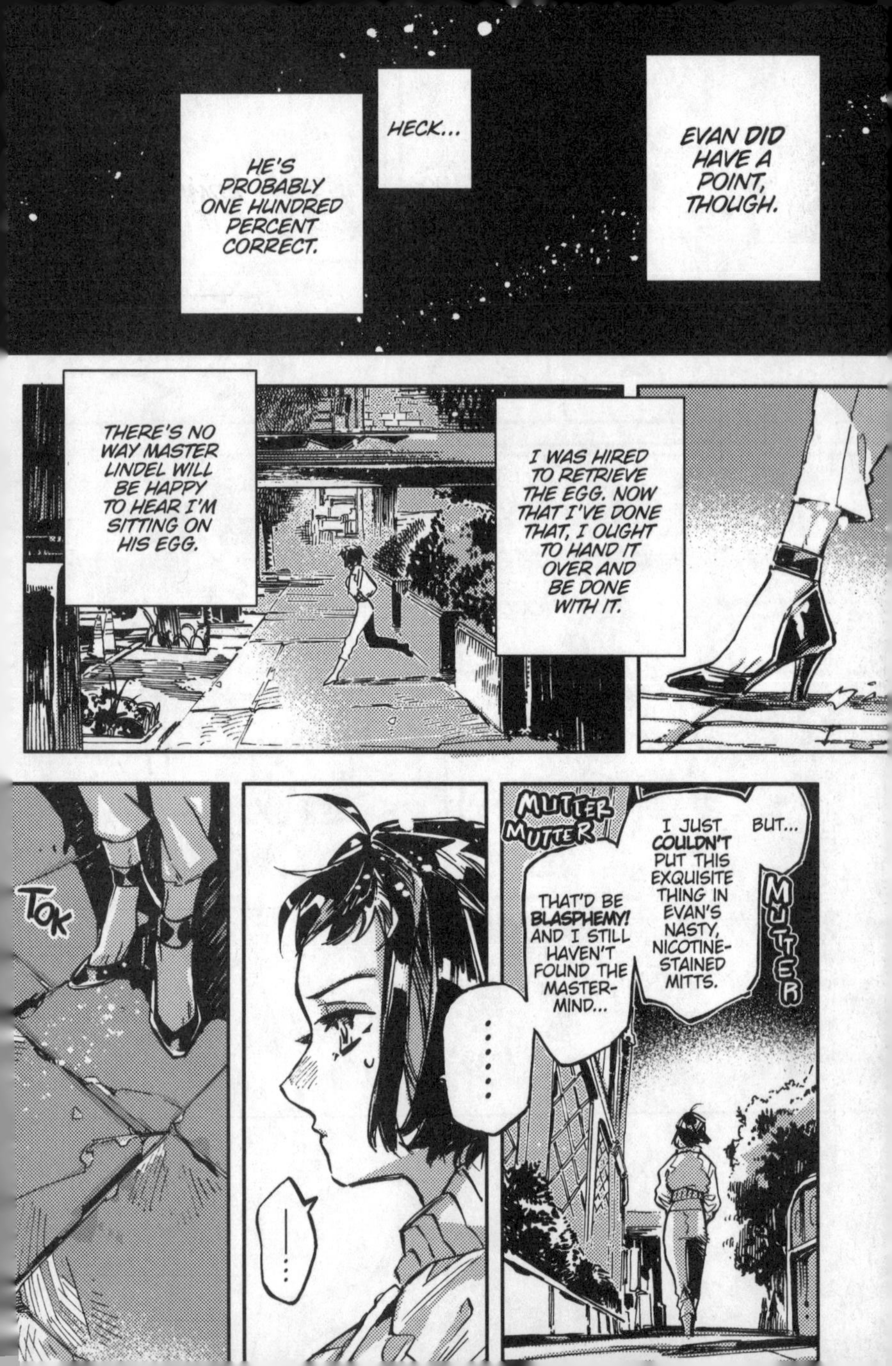
EVAN DID HAVE A POINT, THOUGH.
HECK...
HE'S PROBABLY ONE HUNDRED PERCENT CORRECT.
I WAS HIRED TO RETRIEVE THE EGG. NOW THAT I'VE DONE THAT, I OUGHT TO HAND IT OVER AND BE DONE WITH IT.
THERE'S NO WAY MASTER LINDEL WILL BE HAPPY TO HEAR I'M SITTING ON HIS EGG.
MUTTER
BUT...
I JUST COULDN'T PUT THIS EXQUISITE THING IN EVAN'S NASTY, NICOTINE-STAINED MITTS.
MUTTER MUTTER
THAT'D BE BLASPHEMY! AND I STILL HAVEN'T FOUND THE MASTER-MIND...
......
......
TOK

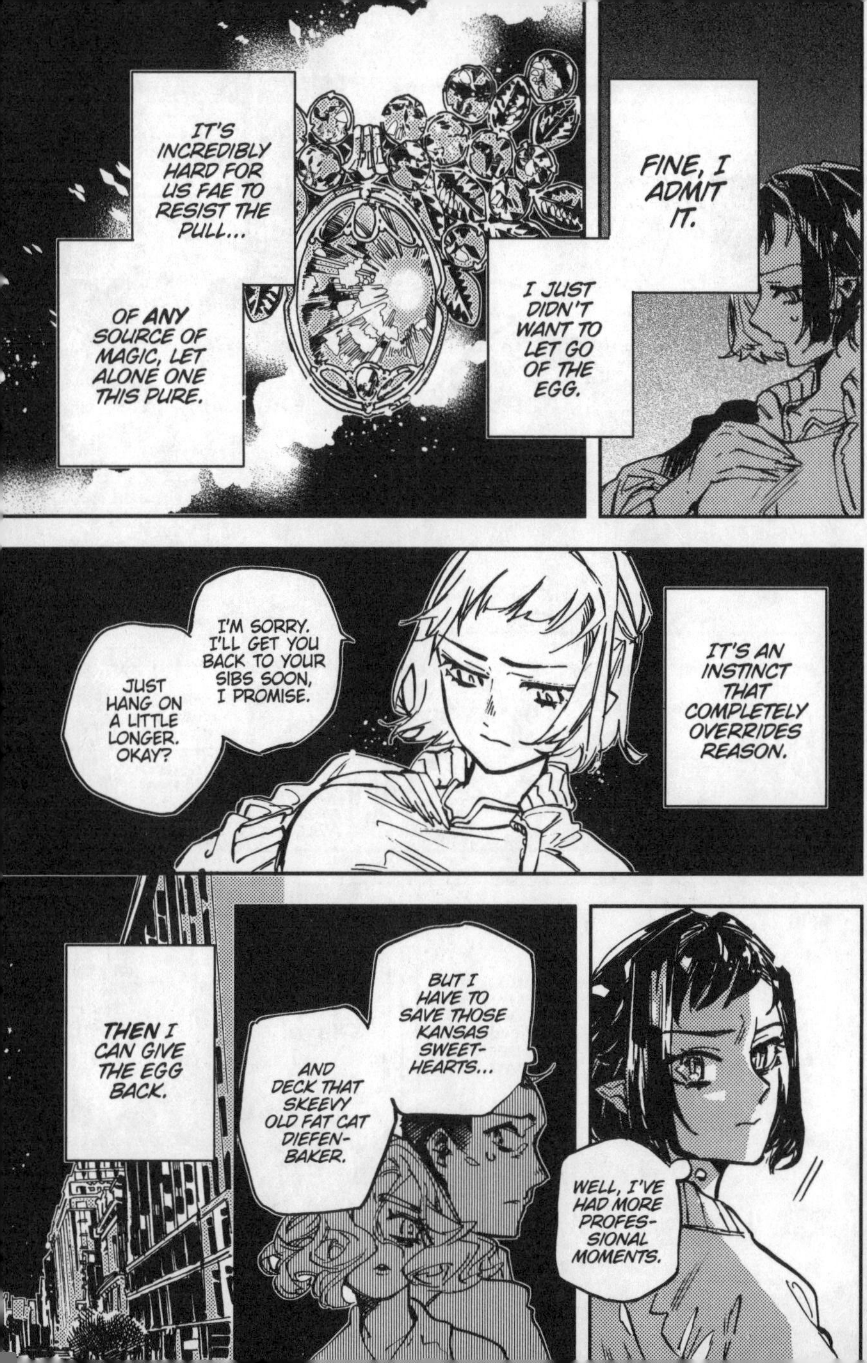
FINE, I ADMIT IT.
I JUST DIDN'T WANT TO LET GO OF THE EGG.
IT'S INCREDIBLY HARD FOR US FAE TO RESIST THE PULL...
OF ANY SOURCE OF MAGIC, LET ALONE ONE THIS PURE.
IT'S AN INSTINCT THAT COMPLETELY OVERRIDES REASON.
I'M SORRY. I'LL GET YOU BACK TO YOUR SIBS SOON, I PROMISE.
JUST HANG ON A LITTLE LONGER. OKAY?
WELL, I'VE HAD MORE PROFES-SIONAL MOMENTS.
BUT I HAVE TO SAVE THOSE KANSAS SWEET-HEARTS...
AND DECK THAT SKEEVY OLD FAT CAT DIEFEN-BAKER.
THEN I CAN GIVE THE EGG BACK.

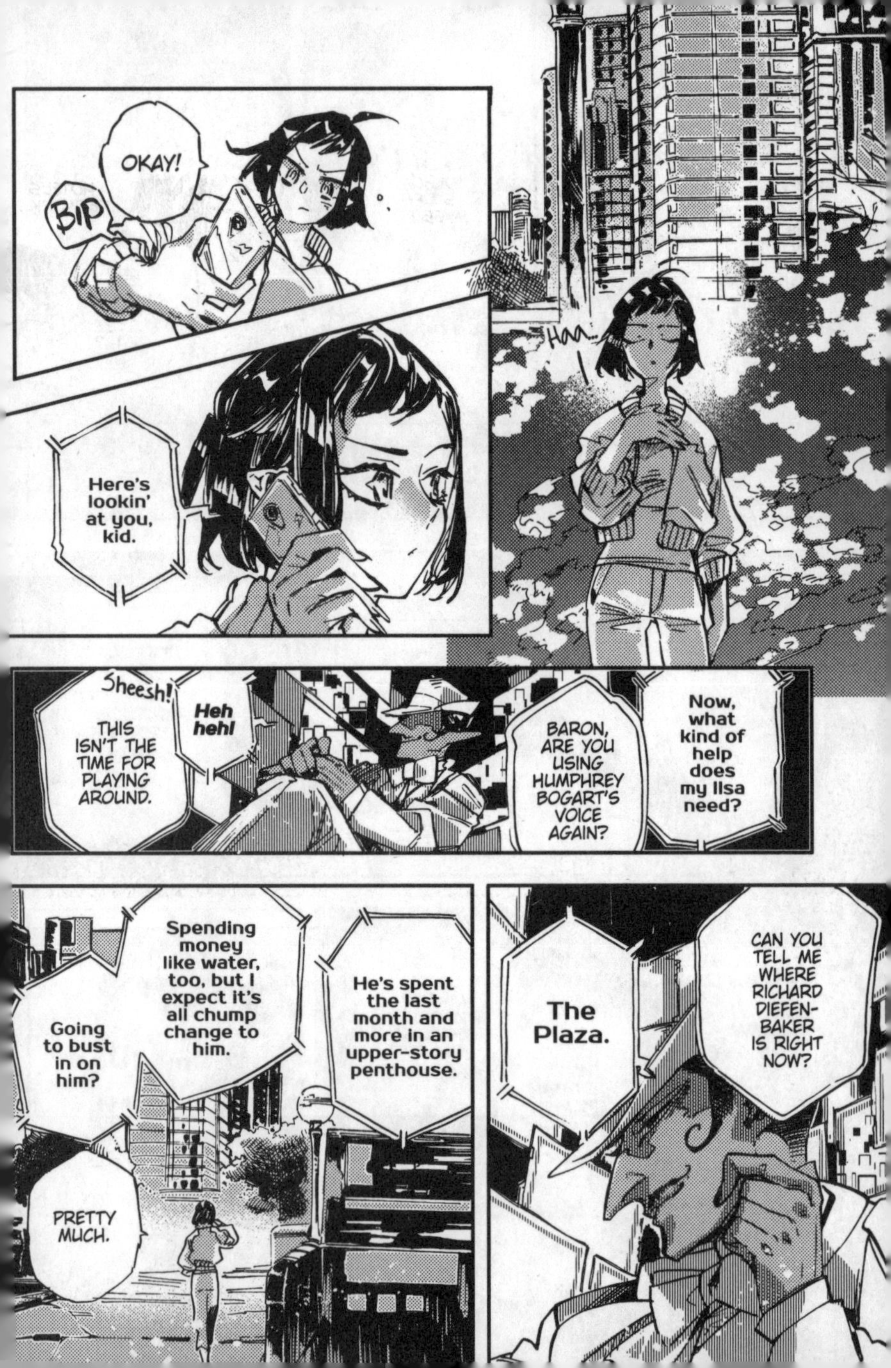
Hmm...
OKAY!
BIP
Here's lookin' at you, kid.
Now, what kind of help does my Ilsa need?
BARON, ARE YOU USING HUMPHREY BOGART'S VOICE AGAIN?
Heh heh!
Sheesh!
THIS ISN'T THE TIME FOR PLAYING AROUND.
CAN YOU TELL ME WHERE RICHARD DIEFEN-BAKER IS RIGHT NOW?
The Plaza.
He's spent the last month and more in an upper-story penthouse.
Spending money like water, too, but I expect it's all chump change to him.
Going to bust in on him?
PRETTY MUCH.

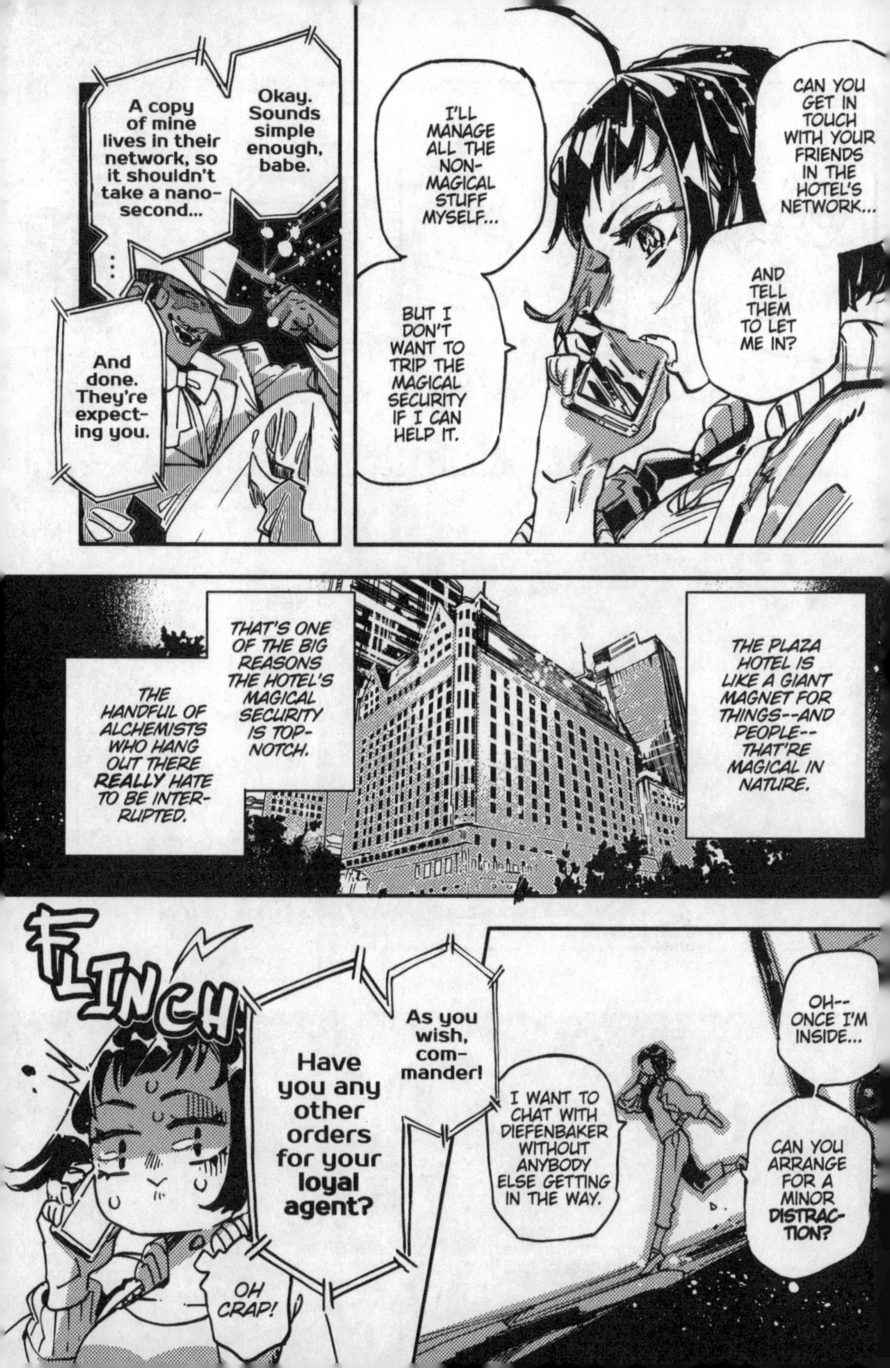
CAN YOU GET IN TOUCH WITH YOUR FRIENDS IN THE HOTEL'S NETWORK...
AND TELL THEM TO LET ME IN?
I'LL MANAGE ALL THE NON-MAGICAL STUFF MYSELF...
BUT I DON'T WANT TO TRIP THE MAGICAL SECURITY IF I CAN HELP IT.
Okay. Sounds simple enough, babe.
A copy of mine lives in their network, so it shouldn't take a nano-second...
...
And done. They're expecting you.
THE PLAZA HOTEL IS LIKE A GIANT MAGNET FOR THINGS--AND PEOPLE--THAT'RE MAGICAL IN NATURE.
THAT'S ONE OF THE BIG REASONS THE HOTEL'S MAGICAL SECURITY IS TOP-NOTCH.
THE HANDFUL OF ALCHEMISTS WHO HANG OUT THERE REALLY HATE TO BE INTER-RUPTED.
OH-- ONCE I'M INSIDE...
CAN YOU ARRANGE FOR A MINOR DISTRACTION?
I WANT TO CHAT WITH DIEFENBAKER WITHOUT ANYBODY ELSE GETTING IN THE WAY.
As you wish, com-mander!
Have you any other orders for your loyal agent?
FLINCH
OH CRAP!

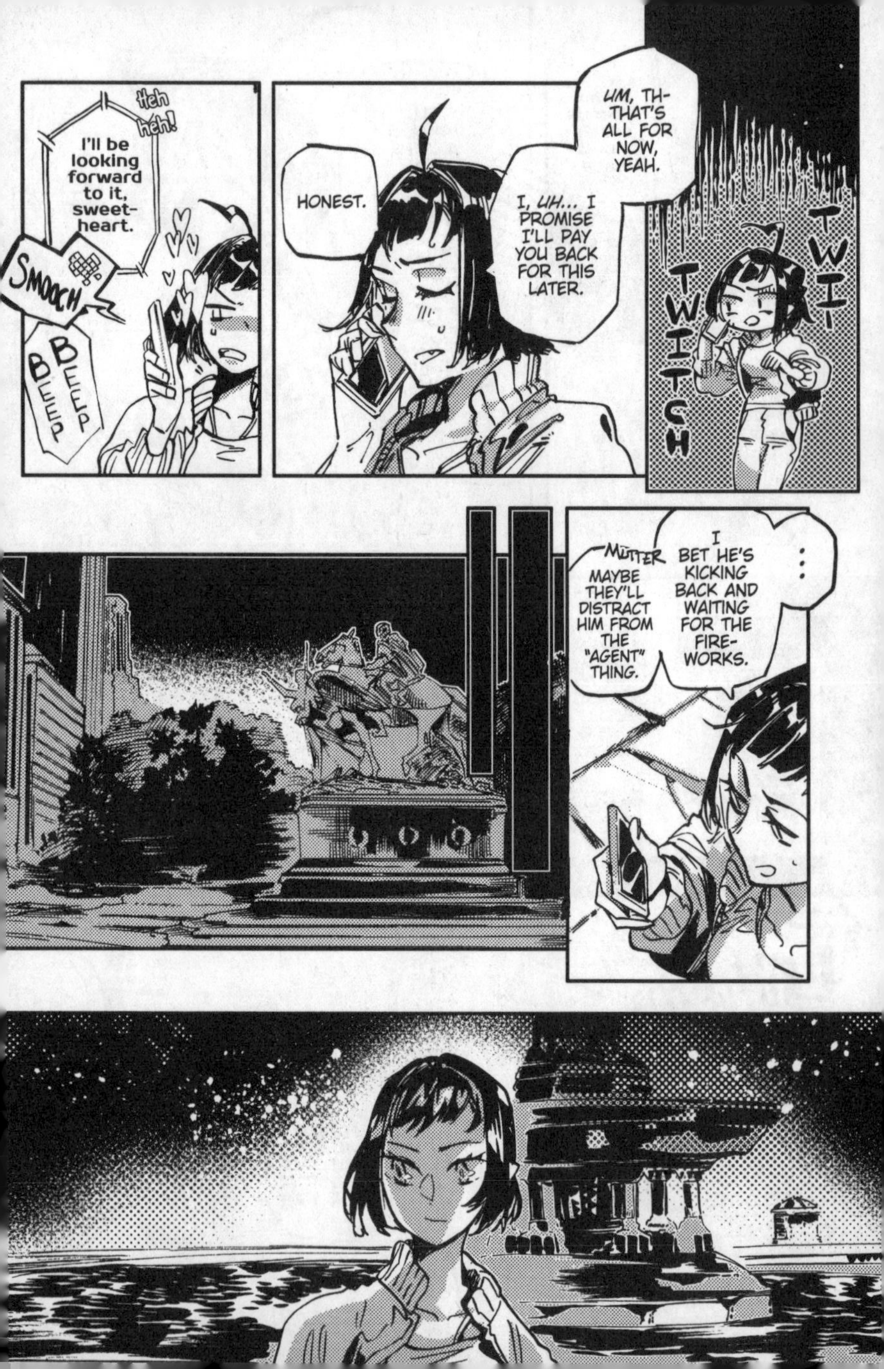
UM, TH-THAT'S ALL FOR NOW, YEAH.
TWI-
TWITCH
I, UH... I PROMISE I'LL PAY YOU BACK FOR THIS LATER.
HONEST.
heh heh!
I'll be looking forward to it, sweetheart.
SMOOCH
BEEP BEEP
...
I BET HE'S KICKING BACK AND WAITING FOR THE FIRE-WORKS.
MUTTER
MAYBE THEY'LL DISTRACT HIM FROM THE "AGENT" THING.

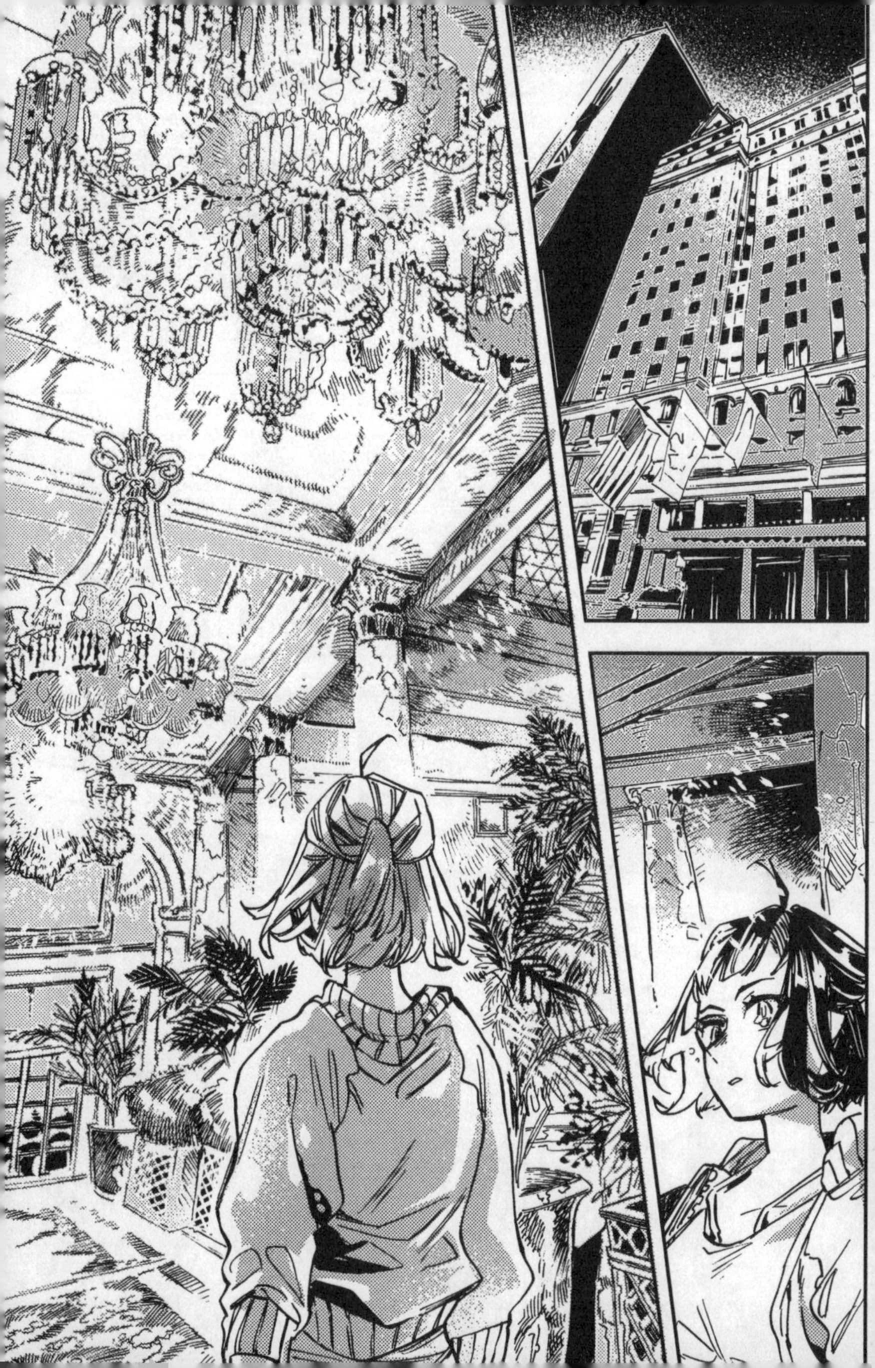

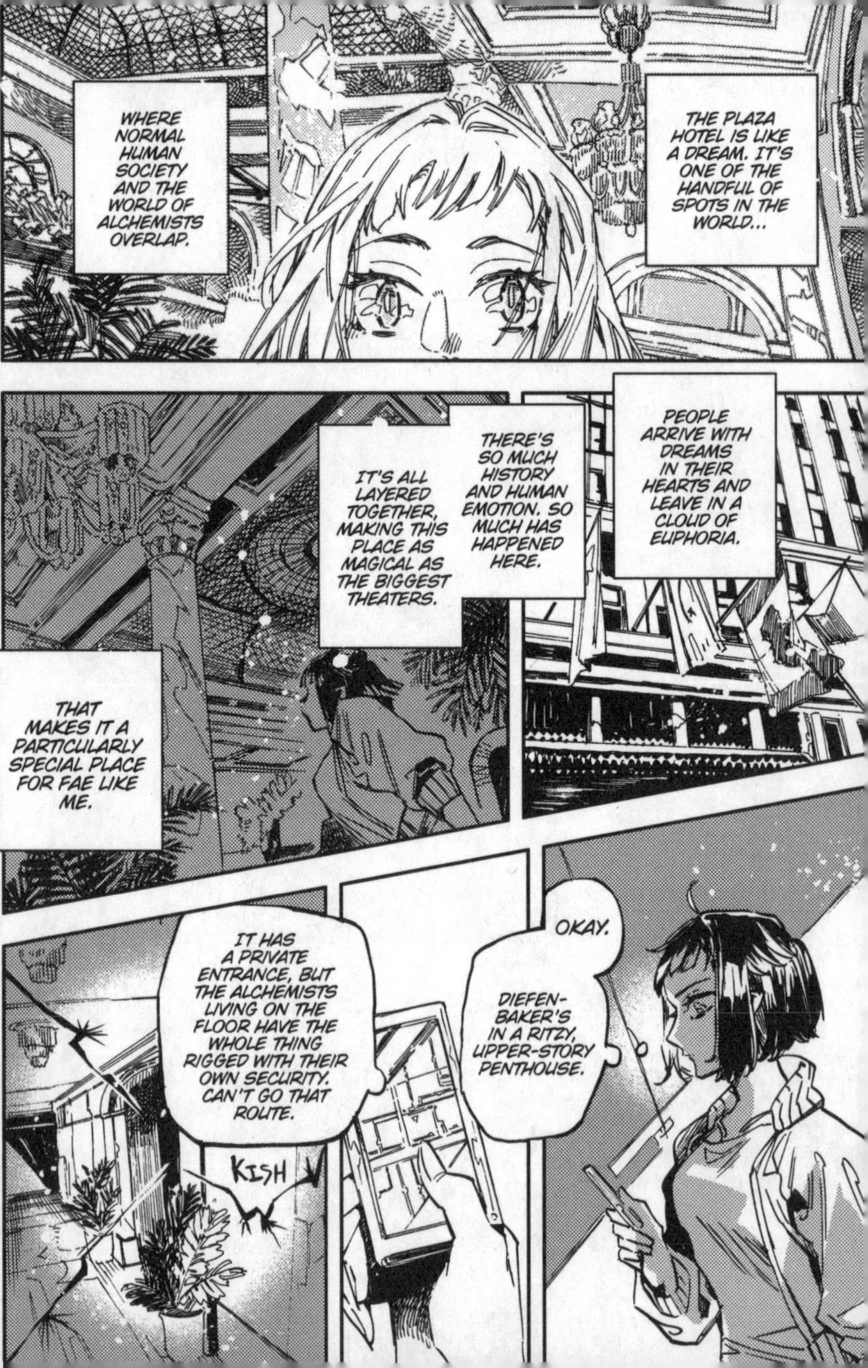
THE PLAZA HOTEL IS LIKE A DREAM. IT'S ONE OF THE HANDFUL OF SPOTS IN THE WORLD...
WHERE NORMAL HUMAN SOCIETY AND THE WORLD OF ALCHEMISTS OVERLAP.
PEOPLE ARRIVE WITH DREAMS IN THEIR HEARTS AND LEAVE IN A CLOUD OF EUPHORIA.
THERE'S SO MUCH HISTORY AND HUMAN EMOTION. SO MUCH HAS HAPPENED HERE.
IT'S ALL LAYERED TOGETHER, MAKING THIS PLACE AS MAGICAL AS THE BIGGEST THEATERS.
THAT MAKES IT A PARTICULARLY SPECIAL PLACE FOR FAE LIKE ME.
OKAY.
DIEFEN-BAKER'S IN A RITZY, UPPER-STORY PENTHOUSE.
IT HAS A PRIVATE ENTRANCE, BUT THE ALCHEMISTS LIVING ON THE FLOOR HAVE THE WHOLE THING RIGGED WITH THEIR OWN SECURITY. CAN'T GO THAT ROUTE.
KISH

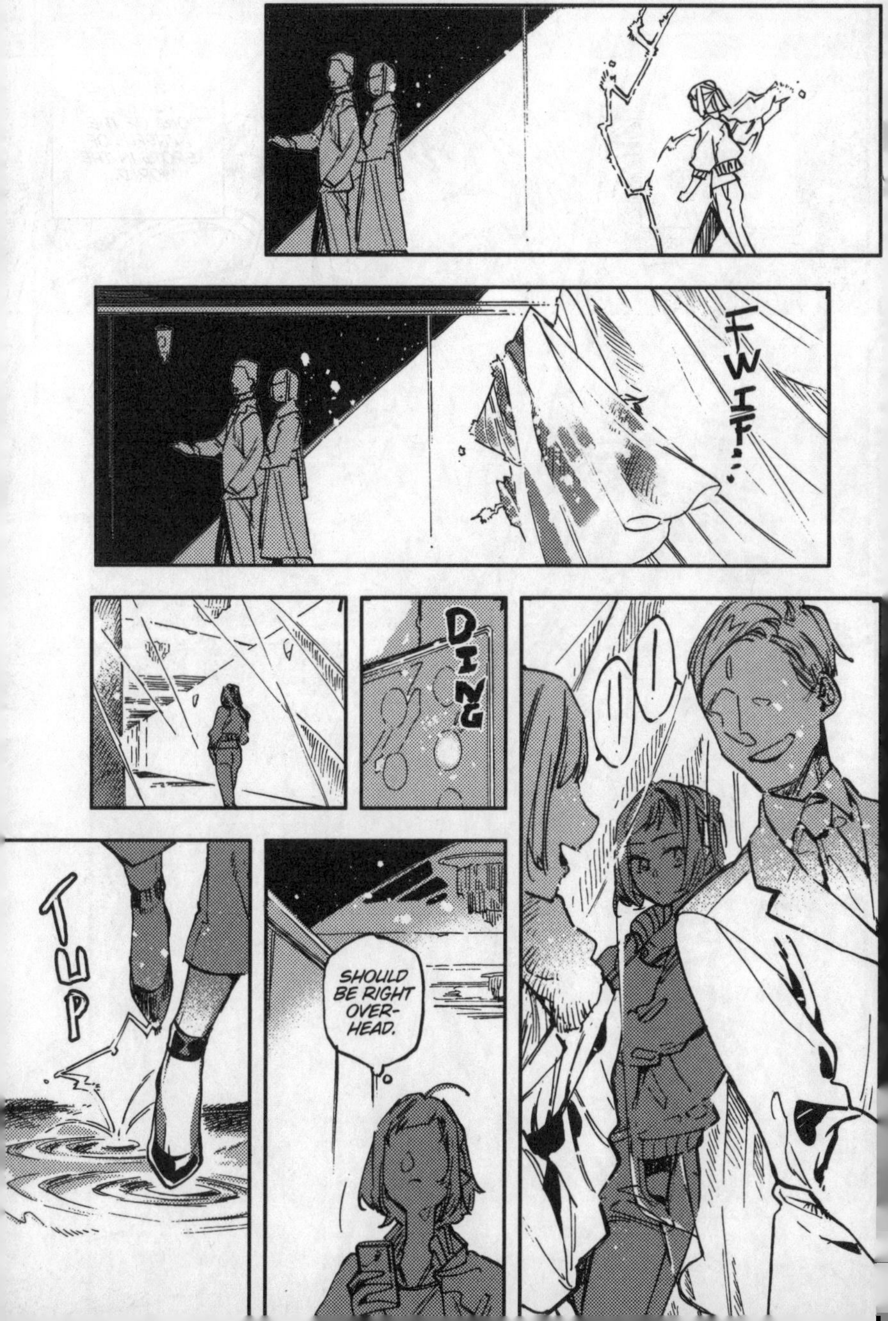
FWIF
DING
SHOULD BE RIGHT OVER-HEAD.
TUP

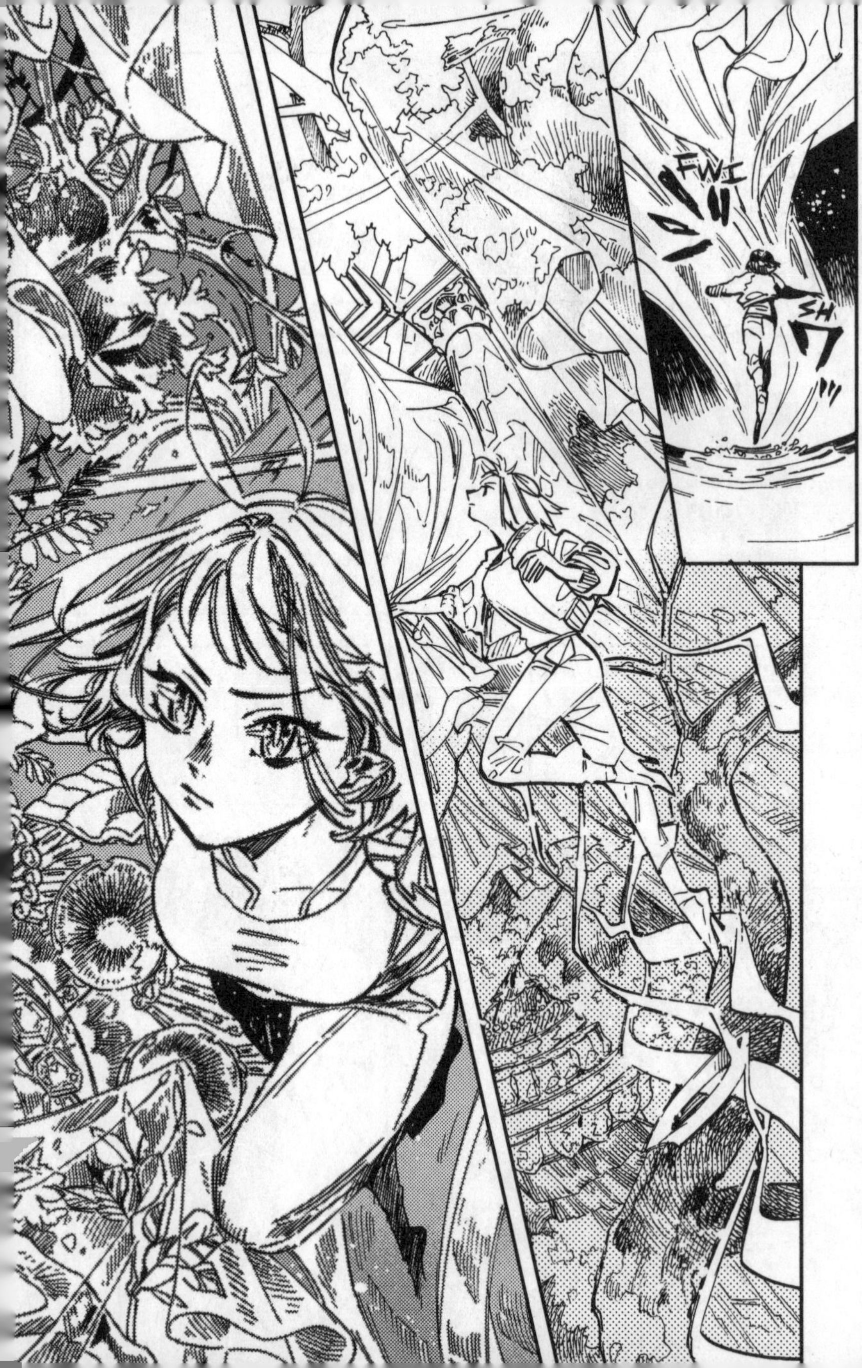
FWI
SH

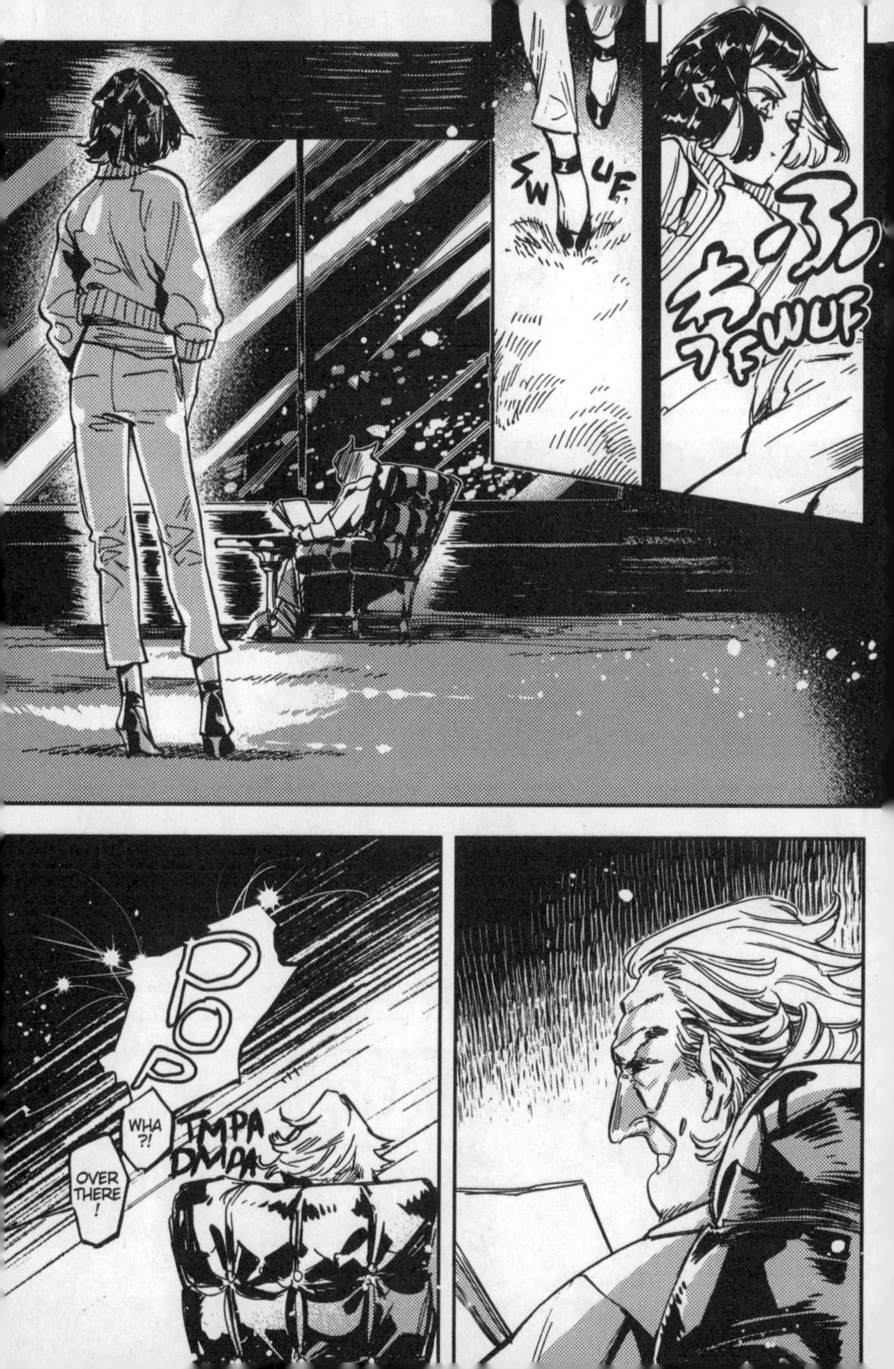
ふわ
FWUF
SWUF
POP
WHA?!
TMPA DMPA
OVER THERE!

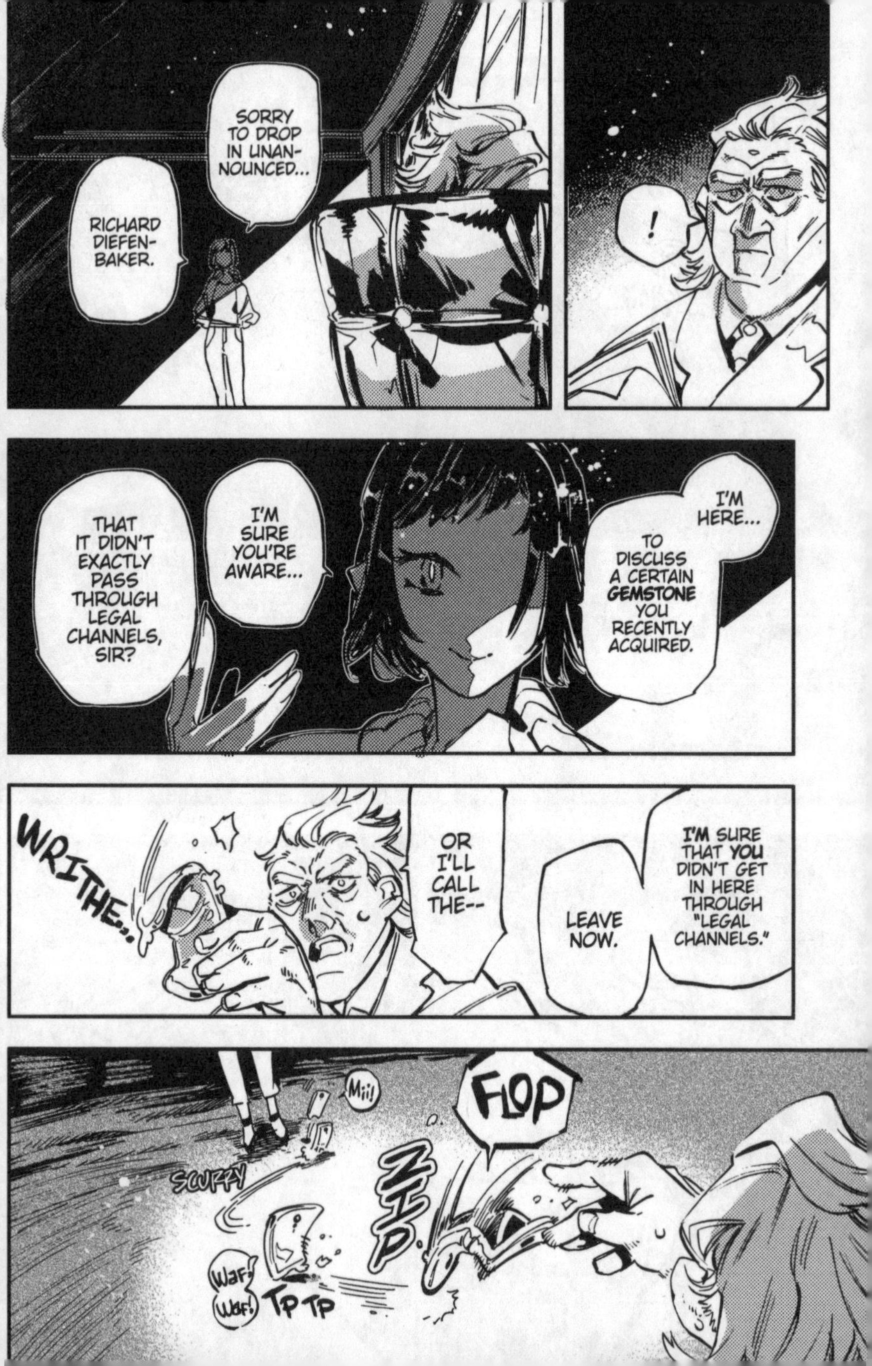
!
SORRY TO DROP IN UNANNOUNCED...
RICHARD DIEFENBAKER.
I'M HERE...
TO DISCUSS A CERTAIN **GEMSTONE** YOU RECENTLY ACQUIRED.
I'M SURE YOU'RE AWARE...
THAT IT DIDN'T EXACTLY PASS THROUGH LEGAL CHANNELS, SIR?
I'M SURE THAT **YOU** DIDN'T GET IN HERE THROUGH "LEGAL CHANNELS."
LEAVE NOW.
OR I'LL CALL THE--
WRITHE...
FLOP
Mi!
ZIP
SCURRY
Waf! Waf!
TP TP

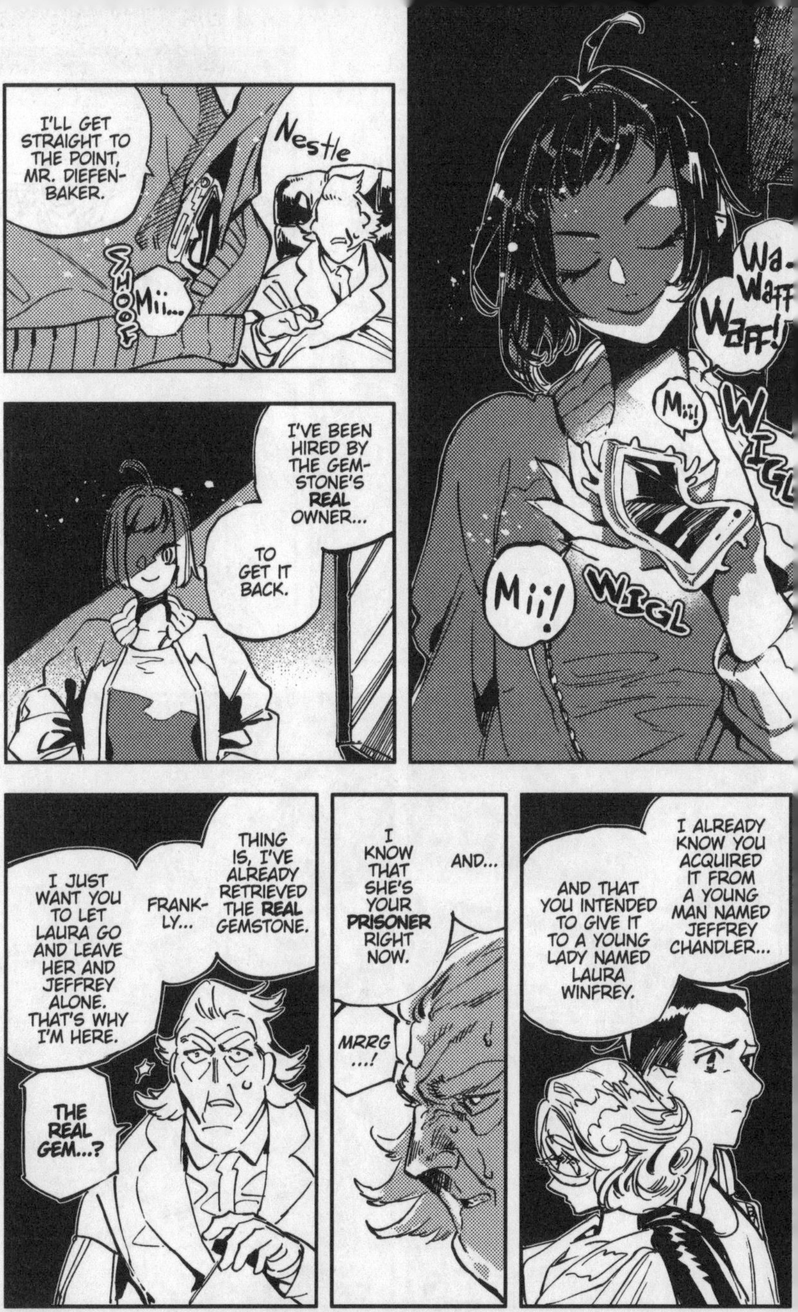
Wa-Waff Waff!
WIGL
Mii!
Mii!
WIGL
I'LL GET STRAIGHT TO THE POINT, MR. DIEFEN-BAKER.
Nestle
Mii...
I'VE BEEN HIRED BY THE GEM-STONE'S **REAL** OWNER...
TO GET IT BACK.
I ALREADY KNOW YOU ACQUIRED IT FROM A YOUNG MAN NAMED JEFFREY CHANDLER...
AND THAT YOU INTENDED TO GIVE IT TO A YOUNG LADY NAMED LAURA WINFREY.
AND...
I KNOW THAT SHE'S YOUR **PRISONER** RIGHT NOW.
MRRG ...!
THING IS, I'VE ALREADY RETRIEVED THE **REAL** GEMSTONE.
FRANK-LY...
I JUST WANT YOU TO LET LAURA GO AND LEAVE HER AND JEFFREY ALONE. THAT'S WHY I'M HERE.
THE REAL GEM...?

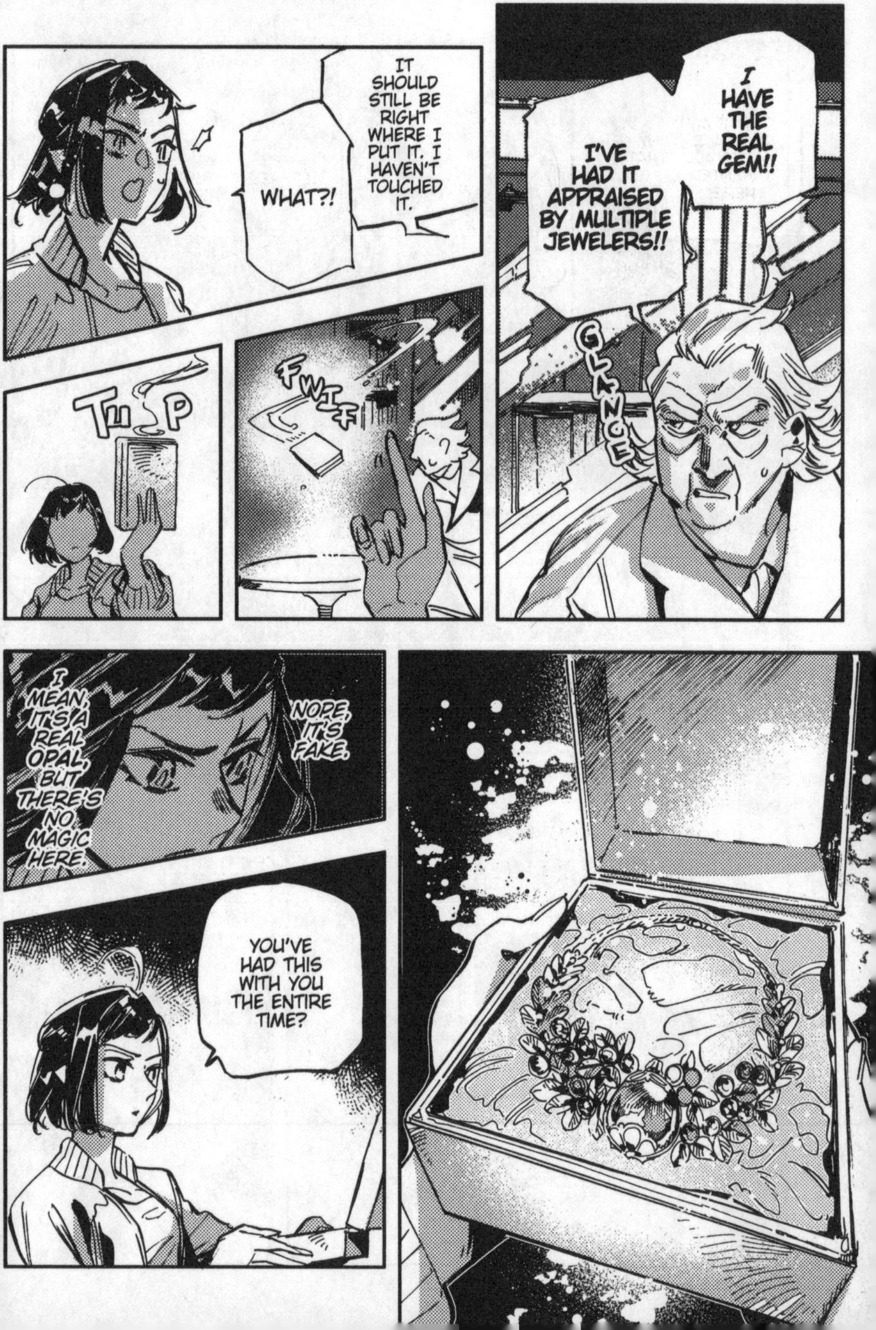
I HAVE THE REAL GEM!!
I'VE HAD IT APPRAISED BY MULTIPLE JEWELERS!!
GLANCE
IT SHOULD STILL BE RIGHT WHERE I PUT IT. I HAVEN'T TOUCHED IT.
WHAT?!
FWIF
TUP
NOPE, IT'S FAKE.
I MEAN, IT'S A REAL OPAL, BUT THERE'S NO MAGIC HERE.
YOU'VE HAD THIS WITH YOU THE ENTIRE TIME?

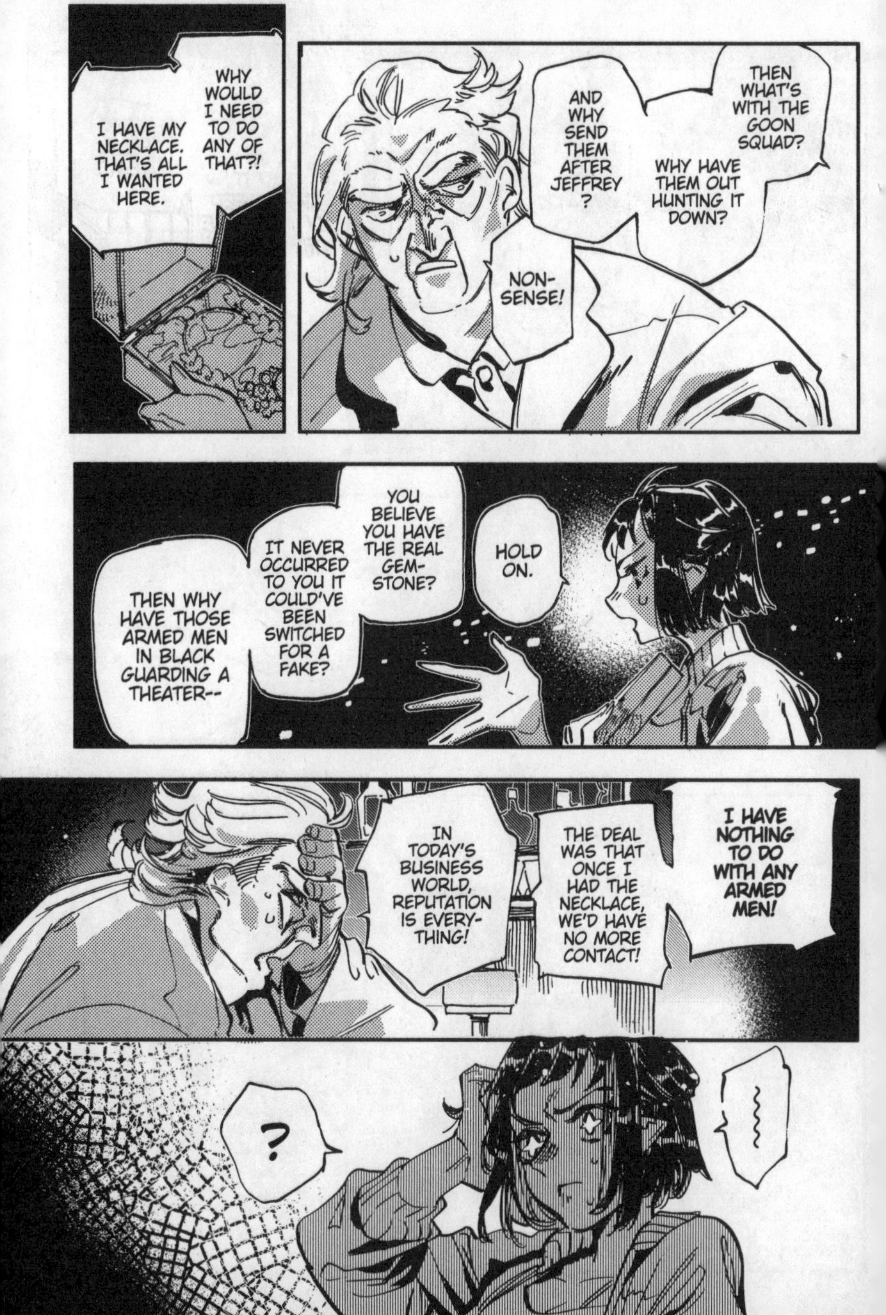
THEN WHAT'S WITH THE GOON SQUAD?
WHY HAVE THEM OUT HUNTING IT DOWN?
AND WHY SEND THEM AFTER JEFFREY?
NON-SENSE!
WHY WOULD I NEED TO DO ANY OF THAT?!
I HAVE MY NECKLACE. THAT'S ALL I WANTED HERE.
HOLD ON.
YOU BELIEVE YOU HAVE THE REAL GEM-STONE?
IT NEVER OCCURRED TO YOU IT COULD'VE BEEN SWITCHED FOR A FAKE?
THEN WHY HAVE THOSE ARMED MEN IN BLACK GUARDING A THEATER--
I HAVE NOTHING TO DO WITH ANY ARMED MEN!
THE DEAL WAS THAT ONCE I HAD THE NECKLACE, WE'D HAVE NO MORE CONTACT!
IN TODAY'S BUSINESS WORLD, REPUTATION IS EVERY-THING!
......
?

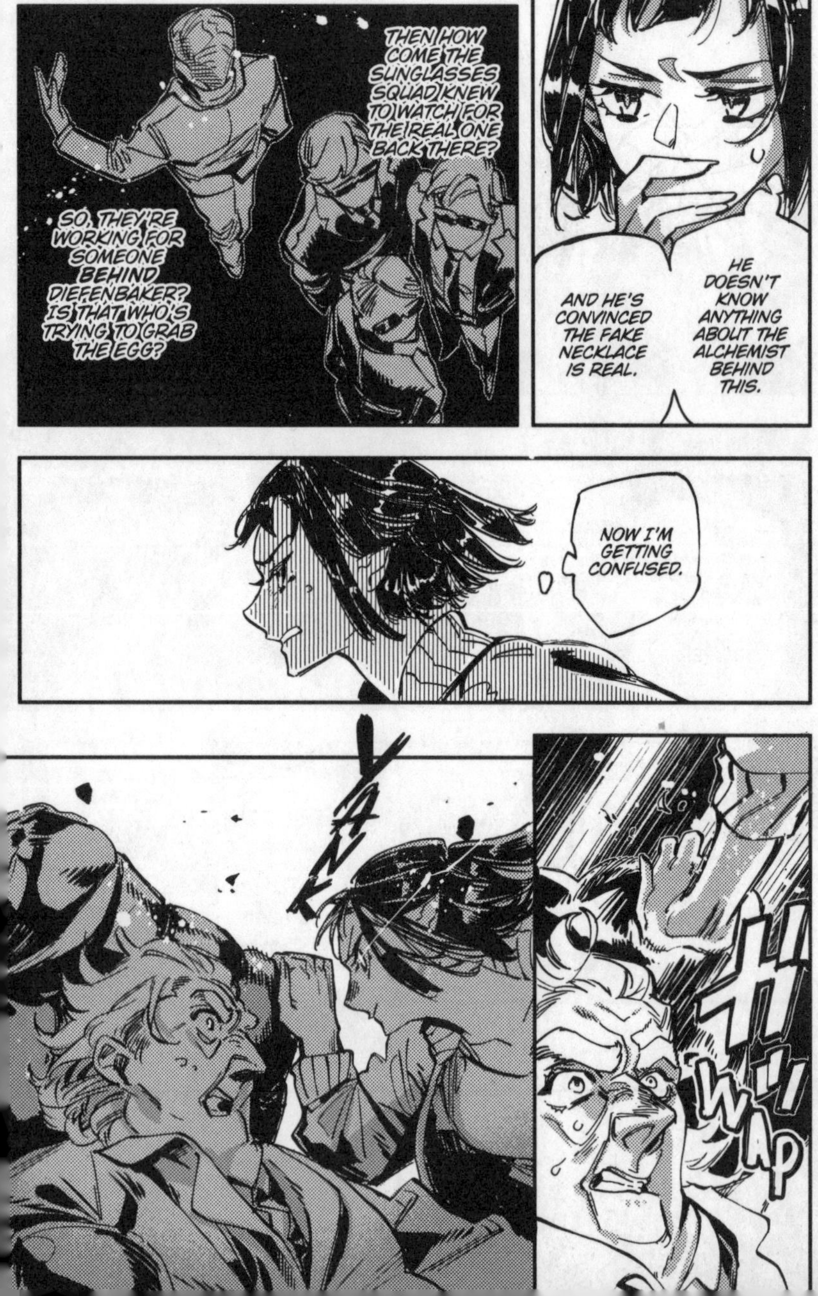
HE DOESN'T KNOW ANYTHING ABOUT THE ALCHEMIST BEHIND THIS.
AND HE'S CONVINCED THE FAKE NECKLACE IS REAL.
THEN HOW COME THE SUNGLASSES SQUAD KNEW TO WATCH FOR THE REAL ONE BACK THERE?
SO, THEY'RE WORKING FOR SOMEONE BEHIND DIEFENBAKER? IS THAT WHO'S TRYING TO GRAB THE EGG?
NOW I'M GETTING CONFUSED.
YANK

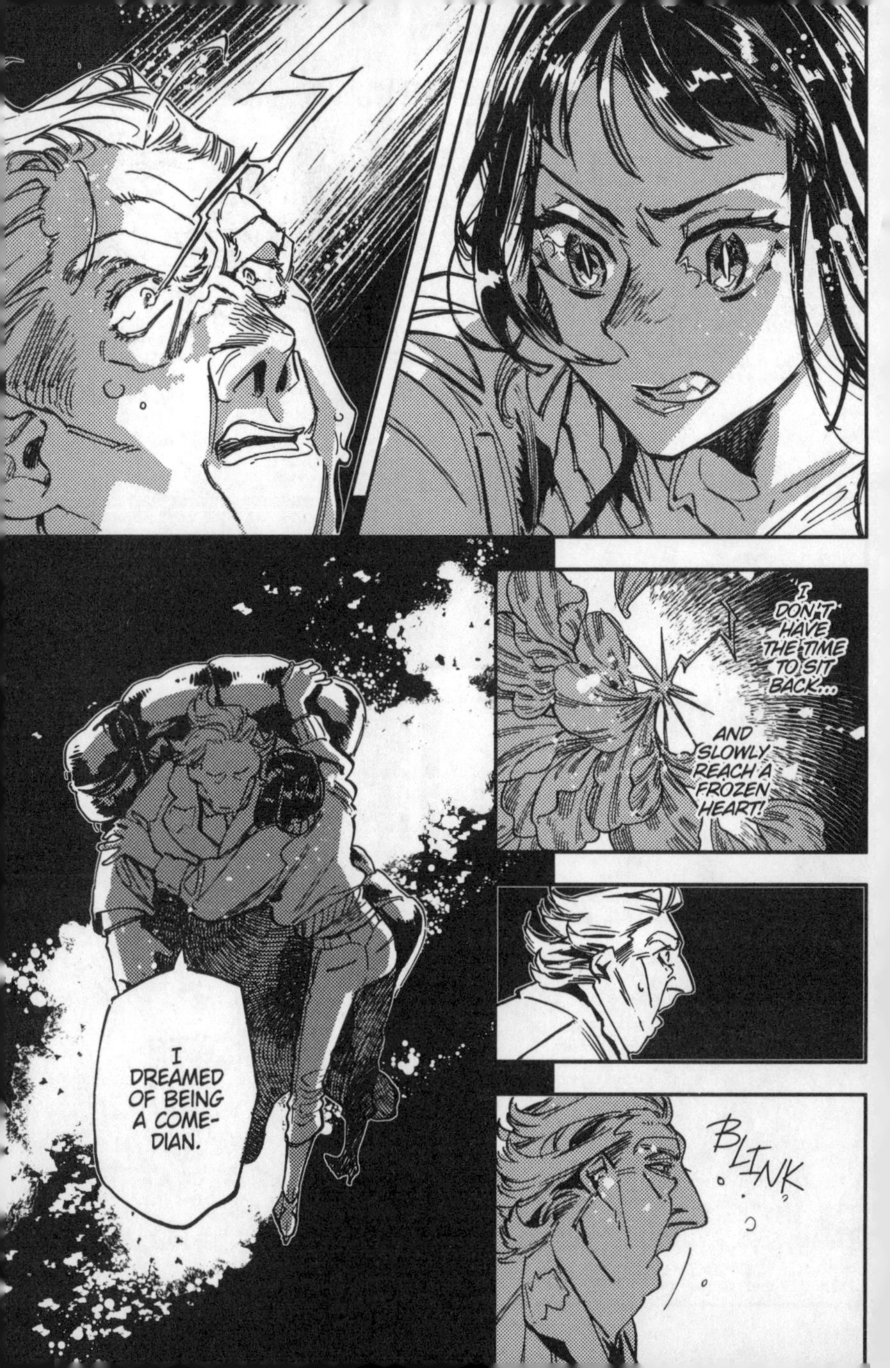
I DON'T HAVE THE TIME TO SIT BACK...
AND SLOWLY REACH A FROZEN HEART!
BLINK
I DREAMED OF BEING A COME-DIAN.

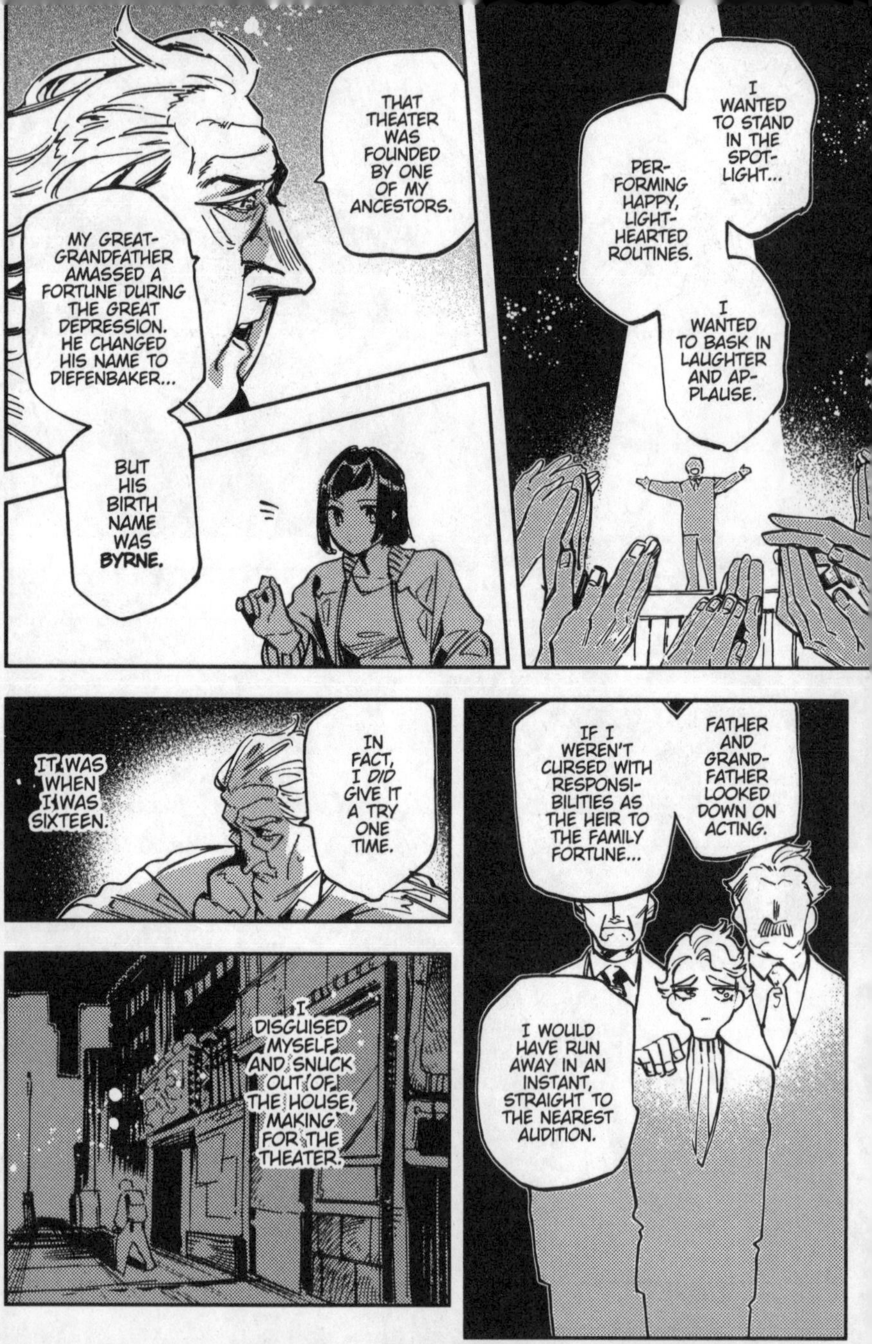
I WANTED TO STAND IN THE SPOTLIGHT...
PERFORMING HAPPY, LIGHTHEARTED ROUTINES.
I WANTED TO BASK IN LAUGHTER AND APPLAUSE.
THAT THEATER WAS FOUNDED BY ONE OF MY ANCESTORS.
MY GREAT-GRANDFATHER AMASSED A FORTUNE DURING THE GREAT DEPRESSION. HE CHANGED HIS NAME TO DIEFENBAKER...
BUT HIS BIRTH NAME WAS BYRNE.
FATHER AND GRANDFATHER LOOKED DOWN ON ACTING.
IF I WEREN'T CURSED WITH RESPONSIBILITIES AS THE HEIR TO THE FAMILY FORTUNE...
I WOULD HAVE RUN AWAY IN AN INSTANT, STRAIGHT TO THE NEAREST AUDITION.
IN FACT, I DID GIVE IT A TRY ONE TIME.
IT WAS WHEN I WAS SIXTEEN.
I DISGUISED MYSELF AND SNUCK OUT OF THE HOUSE, MAKING FOR THE THEATER.

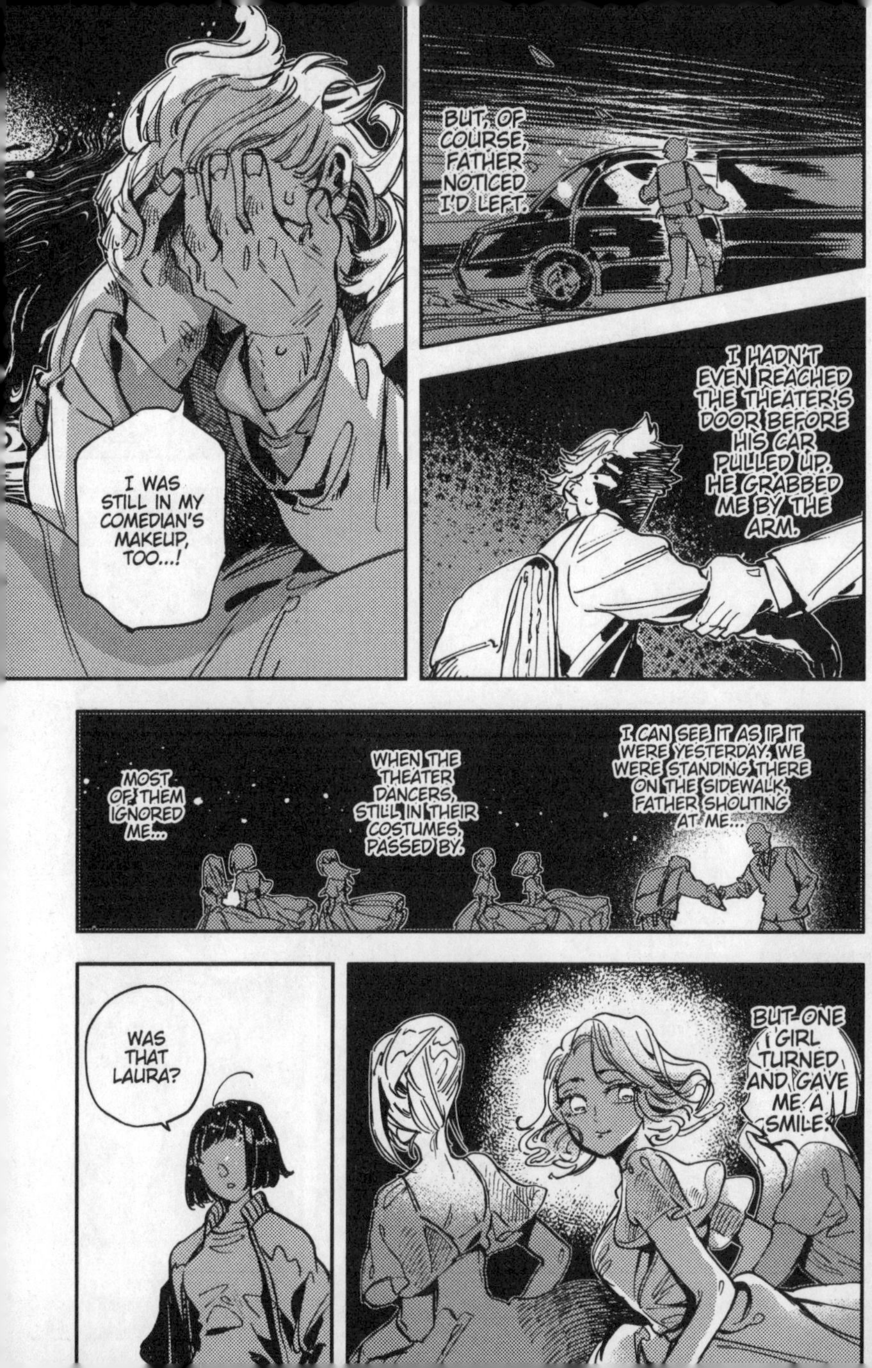
BUT, OF COURSE, FATHER NOTICED I'D LEFT.
I HADN'T EVEN REACHED THE THEATER'S DOOR BEFORE HIS CAR PULLED UP. HE GRABBED ME BY THE ARM.
I WAS STILL IN MY COMEDIAN'S MAKEUP, TOO...!
I CAN SEE IT AS IF IT WERE YESTERDAY. WE WERE STANDING THERE ON THE SIDEWALK, FATHER SHOUTING AT ME...
WHEN THE THEATER DANCERS, STILL IN THEIR COSTUMES, PASSED BY.
MOST OF THEM IGNORED ME...
BUT ONE GIRL TURNED AND GAVE ME A SMILE.
WAS THAT LAURA?

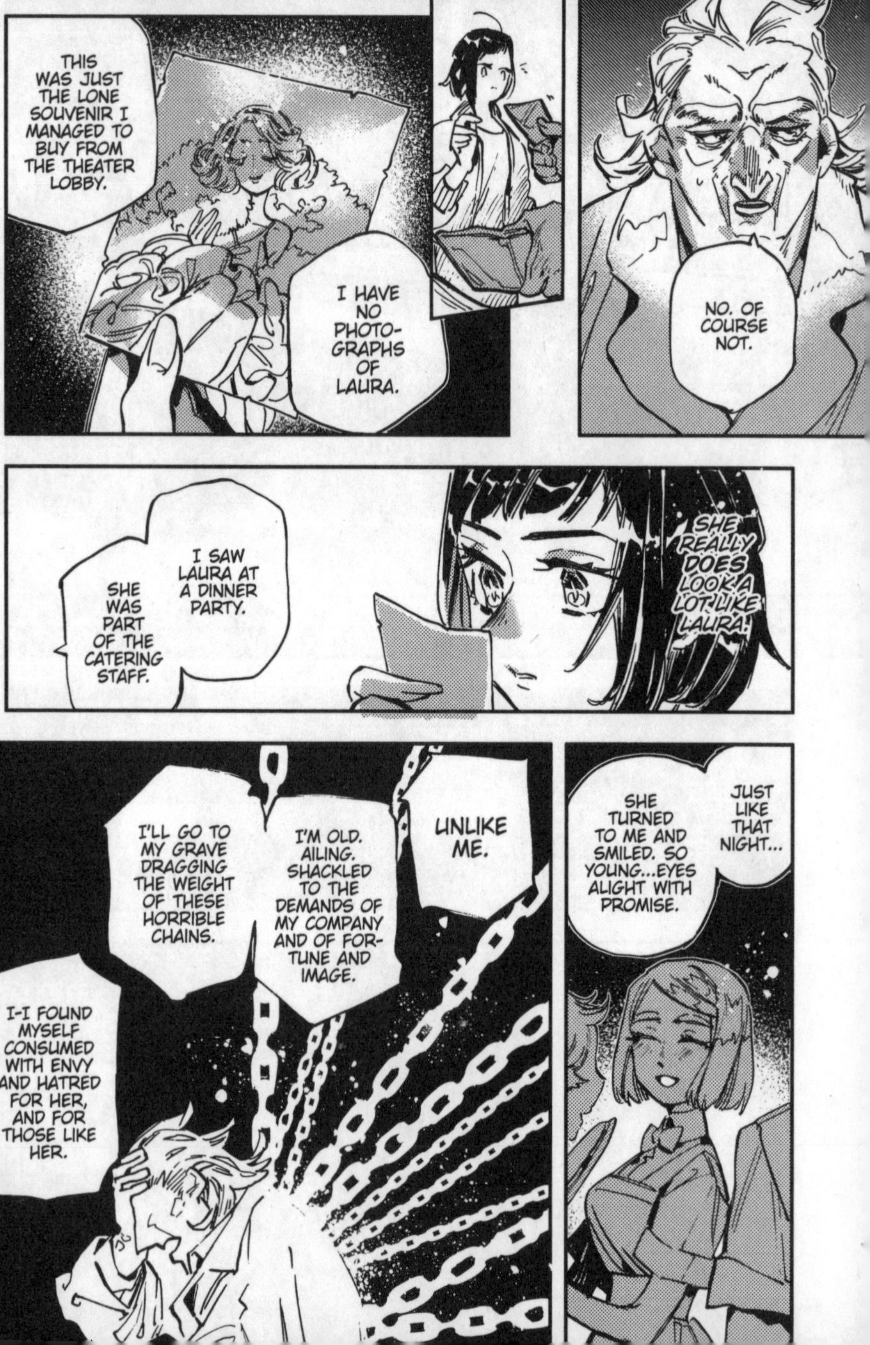
NO. OF COURSE NOT.
I HAVE NO PHOTOGRAPHS OF LAURA.
THIS WAS JUST THE LONE SOUVENIR I MANAGED TO BUY FROM THE THEATER LOBBY.
SHE REALLY DOES LOOK A LOT LIKE LAURA.
I SAW LAURA AT A DINNER PARTY.
SHE WAS PART OF THE CATERING STAFF.
JUST LIKE THAT NIGHT...
SHE TURNED TO ME AND SMILED. SO YOUNG...EYES ALIGHT WITH PROMISE.
UNLIKE ME.
I'M OLD. AILING. SHACKLED TO THE DEMANDS OF MY COMPANY AND OF FORTUNE AND IMAGE.
I'LL GO TO MY GRAVE DRAGGING THE WEIGHT OF THESE HORRIBLE CHAINS.
I-I FOUND MYSELF CONSUMED WITH ENVY AND HATRED FOR HER, AND FOR THOSE LIKE HER.

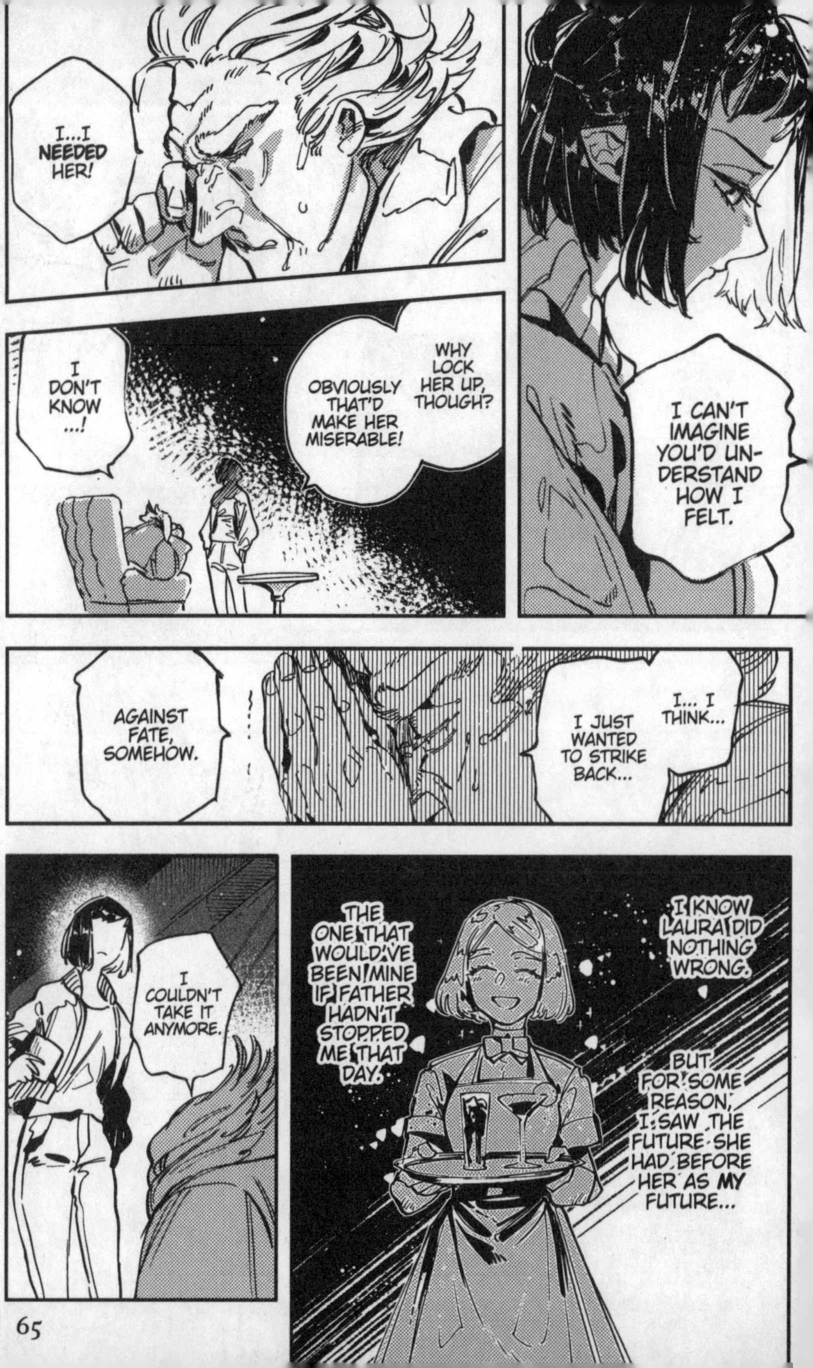
I CAN'T IMAGINE YOU'D UNDERSTAND HOW I FELT.
I...I NEEDED HER!
WHY LOCK HER UP, THOUGH?
OBVIOUSLY THAT'D MAKE HER MISERABLE!
I DON'T KNOW ...!
I... I THINK...
I JUST WANTED TO STRIKE BACK...
AGAINST FATE, SOMEHOW.
I KNOW LAURA DID NOTHING WRONG.
BUT FOR SOME REASON, I SAW THE FUTURE SHE HAD BEFORE HER AS MY FUTURE...
THE ONE THAT WOULD'VE BEEN MINE IF FATHER HADN'T STOPPED ME THAT DAY.
I COULDN'T TAKE IT ANYMORE.

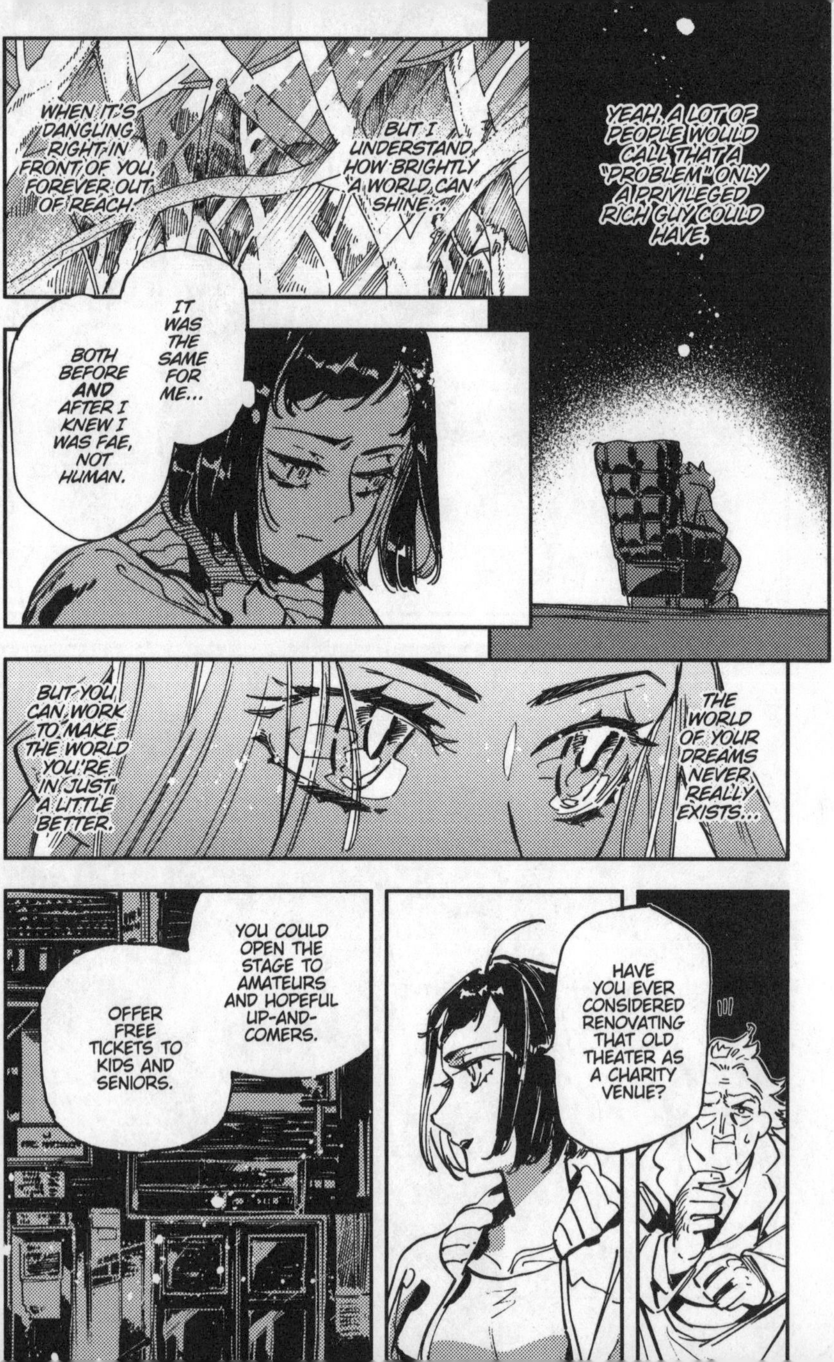
YEAH, A LOT OF PEOPLE WOULD CALL THAT A "PROBLEM" ONLY A PRIVILEGED RICH GUY COULD HAVE.
BUT I UNDERSTAND HOW BRIGHTLY A WORLD CAN SHINE...
WHEN IT'S DANGLING RIGHT IN FRONT OF YOU, FOREVER OUT OF REACH.
IT WAS THE SAME FOR ME...
BOTH BEFORE AND AFTER I KNEW I WAS FAE, NOT HUMAN.
THE WORLD OF YOUR DREAMS NEVER REALLY EXISTS...
BUT YOU CAN WORK TO MAKE THE WORLD YOU'RE IN JUST A LITTLE BETTER.
HAVE YOU EVER CONSIDERED RENOVATING THAT OLD THEATER AS A CHARITY VENUE?
YOU COULD OPEN THE STAGE TO AMATEURS AND HOPEFUL UP-AND-COMERS.
OFFER FREE TICKETS TO KIDS AND SENIORS.

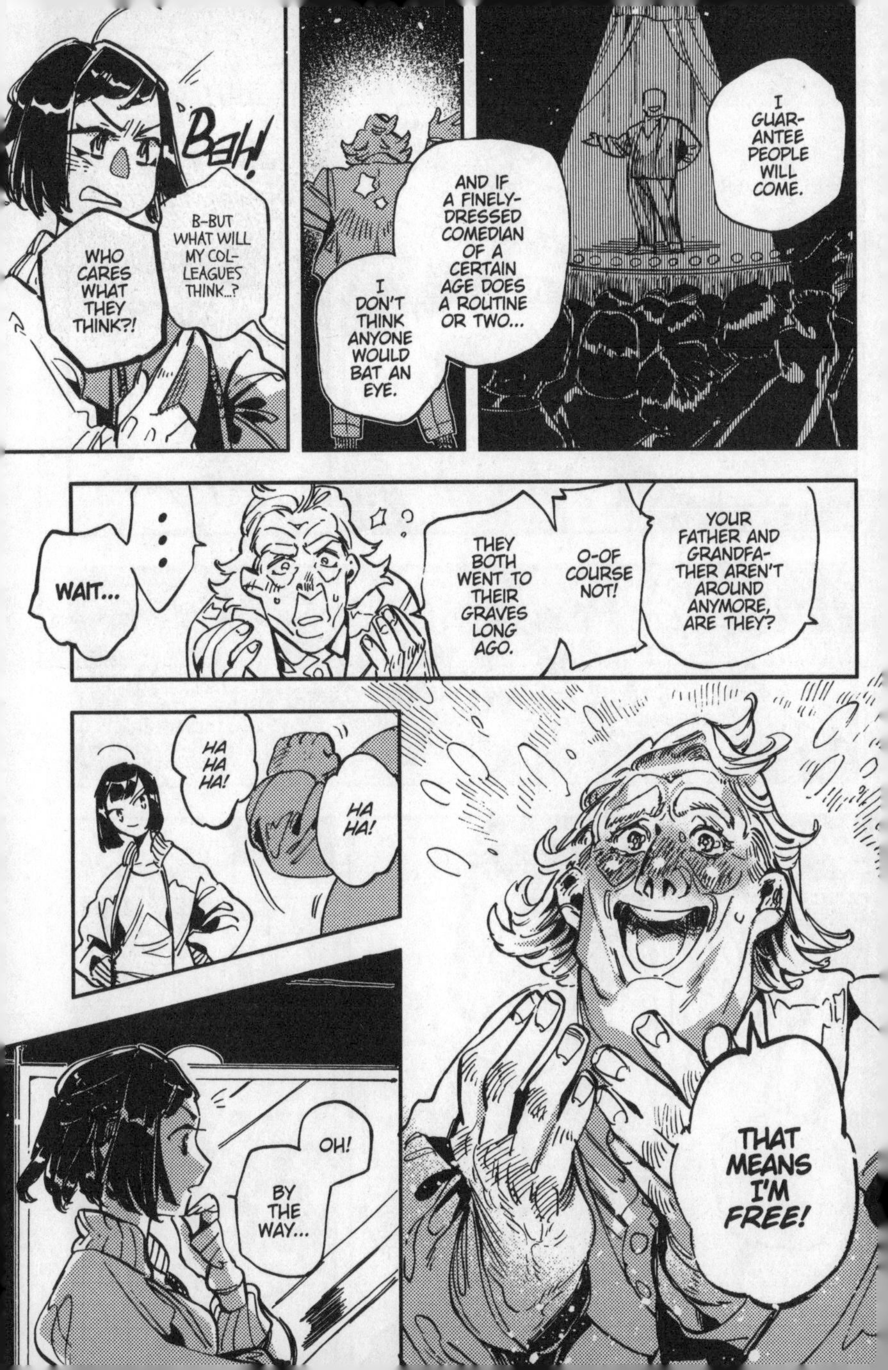
I GUARANTEE PEOPLE WILL COME.
AND IF A FINELY-DRESSED COMEDIAN OF A CERTAIN AGE DOES A ROUTINE OR TWO...
I DON'T THINK ANYONE WOULD BAT AN EYE.
BAH!
B-BUT WHAT WILL MY COLLEAGUES THINK..?
WHO CARES WHAT THEY THINK?!
YOUR FATHER AND GRANDFATHER AREN'T AROUND ANYMORE, ARE THEY?
O-OF COURSE NOT!
THEY BOTH WENT TO THEIR GRAVES LONG AGO.
...
WAIT...
THAT MEANS I'M FREE!
HA HA!
HA HA HA!
OH!
BY THE WAY...

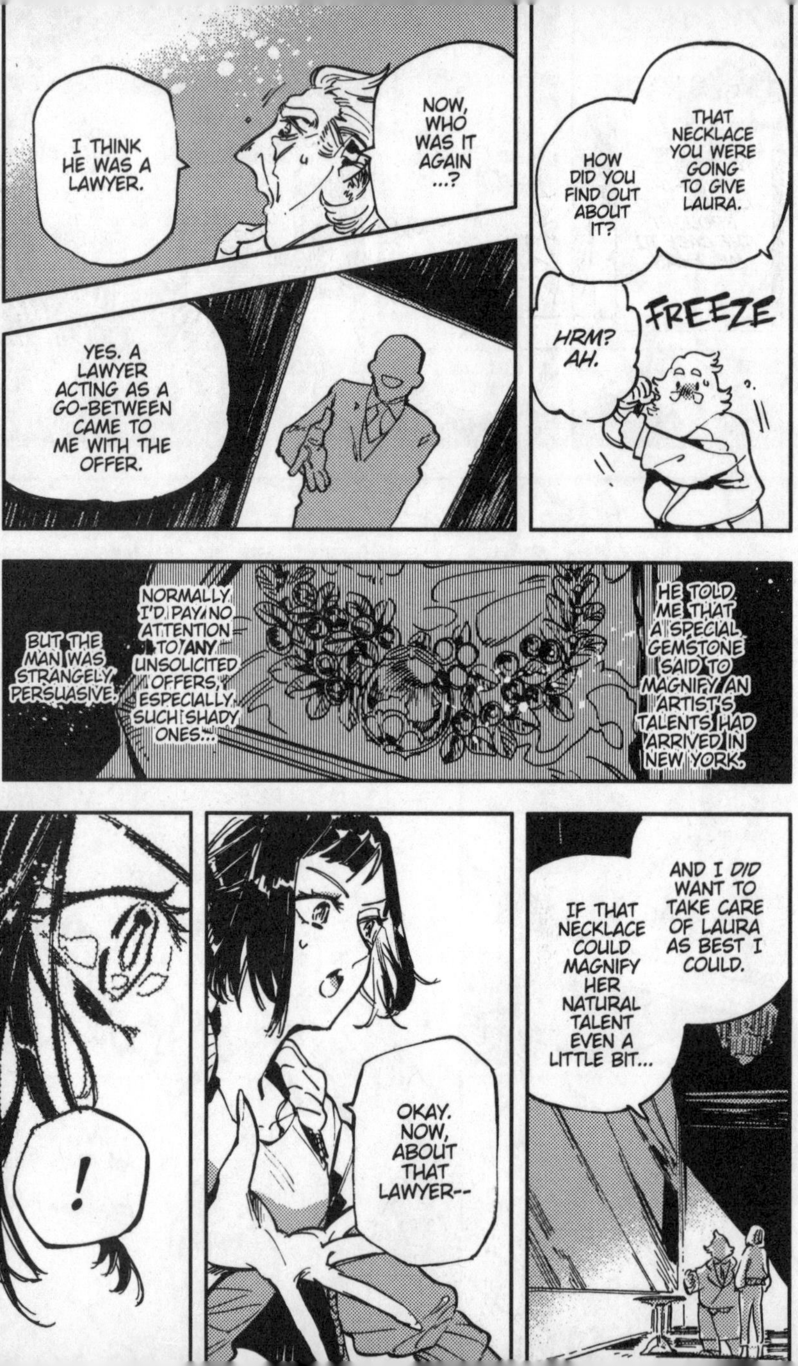
THAT NECKLACE YOU WERE GOING TO GIVE LAURA.
HOW DID YOU FIND OUT ABOUT IT?
FREEZE
HRM? AH.
NOW, WHO WAS IT AGAIN ...?
I THINK HE WAS A LAWYER.
YES. A LAWYER ACTING AS A GO-BETWEEN CAME TO ME WITH THE OFFER.
HE TOLD ME THAT A SPECIAL GEMSTONE SAID TO MAGNIFY AN ARTIST'S TALENTS HAD ARRIVED IN NEW YORK.
NORMALLY I'D PAY NO ATTENTION TO *ANY* UNSOLICITED OFFERS, ESPECIALLY SUCH SHADY ONES...
BUT THE MAN WAS STRANGELY PERSUASIVE.
AND I *DID* WANT TO TAKE CARE OF LAURA AS BEST I COULD.
IF THAT NECKLACE COULD MAGNIFY HER NATURAL TALENT EVEN A LITTLE BIT...
OKAY. NOW, ABOUT THAT LAWYER--
!

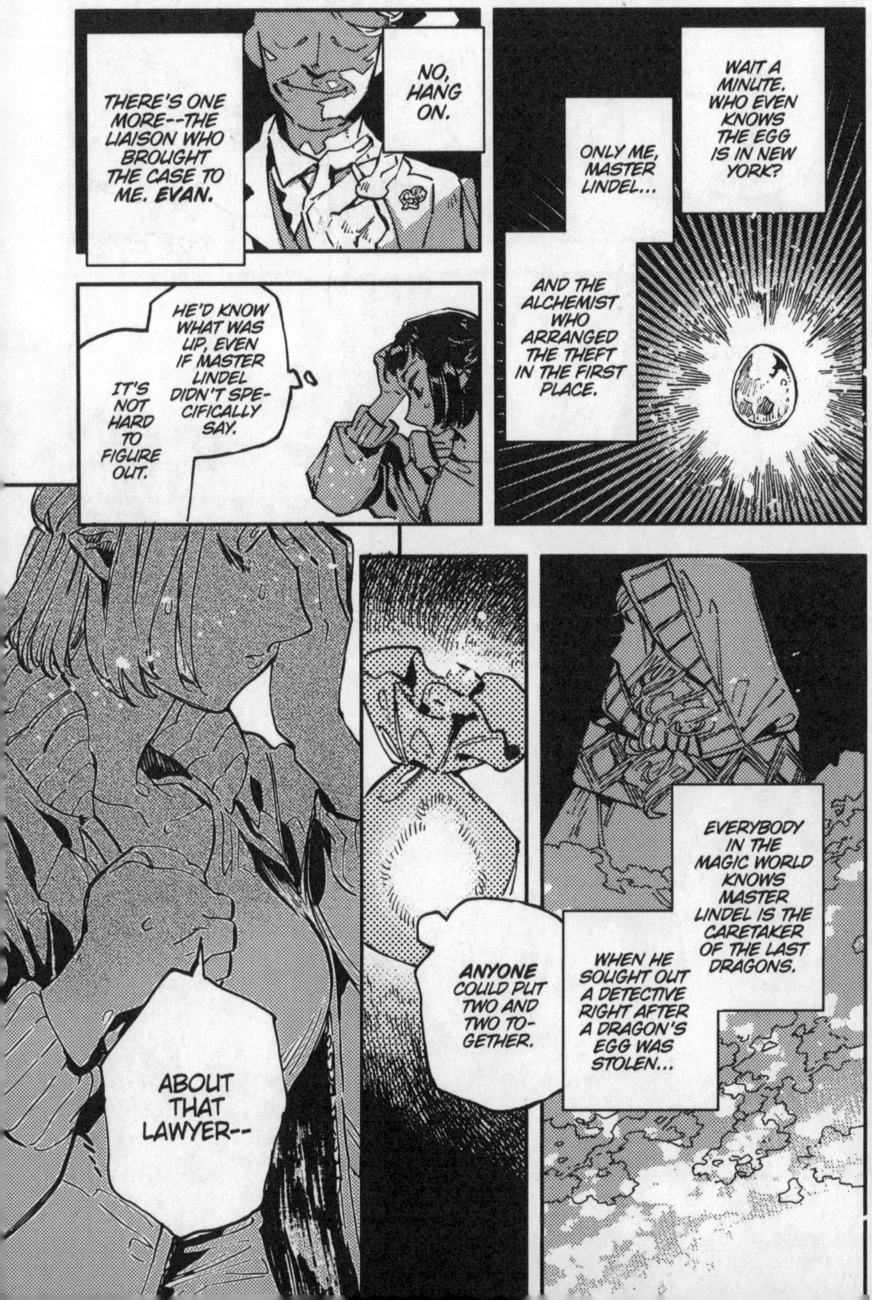
WAIT A MINUTE. WHO EVEN KNOWS THE EGG IS IN NEW YORK?
ONLY ME, MASTER LINDEL...
AND THE ALCHEMIST WHO ARRANGED THE THEFT IN THE FIRST PLACE.
NO, HANG ON.
THERE'S ONE MORE--THE LIAISON WHO BROUGHT THE CASE TO ME. EVAN.
HE'D KNOW WHAT WAS UP, EVEN IF MASTER LINDEL DIDN'T SPECIFICALLY SAY.
IT'S NOT HARD TO FIGURE OUT.
EVERYBODY IN THE MAGIC WORLD KNOWS MASTER LINDEL IS THE CARETAKER OF THE LAST DRAGONS.
WHEN HE SOUGHT OUT A DETECTIVE RIGHT AFTER A DRAGON'S EGG WAS STOLEN...
ANYONE COULD PUT TWO AND TWO TOGETHER.
ABOUT THAT LAWYER--

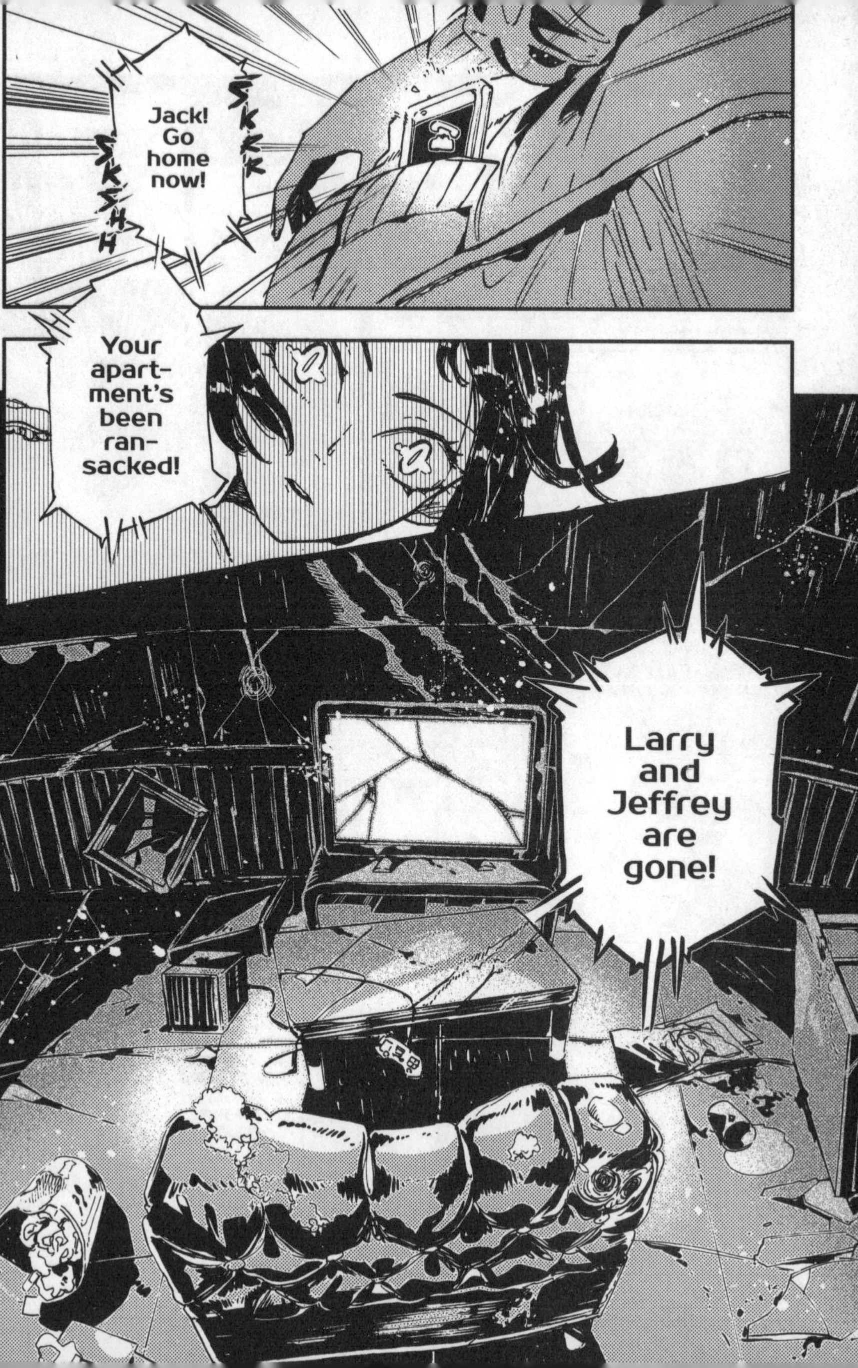
SKKR
Jack! Go home now!
SKSHH
Your apartment's been ransacked!
Larry and Jeffrey are gone!

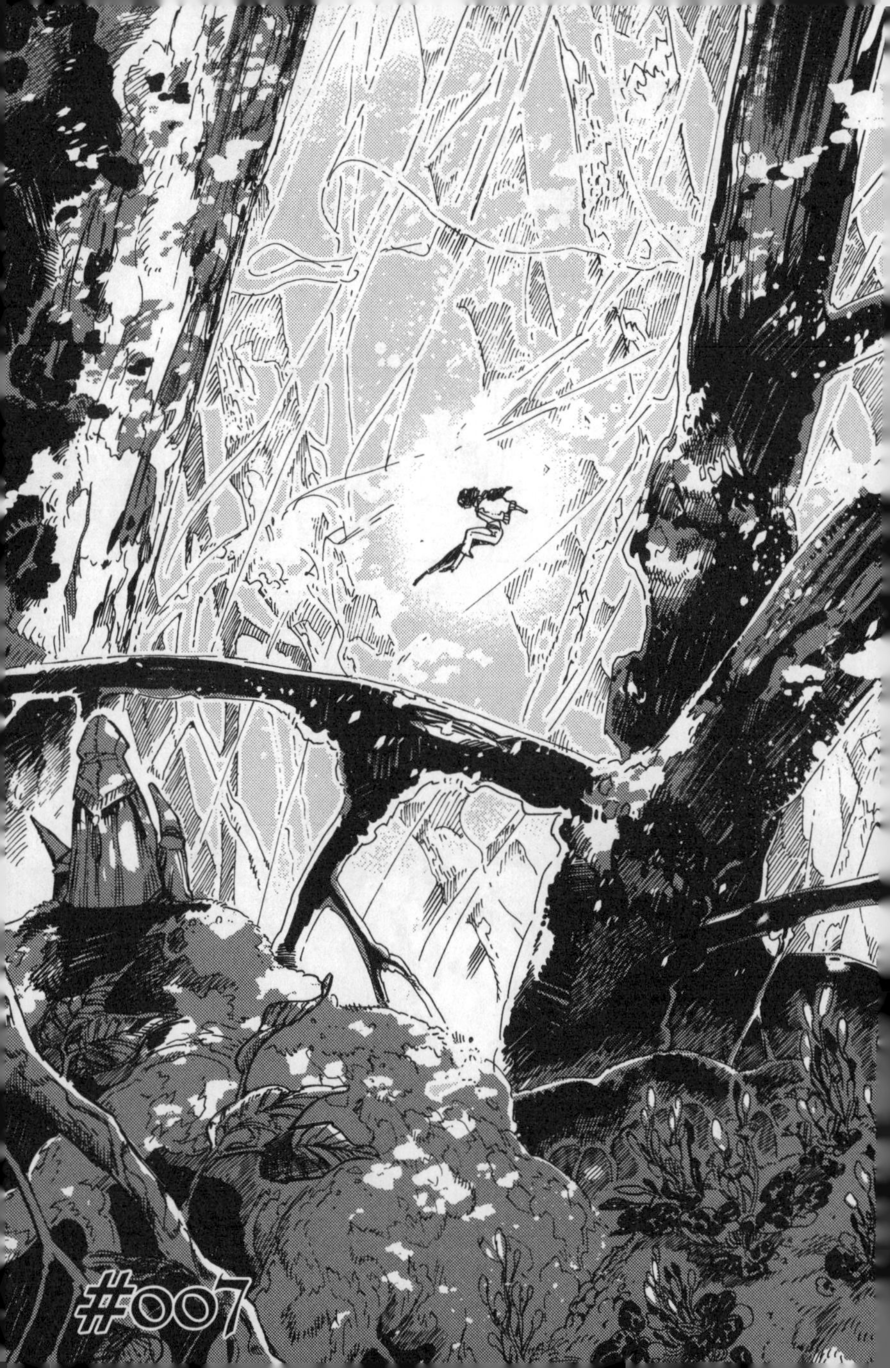
#007

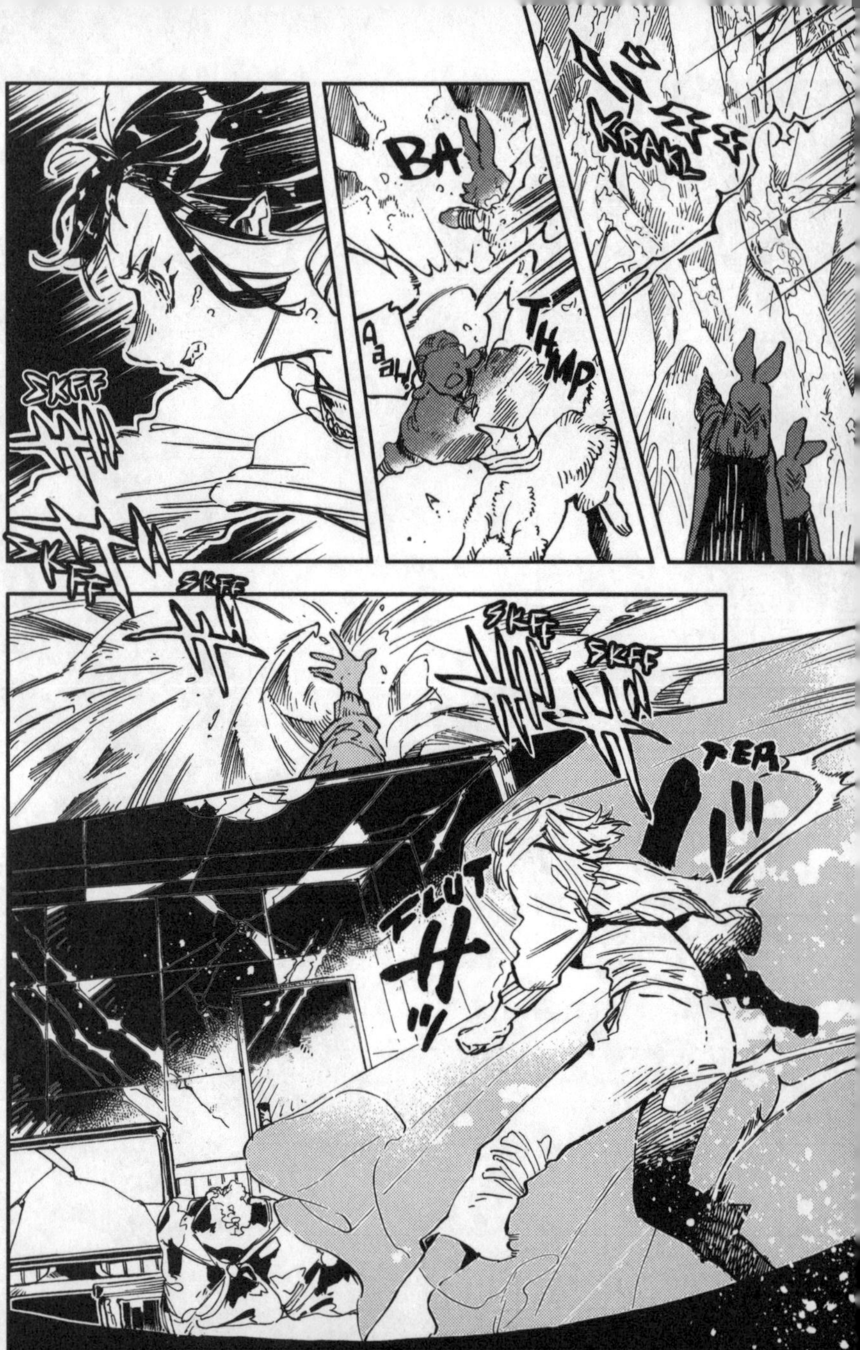
KRAKL
BA
Aaah!
THUMP
SKFF
SKFF
TER
SKFF
SKFF
SKFF
FLUT

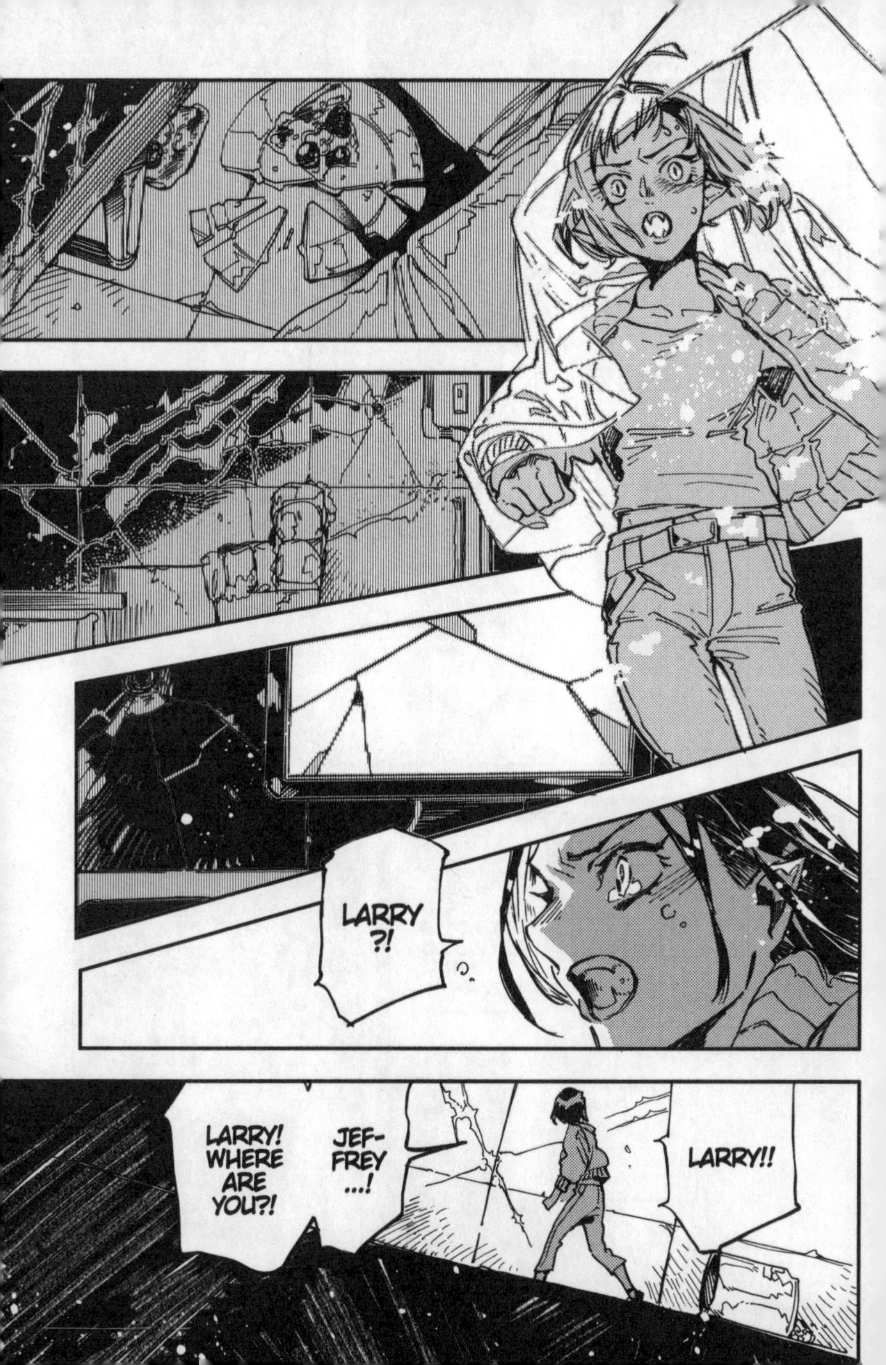
LARRY ?!
LARRY!!
JEF- FREY ...!
LARRY! WHERE ARE YOU?!

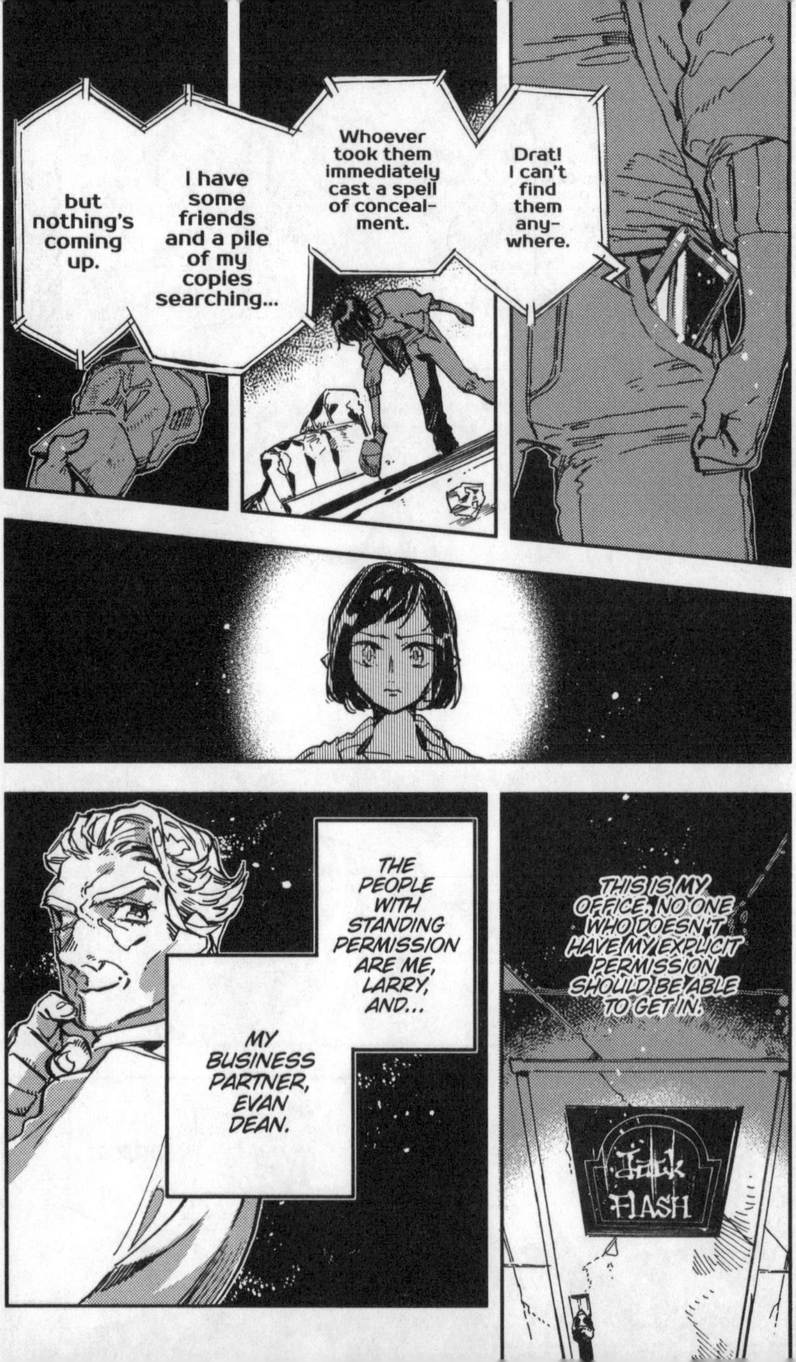
Drat! I can't find them any-where.
Whoever took them immediately cast a spell of conceal-ment.
I have some friends and a pile of my copies searching...
but nothing's coming up.
THIS IS MY OFFICE. NO ONE WHO DOESN'T HAVE MY EXPLICIT PERMISSION SHOULD BE ABLE TO GET IN.
FLASH
THE PEOPLE WITH STANDING PERMISSION ARE ME, LARRY, AND...
MY BUSINESS PARTNER, EVAN DEAN.

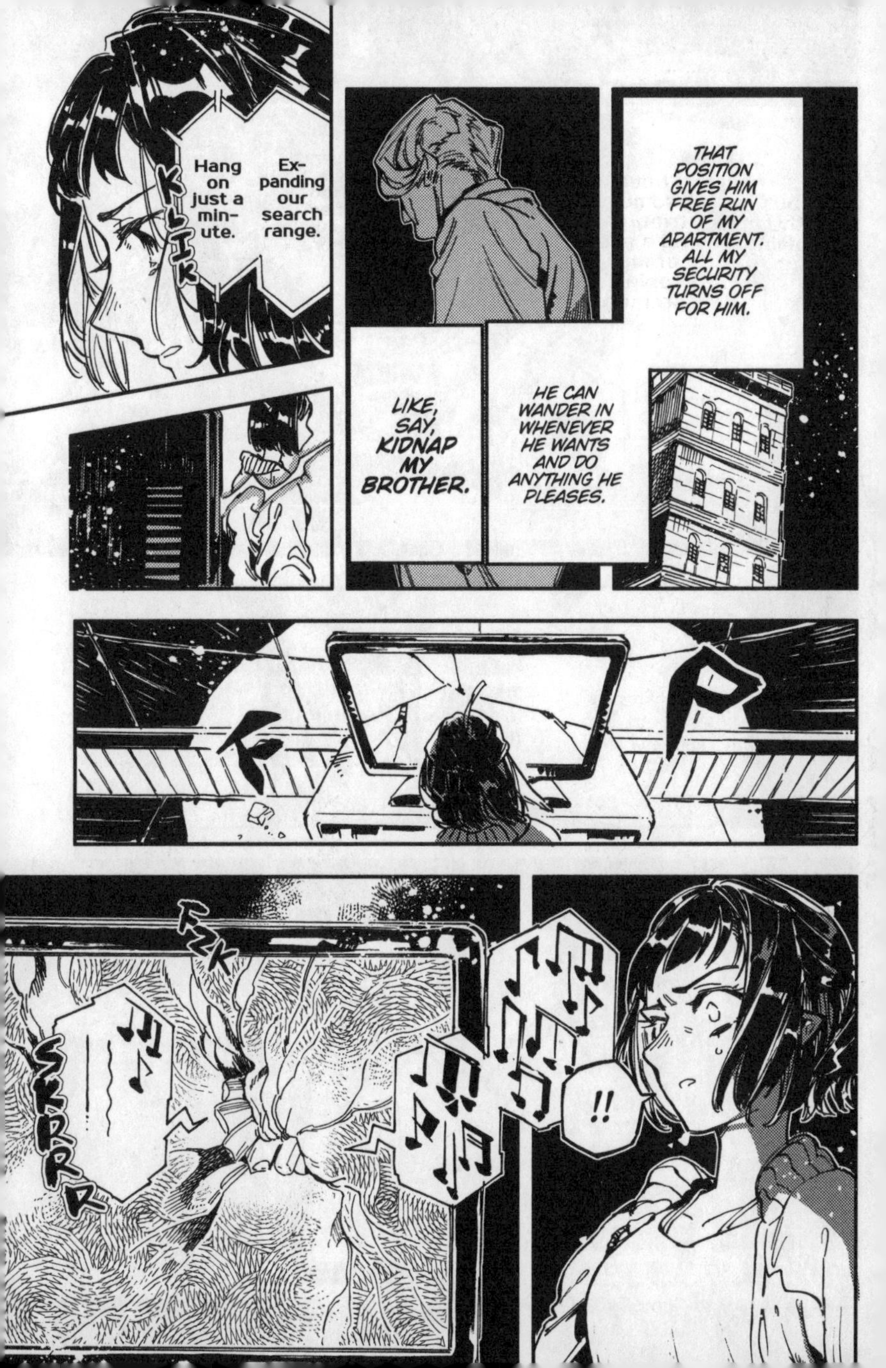
THAT POSITION GIVES HIM FREE RUN OF MY APARTMENT. ALL MY SECURITY TURNS OFF FOR HIM.
HE CAN WANDER IN WHENEVER HE WANTS AND DO ANYTHING HE PLEASES.
LIKE, SAY, KIDNAP MY BROTHER.
Expanding our search range.
Hang on just a minute.
KLIK
!!
FZK
SKRRRA

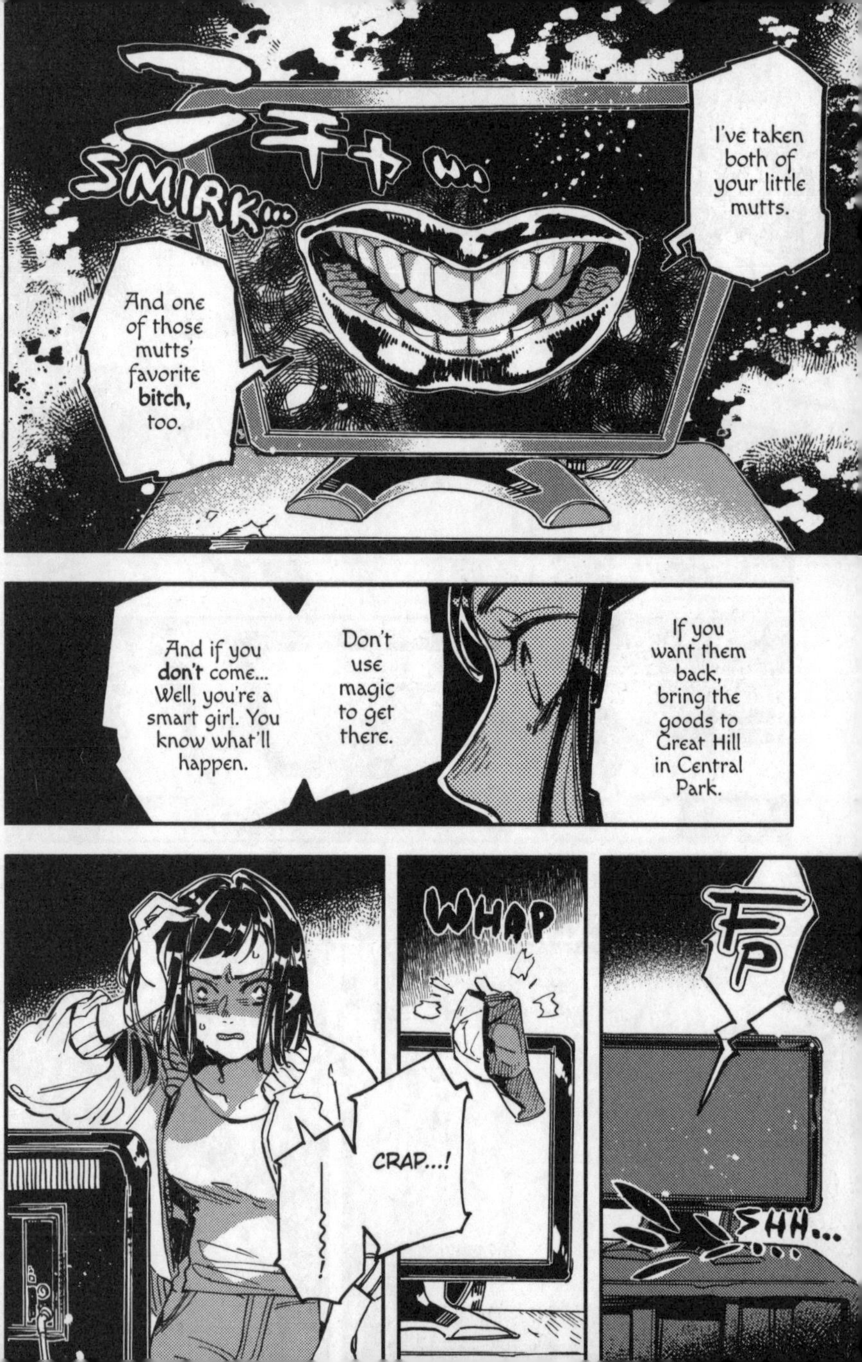
I've taken both of your little mutts.
SMIRK...
And one of those mutts' favorite **bitch,** too.
If you want them back, bring the goods to Great Hill in Central Park.
Don't use magic to get there.
And if you **don't** come... Well, you're a smart girl. You know what'll happen.
SHH...
WHAP
CRAP...!

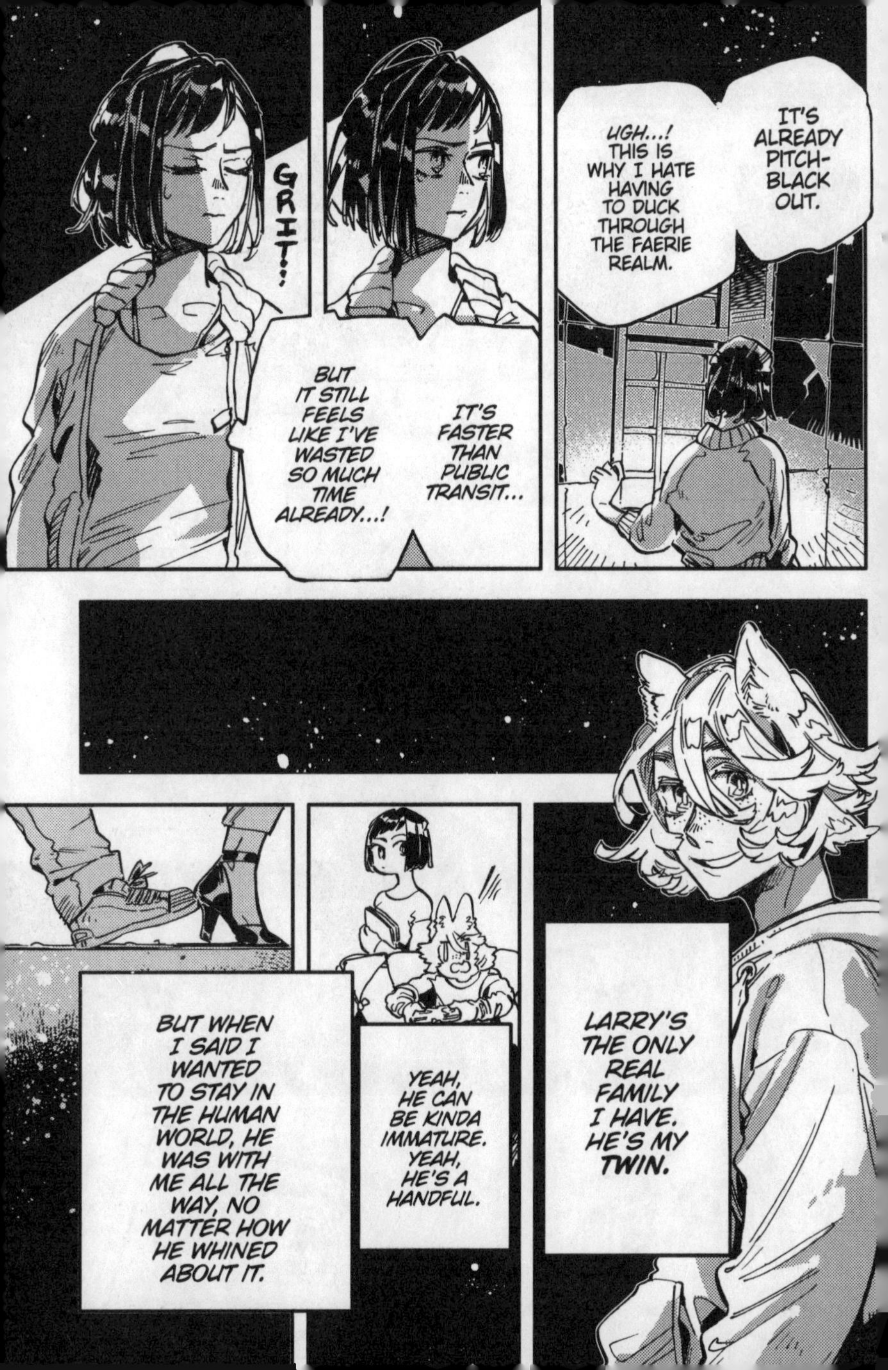
IT'S ALREADY PITCH-BLACK OUT.
UGH...! THIS IS WHY I HATE HAVING TO DUCK THROUGH THE FAERIE REALM.
IT'S FASTER THAN PUBLIC TRANSIT...
BUT IT STILL FEELS LIKE I'VE WASTED SO MUCH TIME ALREADY...!
GRIT!
LARRY'S THE ONLY REAL FAMILY I HAVE. HE'S MY TWIN.
YEAH, HE CAN BE KINDA IMMATURE. YEAH, HE'S A HANDFUL.
BUT WHEN I SAID I WANTED TO STAY IN THE HUMAN WORLD, HE WAS WITH ME ALL THE WAY, NO MATTER HOW HE WHINED ABOUT IT.

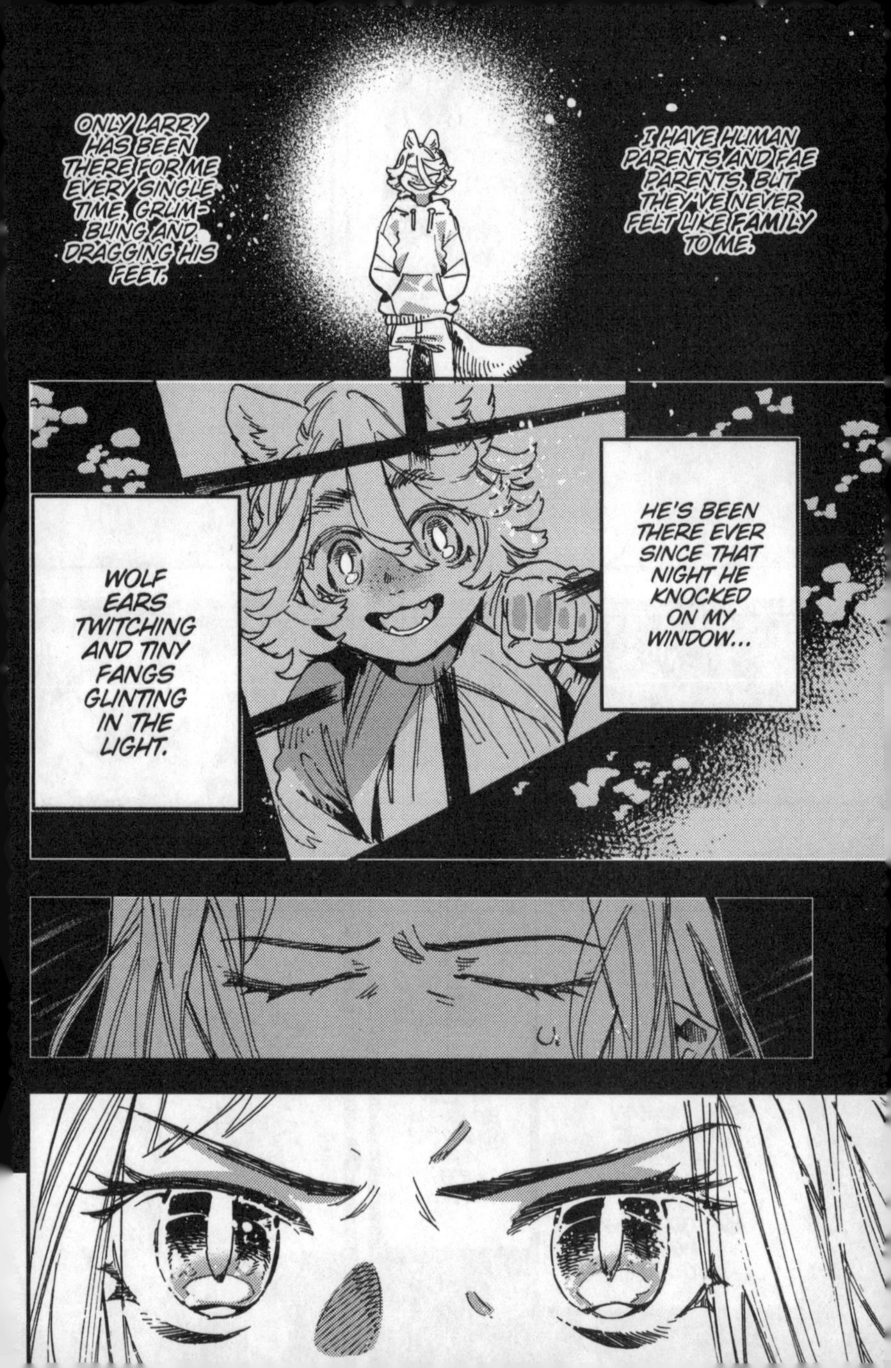
I HAVE HUMAN PARENTS AND FAE PARENTS, BUT THEY'VE NEVER FELT LIKE FAMILY TO ME.
ONLY LARRY HAS BEEN THERE FOR ME EVERY SINGLE TIME, GRUM-BLING AND DRAGGING HIS FEET.
HE'S BEEN THERE EVER SINCE THAT NIGHT HE KNOCKED ON MY WINDOW...
WOLF EARS TWITCHING AND TINY FANGS GLINTING IN THE LIGHT.

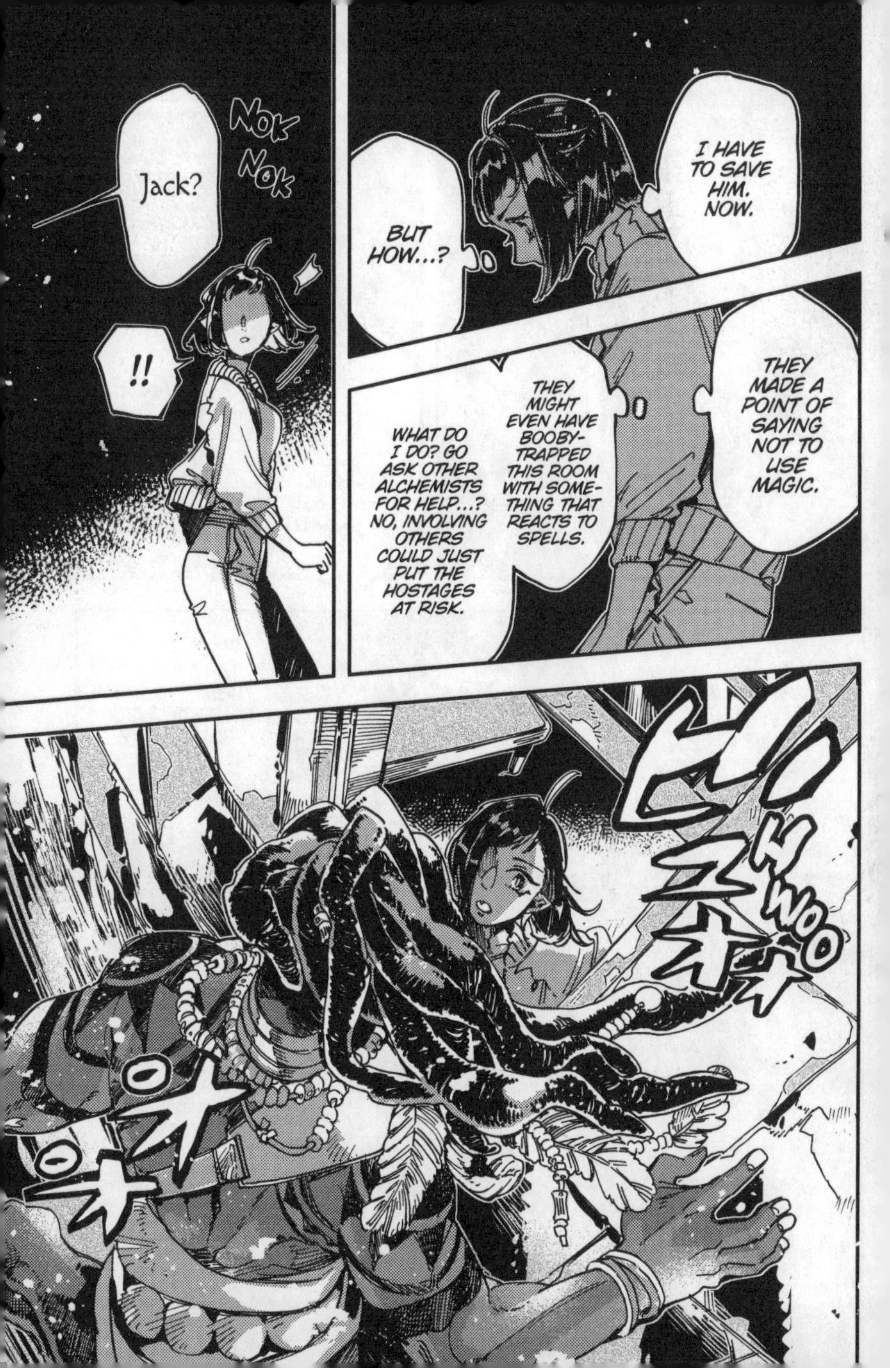
I HAVE TO SAVE HIM. NOW.
BUT HOW...?
THEY MADE A POINT OF SAYING NOT TO USE MAGIC.
THEY MIGHT EVEN HAVE BOOBY-TRAPPED THIS ROOM WITH SOMETHING THAT REACTS TO SPELLS.
WHAT DO I DO? GO ASK OTHER ALCHEMISTS FOR HELP...? NO, INVOLVING OTHERS COULD JUST PUT THE HOSTAGES AT RISK.
NOK NOK
Jack?
!!
WHOO

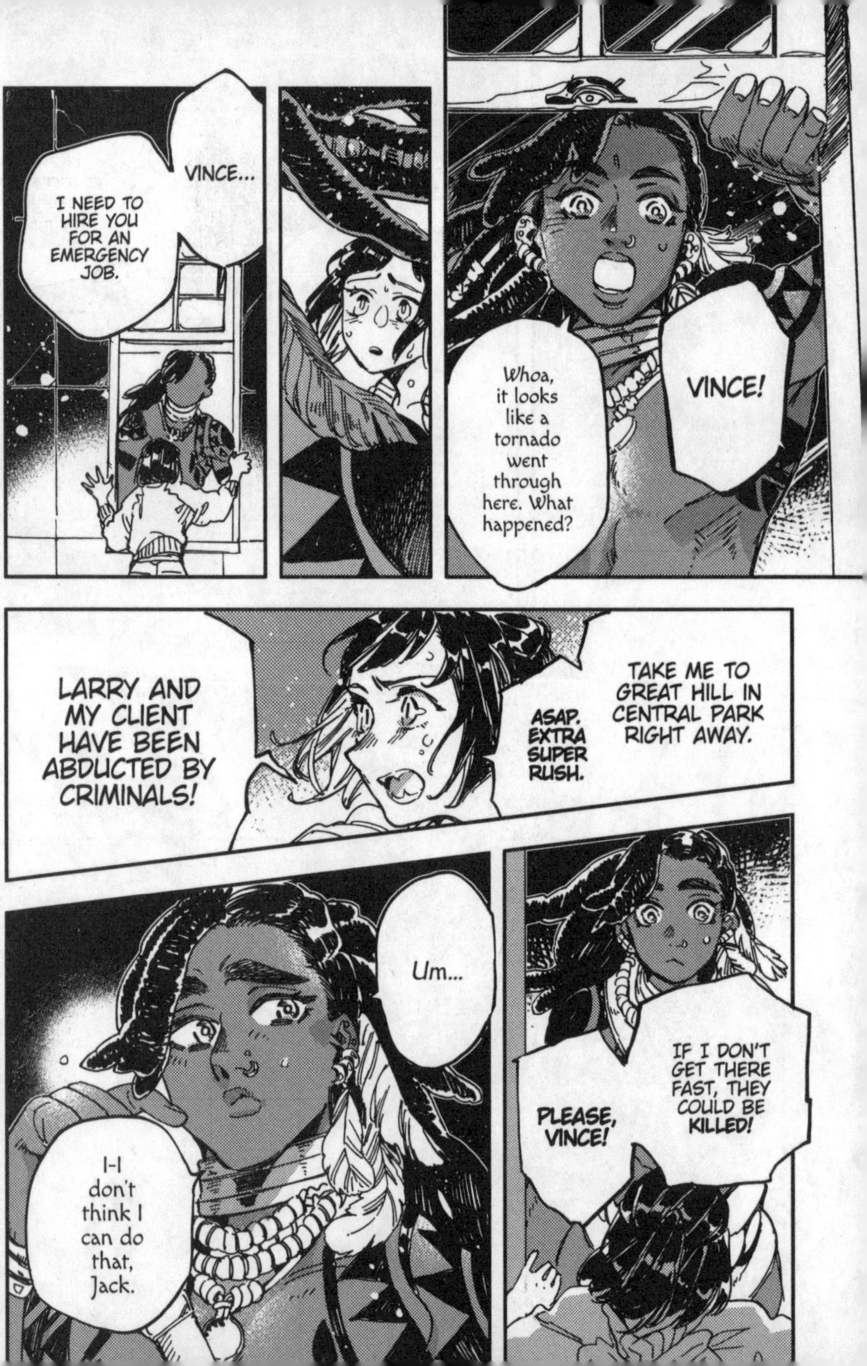
VINCE!
Whoa, it looks like a tornado went through here. What happened?
VINCE...
I NEED TO HIRE YOU FOR AN EMERGENCY JOB.
TAKE ME TO GREAT HILL IN CENTRAL PARK RIGHT AWAY.
ASAP. EXTRA SUPER RUSH.
LARRY AND MY CLIENT HAVE BEEN ABDUCTED BY CRIMINALS!
IF I DON'T GET THERE FAST, THEY COULD BE KILLED!
PLEASE, VINCE!
Um...
I-I don't think I can do that, Jack.

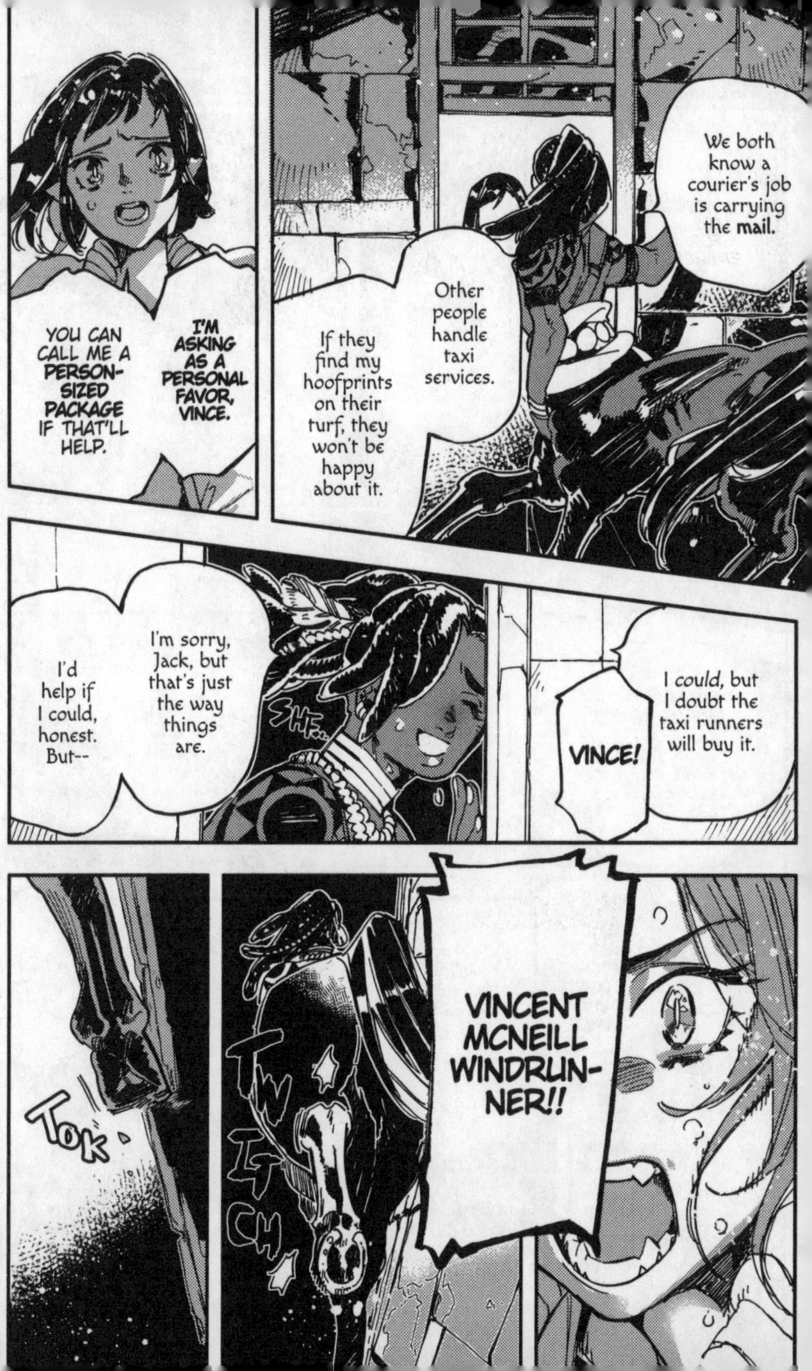
We both know a courier's job is carrying the **mail.**
Other people handle taxi services.
If they find my hoofprints on their turf, they won't be happy about it.
I'M ASKING AS A PERSONAL FAVOR, VINCE.
YOU CAN CALL ME A PERSON-SIZED PACKAGE IF THAT'LL HELP.
I *could,* but I doubt the taxi runners will buy it.
VINCE!
I'm sorry, Jack, but that's just the way things are.
I'd help if I could, honest. But--
SHF...
VINCENT MCNEILL WINDRUN-NER!!
TWITCH
TOK

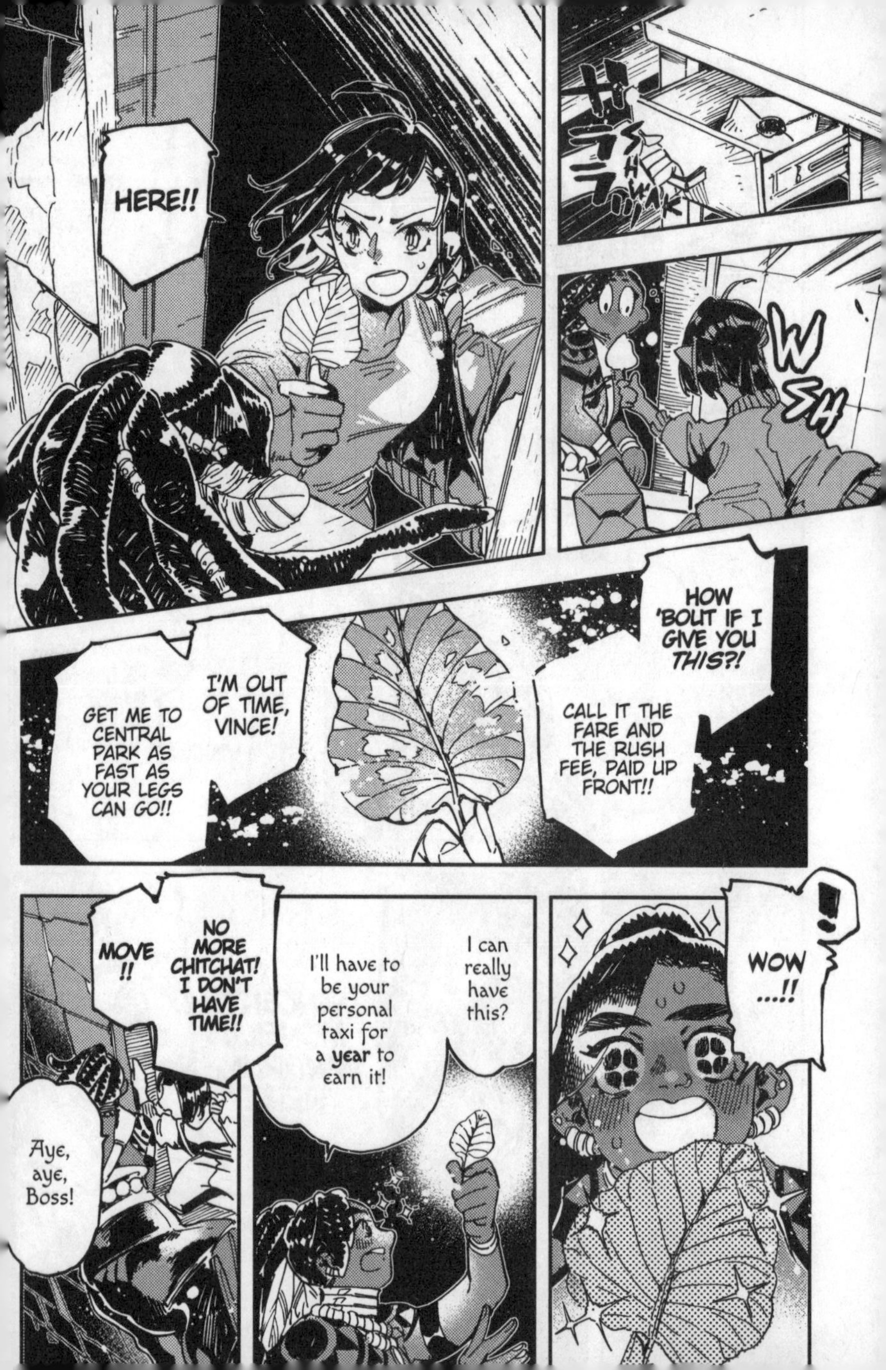
SHWAK
WSH
HERE!!
HOW 'BOUT IF I GIVE YOU THIS?!
CALL IT THE FARE AND THE RUSH FEE, PAID UP FRONT!!
I'M OUT OF TIME, VINCE!
GET ME TO CENTRAL PARK AS FAST AS YOUR LEGS CAN GO!!
!
WOW ...!!
I can really have this?
I'll have to be your personal taxi for a year to earn it!
NO MORE CHITCHAT! I DON'T HAVE TIME!!
MOVE !!
Aye, aye, Boss!

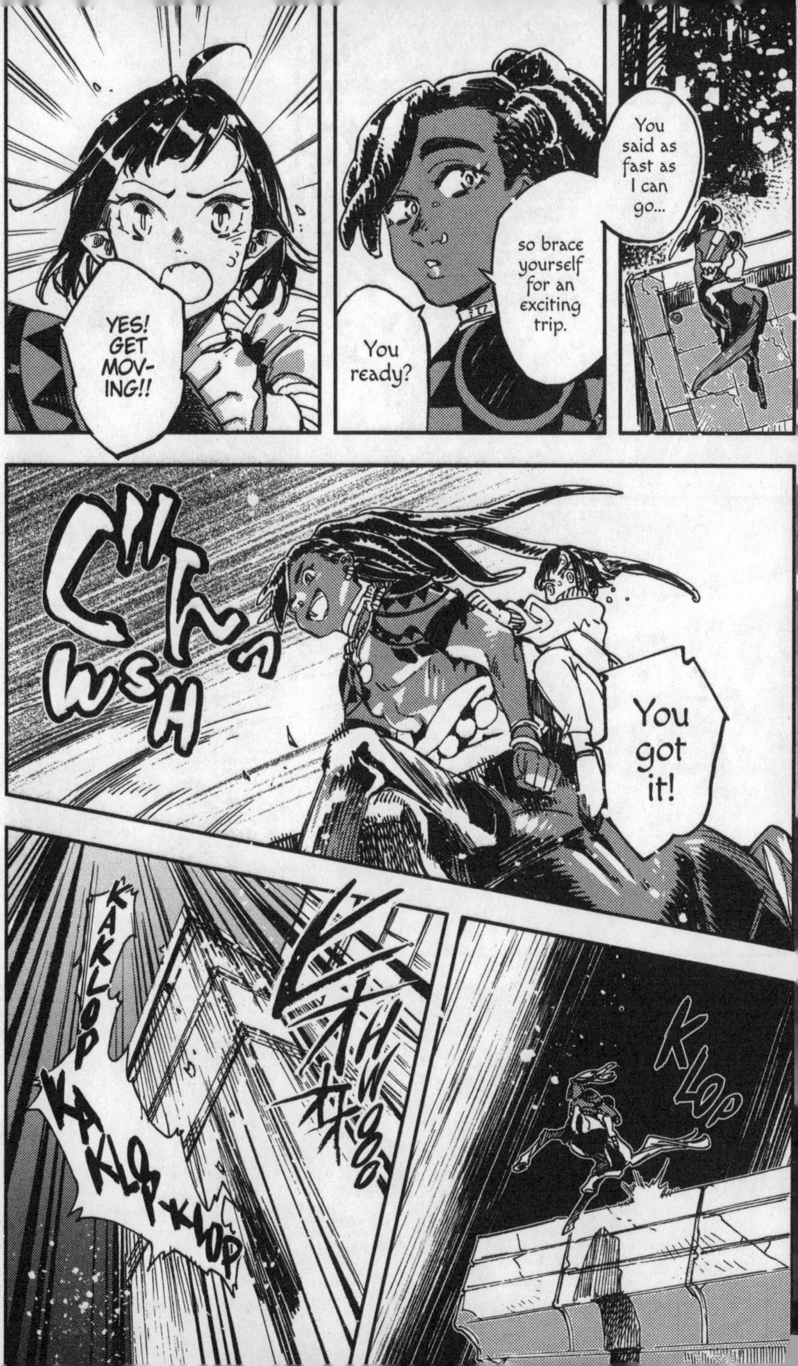

You said as fast as I can go...
so brace yourself for an exciting trip.
You ready?
YES! GET MOVING!!
You got it!
WSH
KLOP
KAKLOP
KAKLOP-KLOP

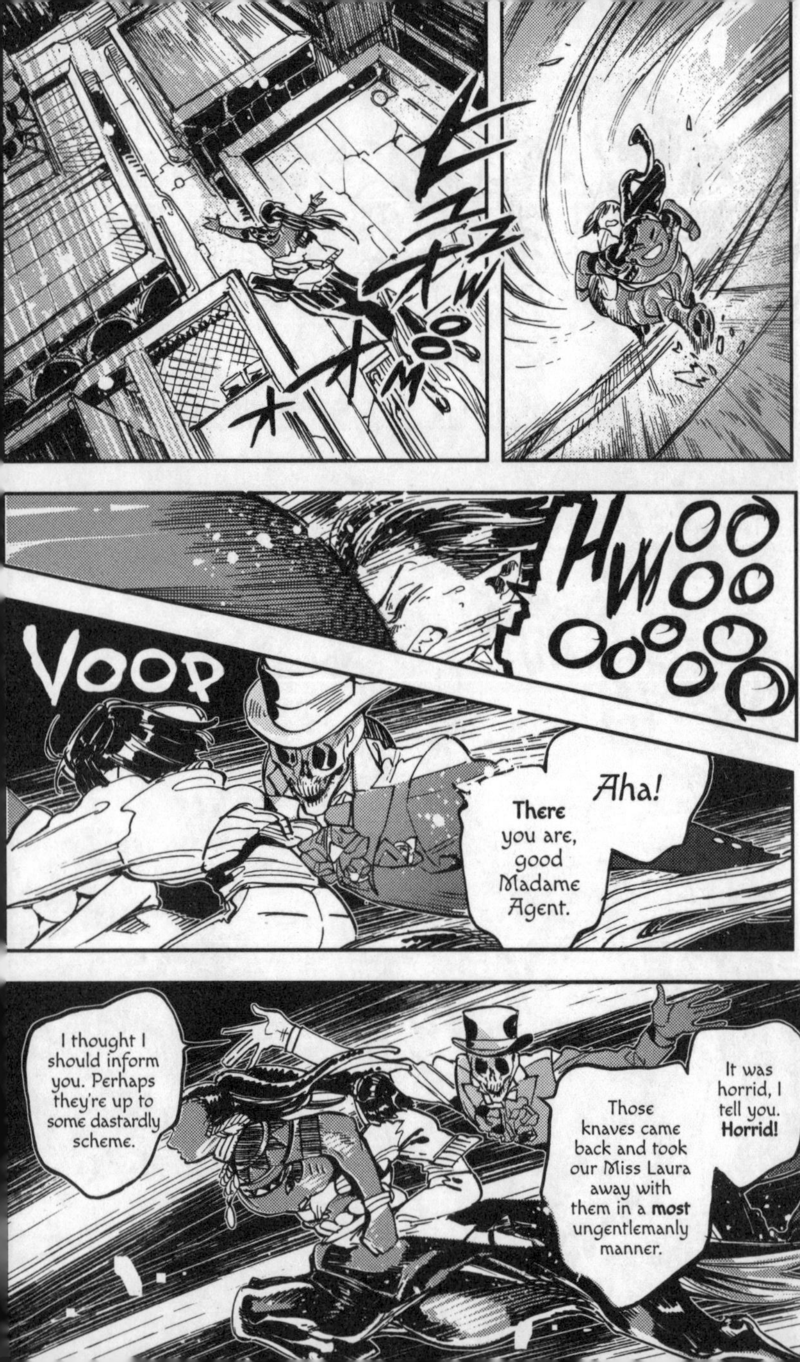
ZZZWOOM
HWOOOOOOOOOOO
VOOP
Aha! **There** you are, good Madame Agent.
It was horrid, I tell you. **Horrid!**
Those knaves came back and took our Miss Laura away with them in a **most** ungentlemanly manner.
I thought I should inform you. Perhaps they're up to some dastardly scheme.

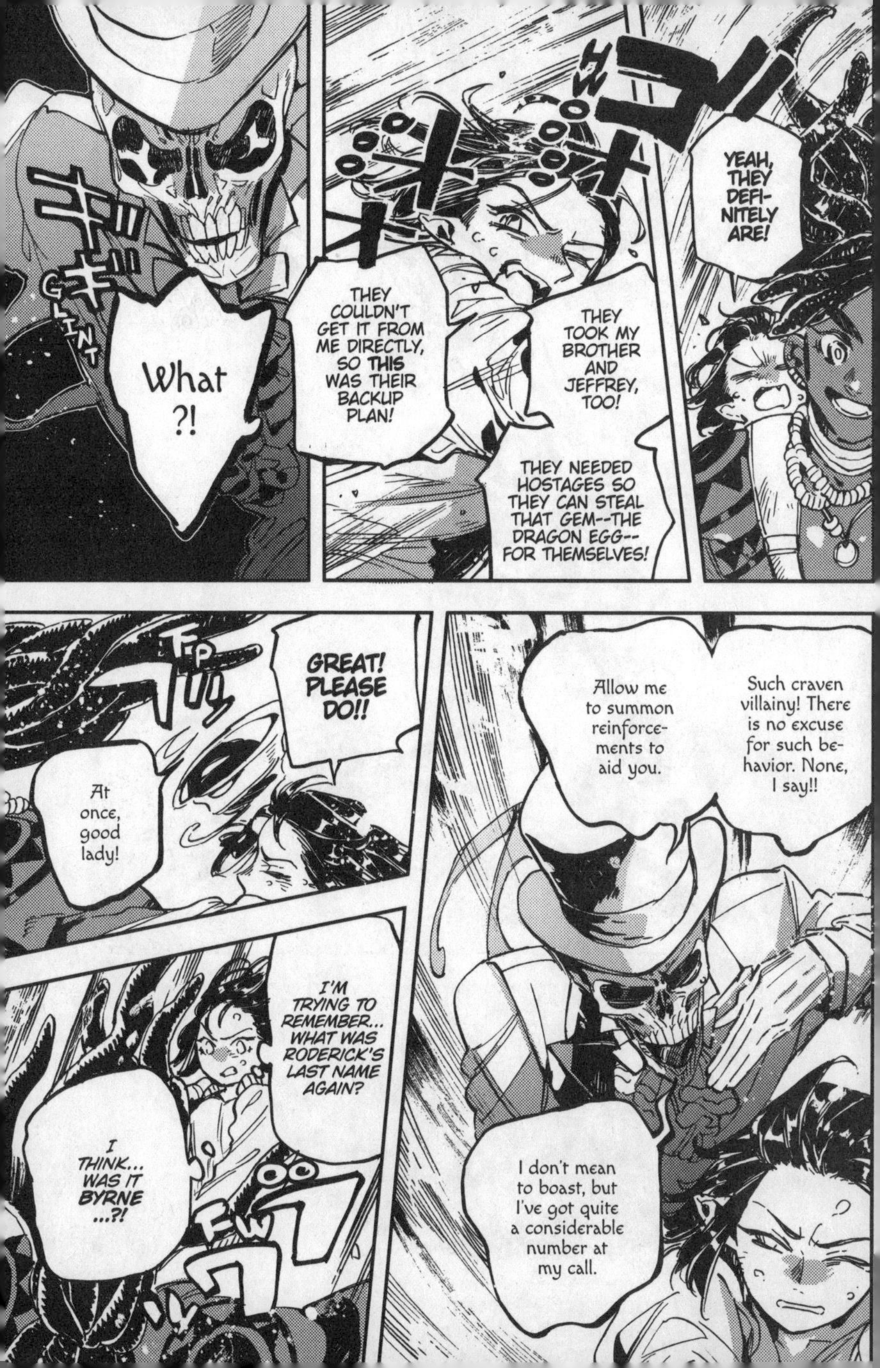
YEAH, THEY DEFINITELY ARE!
THEY TOOK MY BROTHER AND JEFFREY, TOO!
THEY NEEDED HOSTAGES SO THEY CAN STEAL THAT GEM--THE DRAGON EGG--FOR THEMSELVES!
THEY COULDN'T GET IT FROM ME DIRECTLY, SO THIS WAS THEIR BACKUP PLAN!
GLINT
What ?!
Such craven villainy! There is no excuse for such behavior. None, I say!!
Allow me to summon reinforcements to aid you.
I don't mean to boast, but I've got quite a considerable number at my call.
GREAT! PLEASE DO!!
At once, good lady!
I'M TRYING TO REMEMBER... WHAT WAS RODERICK'S LAST NAME AGAIN?
I THINK... WAS IT BYRNE ...?!

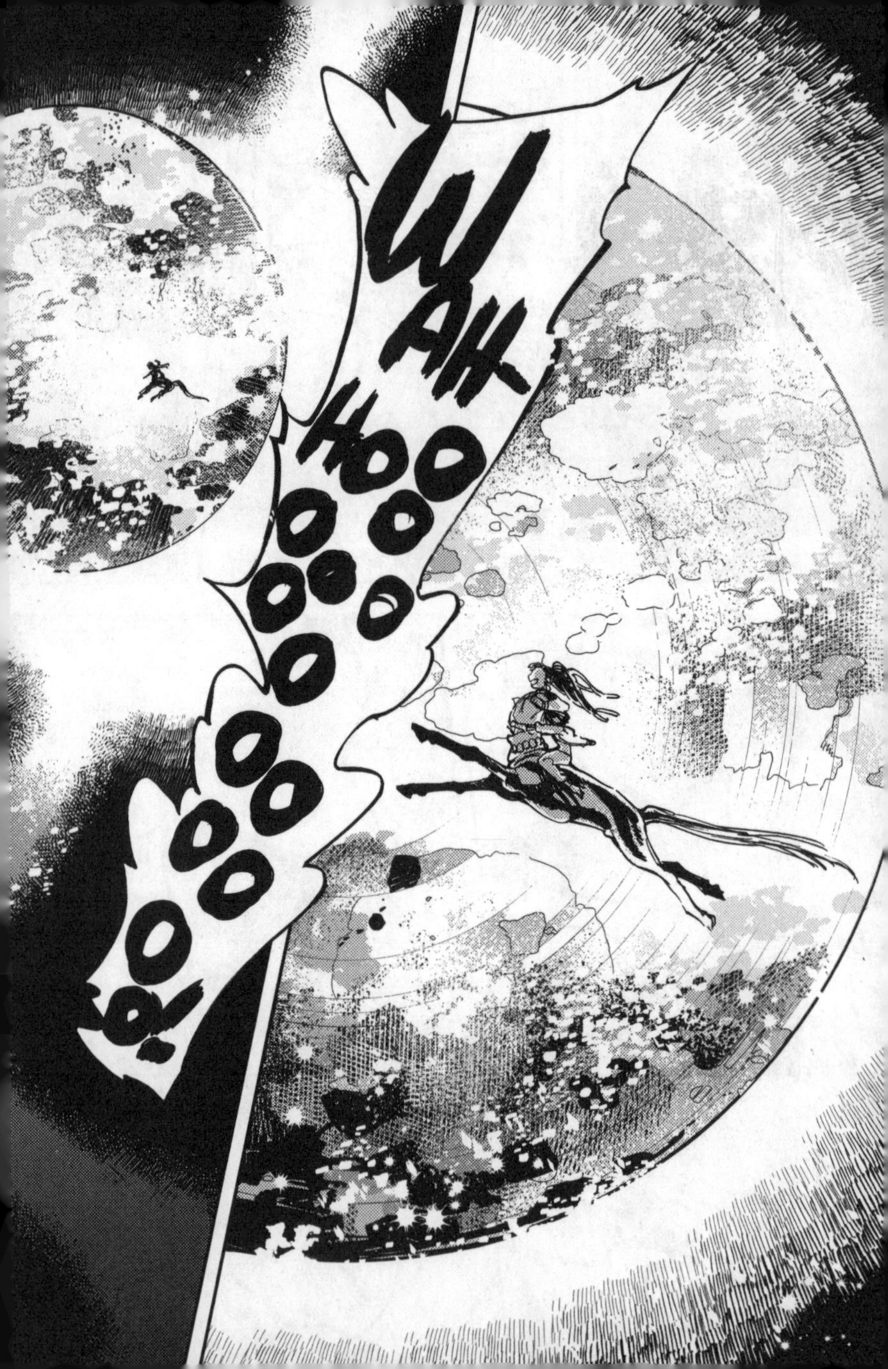
WAH HOOOOOOOOOOOOOOOOO!

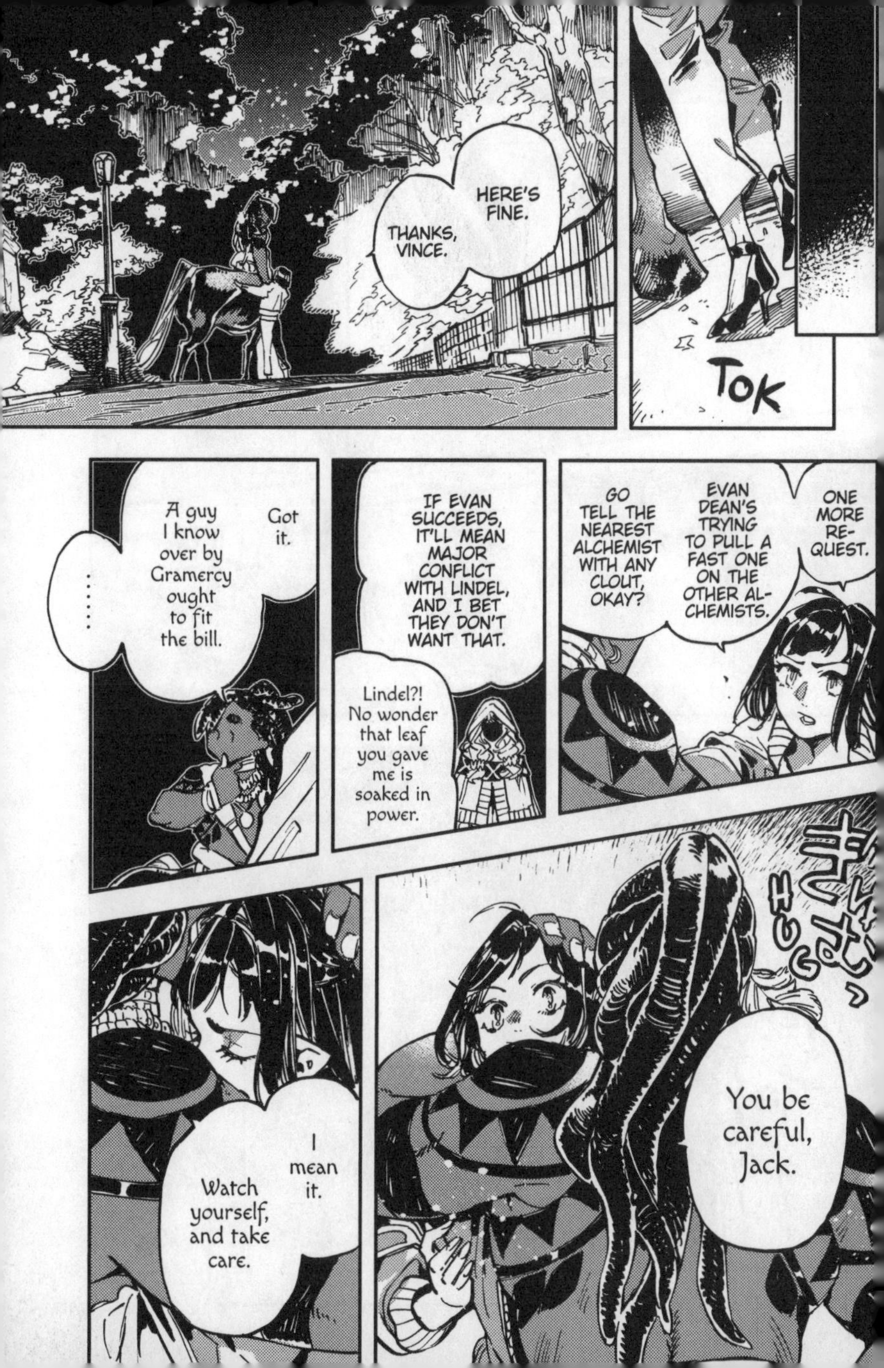
TOK
HERE'S FINE.
THANKS, VINCE.
ONE MORE RE-QUEST.
EVAN DEAN'S TRYING TO PULL A FAST ONE ON THE OTHER AL-CHEMISTS.
GO TELL THE NEAREST ALCHEMIST WITH ANY CLOUT, OKAY?
IF EVAN SUCCEEDS, IT'LL MEAN MAJOR CONFLICT WITH LINDEL, AND I BET THEY DON'T WANT THAT.
Lindel?! No wonder that leaf you gave me is soaked in power.
Got it.
A guy I know over by Gramercy ought to fit the bill.
......
HUG
You be careful, Jack.
I mean it.
Watch yourself, and take care.

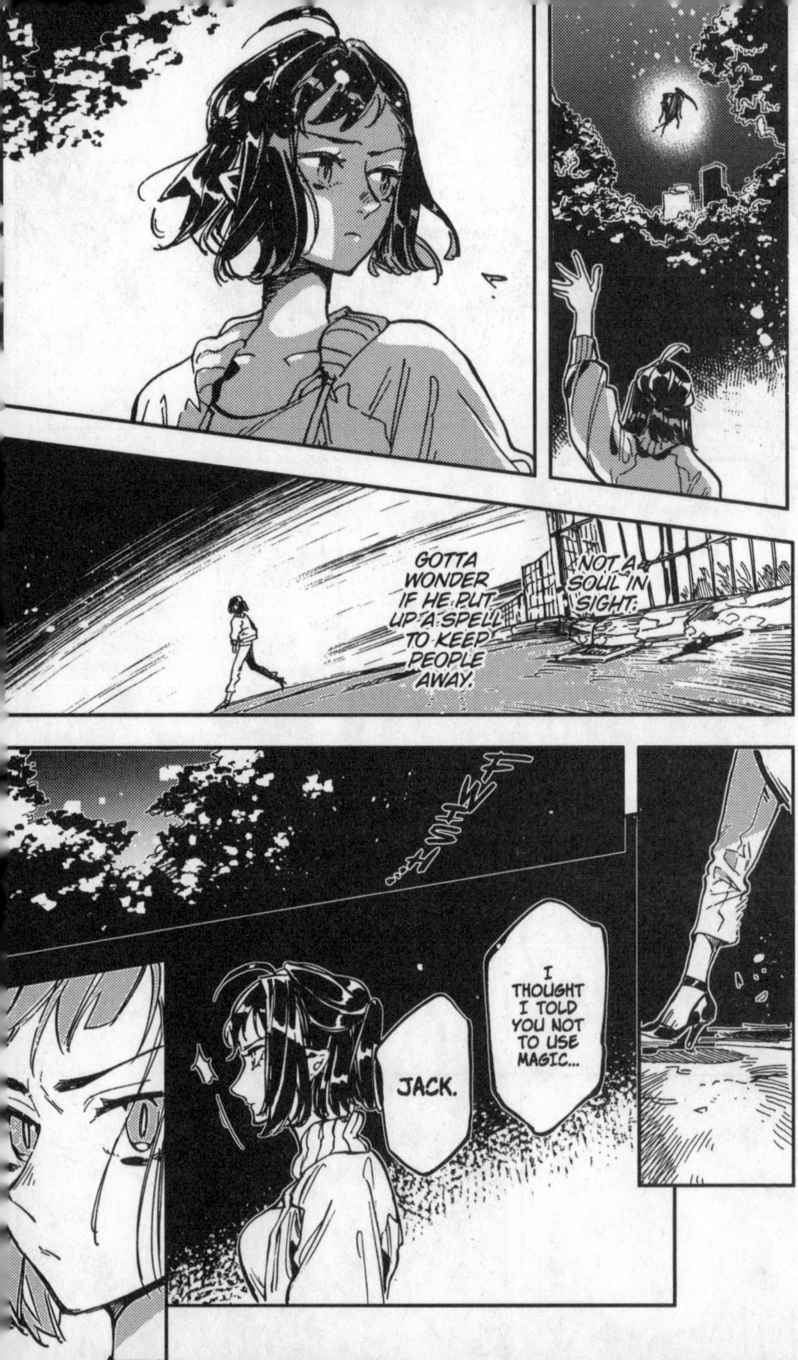
?
NOT A SOUL IN SIGHT.
GOTTA WONDER IF HE PUT UP A SPELL TO KEEP PEOPLE AWAY.
...HSHWFF
I THOUGHT I TOLD YOU NOT TO USE MAGIC...
JACK.

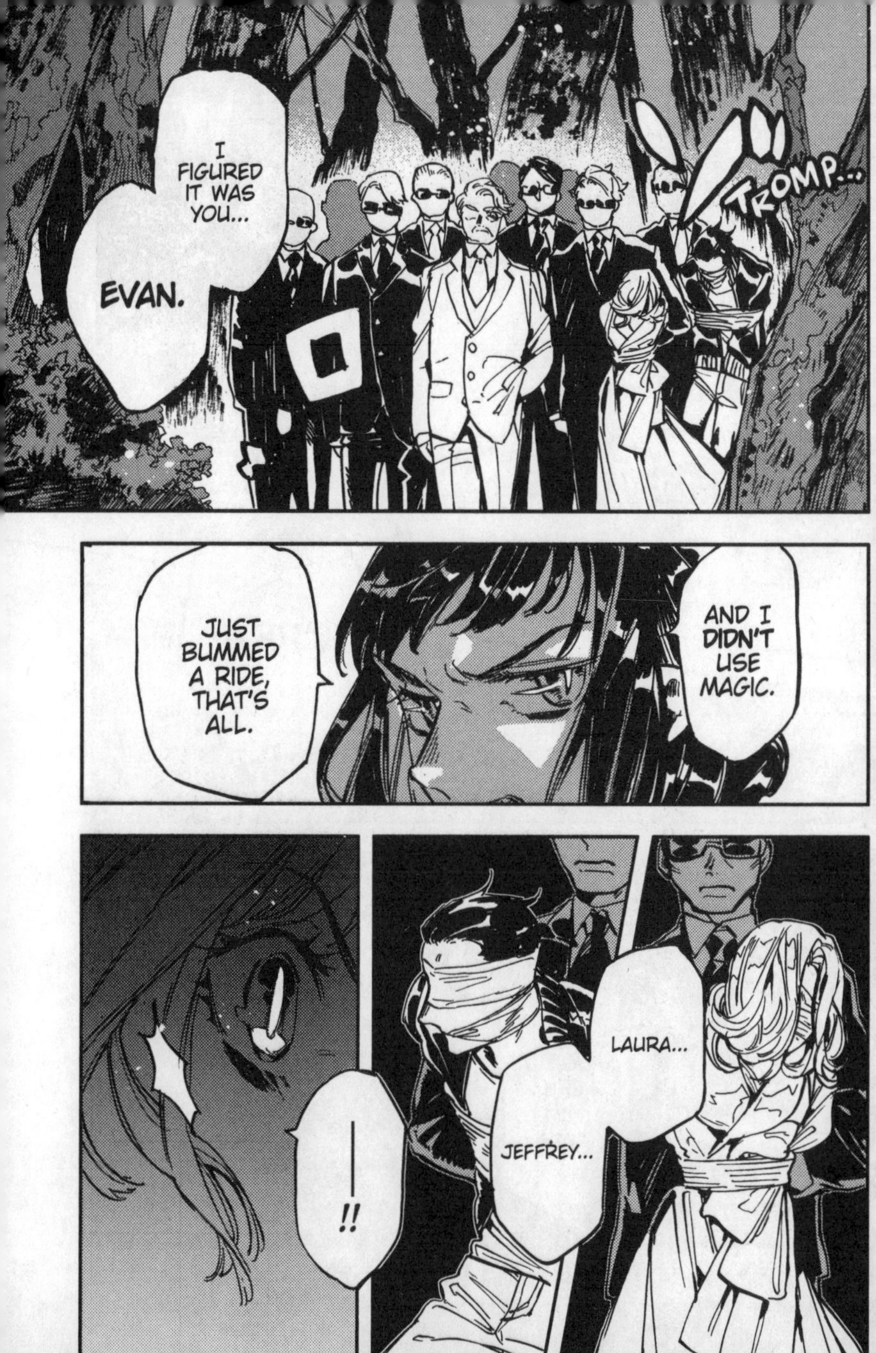
TROMP...
I FIGURED IT WAS YOU...
EVAN.
AND I DIDN'T USE MAGIC.
JUST BUMMED A RIDE, THAT'S ALL.
LAURA...
JEFFREY...
—!!

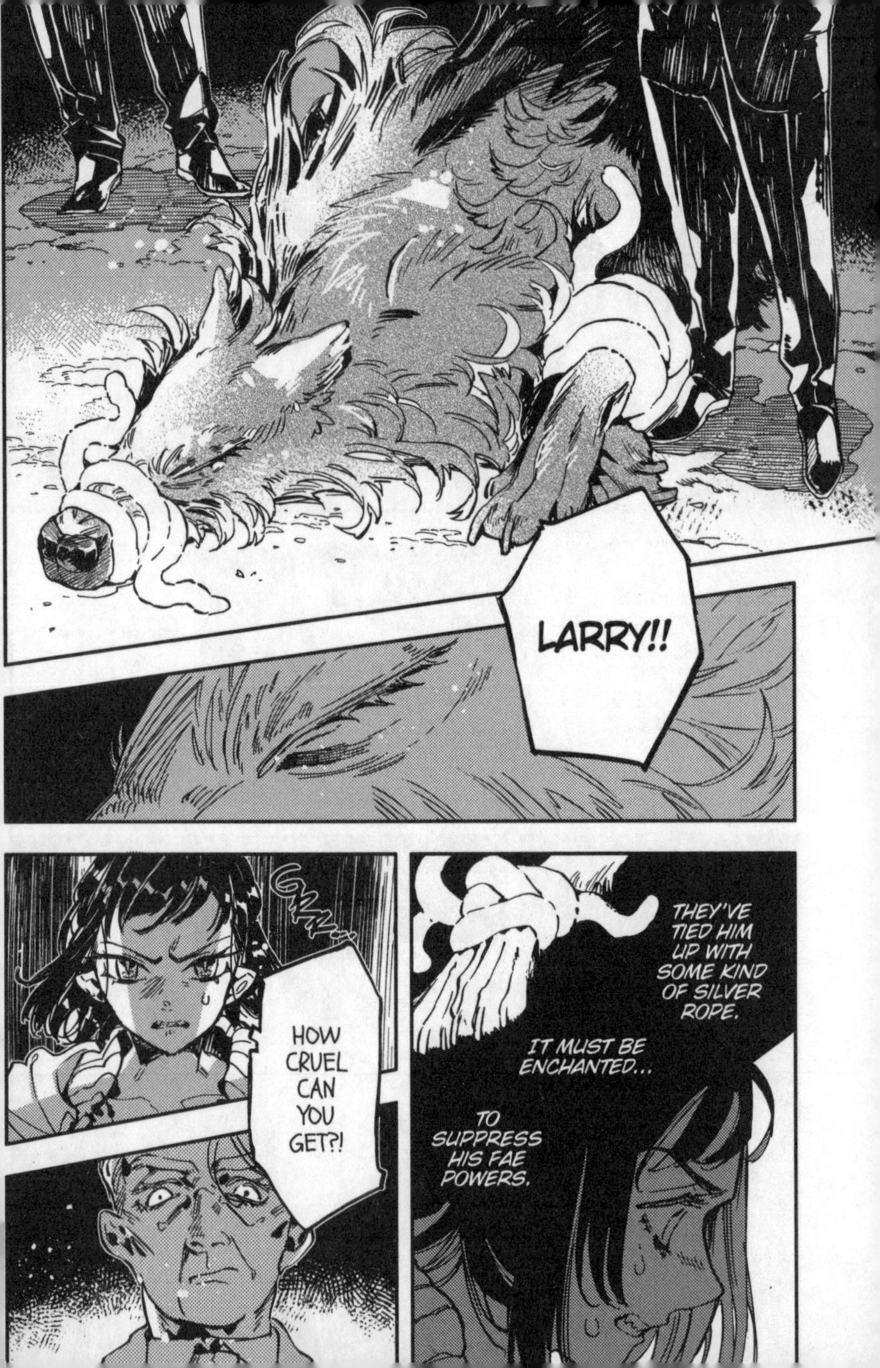
LARRY!!
THEY'VE TIED HIM UP WITH SOME KIND OF SILVER ROPE.
IT MUST BE ENCHANTED...
TO SUPPRESS HIS FAE POWERS.
GNNN...
HOW CRUEL CAN YOU GET?!

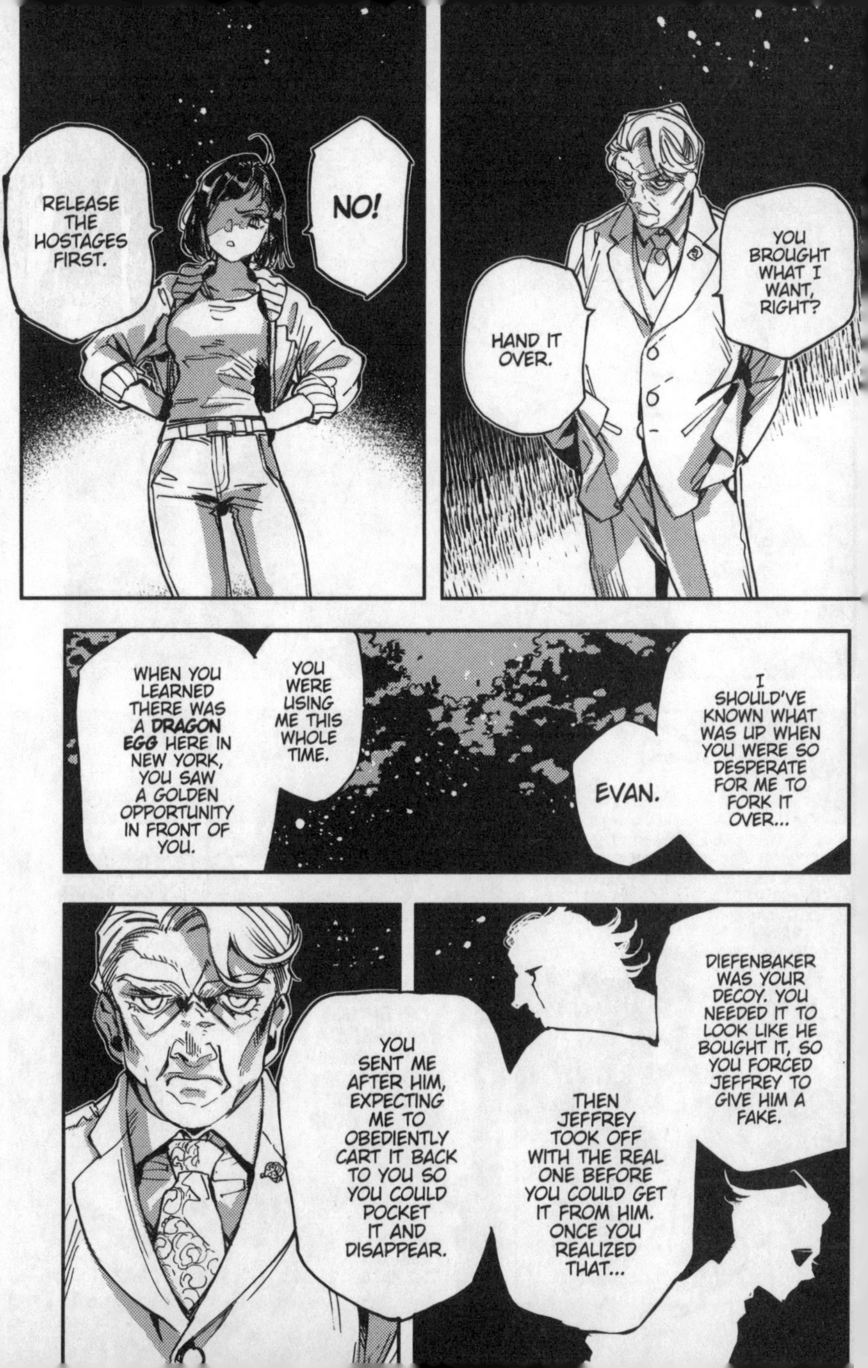
YOU BROUGHT WHAT I WANT, RIGHT?
HAND IT OVER.
NO!
RELEASE THE HOSTAGES FIRST.
I SHOULD'VE KNOWN WHAT WAS UP WHEN YOU WERE SO DESPERATE FOR ME TO FORK IT OVER...
EVAN.
YOU WERE USING ME THIS WHOLE TIME.
WHEN YOU LEARNED THERE WAS A **DRAGON EGG** HERE IN NEW YORK, YOU SAW A GOLDEN OPPORTUNITY IN FRONT OF YOU.
DIEFENBAKER WAS YOUR DECOY. YOU NEEDED IT TO LOOK LIKE HE BOUGHT IT, SO YOU FORCED JEFFREY TO GIVE HIM A FAKE.
THEN JEFFREY TOOK OFF WITH THE REAL ONE BEFORE YOU COULD GET IT FROM HIM. ONCE YOU REALIZED THAT...
YOU SENT ME AFTER HIM, EXPECTING ME TO OBEDIENTLY CART IT BACK TO YOU SO YOU COULD POCKET IT AND DISAPPEAR.

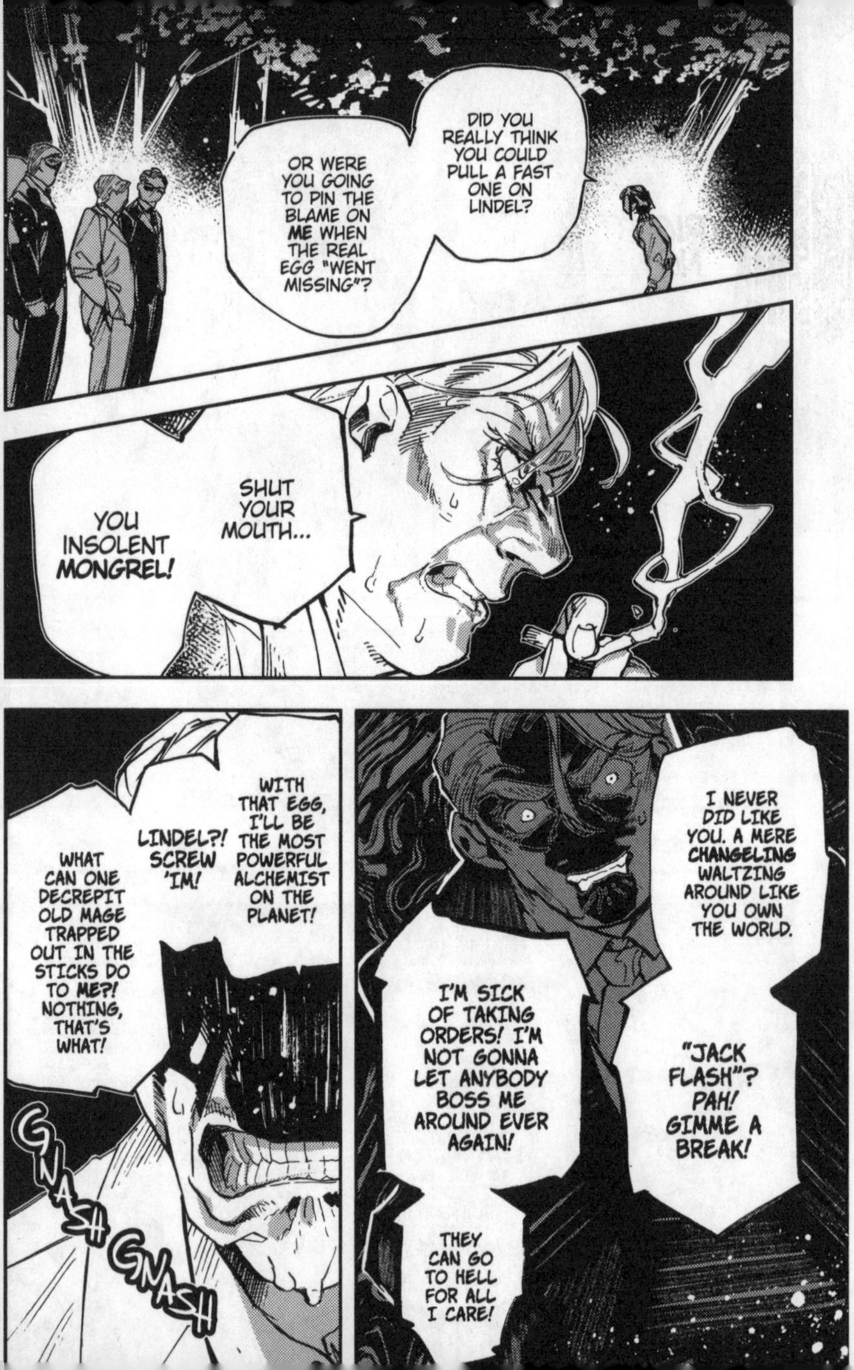
DID YOU REALLY THINK YOU COULD PULL A FAST ONE ON LINDEL?
OR WERE YOU GOING TO PIN THE BLAME ON **ME** WHEN THE REAL EGG "WENT MISSING"?
SHUT YOUR MOUTH...
YOU INSOLENT **MONGREL!**
I NEVER DID LIKE YOU. A MERE **CHANGELING** WALTZING AROUND LIKE YOU OWN THE WORLD.
"JACK FLASH"? PAH! GIMME A BREAK!
I'M SICK OF TAKING ORDERS! I'M NOT GONNA LET ANYBODY BOSS ME AROUND EVER AGAIN!
THEY CAN GO TO HELL FOR ALL I CARE!
WITH THAT EGG, I'LL BE THE MOST POWERFUL ALCHEMIST ON THE PLANET!
LINDEL?! SCREW 'IM!
WHAT CAN ONE DECREPIT OLD MAGE TRAPPED OUT IN THE STICKS DO TO ME?! NOTHING, THAT'S WHAT!
GNASH GNASH

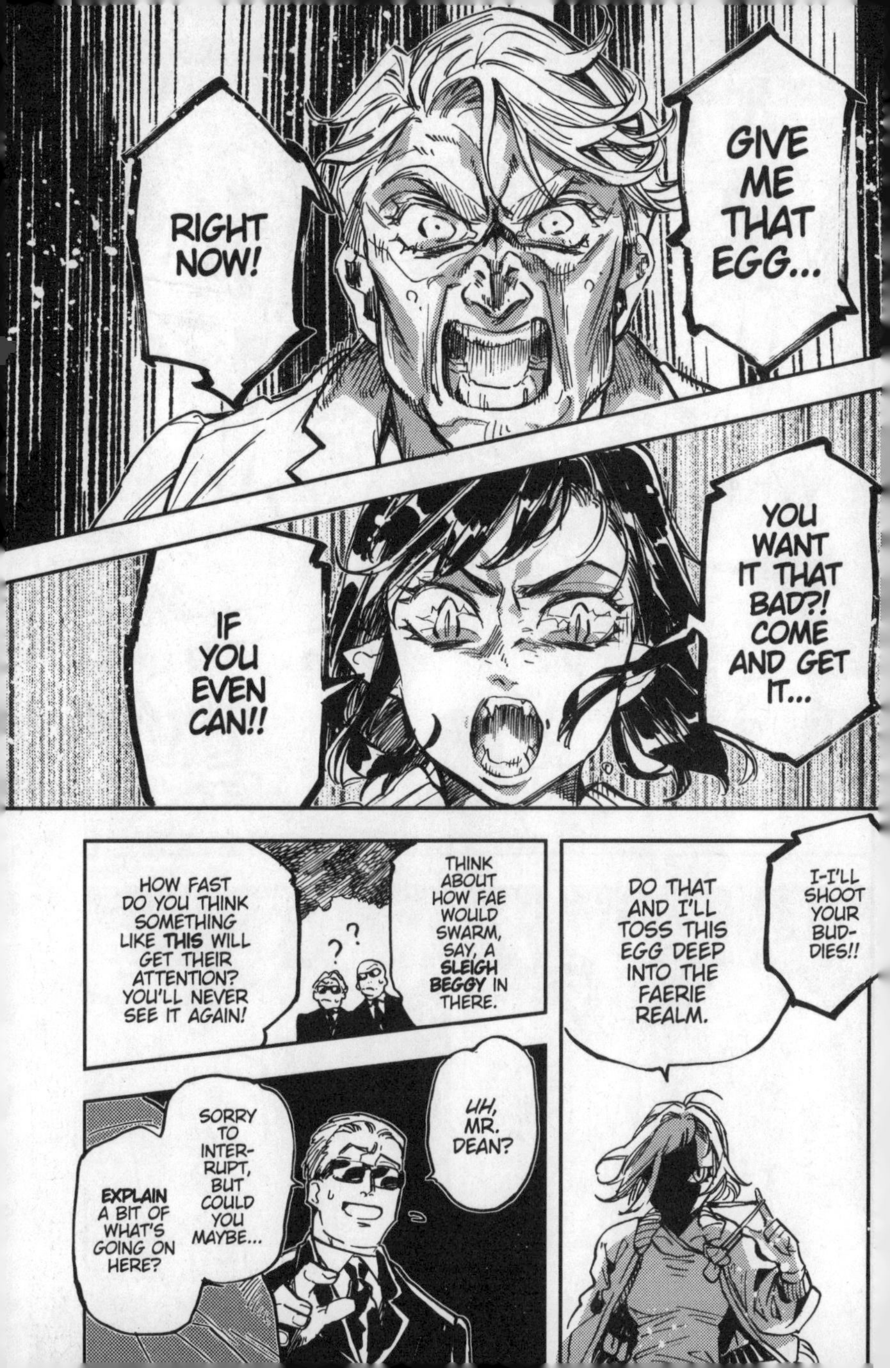
GIVE ME THAT EGG...
RIGHT NOW!
YOU WANT IT THAT BAD?! COME AND GET IT...
IF YOU EVEN CAN!!
I-I'LL SHOOT YOUR BUD-DIES!!
DO THAT AND I'LL TOSS THIS EGG DEEP INTO THE FAERIE REALM.
THINK ABOUT HOW FAE WOULD SWARM, SAY, A **SLEIGH BEGGY** IN THERE.
HOW FAST DO YOU THINK SOMETHING LIKE **THIS** WILL GET THEIR ATTENTION? YOU'LL NEVER SEE IT AGAIN!
? ?
UH, MR. DEAN?
SORRY TO INTER-RUPT, BUT COULD YOU MAYBE...
EXPLAIN A BIT OF WHAT'S GOING ON HERE?

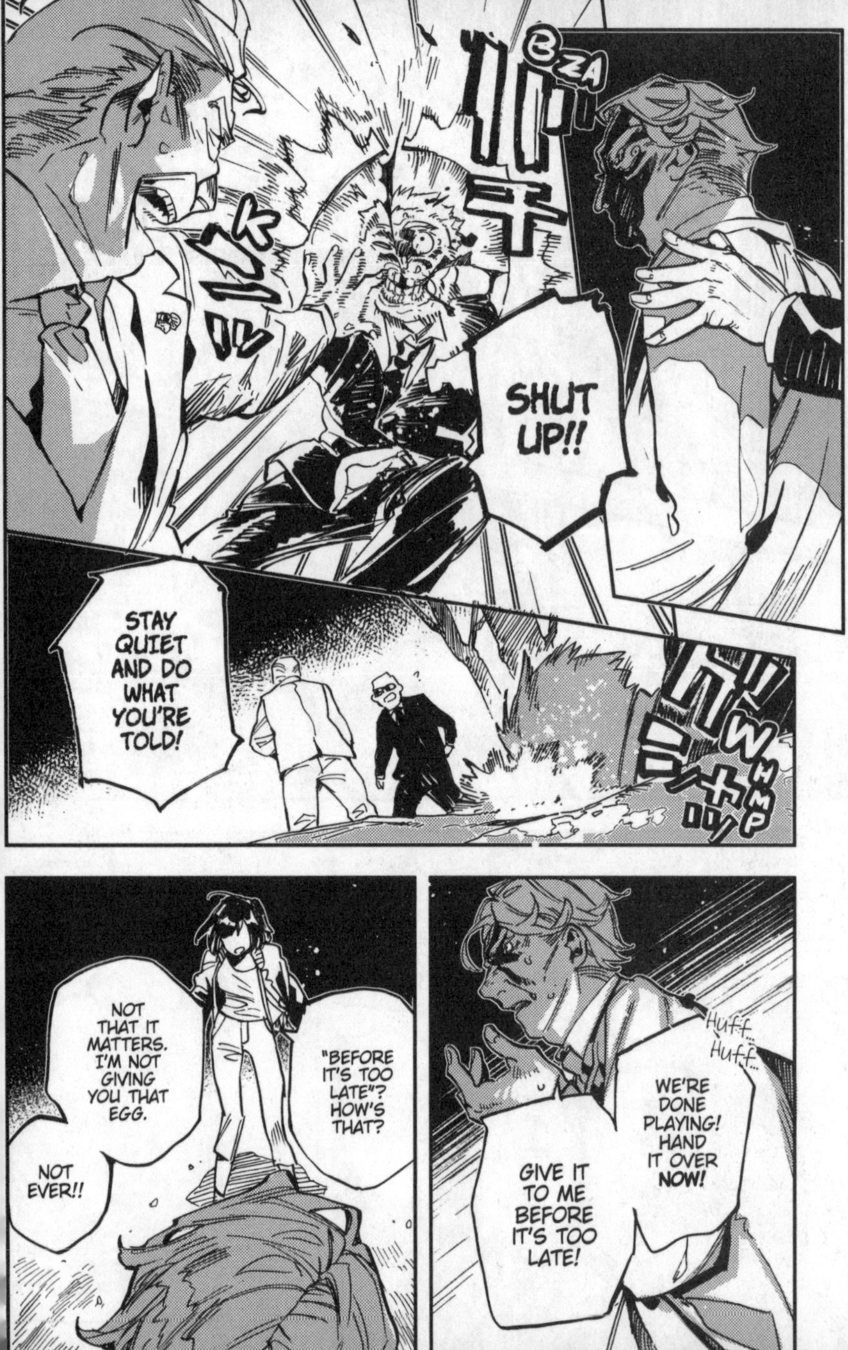
BZA
SHUT UP!!
K
WHMP
STAY QUIET AND DO WHAT YOU'RE TOLD!
Huff... Huff...
WE'RE DONE PLAYING! HAND IT OVER NOW!
GIVE IT TO ME BEFORE IT'S TOO LATE!
"BEFORE IT'S TOO LATE"? HOW'S THAT?
NOT THAT IT MATTERS. I'M NOT GIVING YOU THAT EGG.
NOT EVER!!

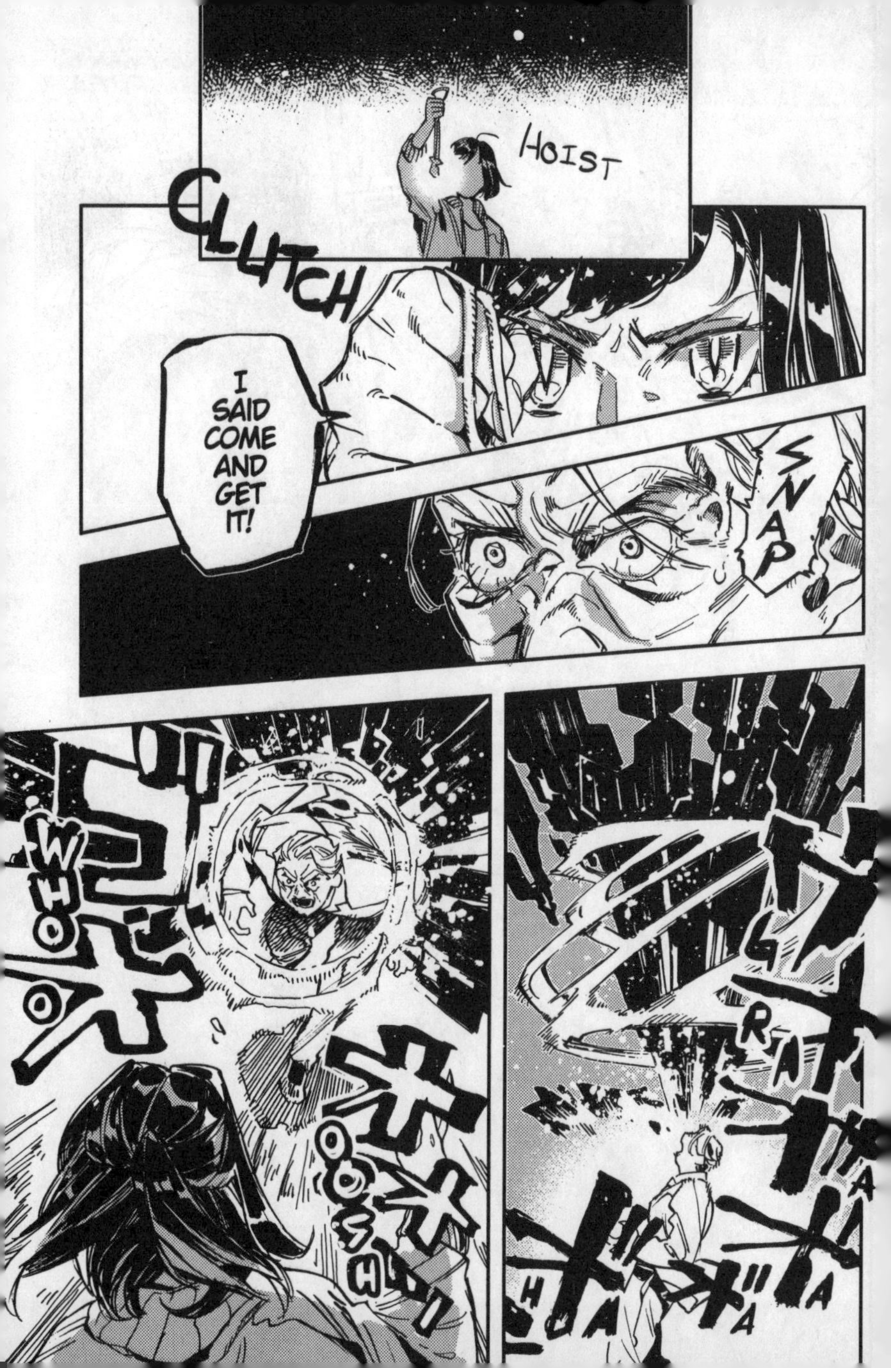
HOIST
CLUTCH
I SAID COME AND GET IT!
SNAP
GRA
WHOOO
OOOSH

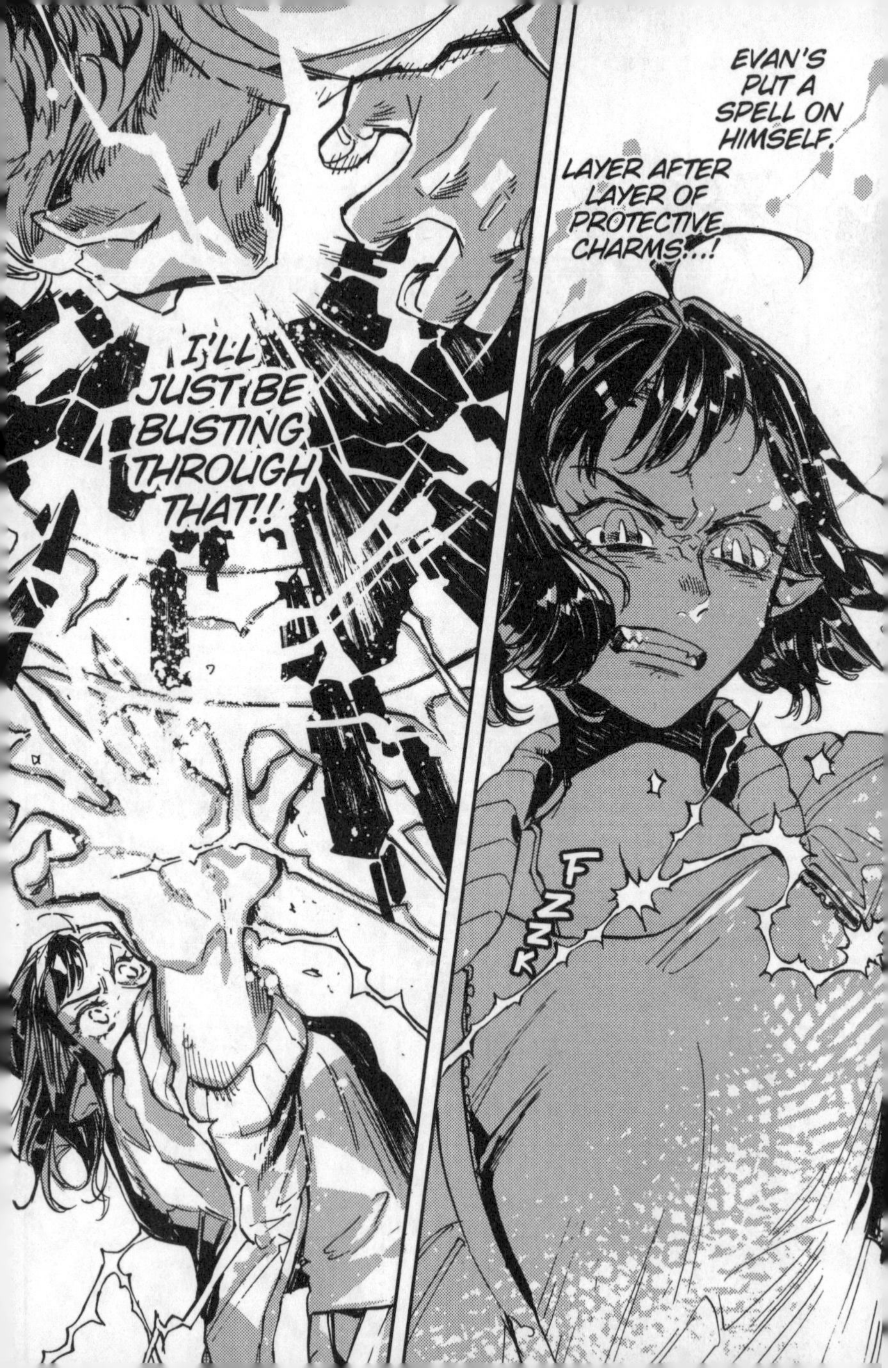
EVAN'S PUT A SPELL ON HIMSELF.
LAYER AFTER LAYER OF PROTECTIVE CHARMS...!
FZZK
I'LL JUST BE BUSTING THROUGH THAT!!

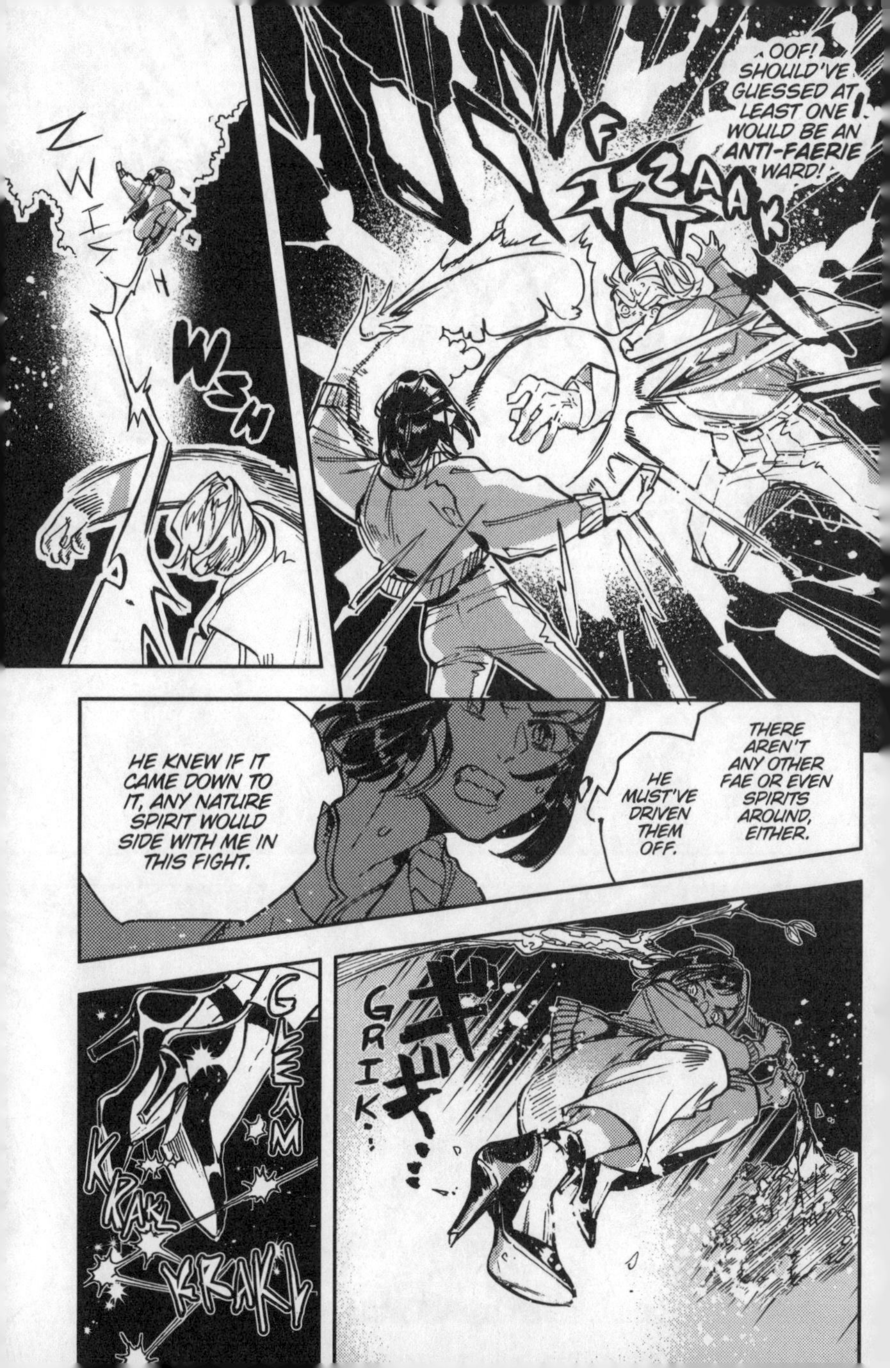
OOF! SHOULD'VE GUESSED AT LEAST ONE WOULD BE AN ANTI-FAERIE WARD!
FZAAK
WSH
THERE AREN'T ANY OTHER FAE OR EVEN SPIRITS AROUND, EITHER.
HE MUST'VE DRIVEN THEM OFF.
HE KNEW IF IT CAME DOWN TO IT, ANY NATURE SPIRIT WOULD SIDE WITH ME IN THIS FIGHT.
GRIK
GLEAM
KRAK
KRAK

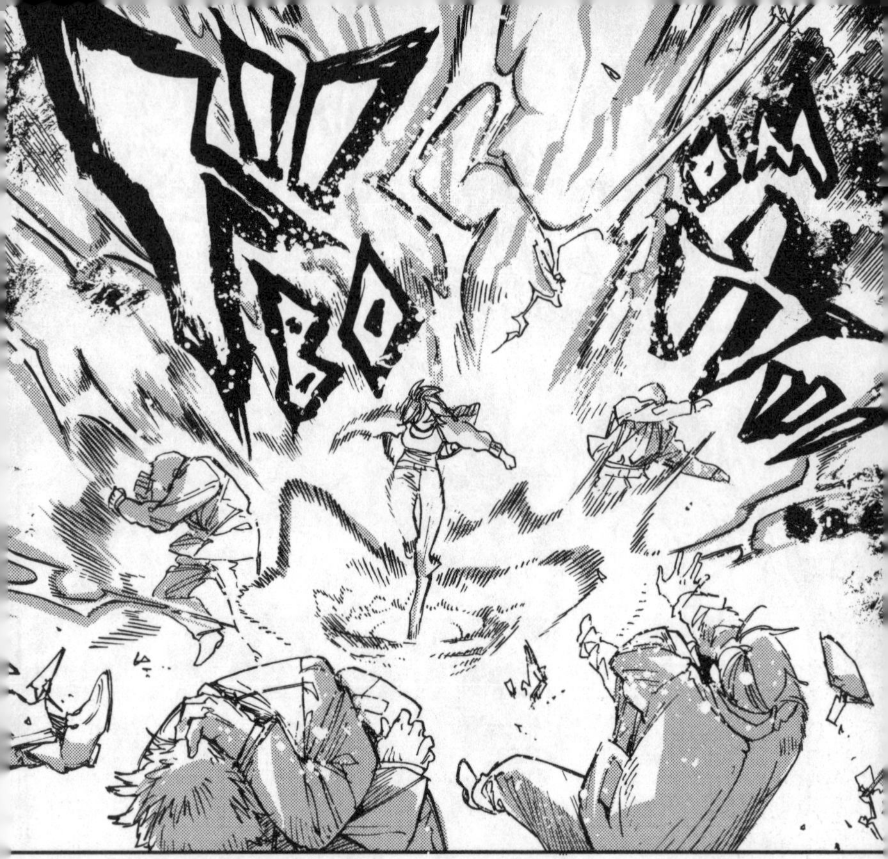

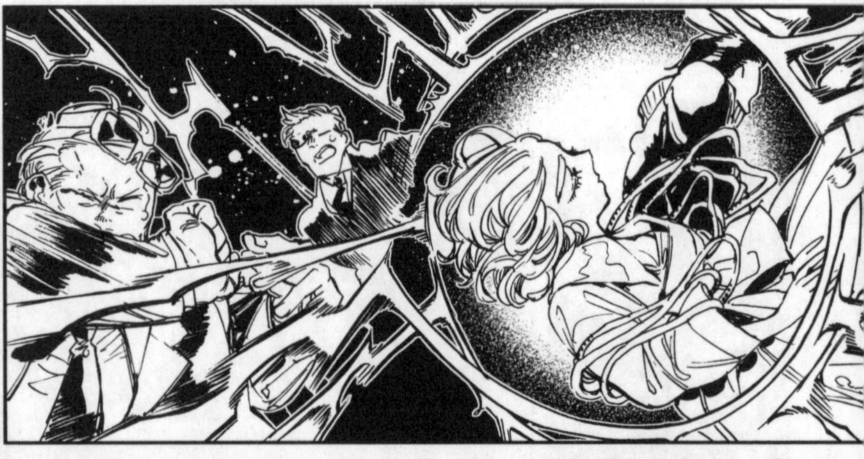

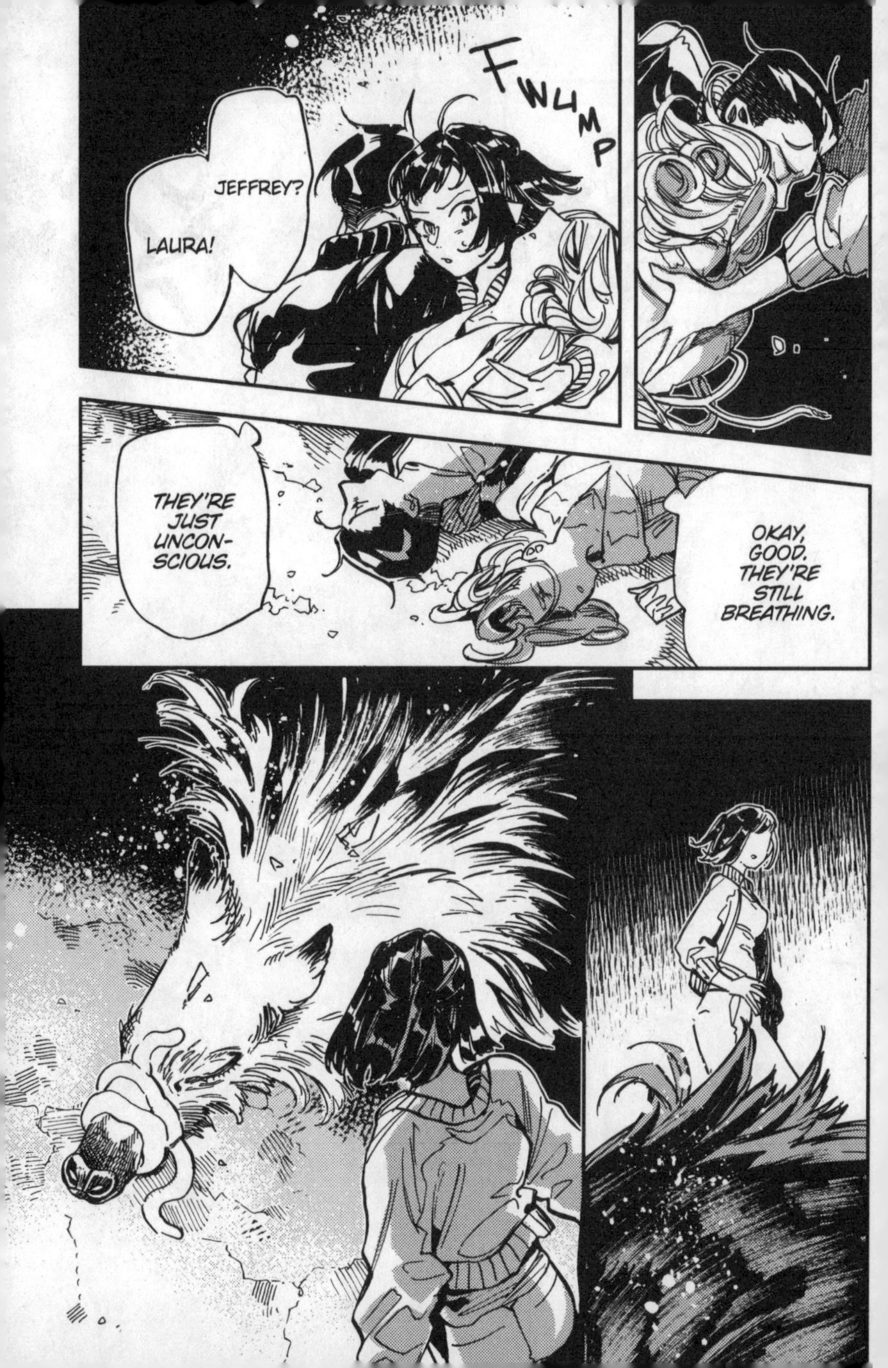
FWUMP
JEFFREY? LAURA!
OKAY, GOOD. THEY'RE STILL BREATHING.
THEY'RE JUST UNCONSCIOUS.

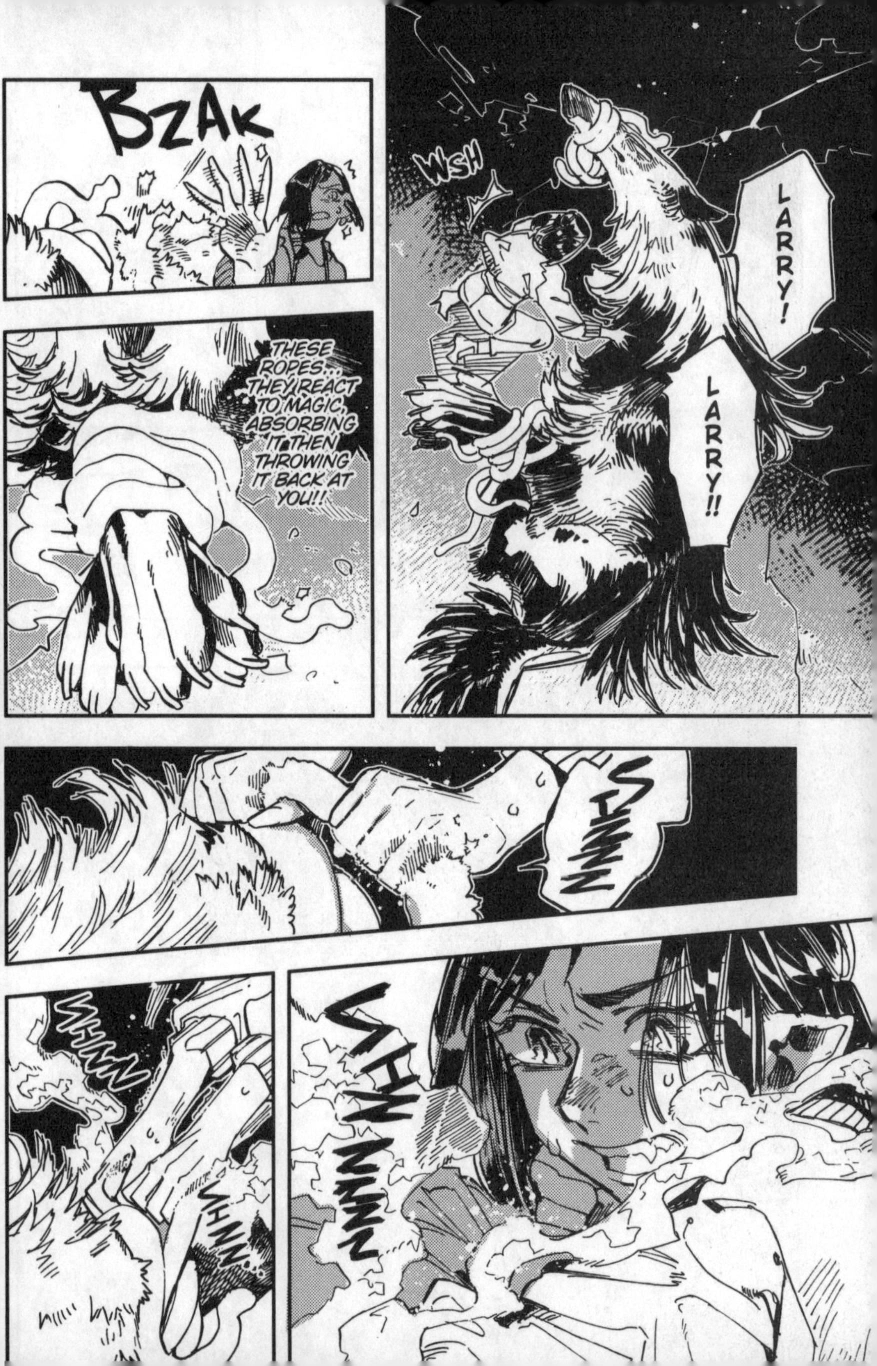
LARRY!
LARRY!!
WSH
BZAK
THESE ROPES... THEY REACT TO MAGIC, ABSORBING IT THEN THROWING IT BACK AT YOU!!

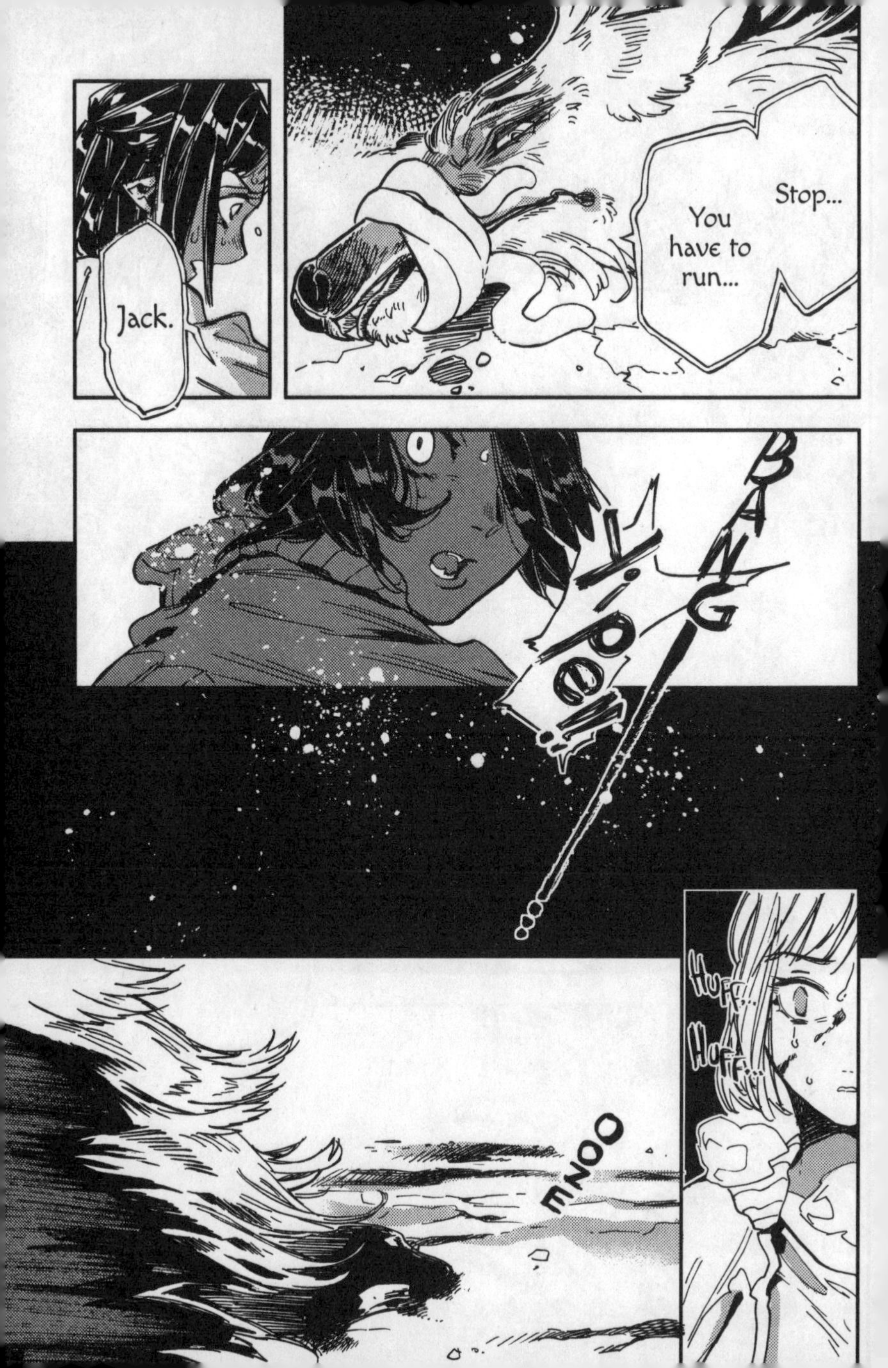
Stop... You have to run...
Jack.
BLANG
YIPE!!
Huff... Huff...

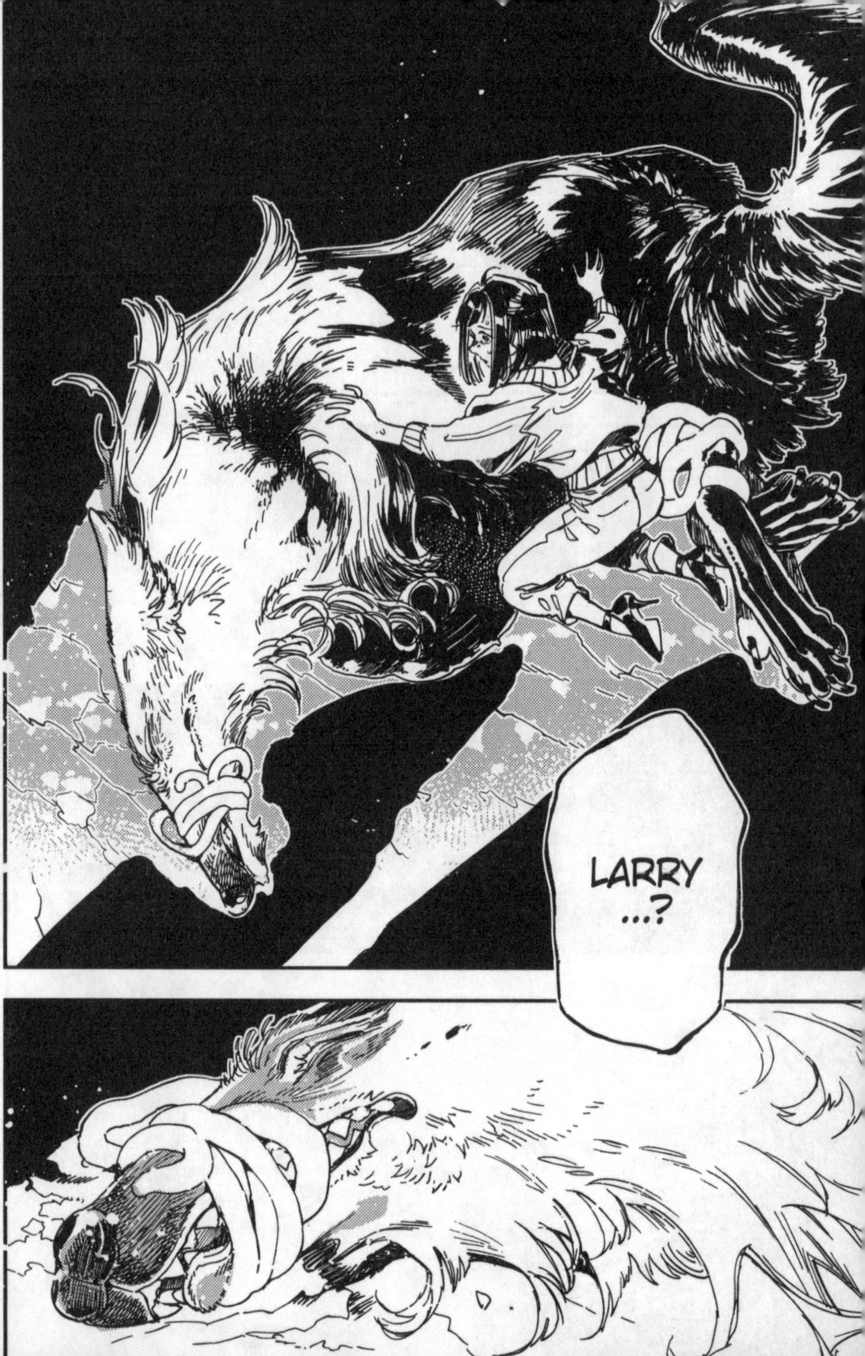
LARRY
...?

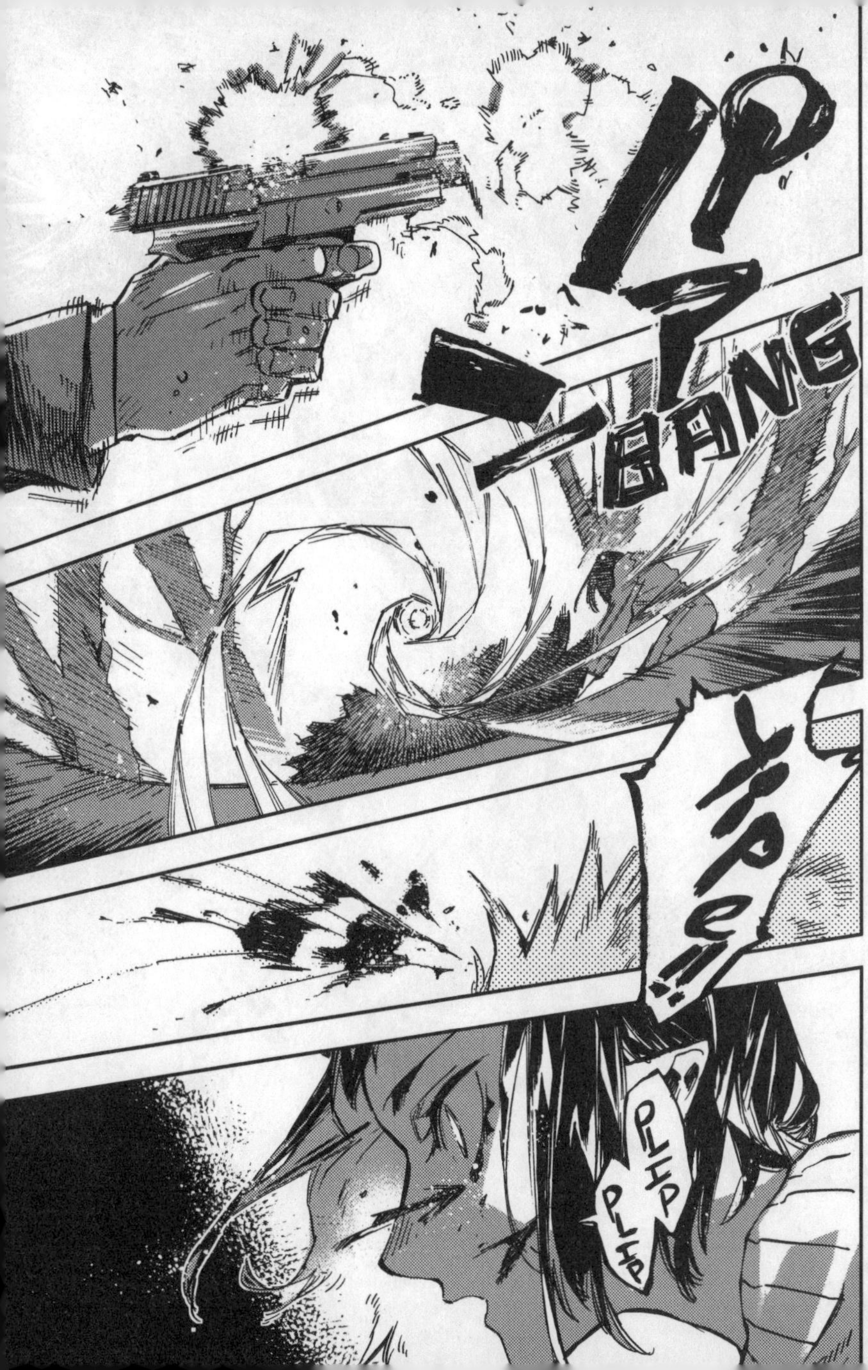
BANG
BANG
Yipe!!
PLIP
PLIP
PLIP

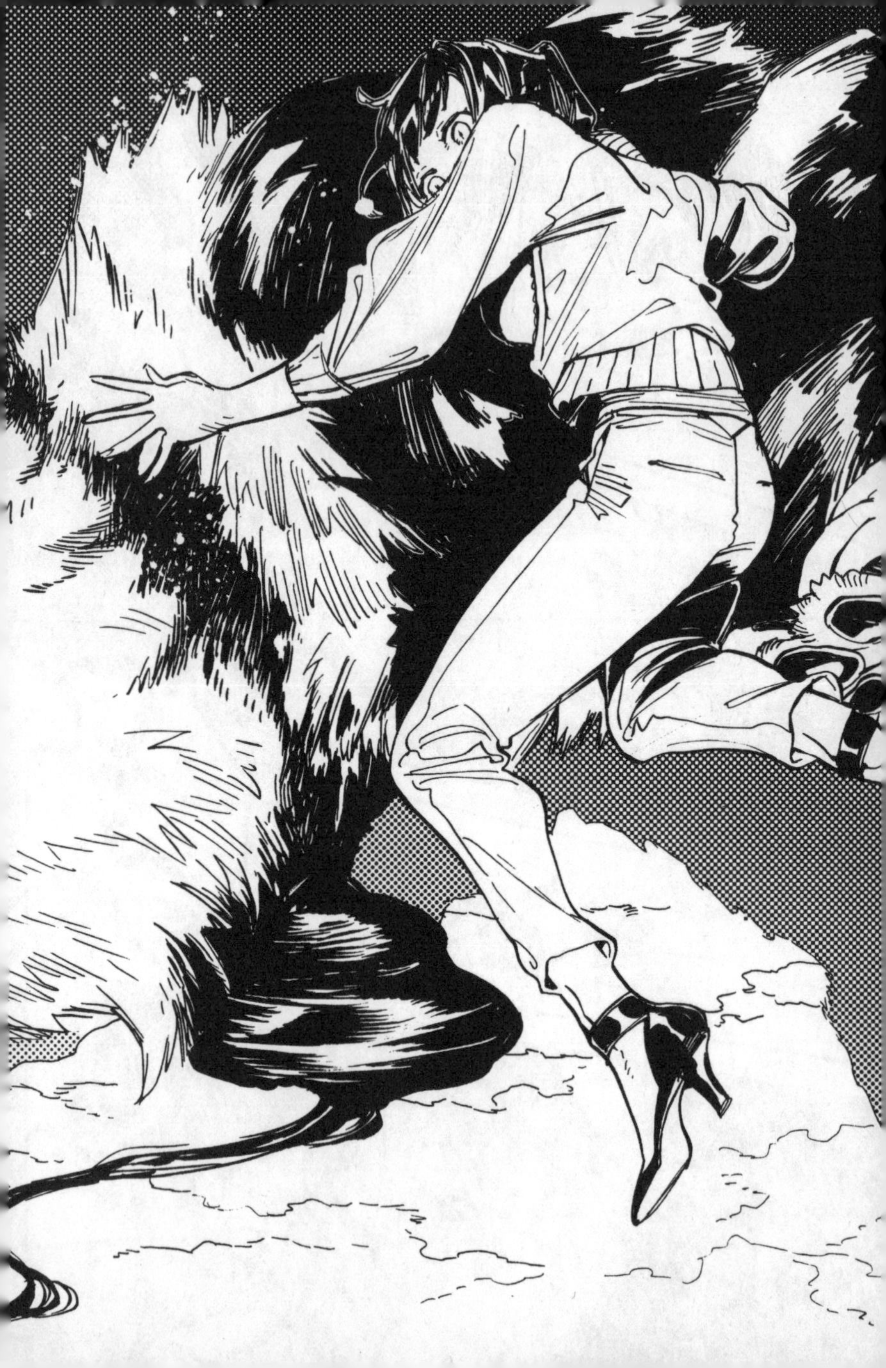

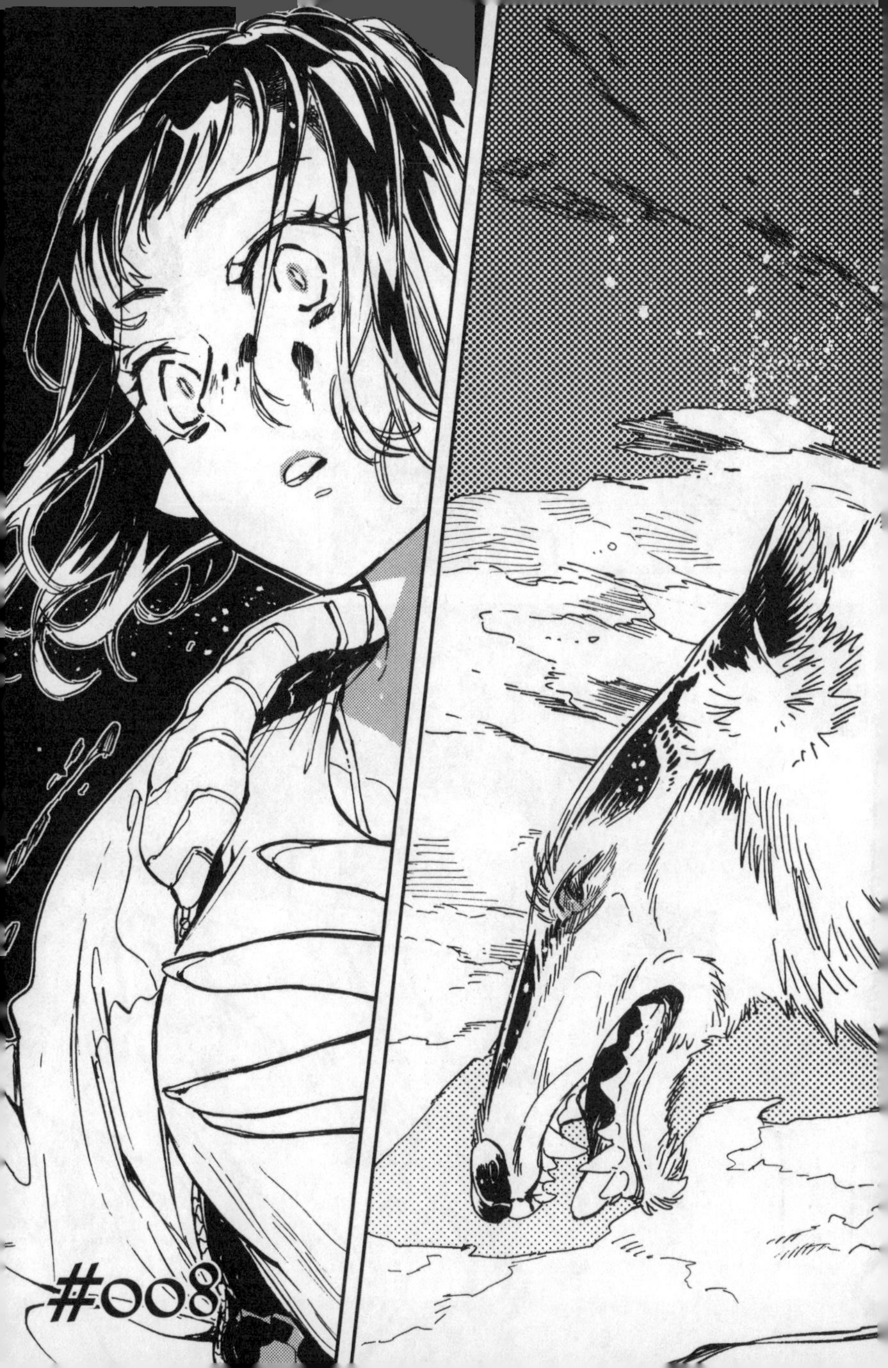
#008

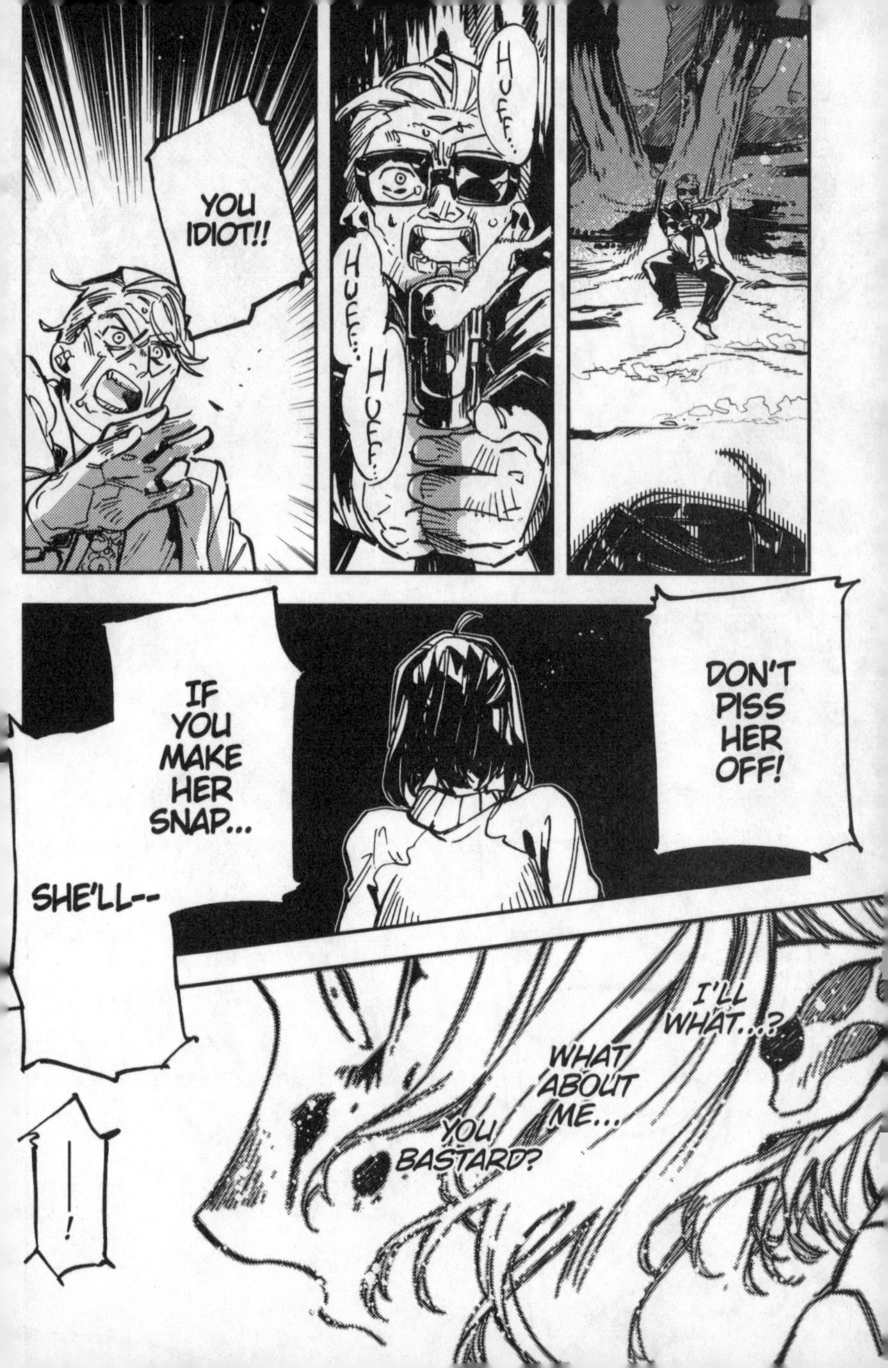

HUFF...
HUFF... HUFF...
YOU IDIOT!!
DON'T PISS HER OFF!
IF YOU MAKE HER SNAP...
SHE'LL--
I'LL WHAT...?
WHAT ABOUT ME...
YOU BASTARD?
--!

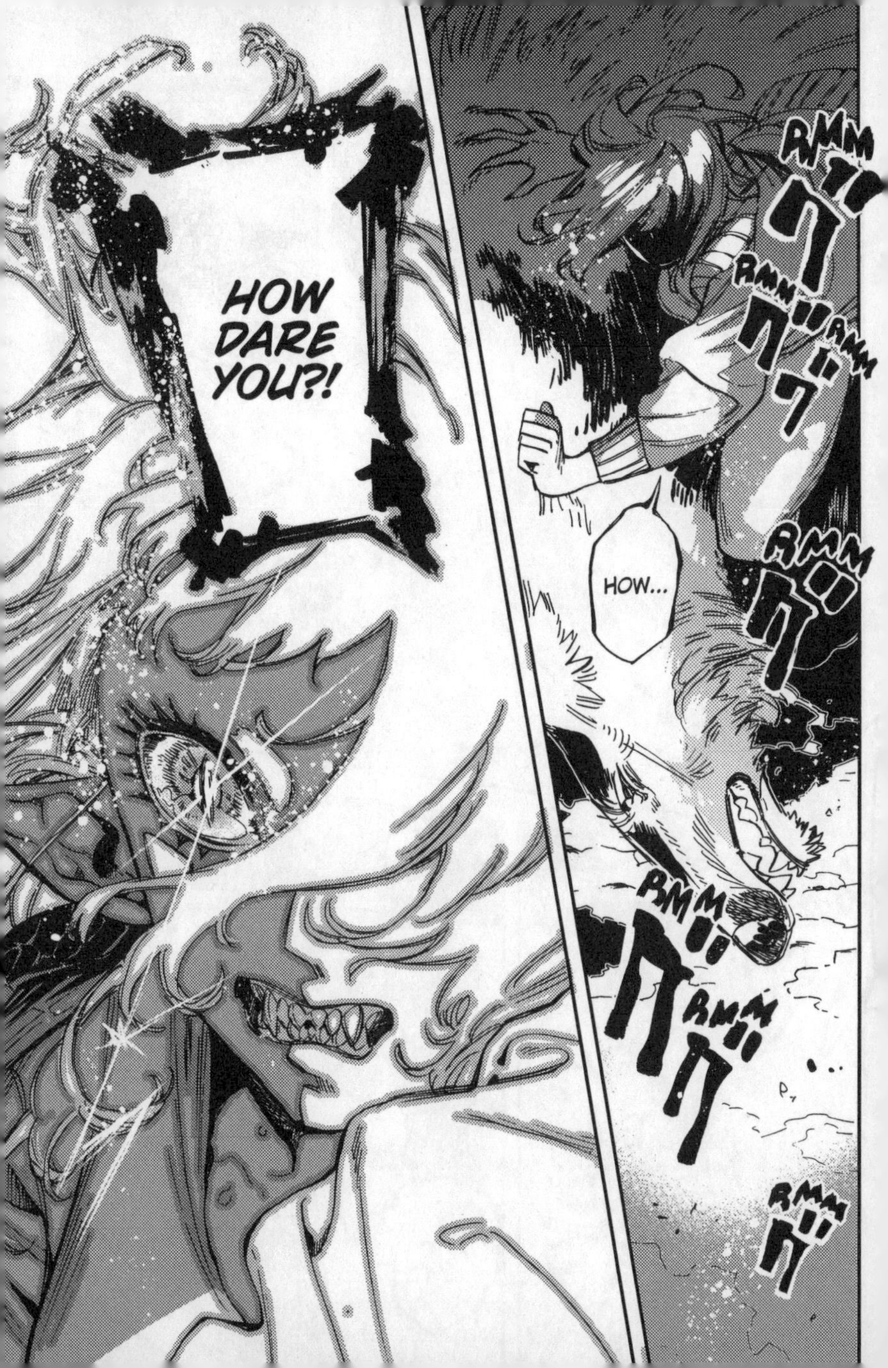
RMM
RMM
RMM
RMM
HOW...
RMM
RMM
RMM
HOW DARE YOU?!

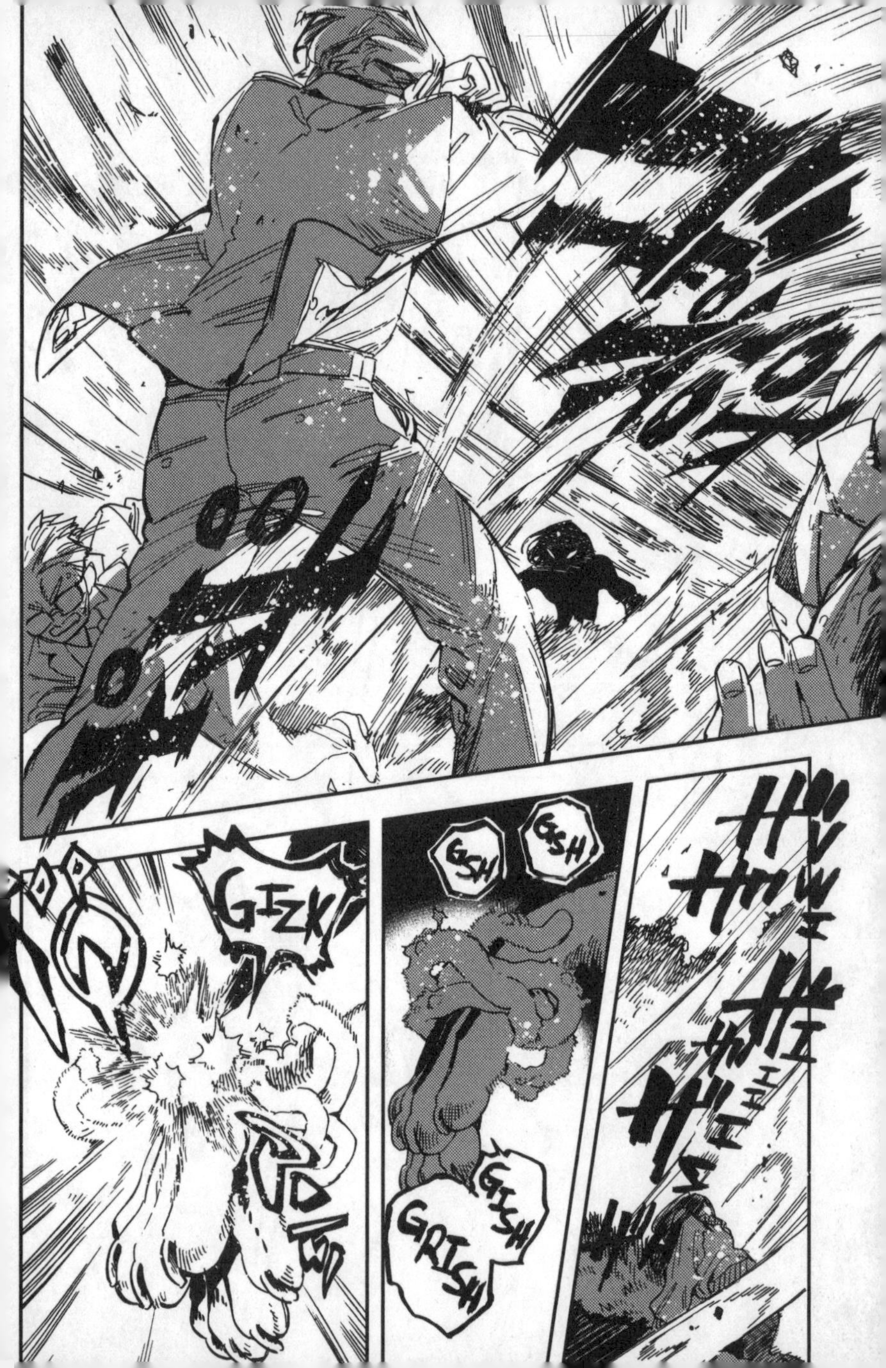

GISH
GISH
GISH
GRISH
GIZK

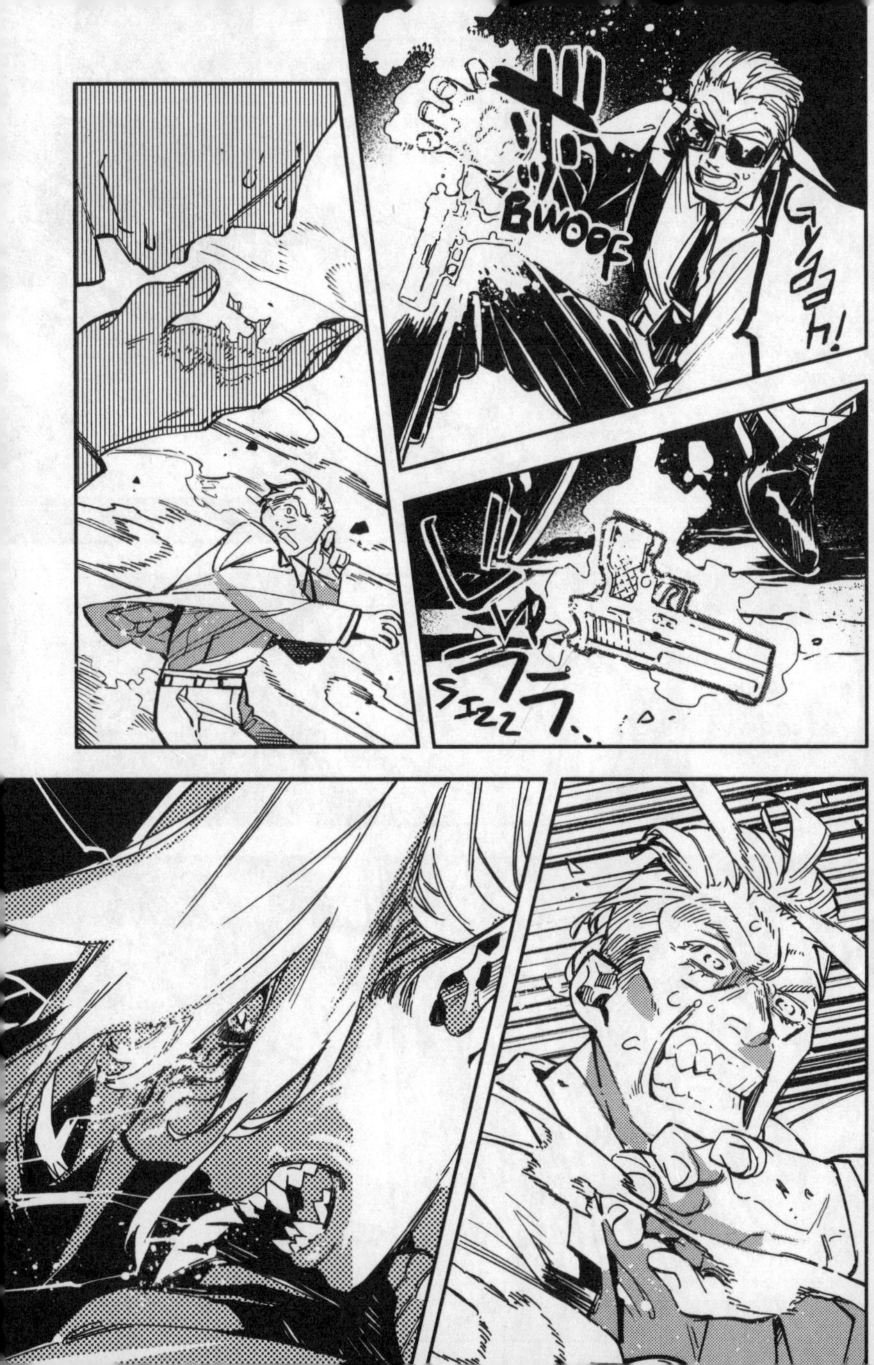
Gyaaah!
BWOOF
SIZZZ

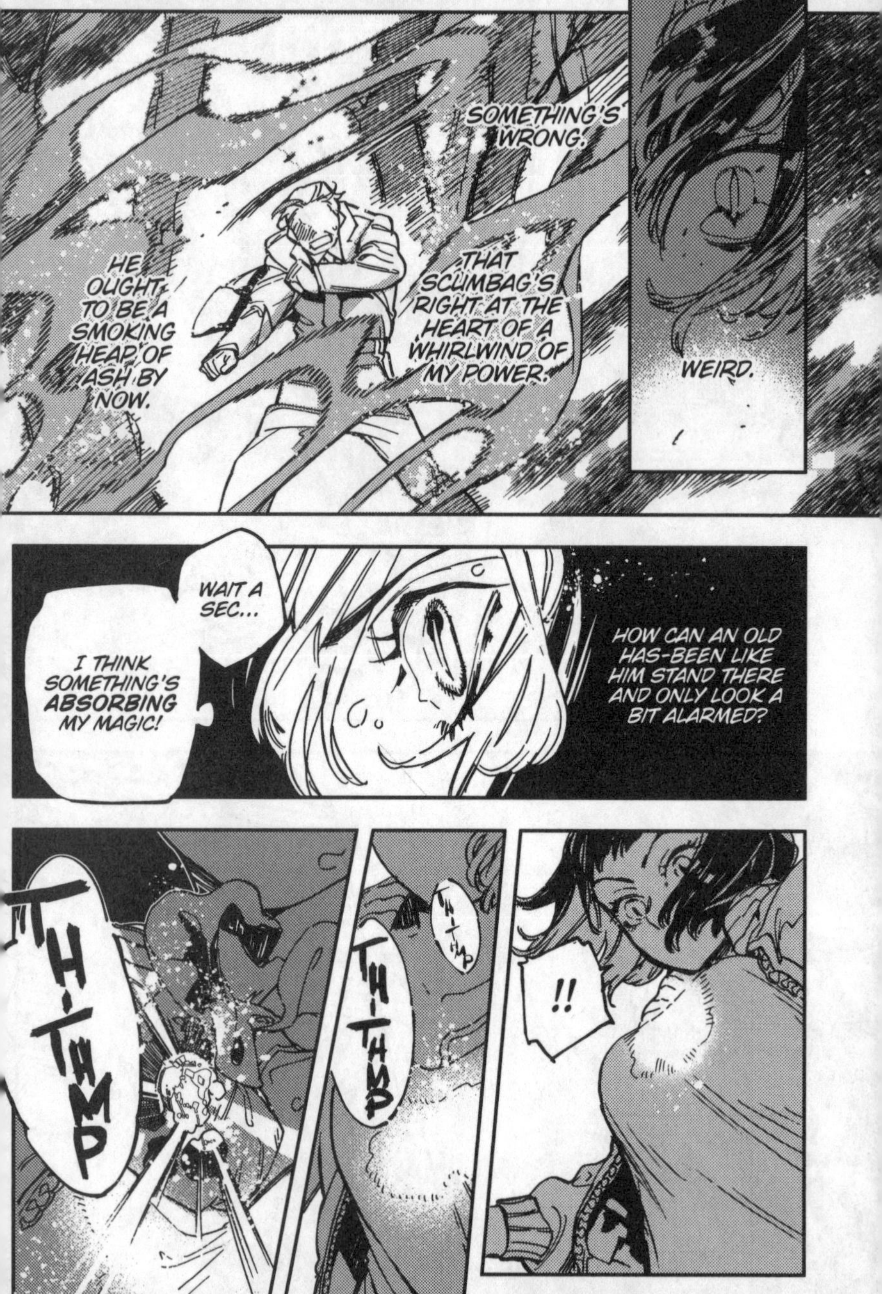
WEIRD.
SOMETHING'S WRONG.
THAT SCUMBAG'S RIGHT AT THE HEART OF A WHIRLWIND OF MY POWER.
HE OUGHT TO BE A SMOKING HEAP OF ASH BY NOW.
HOW CAN AN OLD HAS-BEEN LIKE HIM STAND THERE AND ONLY LOOK A BIT ALARMED?
WAIT A SEC...
I THINK SOMETHING'S **ABSORBING** MY MAGIC!
!!
TH-THUMP
TH-THUMP
TH-THUMP

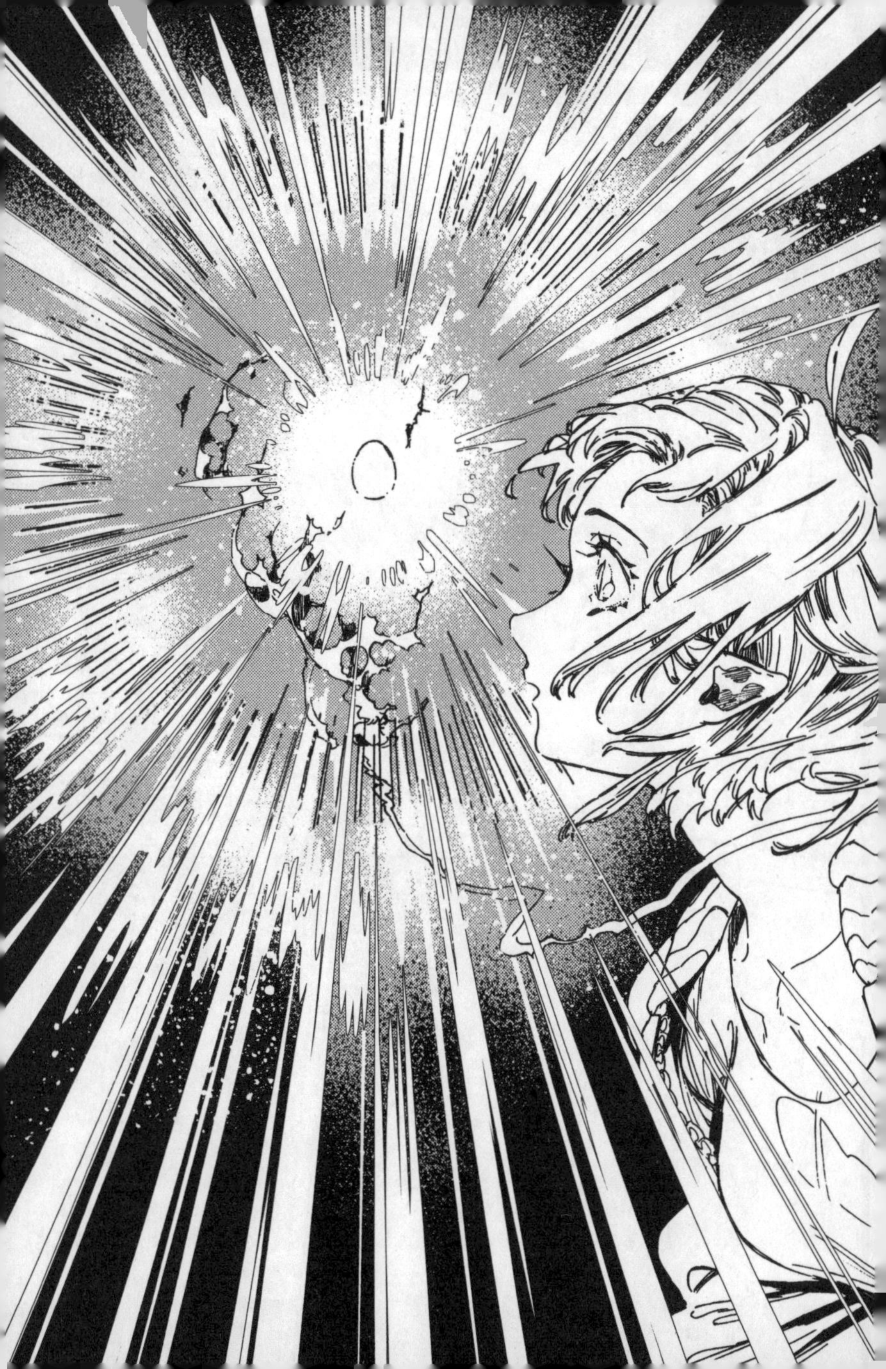

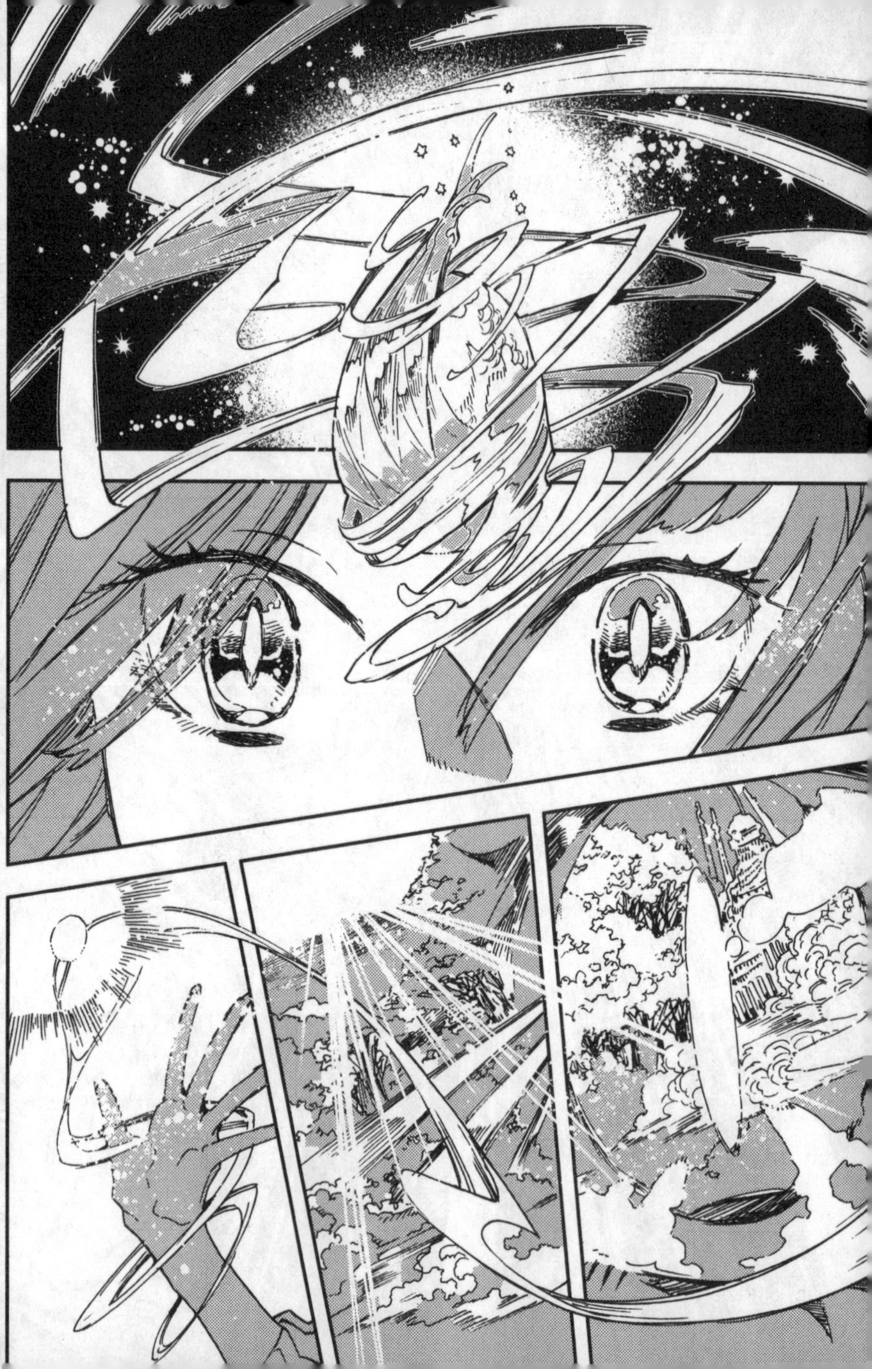

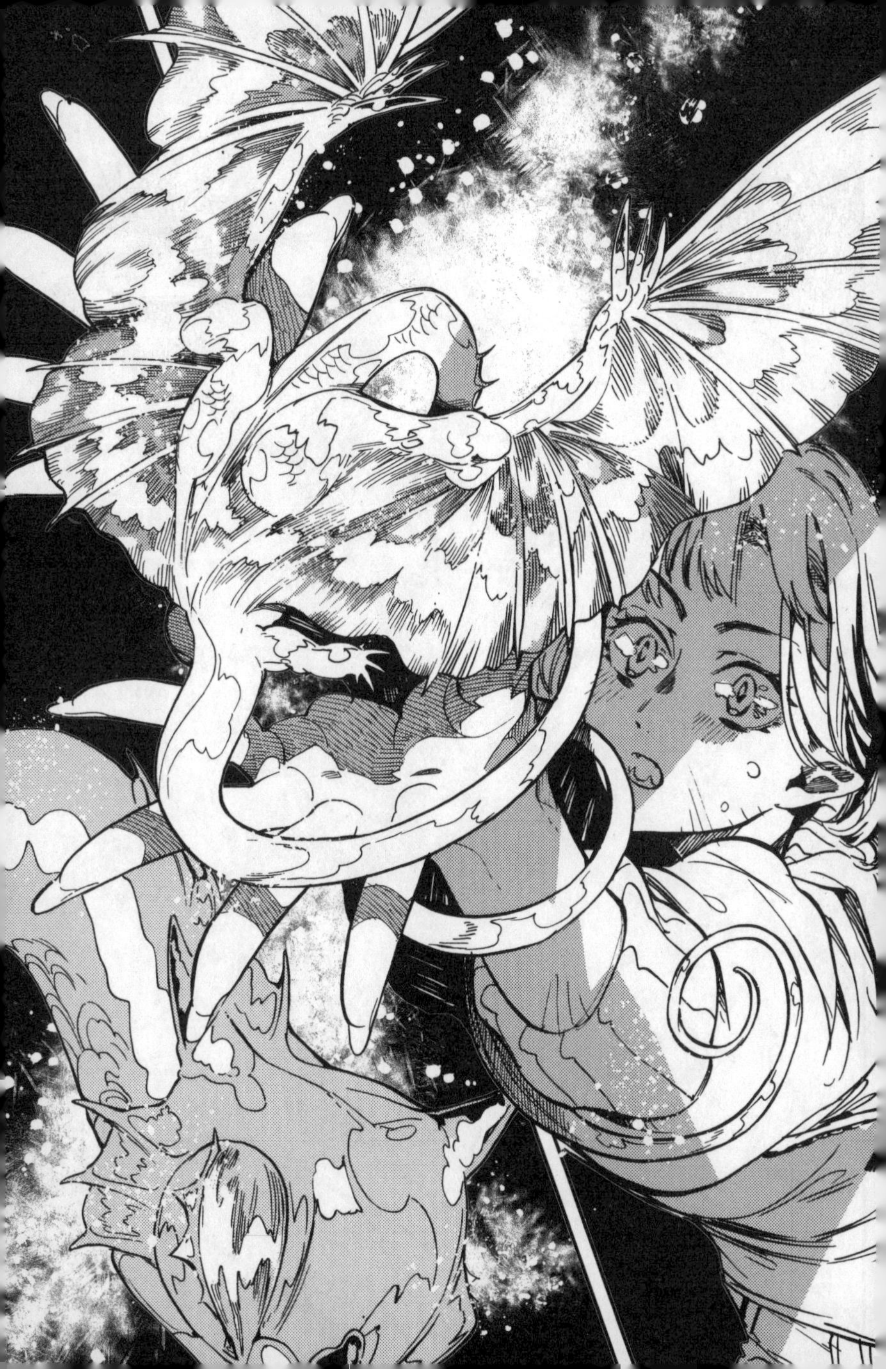

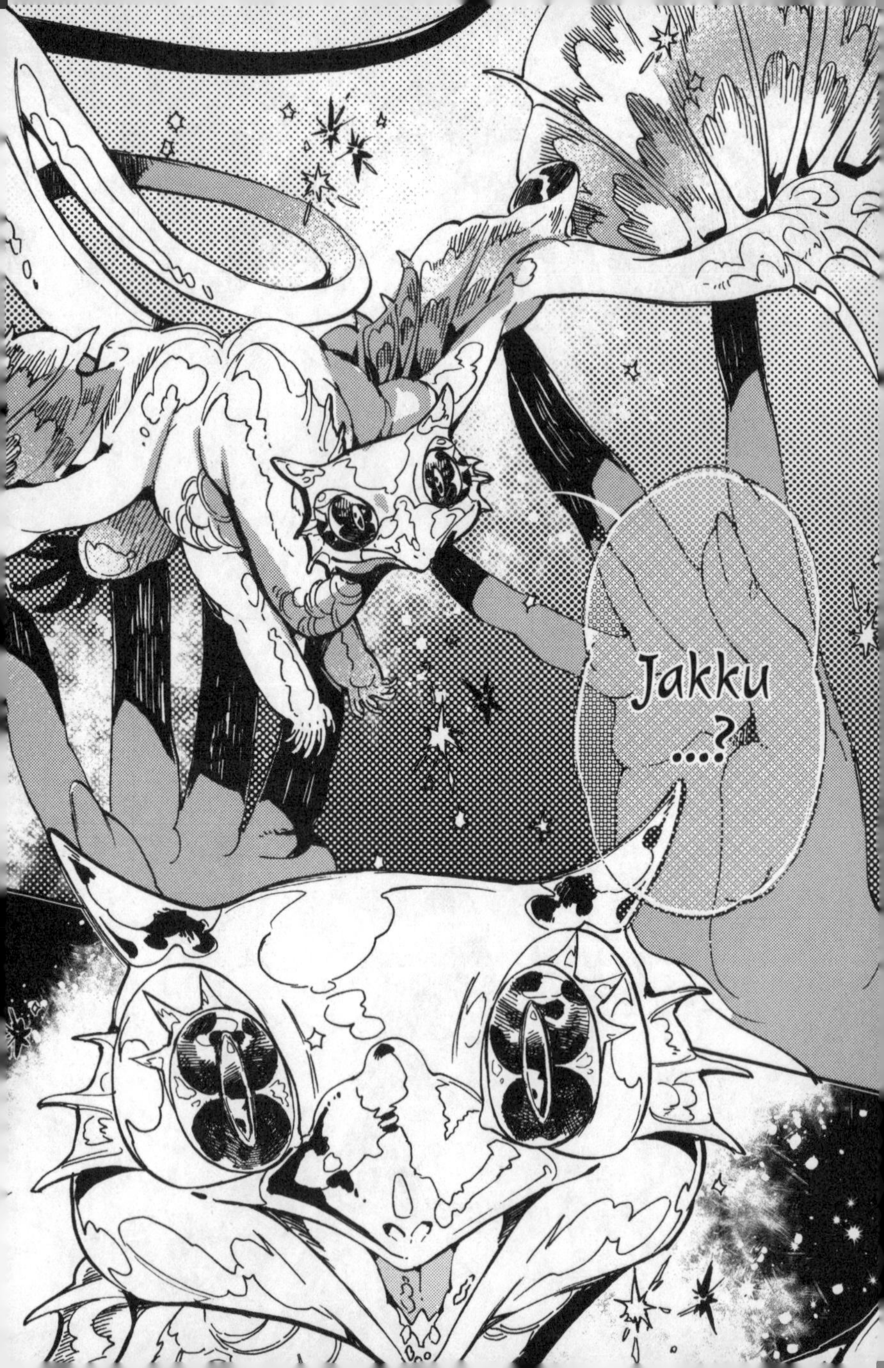
Jakku ...?

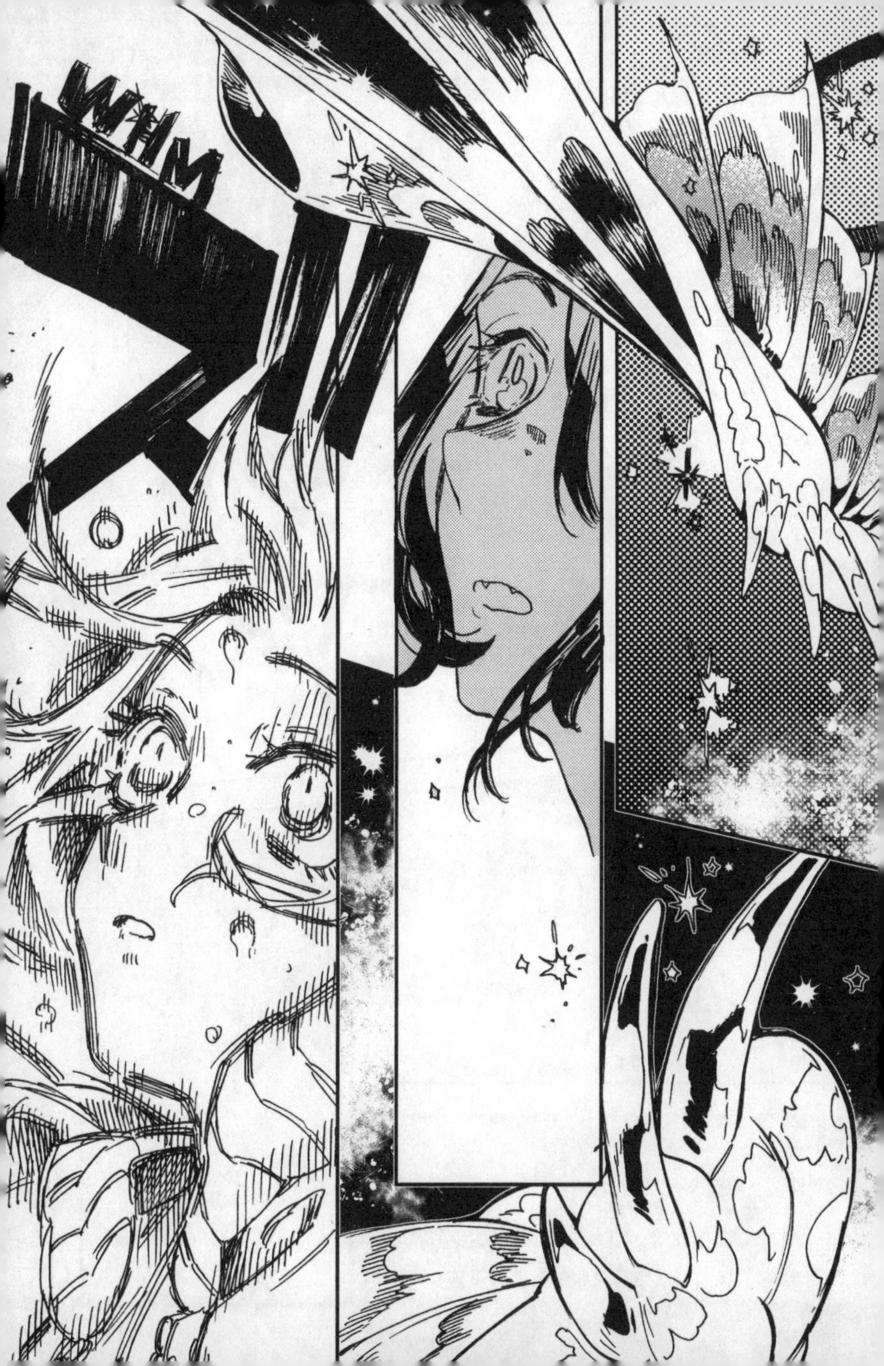
WHM

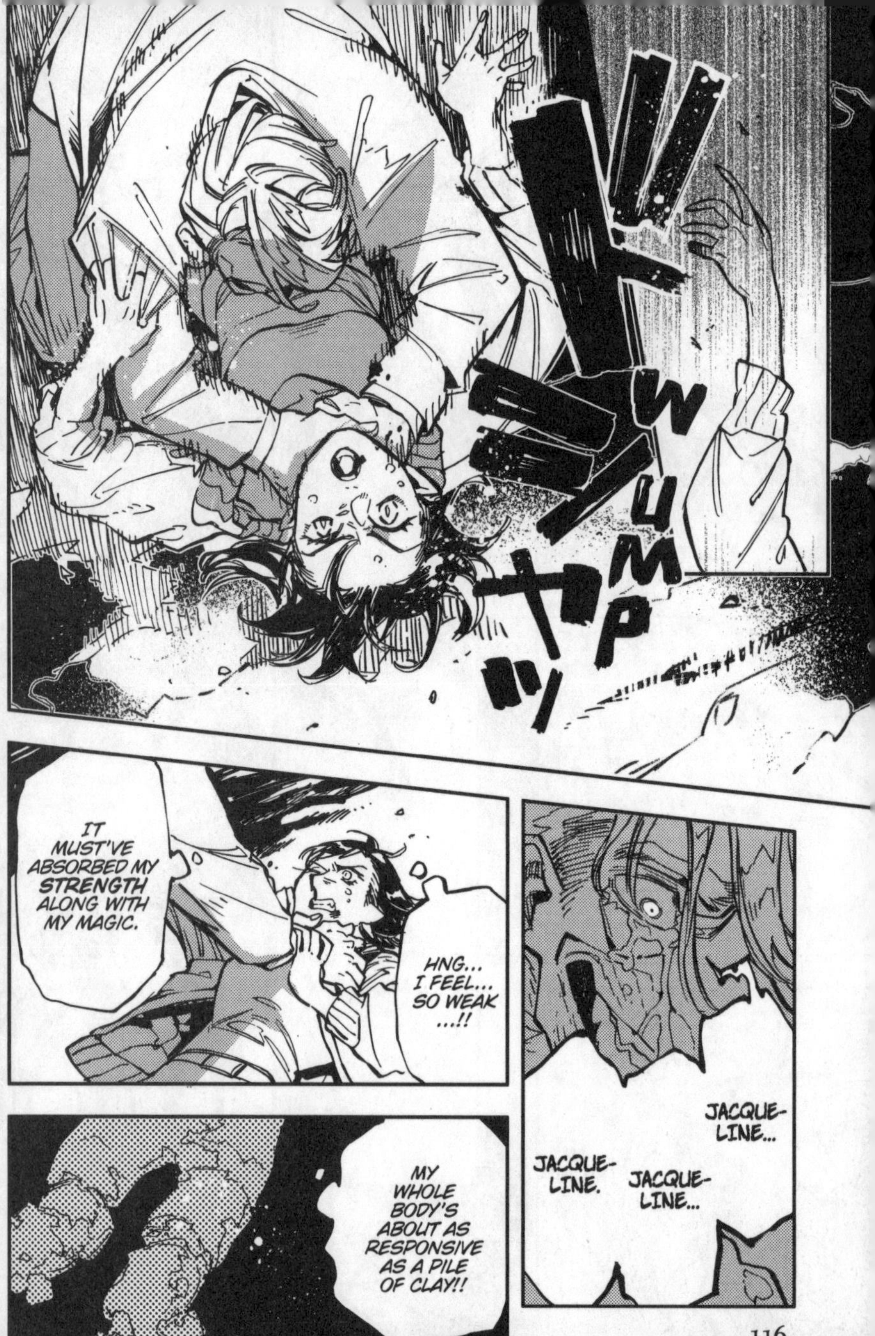
WUMP
JACQUE-LINE...
JACQUE-LINE...
JACQUE-LINE.
HNG... I FEEL... SO WEAK ...!!
IT MUST'VE ABSORBED MY STRENGTH ALONG WITH MY MAGIC.
MY WHOLE BODY'S ABOUT AS RESPONSIVE AS A PILE OF CLAY!!

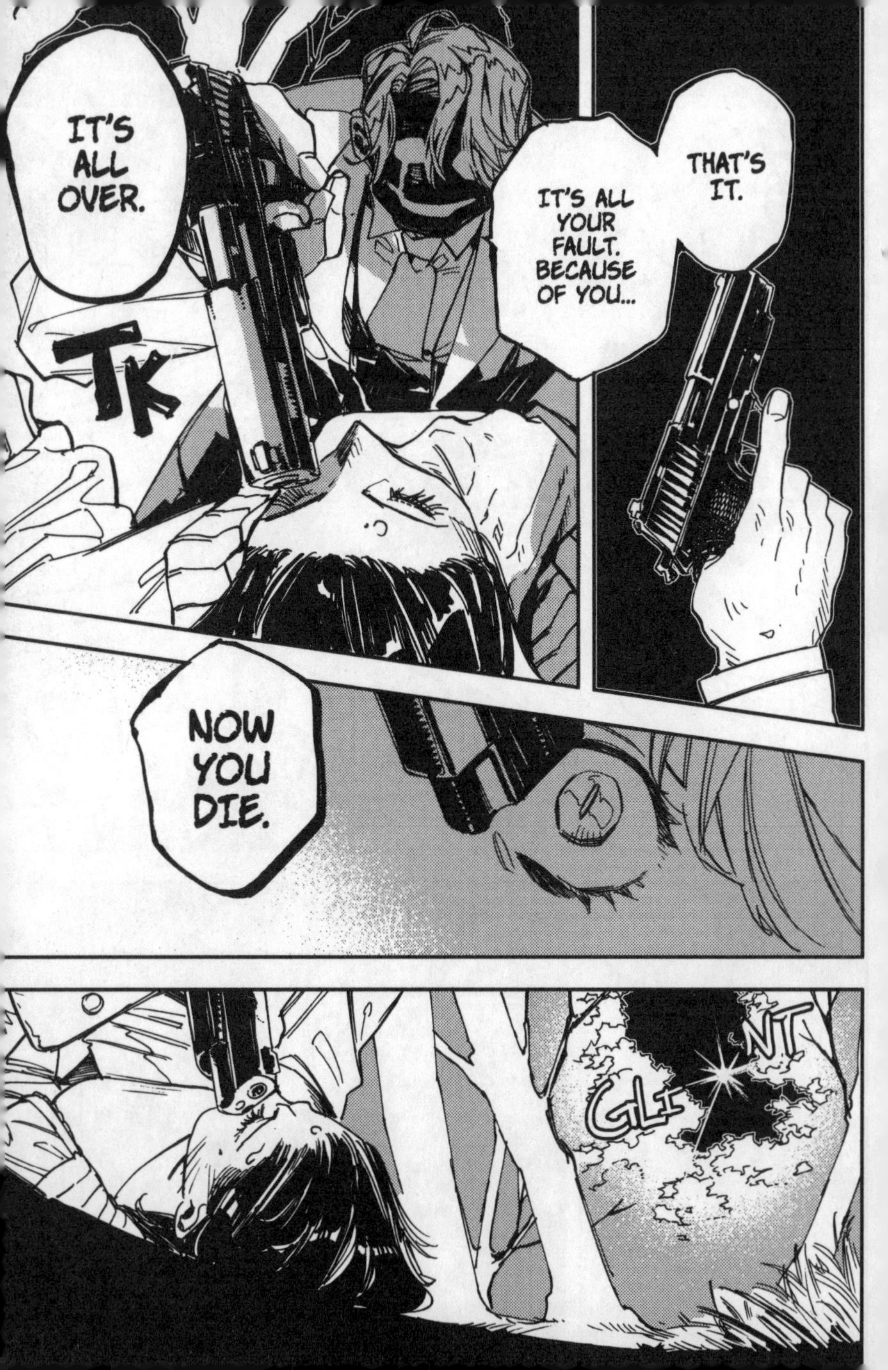
THAT'S IT.
IT'S ALL YOUR FAULT. BECAUSE OF YOU...
IT'S ALL OVER.
TK
NOW YOU DIE.
GLINT

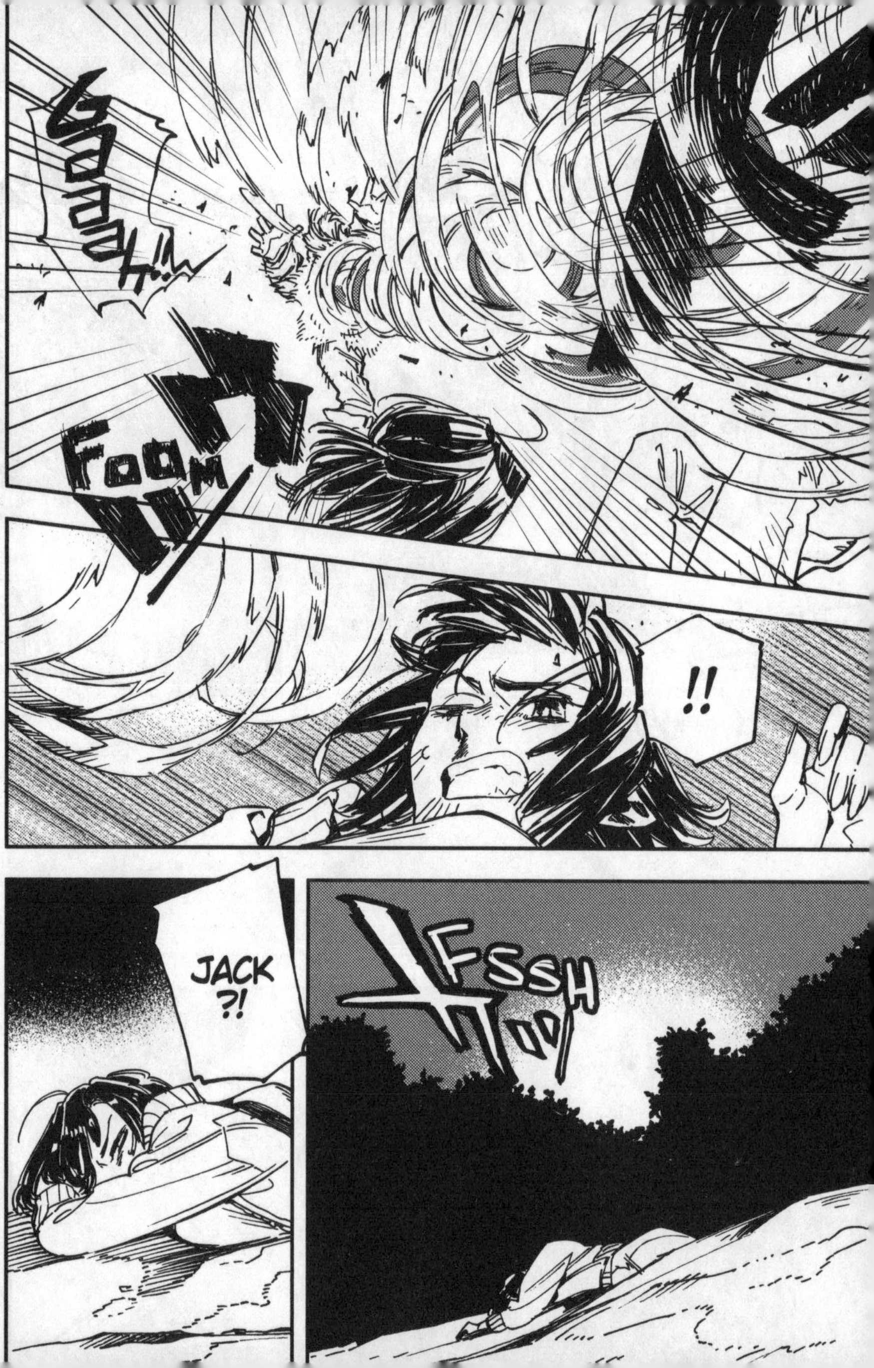
Gaaaah!!
Foom
!!
FSSH
JACK ?!

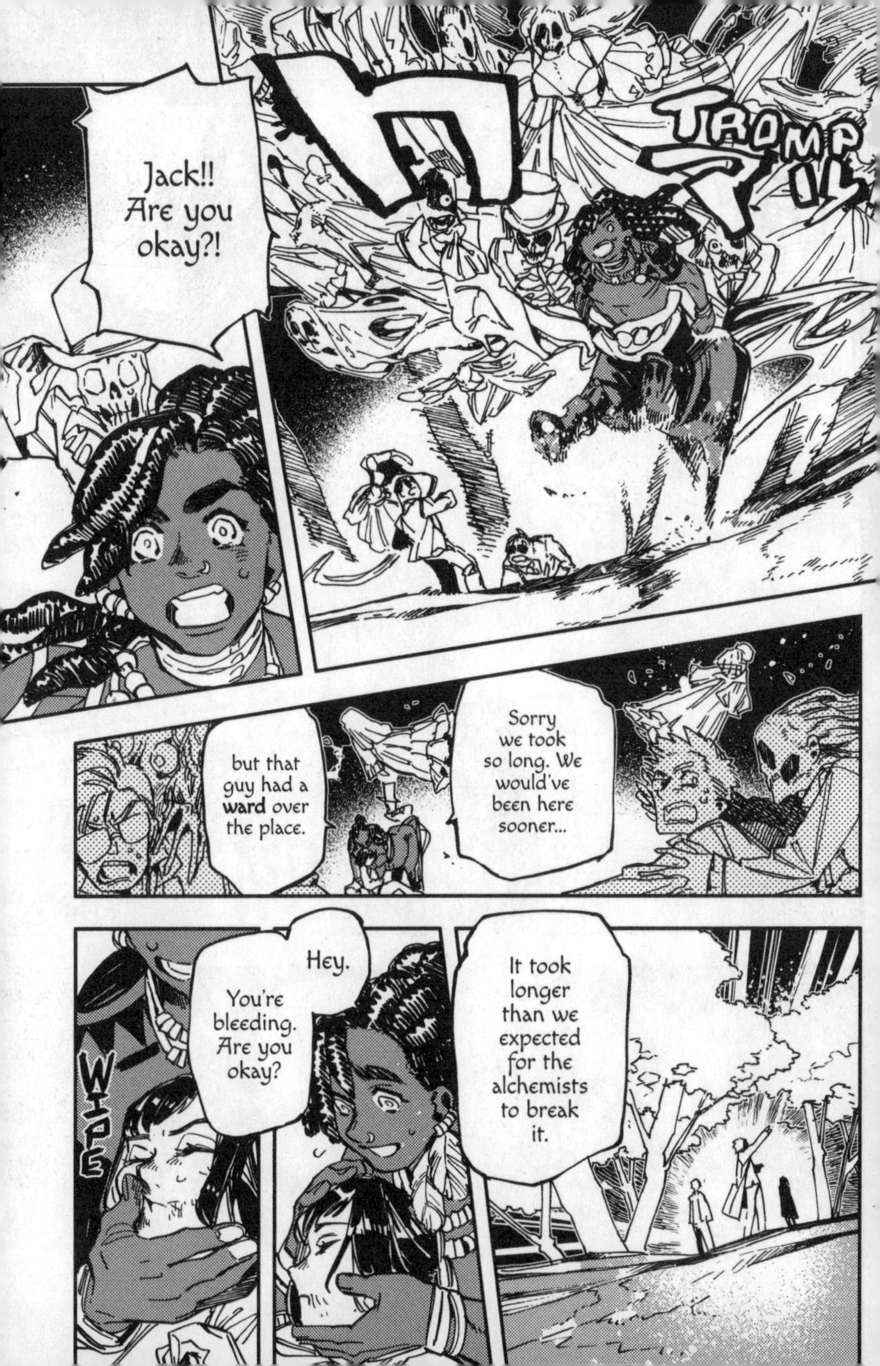
TROMP
Jack!! Are you okay?!
Sorry we took so long. We would've been here sooner...
but that guy had a **ward** over the place.
It took longer than we expected for the alchemists to break it.
Hey.
You're bleeding. Are you okay?
WIPE

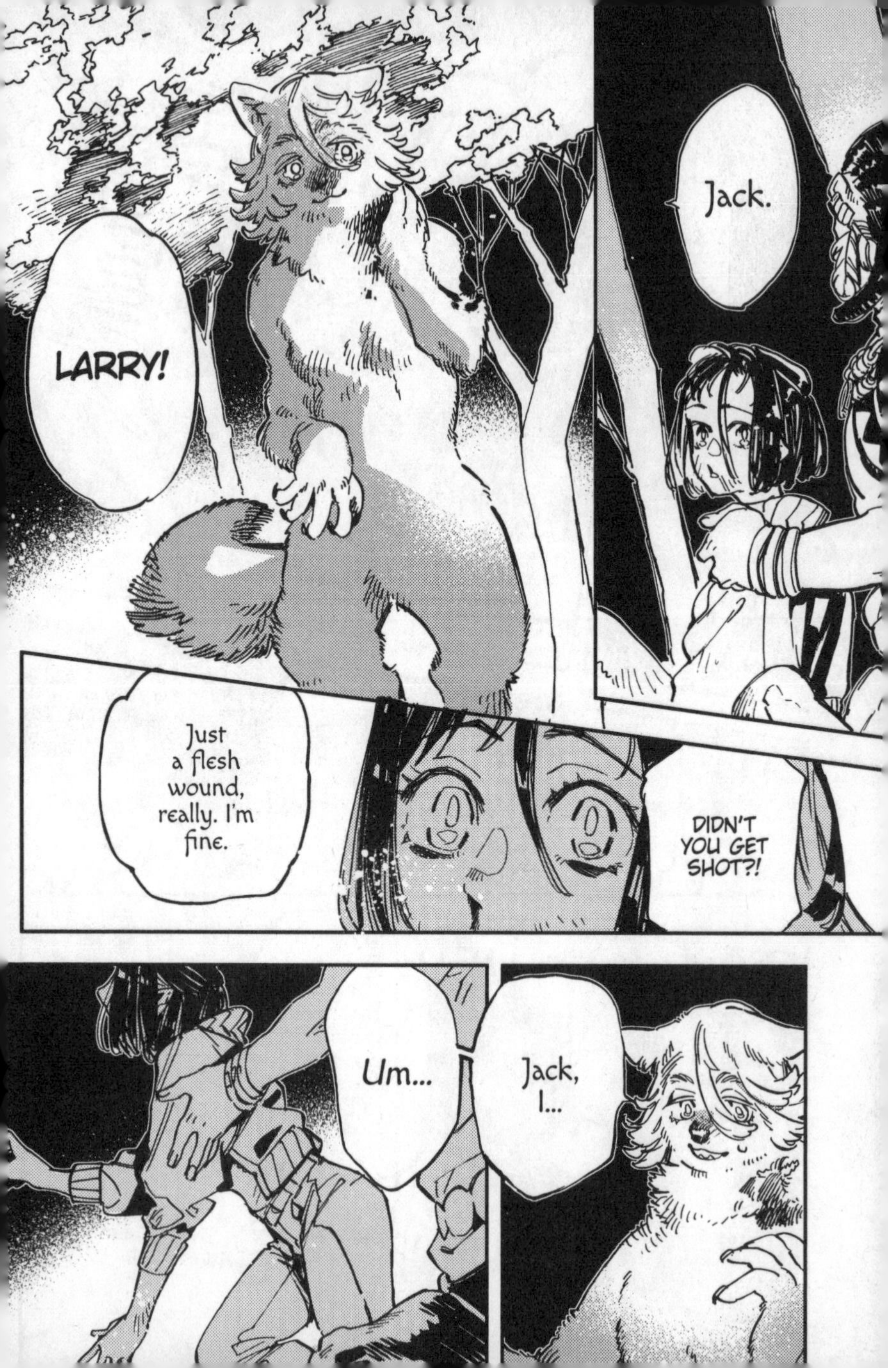
Jack.
LARRY!
DIDN'T YOU GET SHOT?!
Just a flesh wound, really. I'm fine.
Jack, I...
Um...

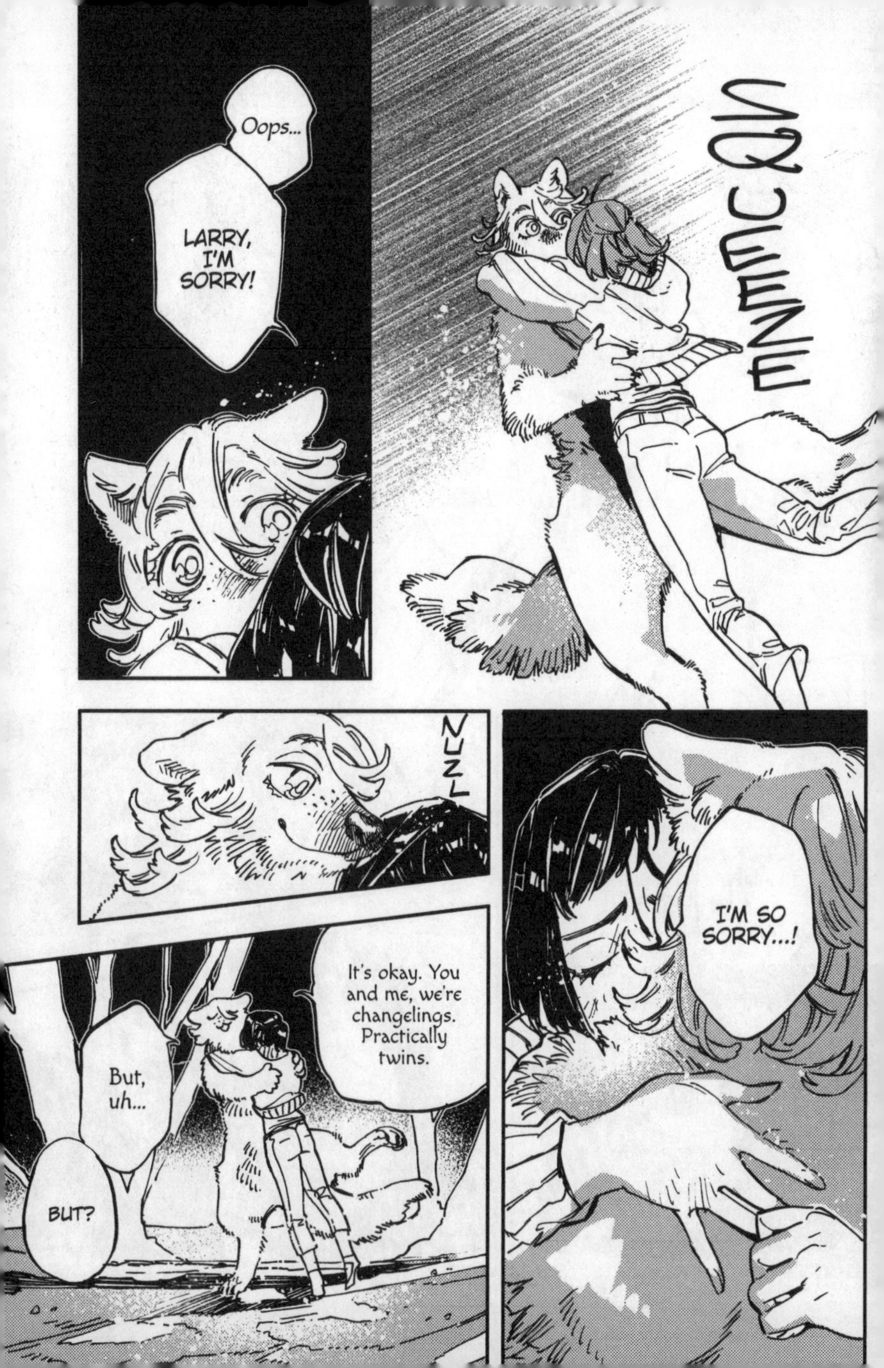
SQUEEZE
Oops...
LARRY, I'M SORRY!
I'M SO SORRY...!
NUZL
It's okay. You and me, we're changelings. Practically twins.
But, uh...
BUT?

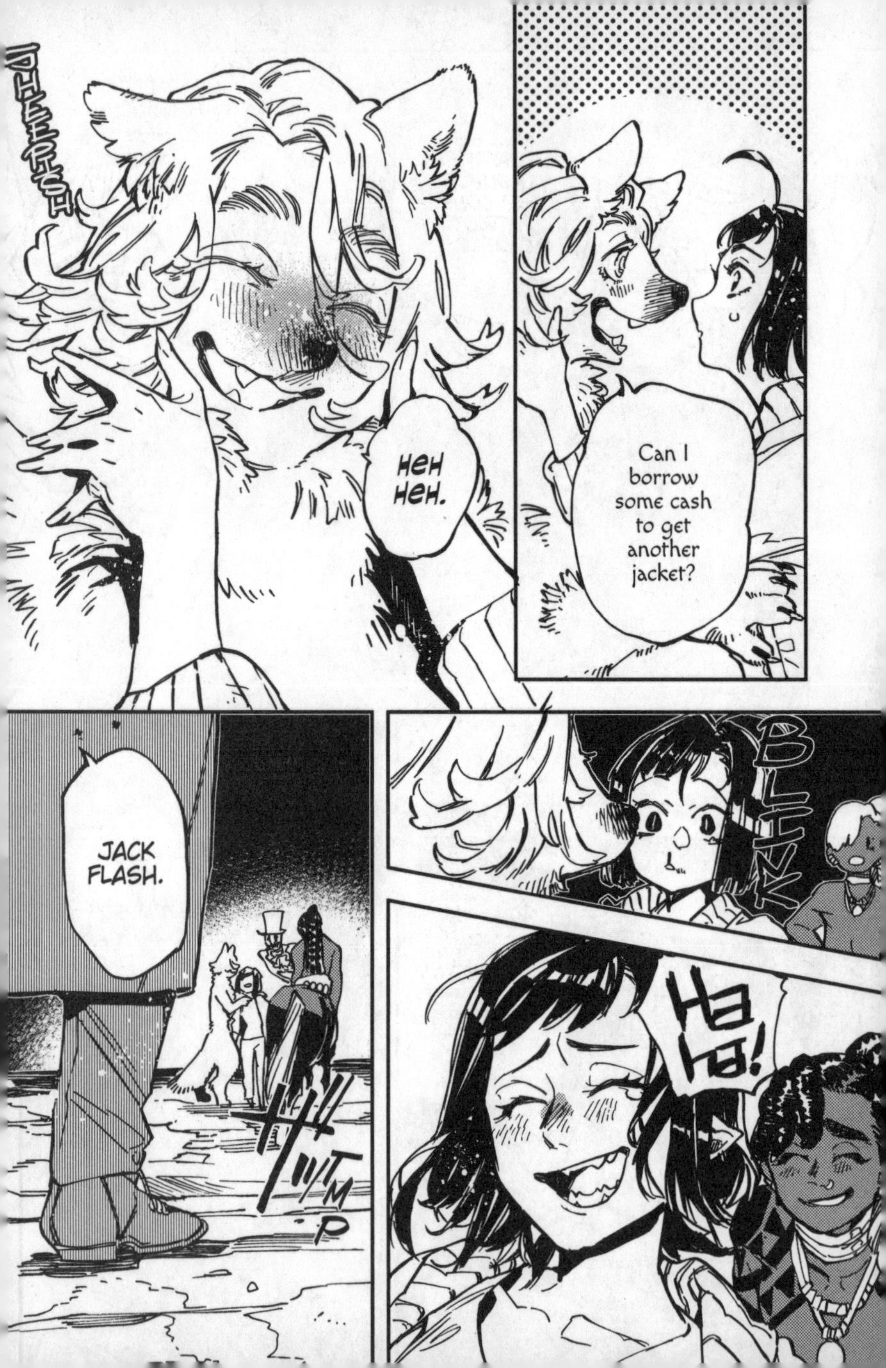
Can I borrow some cash to get another jacket?
SHEERISH
HEH HEH.
BLINK
HA HA!
JACK FLASH.
THUMP

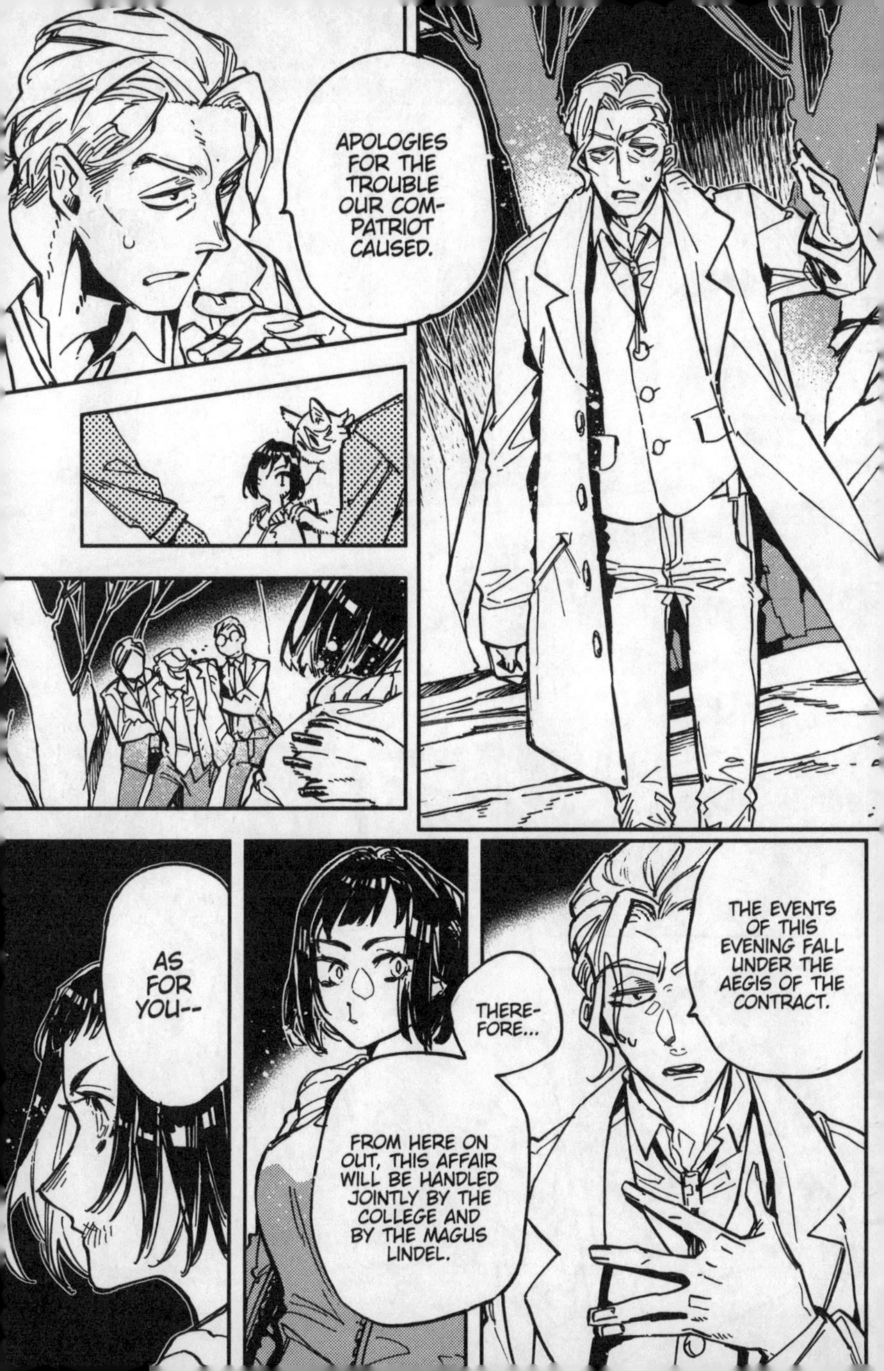
APOLOGIES FOR THE TROUBLE OUR COM-PATRIOT CAUSED.
THE EVENTS OF THIS EVENING FALL UNDER THE AEGIS OF THE CONTRACT.
THERE-FORE...
FROM HERE ON OUT, THIS AFFAIR WILL BE HANDLED JOINTLY BY THE COLLEGE AND BY THE MAGUS LINDEL.
AS FOR YOU--

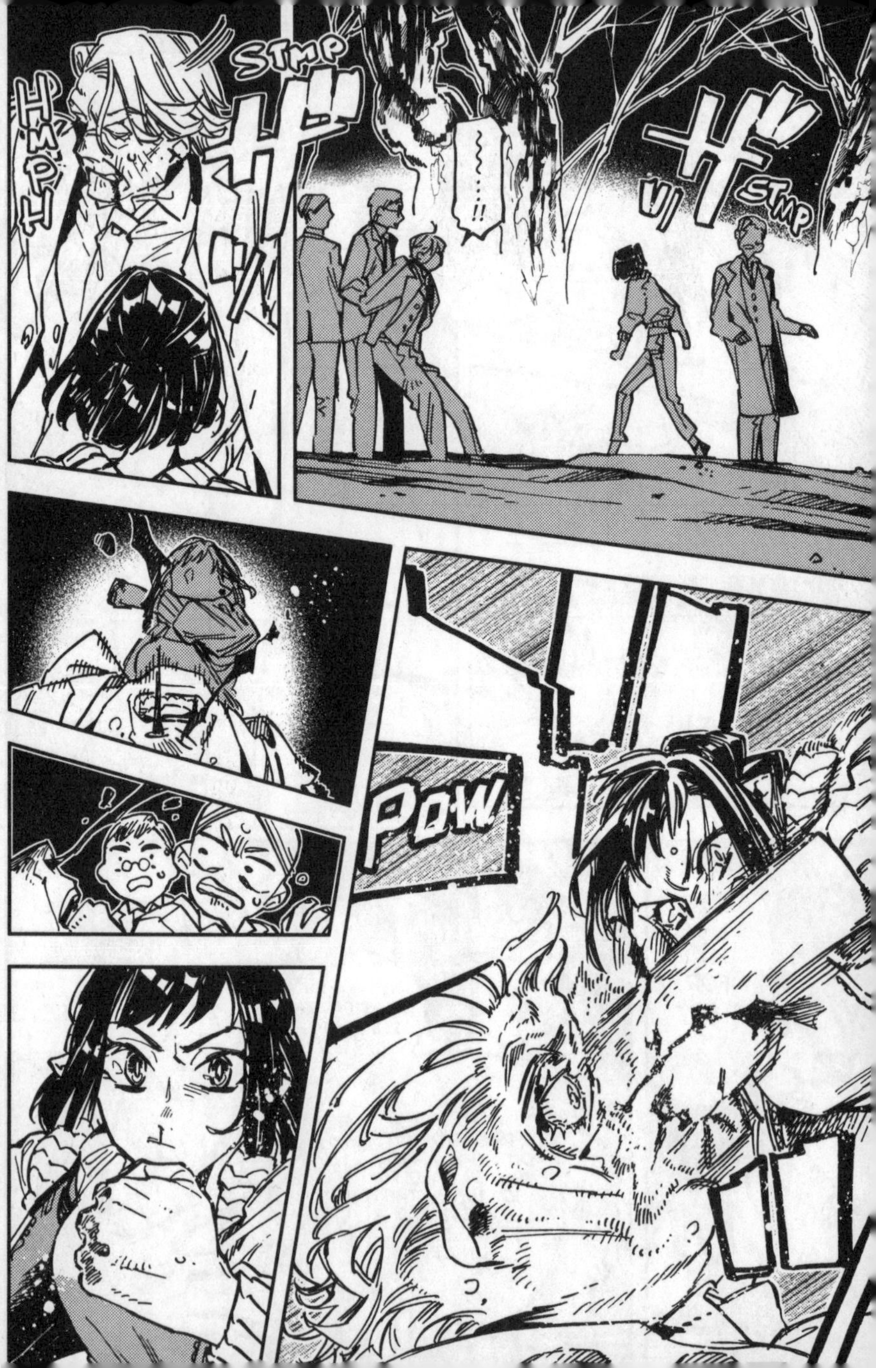
...!!
STMP
HMPH
STMP
POW

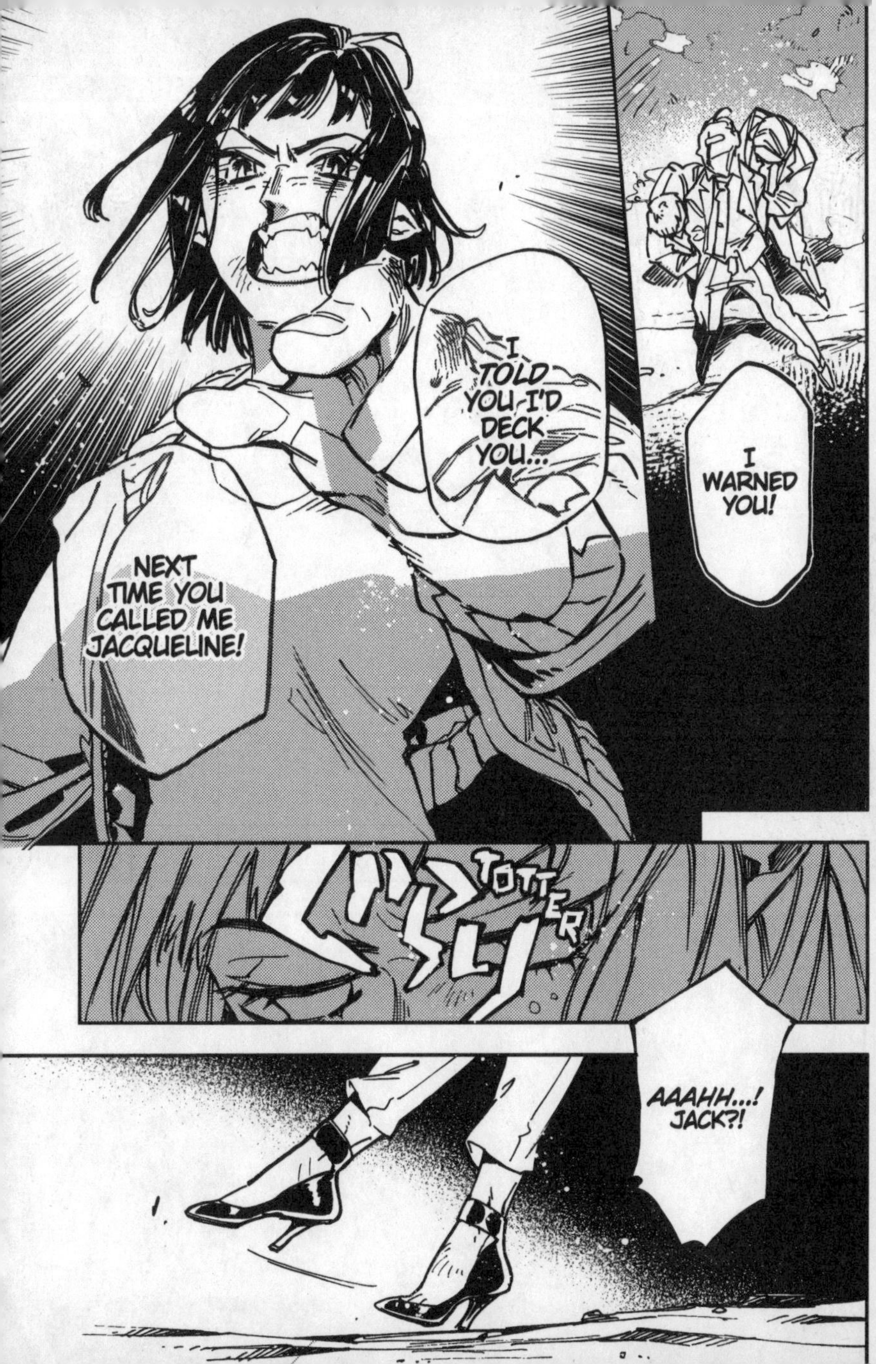
I WARNED YOU!
I TOLD YOU I'D DECK YOU...
NEXT TIME YOU CALLED ME JACQUELINE!
TOTTER
AAAHH...! JACK?!

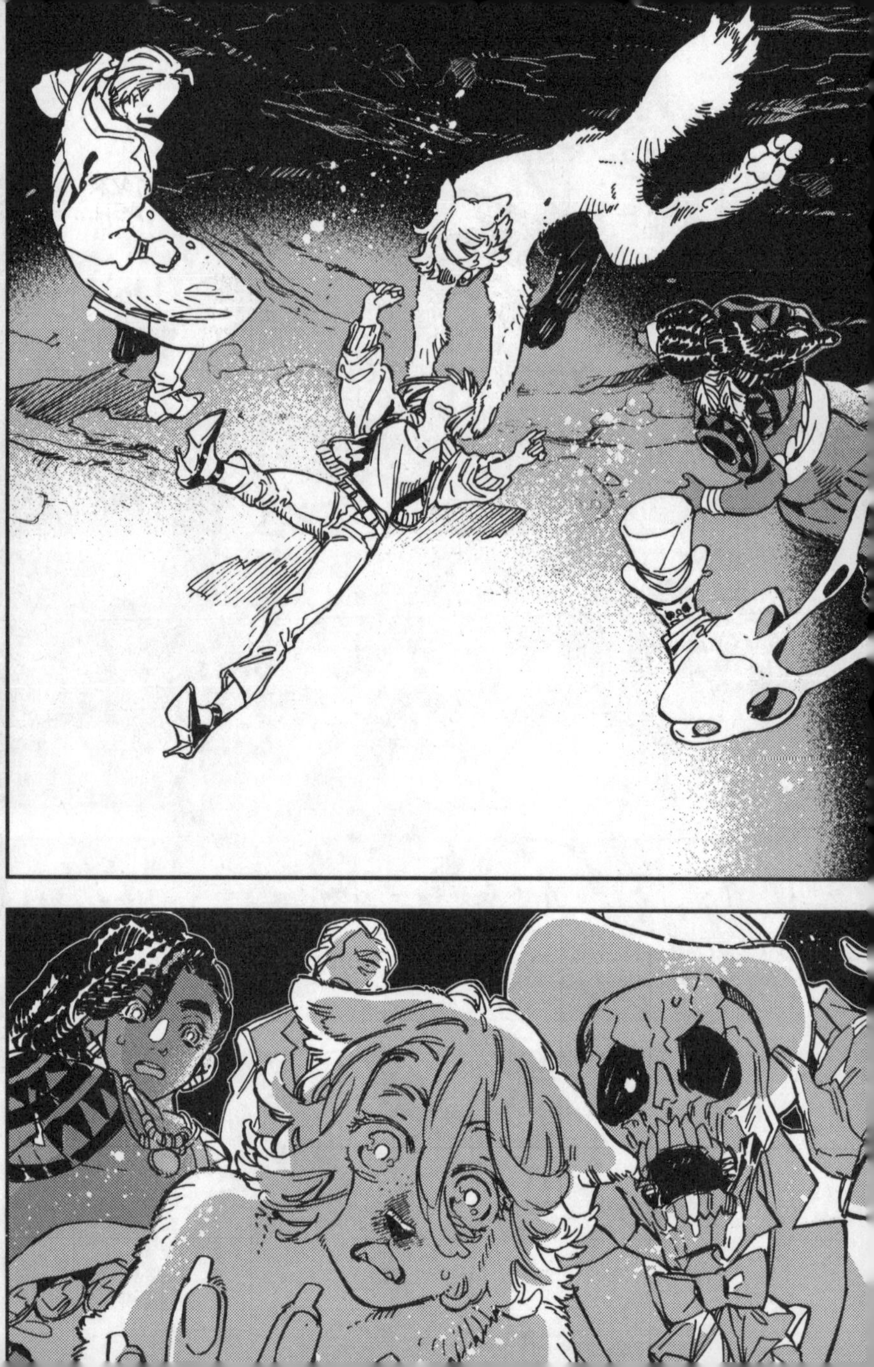

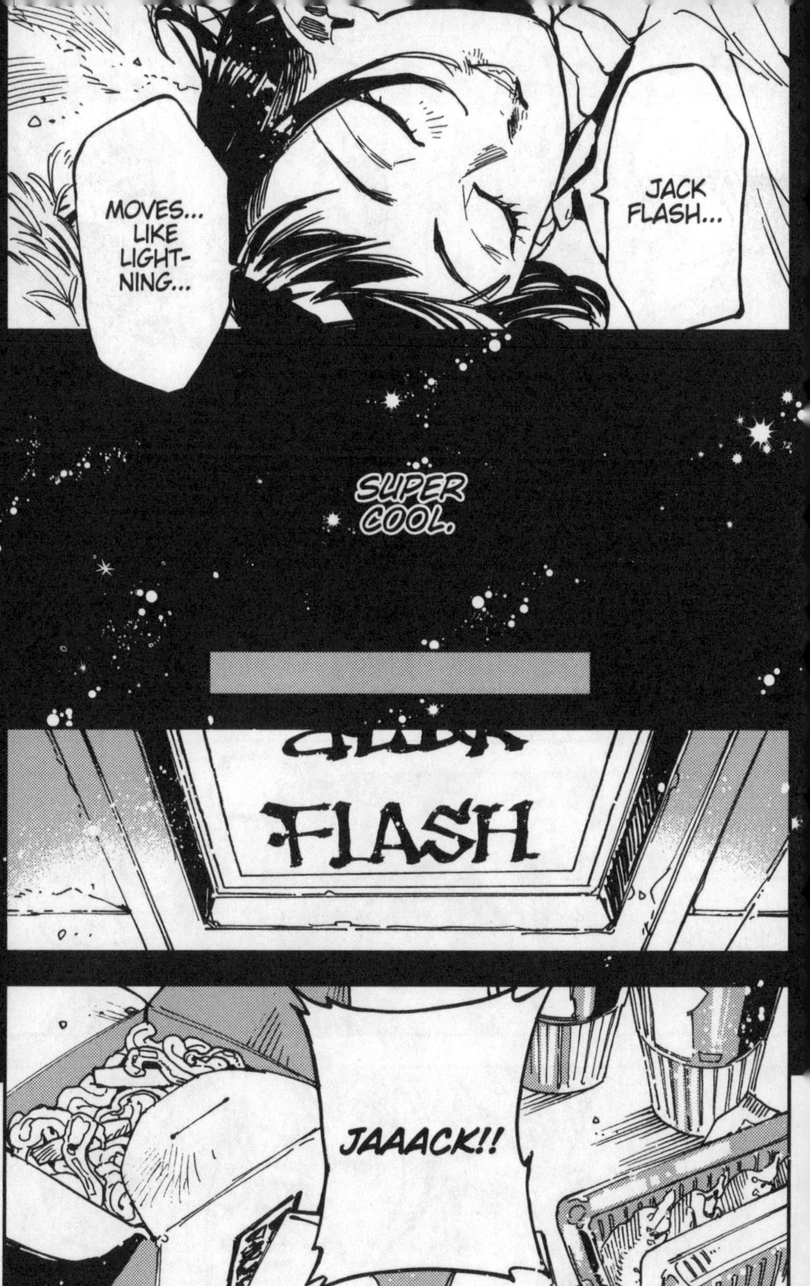
JACK FLASH...
MOVES... LIKE LIGHTNING...
SUPER COOL.
FLASH
JAAACK!!

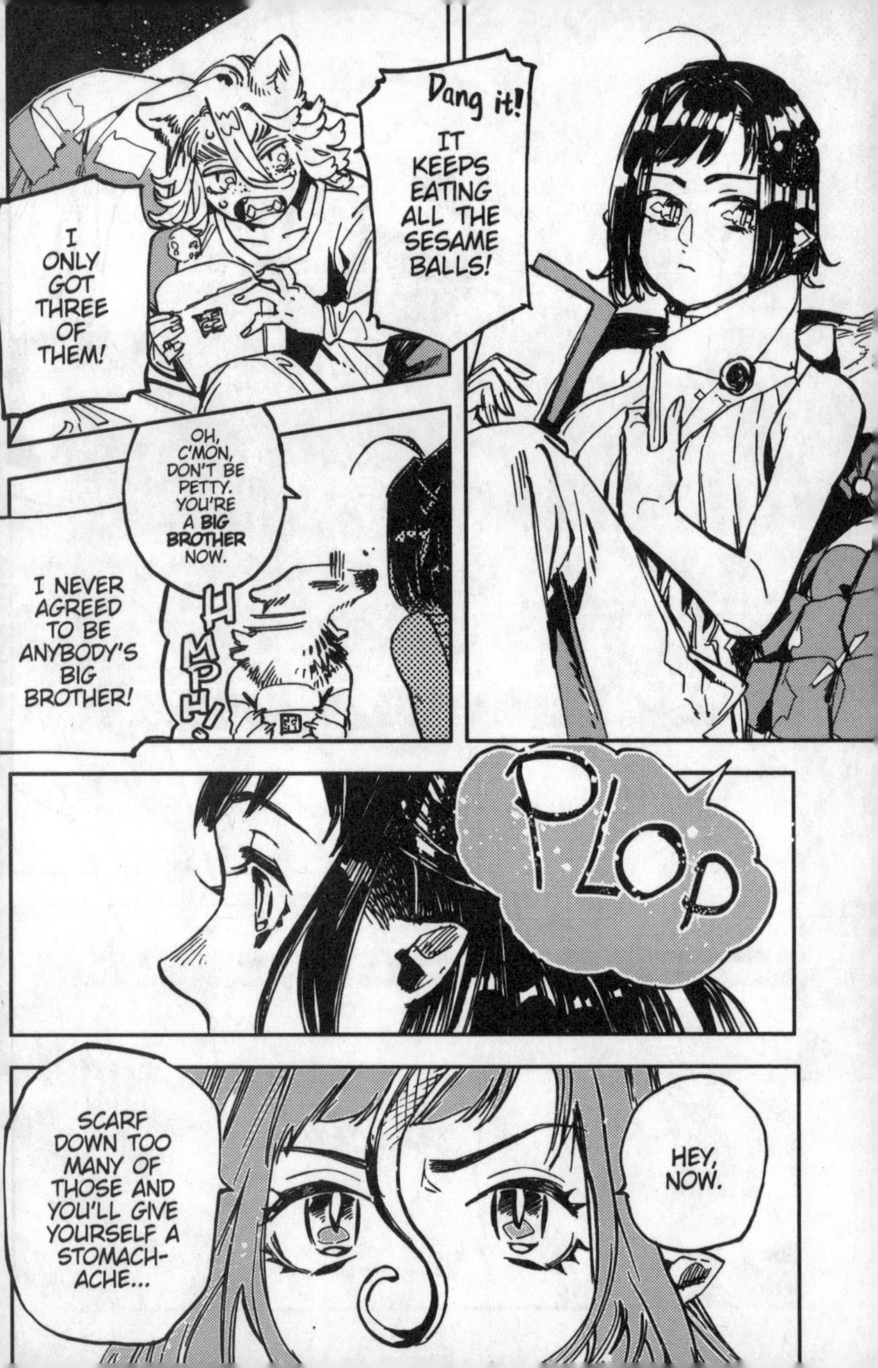
Dang it! IT KEEPS EATING ALL THE SESAME BALLS!
I ONLY GOT THREE OF THEM!
OH, C'MON, DON'T BE PETTY. YOU'RE A **BIG BROTHER** NOW.
HMPH!
I NEVER AGREED TO BE ANYBODY'S BIG BROTHER!
PLOP
HEY, NOW.
SCARF DOWN TOO MANY OF THOSE AND YOU'LL GIVE YOURSELF A STOMACH-ACHE...

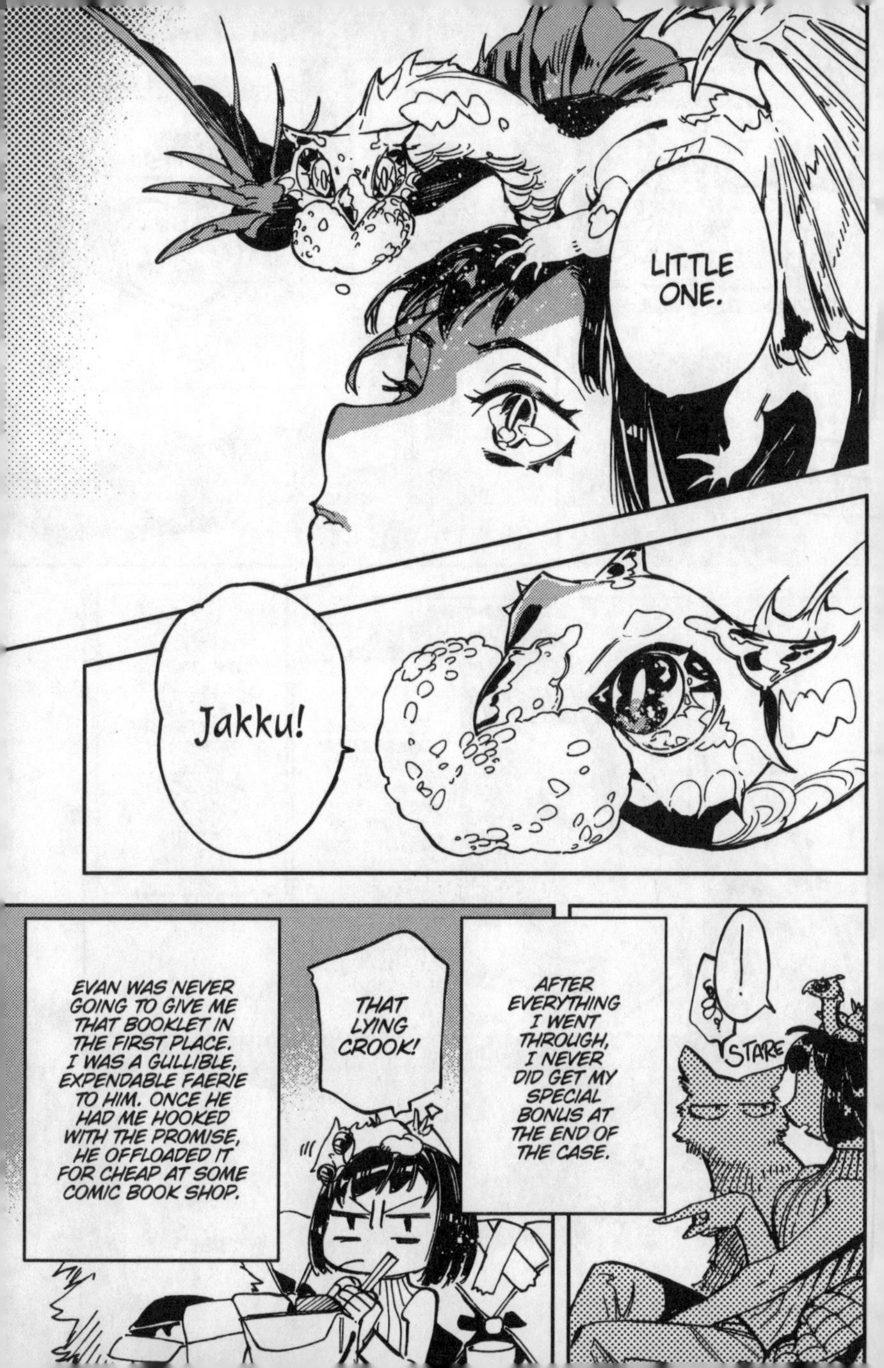
LITTLE ONE.
Jakku!
!
STARE
AFTER EVERYTHING I WENT THROUGH, I NEVER DID GET MY SPECIAL BONUS AT THE END OF THE CASE.
THAT LYING CROOK!
EVAN WAS NEVER GOING TO GIVE ME THAT BOOKLET IN THE FIRST PLACE. I WAS A GULLIBLE, EXPENDABLE FAERIE TO HIM. ONCE HE HAD ME HOOKED WITH THE PROMISE, HE OFFLOADED IT FOR CHEAP AT SOME COMIC BOOK SHOP.

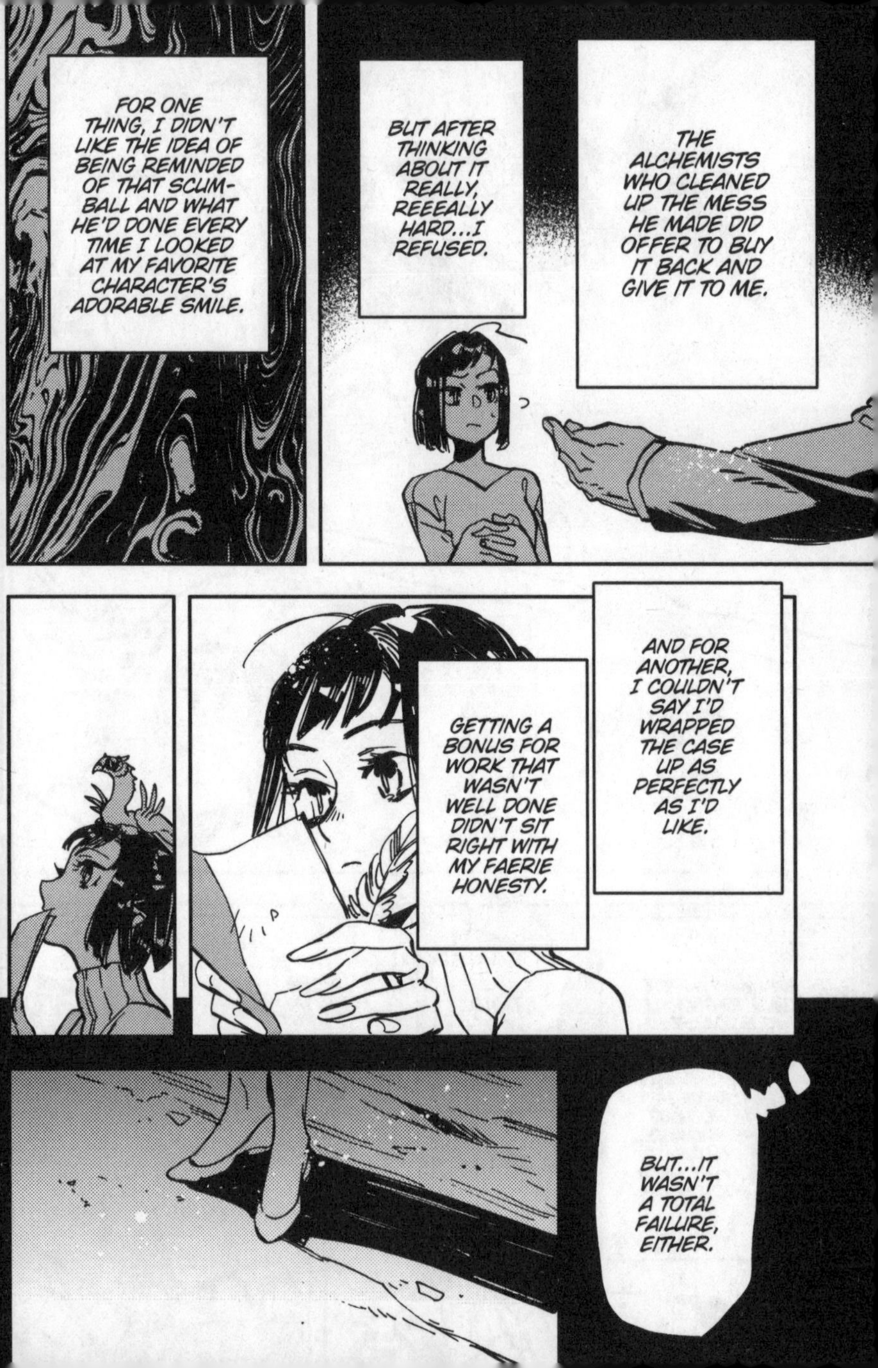
THE ALCHEMISTS WHO CLEANED UP THE MESS HE MADE DID OFFER TO BUY IT BACK AND GIVE IT TO ME.
BUT AFTER THINKING ABOUT IT REALLY, REEEALLY HARD...I REFUSED.
FOR ONE THING, I DIDN'T LIKE THE IDEA OF BEING REMINDED OF THAT SCUM-BALL AND WHAT HE'D DONE EVERY TIME I LOOKED AT MY FAVORITE CHARACTER'S ADORABLE SMILE.
AND FOR ANOTHER, I COULDN'T SAY I'D WRAPPED THE CASE UP AS PERFECTLY AS I'D LIKE.
GETTING A BONUS FOR WORK THAT WASN'T WELL DONE DIDN'T SIT RIGHT WITH MY FAERIE HONESTY.
BUT...IT WASN'T A TOTAL FAILURE, EITHER.

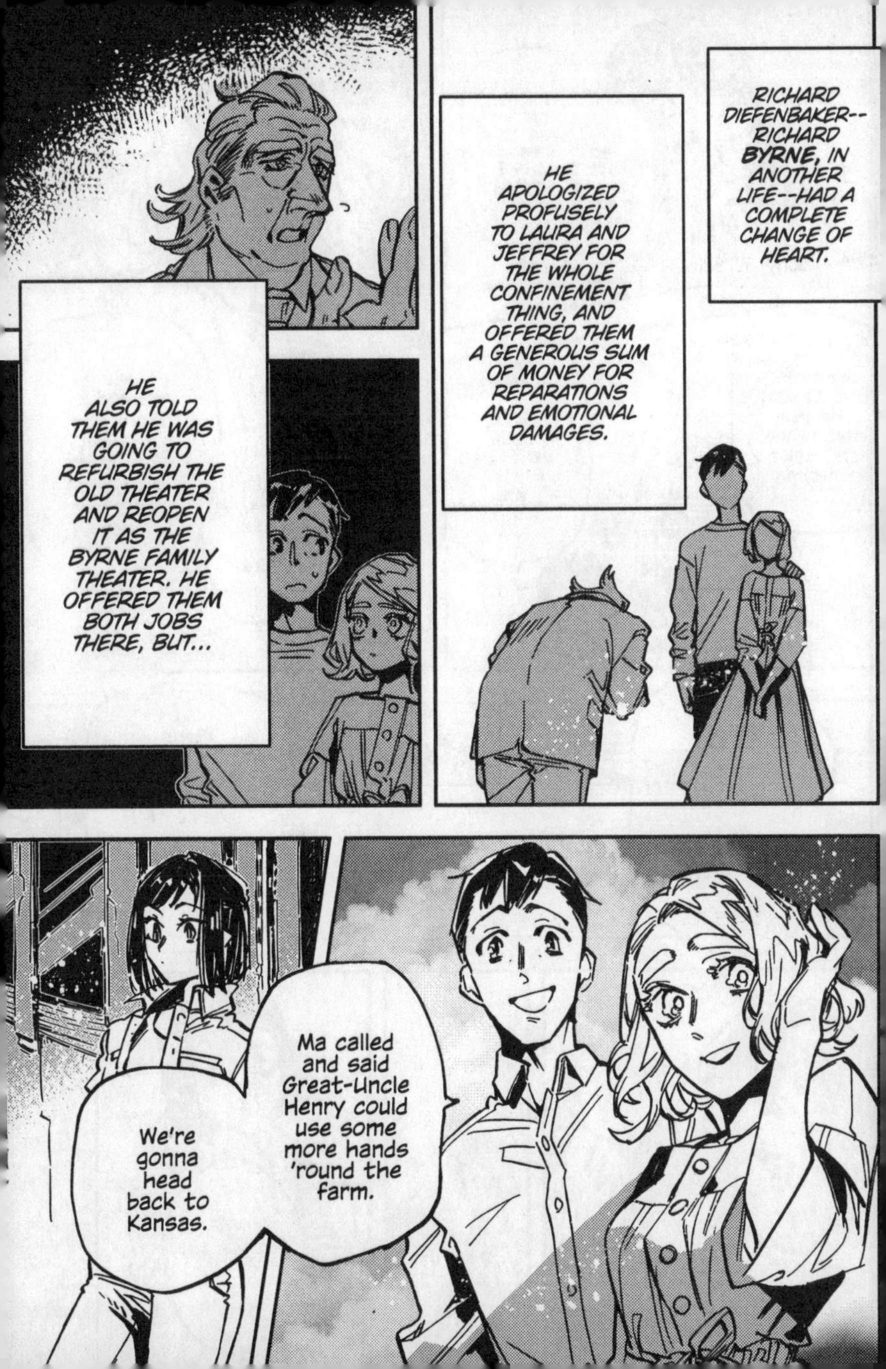
RICHARD DIEFENBAKER-- RICHARD BYRNE, IN ANOTHER LIFE--HAD A COMPLETE CHANGE OF HEART.
HE APOLOGIZED PROFUSELY TO LAURA AND JEFFREY FOR THE WHOLE CONFINEMENT THING, AND OFFERED THEM A GENEROUS SUM OF MONEY FOR REPARATIONS AND EMOTIONAL DAMAGES.
HE ALSO TOLD THEM HE WAS GOING TO REFURBISH THE OLD THEATER AND REOPEN IT AS THE BYRNE FAMILY THEATER. HE OFFERED THEM BOTH JOBS THERE, BUT...
Ma called and said Great-Uncle Henry could use some more hands 'round the farm.
We're gonna head back to Kansas.

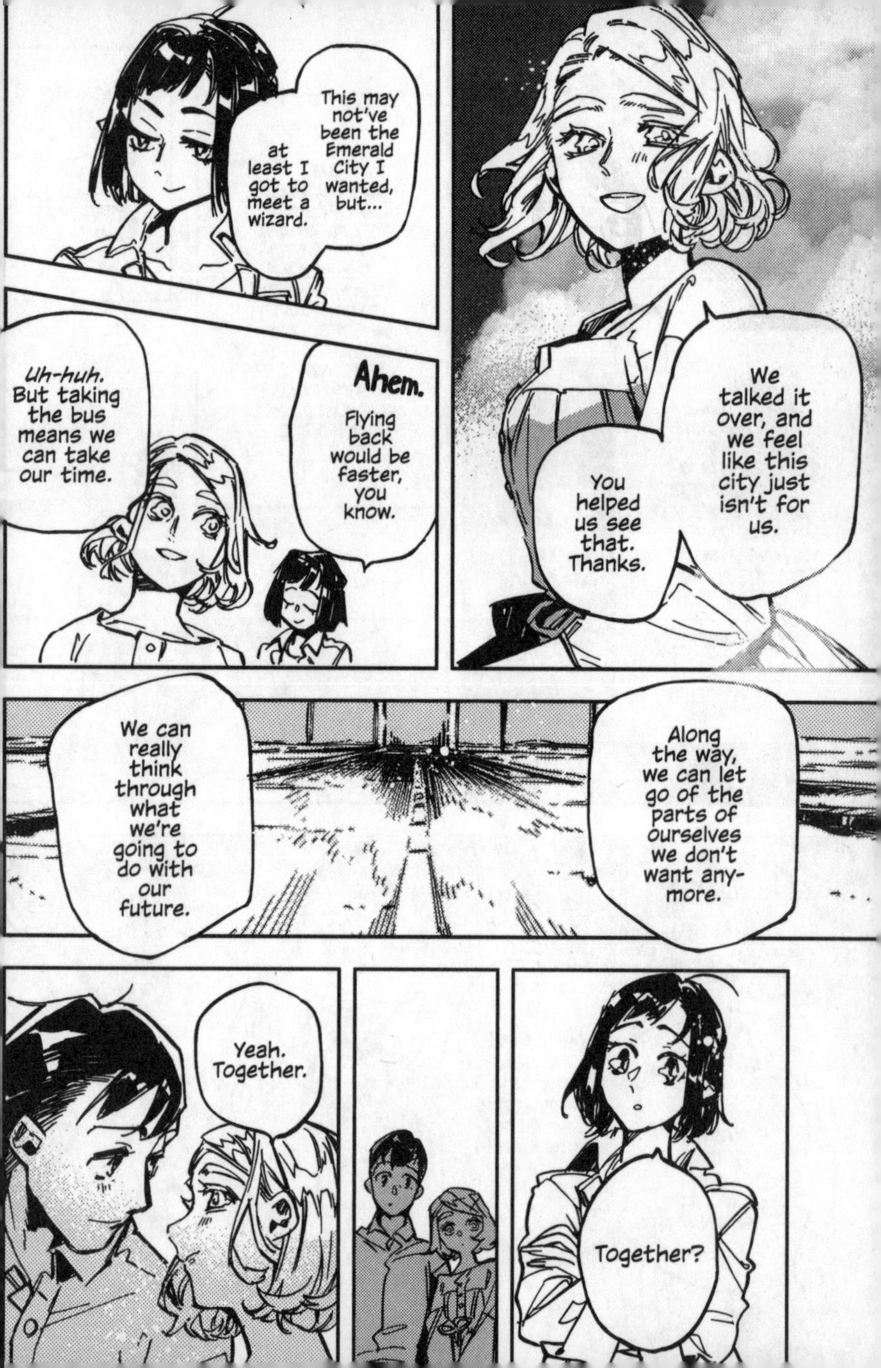
We talked it over, and we feel like this city just isn't for us.
You helped us see that. Thanks.
This may not've been the Emerald City I wanted, but...
at least I got to meet a wizard.
Ahem.
Flying back would be faster, you know.
Uh-huh. But taking the bus means we can take our time.
Along the way, we can let go of the parts of ourselves we don't want any-more.
We can really think through what we're going to do with our future.
Together?
Yeah. Together.

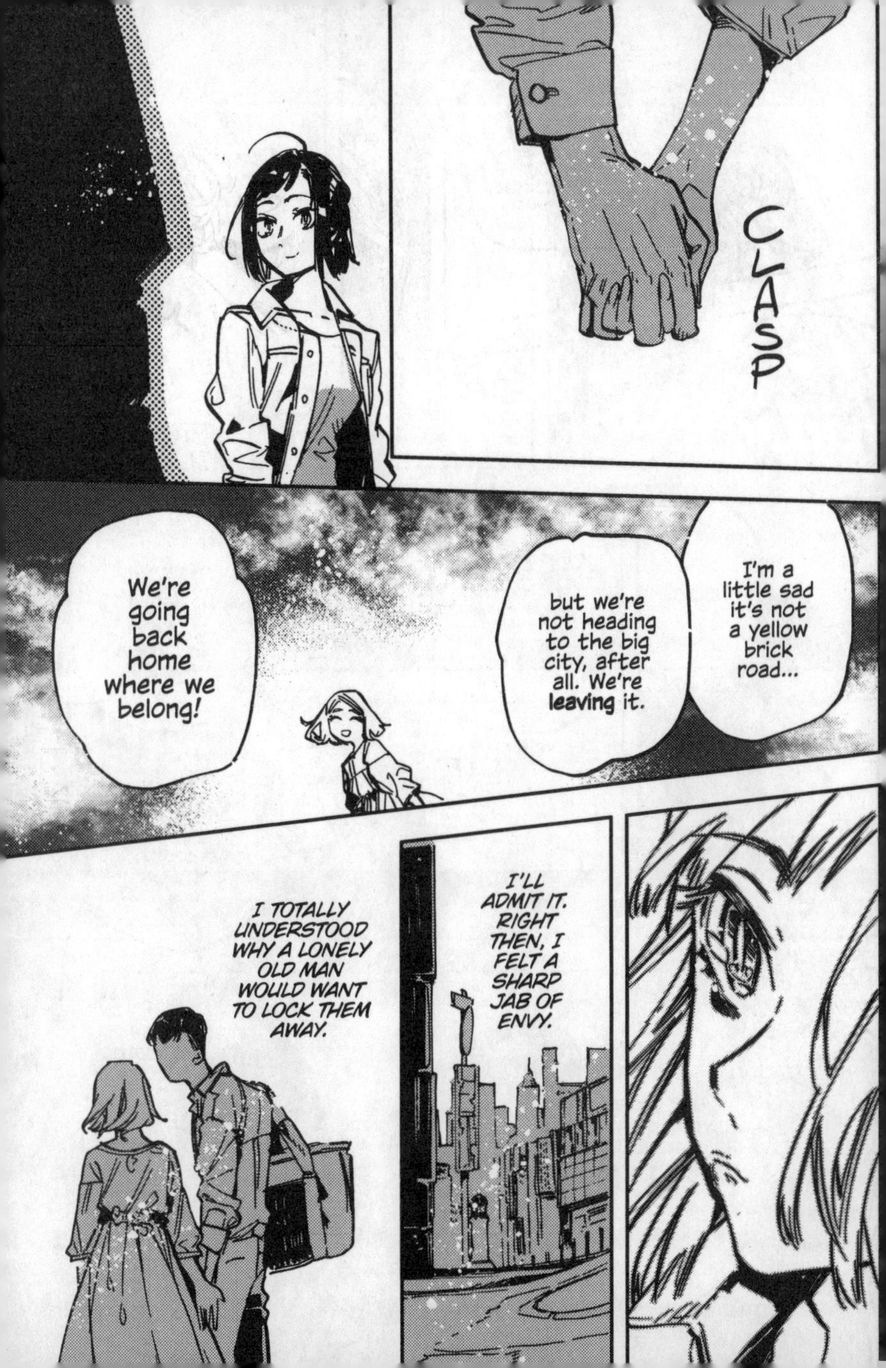
CLASP
I'm a little sad it's not a yellow brick road...
but we're not heading to the big city, after all. We're **leaving** it.
We're going back home where we belong!
I'LL ADMIT IT. RIGHT THEN, I FELT A SHARP JAB OF ENVY.
I TOTALLY UNDERSTOOD WHY A LONELY OLD MAN WOULD WANT TO LOCK THEM AWAY.

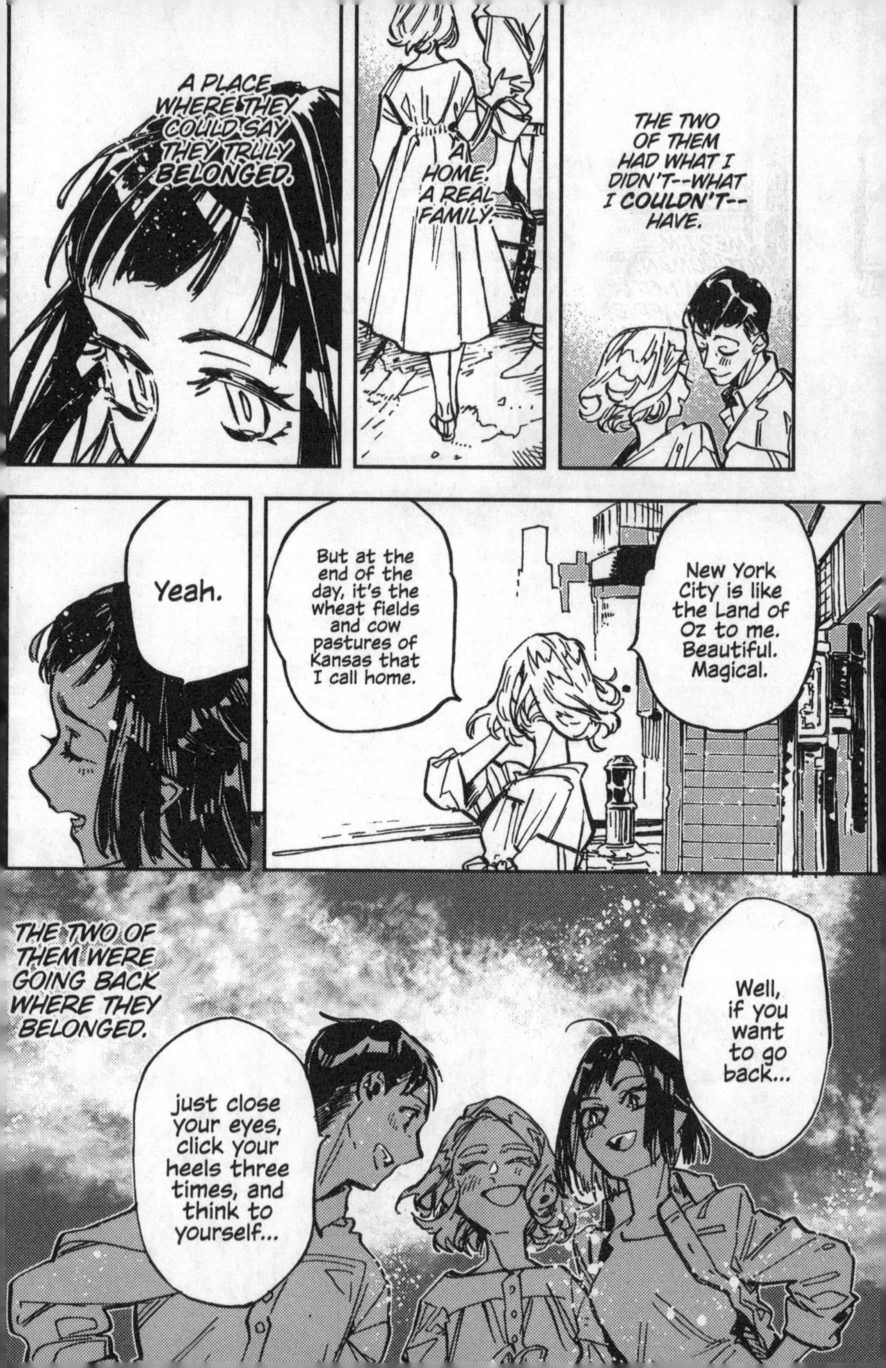
THE TWO OF THEM HAD WHAT I DIDN'T--WHAT I COULDN'T--HAVE.
A HOME. A REAL FAMILY.
A PLACE WHERE THEY COULD SAY THEY TRULY BELONGED.
New York City is like the Land of Oz to me. Beautiful. Magical.
But at the end of the day, it's the wheat fields and cow pastures of Kansas that I call home.
Yeah.
Well, if you want to go back...
THE TWO OF THEM WERE GOING BACK WHERE THEY BELONGED.
just close your eyes, click your heels three times, and think to yourself...

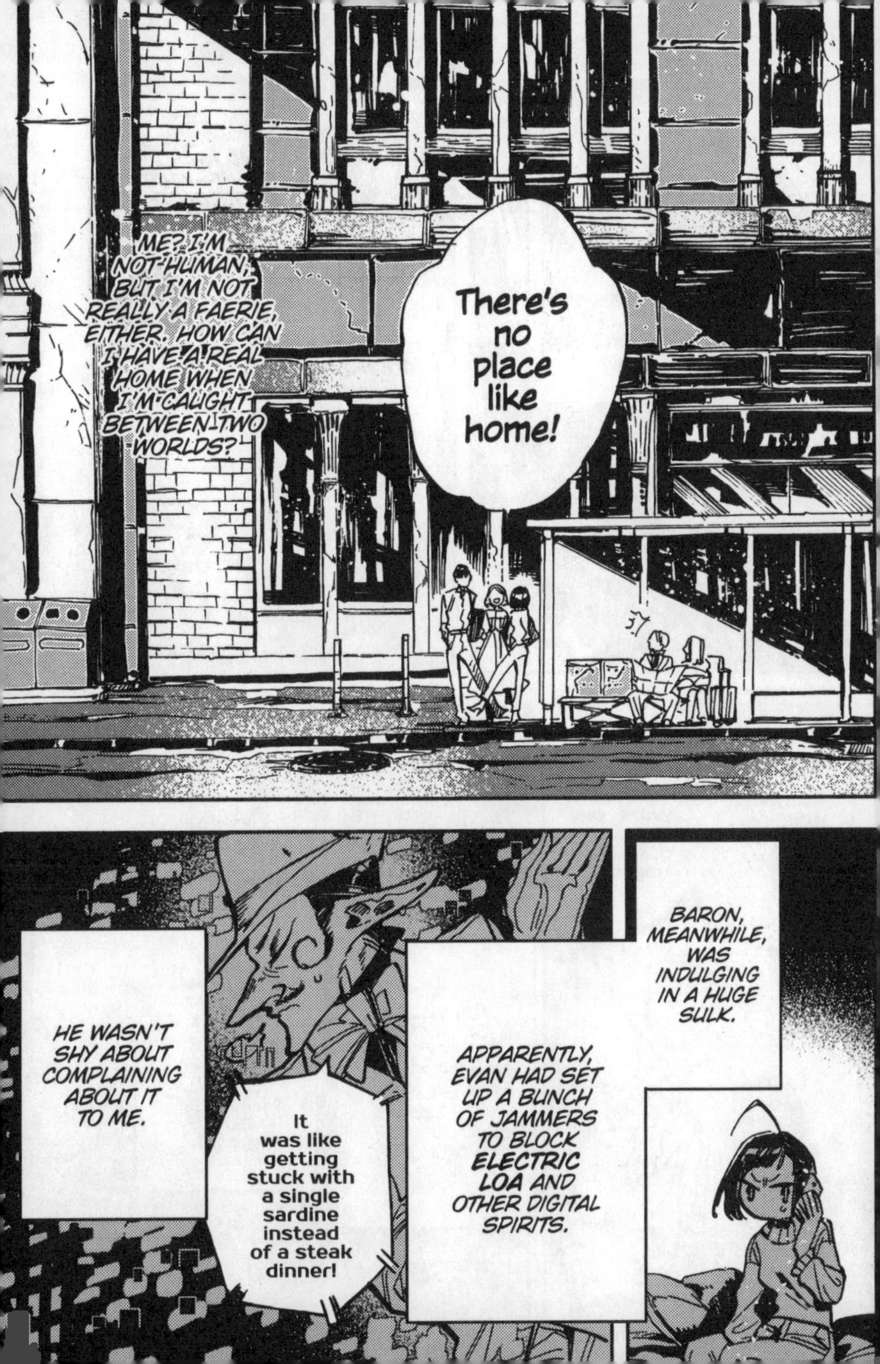
There's no place like home!
ME? I'M NOT HUMAN, BUT I'M NOT REALLY A FAERIE, EITHER. HOW CAN I HAVE A REAL HOME WHEN I'M CAUGHT BETWEEN TWO WORLDS?
BARON, MEANWHILE, WAS INDULGING IN A HUGE SULK.
APPARENTLY, EVAN HAD SET UP A BUNCH OF JAMMERS TO BLOCK ELECTRIC LOA AND OTHER DIGITAL SPIRITS.
HE WASN'T SHY ABOUT COMPLAINING ABOUT IT TO ME.
It was like getting stuck with a single sardine instead of a steak dinner!

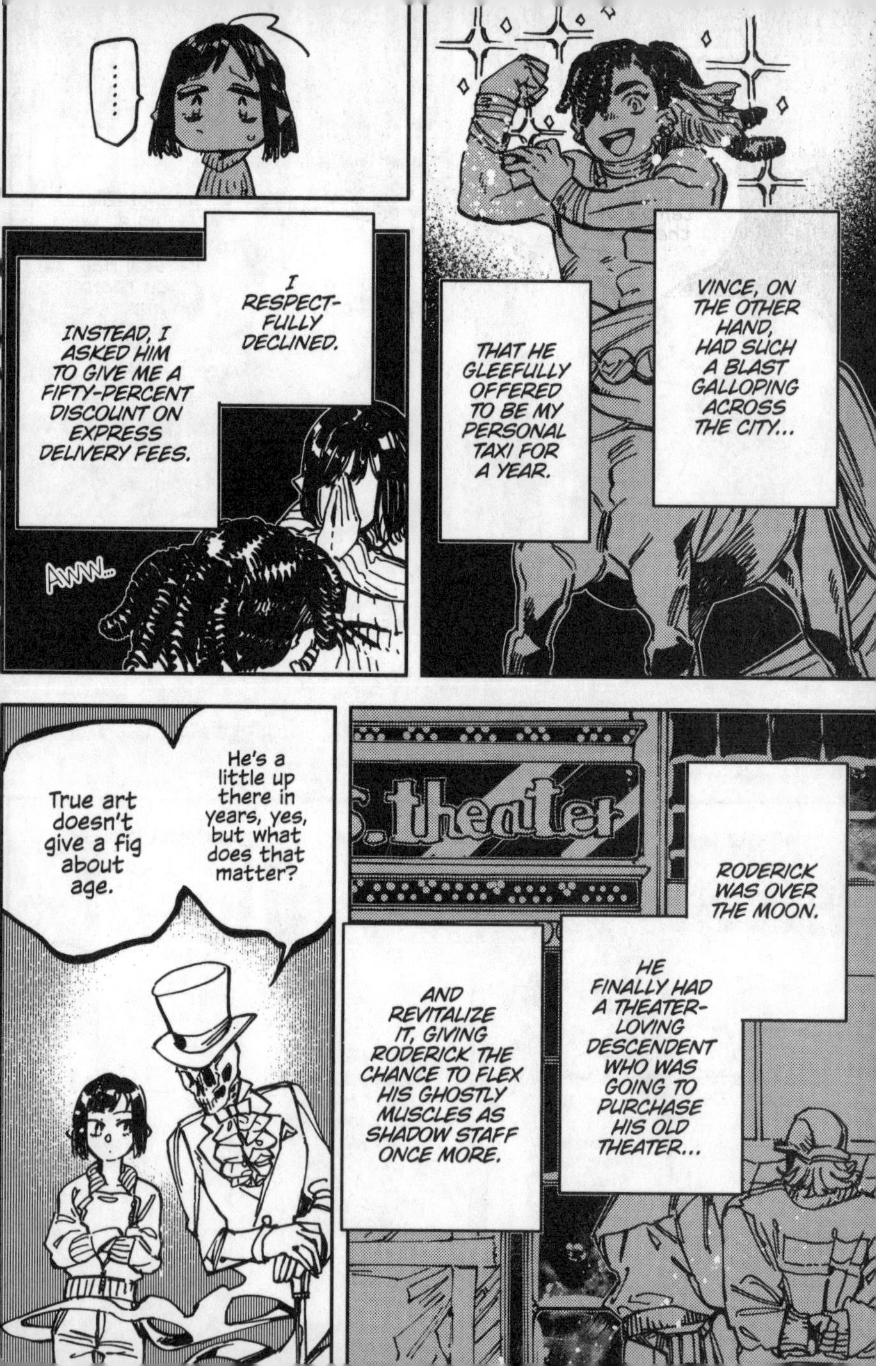
VINCE, ON THE OTHER HAND, HAD SUCH A BLAST GALLOPING ACROSS THE CITY...
THAT HE GLEEFULLY OFFERED TO BE MY PERSONAL TAXI FOR A YEAR.
……
I RESPECT-FULLY DECLINED.
INSTEAD, I ASKED HIM TO GIVE ME A FIFTY-PERCENT DISCOUNT ON EXPRESS DELIVERY FEES.
AWW...
RODERICK WAS OVER THE MOON.
HE FINALLY HAD A THEATER-LOVING DESCENDENT WHO WAS GOING TO PURCHASE HIS OLD THEATER...
AND REVITALIZE IT, GIVING RODERICK THE CHANCE TO FLEX HIS GHOSTLY MUSCLES AS SHADOW STAFF ONCE MORE.
S. theater
He's a little up there in years, yes, but what does that matter?
True art doesn't give a fig about age.

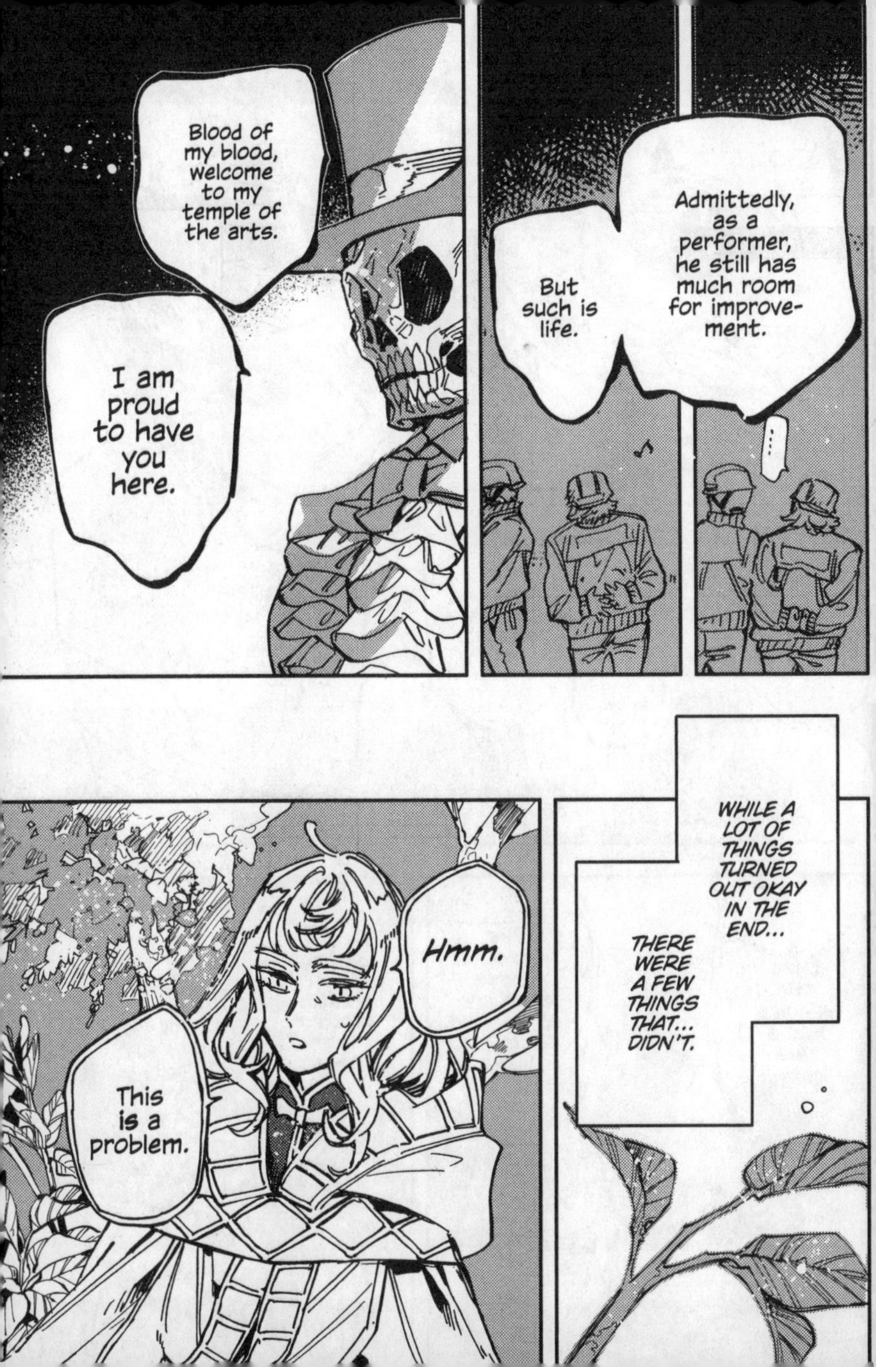
Admittedly, as a performer, he still has much room for improvement.
....
But such is life.
Blood of my blood, welcome to my temple of the arts.
I am proud to have you here.
WHILE A LOT OF THINGS TURNED OUT OKAY IN THE END...
THERE WERE A FEW THINGS THAT... DIDN'T.
Hmm.
This is a problem.

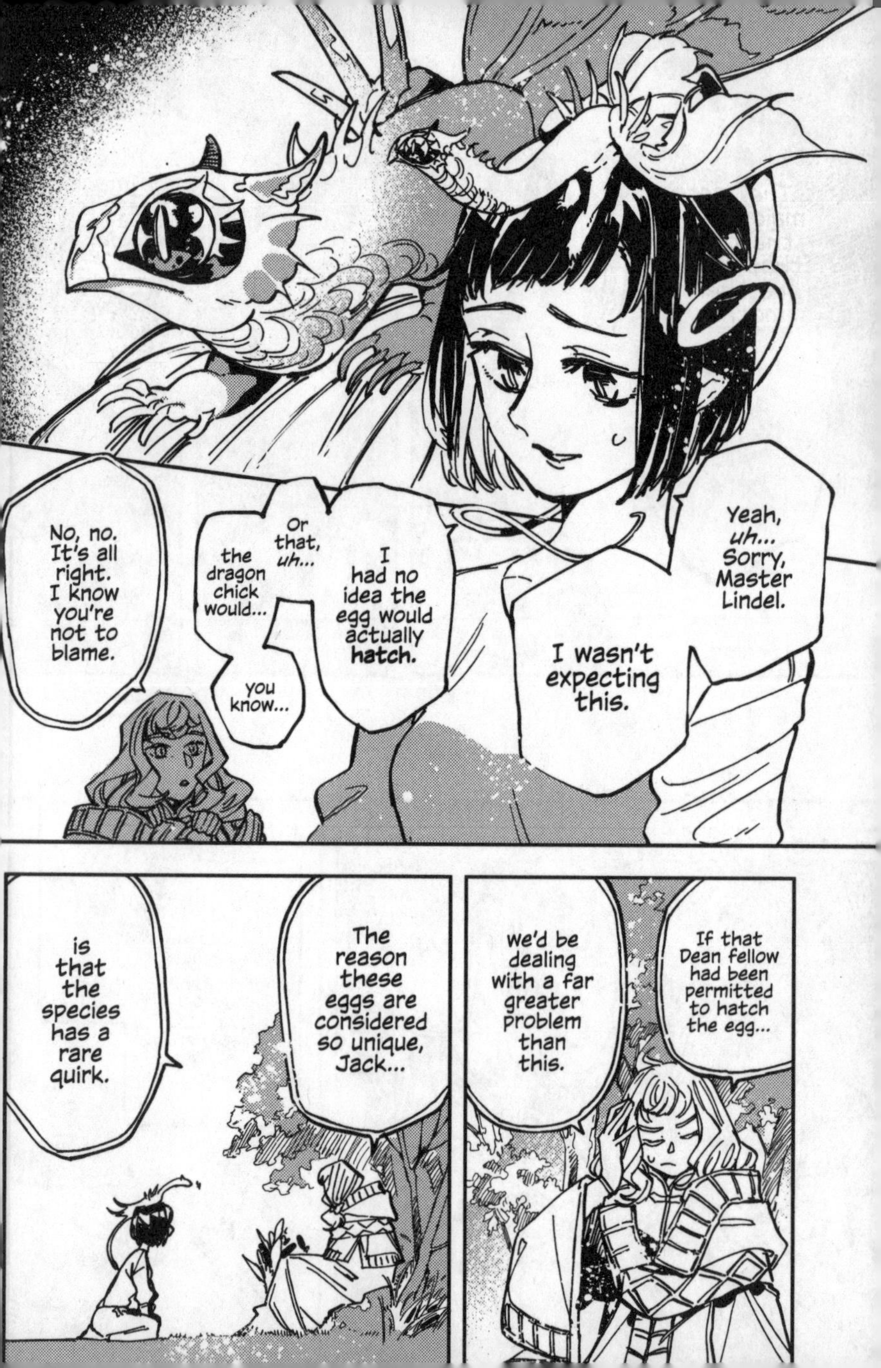
Yeah, *uh*... Sorry, Master Lindel.
I wasn't expecting this.
I had no idea the egg would actually **hatch.**
Or that, *uh*...
the dragon chick would...
you know...
No, no. It's all right. I know you're not to blame.
If that Dean fellow had been permitted to hatch the egg...
we'd be dealing with a far greater problem than this.
The reason these eggs are considered so unique, Jack...
is that the species has a rare quirk.

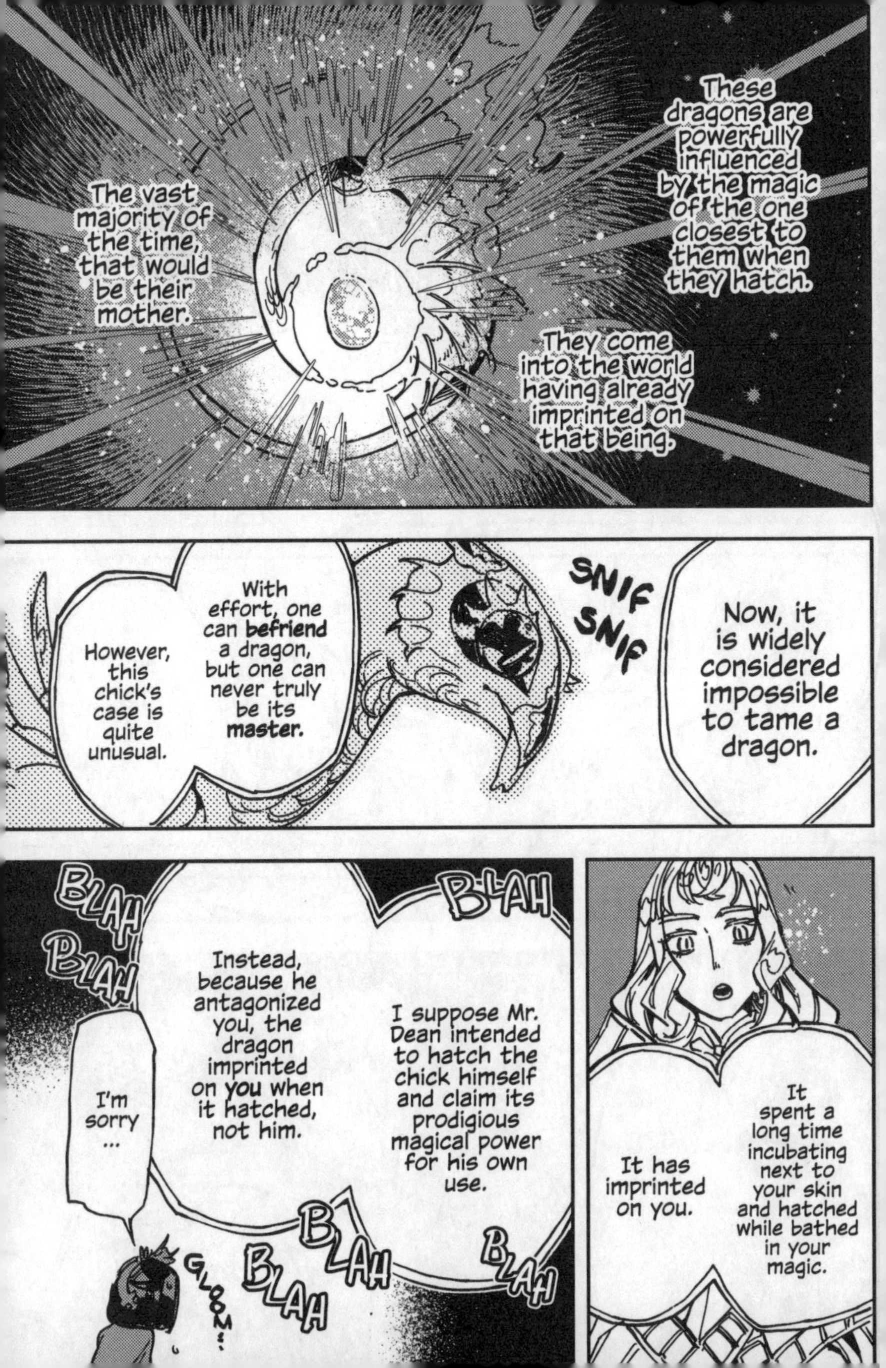
These dragons are powerfully influenced by the magic of the one closest to them when they hatch.
The vast majority of the time, that would be their mother.
They come into the world having already imprinted on that being.
Now, it is widely considered impossible to tame a dragon.
SNIF SNIF
With effort, one can **befriend** a dragon, but one can never truly be its **master.**
However, this chick's case is quite unusual.
It spent a long time incubating next to your skin and hatched while bathed in your magic.
It has imprinted on you.
BLAH
I suppose Mr. Dean intended to hatch the chick himself and claim its prodigious magical power for his own use.
Instead, because he antagonized you, the dragon imprinted on **you** when it hatched, not him.
BLAH
BLAH
BLAH
BLAH
BLAH
I'm sorry ...
GLOOM...

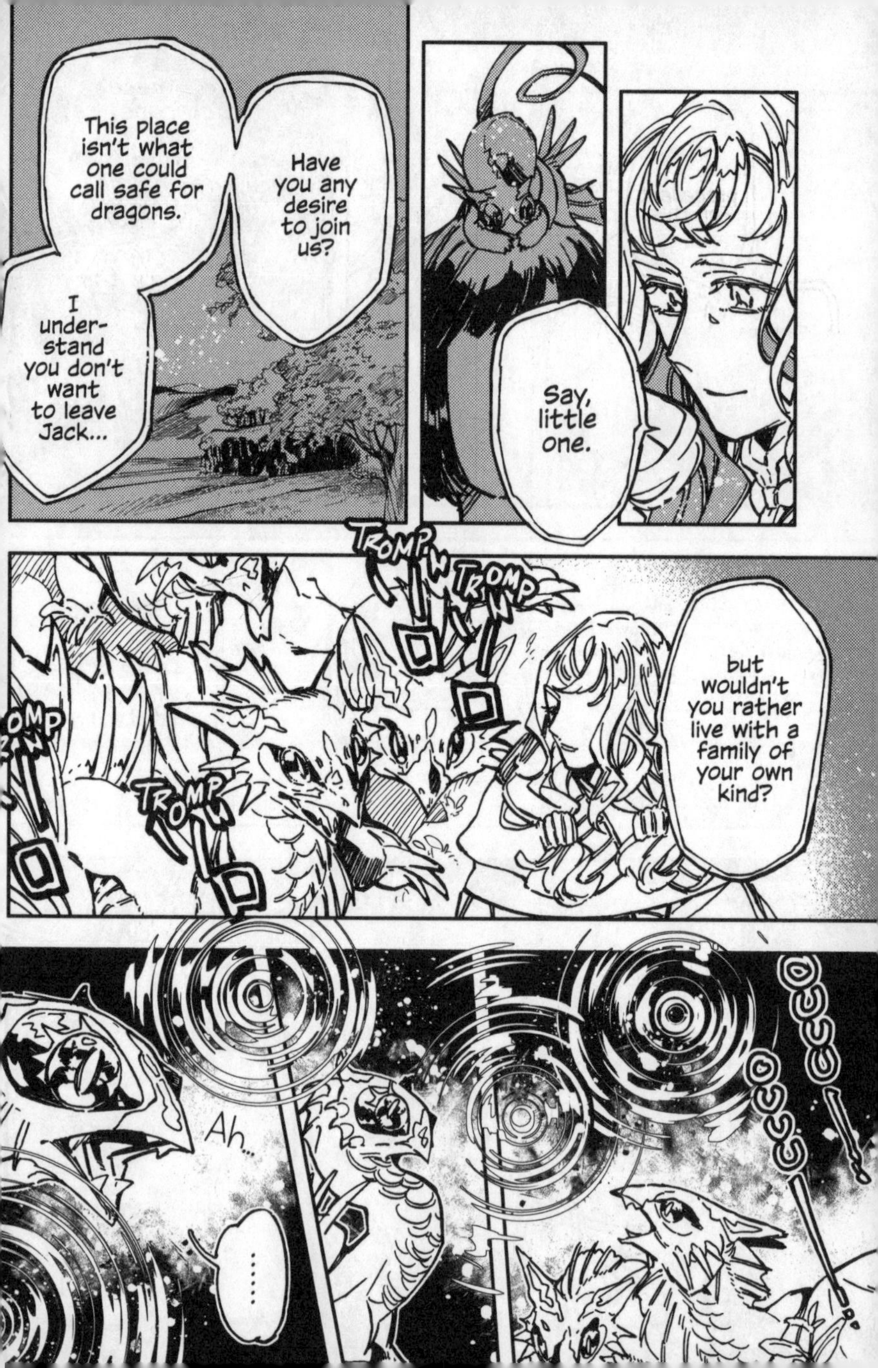
Say, little one.
Have you any desire to join us?
This place isn't what one could call safe for dragons.
I understand you don't want to leave Jack...
TROMP
TROMP
but wouldn't you rather live with a family of your own kind?
TROMP
OMP
Ah...
......

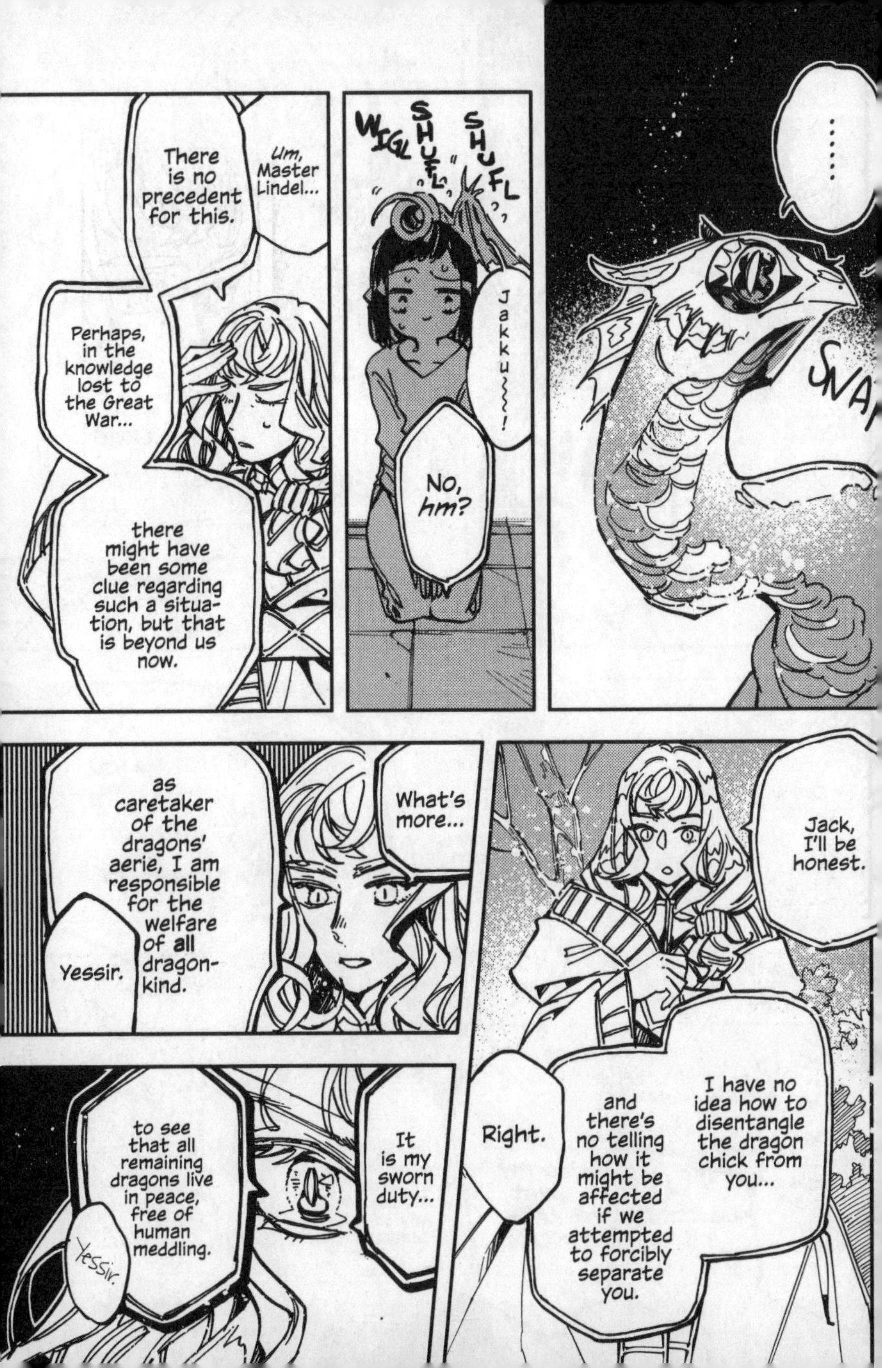
......
SNA
WIGL
SHUFL
SHUFL
Jakku~~~!
No, *hm*?
Um, Master Lindel...
There is no precedent for this.
Perhaps, in the knowledge lost to the Great War...
there might have been some clue regarding such a situation, but that is beyond us now.
Jack, I'll be honest.
I have no idea how to disentangle the dragon chick from you...
and there's no telling how it might be affected if we attempted to forcibly separate you.
Right.
What's more...
as caretaker of the dragons' aerie, I am responsible for the welfare of **all** dragonkind.
Yessir.
It is my sworn duty...
to see that all remaining dragons live in peace, free of human meddling.
Yessir.

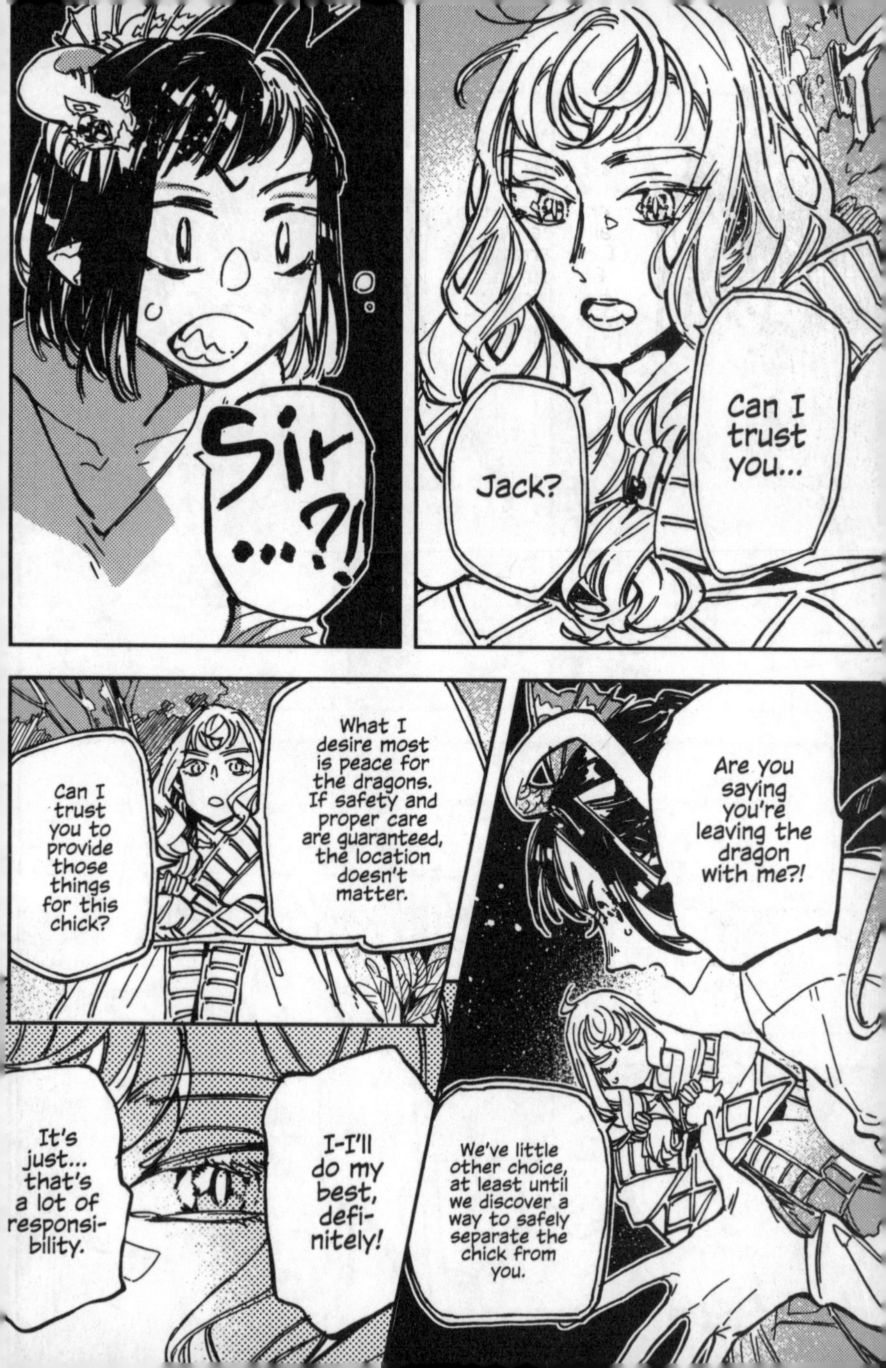
Can I trust you...
Jack?
Sir ...?!
Are you saying you're leaving the dragon with me?!
We've little other choice, at least until we discover a way to safely separate the chick from you.
What I desire most is peace for the dragons. If safety and proper care are guaranteed, the location doesn't matter.
Can I trust you to provide those things for this chick?
I-I'll do my best, defi-nitely!
It's just... that's a lot of responsi-bility.

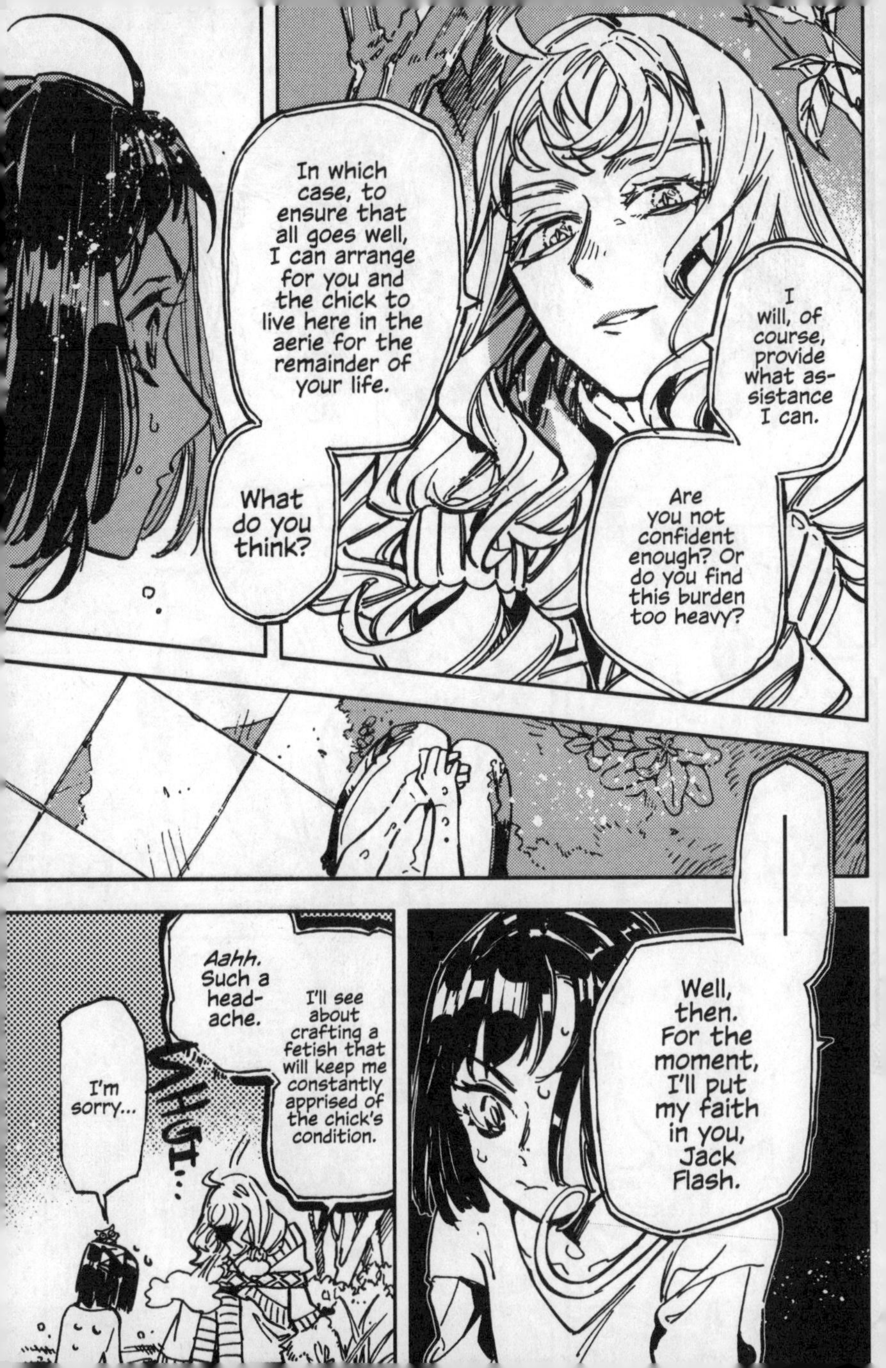
I will, of course, provide what assistance I can.
Are you not confident enough? Or do you find this burden too heavy?
In which case, to ensure that all goes well, I can arrange for you and the chick to live here in the aerie for the remainder of your life.
What do you think?
Well, then. For the moment, I'll put my faith in you, Jack Flash.
Aahh. Such a headache.
I'll see about crafting a fetish that will keep me constantly apprised of the chick's condition.
I'm sorry...

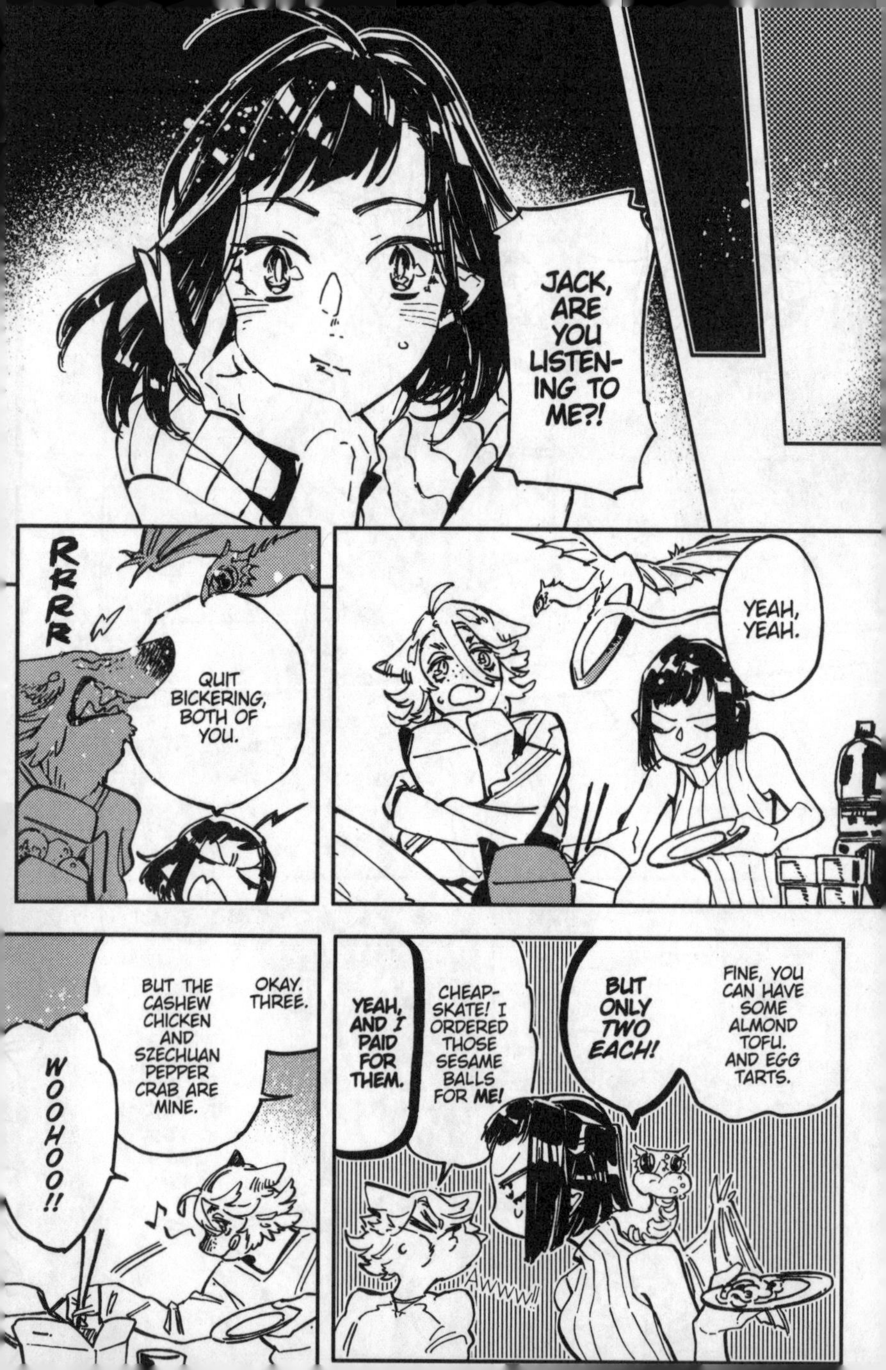
JACK, ARE YOU LISTENING TO ME?!
YEAH, YEAH.
RRRR
QUIT BICKERING, BOTH OF YOU.
FINE, YOU CAN HAVE SOME ALMOND TOFU. AND EGG TARTS.
BUT ONLY TWO EACH!
CHEAPSKATE! I ORDERED THOSE SESAME BALLS FOR ME!
YEAH, AND I PAID FOR THEM.
AWWW!
OKAY. THREE.
BUT THE CASHEW CHICKEN AND SZECHUAN PEPPER CRAB ARE MINE.
WOOHOOO!!

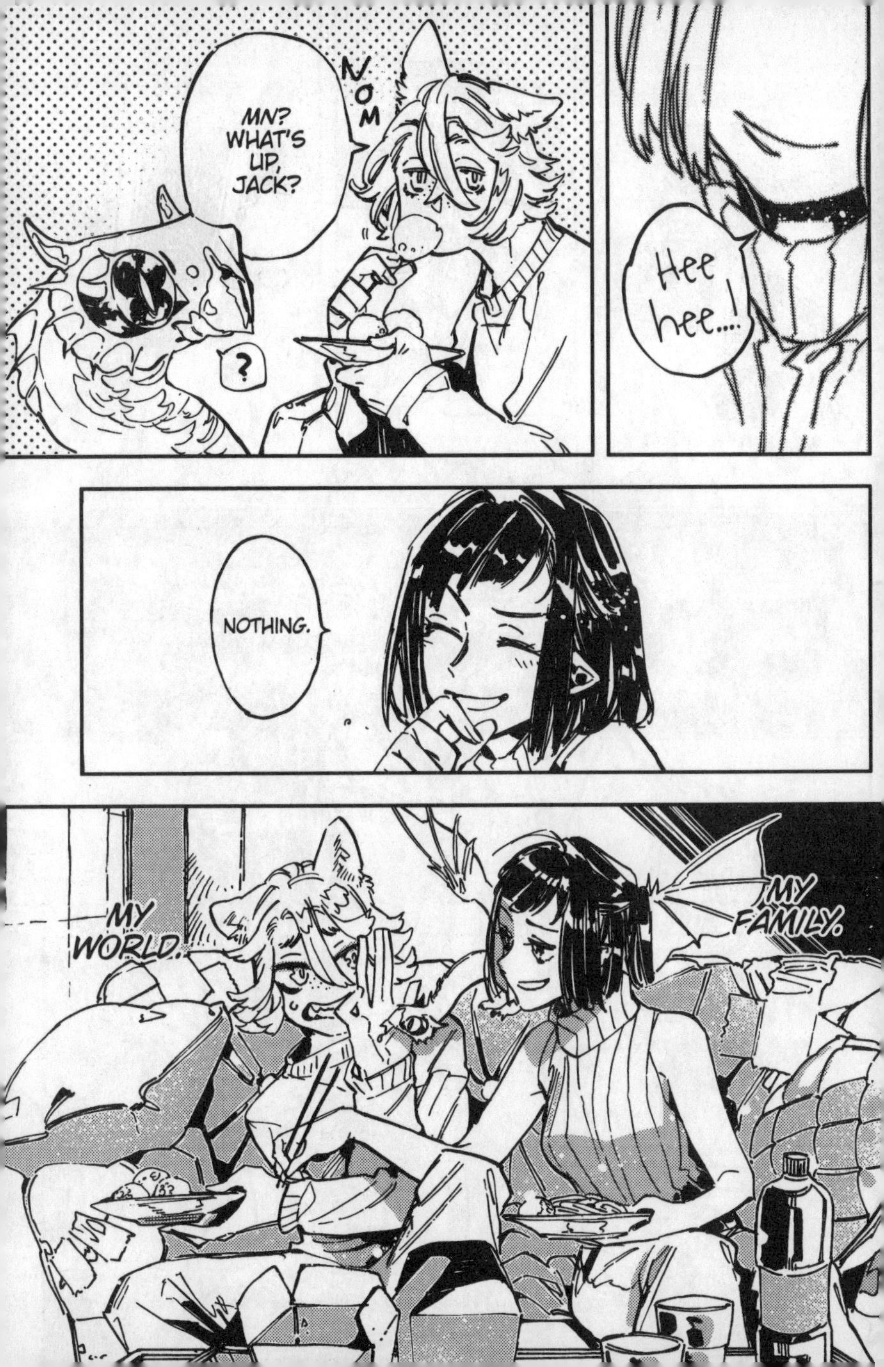
Hee hee...!
NOM
MN? WHAT'S UP, JACK?
?
NOTHING.
MY FAMILY.
MY WORLD.

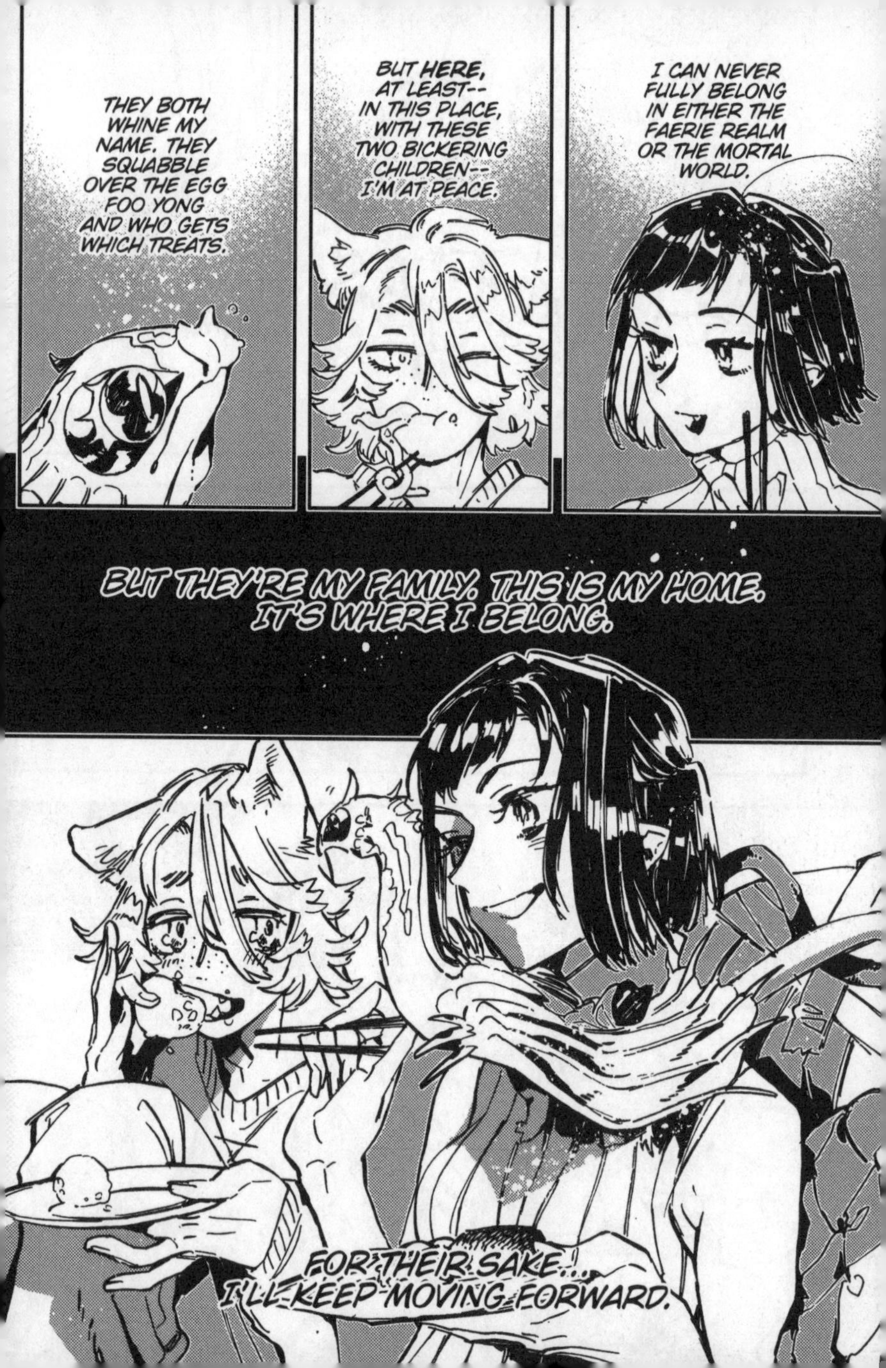
I CAN NEVER FULLY BELONG IN EITHER THE FAERIE REALM OR THE MORTAL WORLD.
BUT HERE, AT LEAST-- IN THIS PLACE, WITH THESE TWO BICKERING CHILDREN-- I'M AT PEACE.
THEY BOTH WHINE MY NAME. THEY SQUABBLE OVER THE EGG FOO YONG AND WHO GETS WHICH TREATS.
BUT THEY'RE MY FAMILY. THIS IS MY HOME. IT'S WHERE I BELONG.
FOR THEIR SAKE... I'LL KEEP MOVING FORWARD.

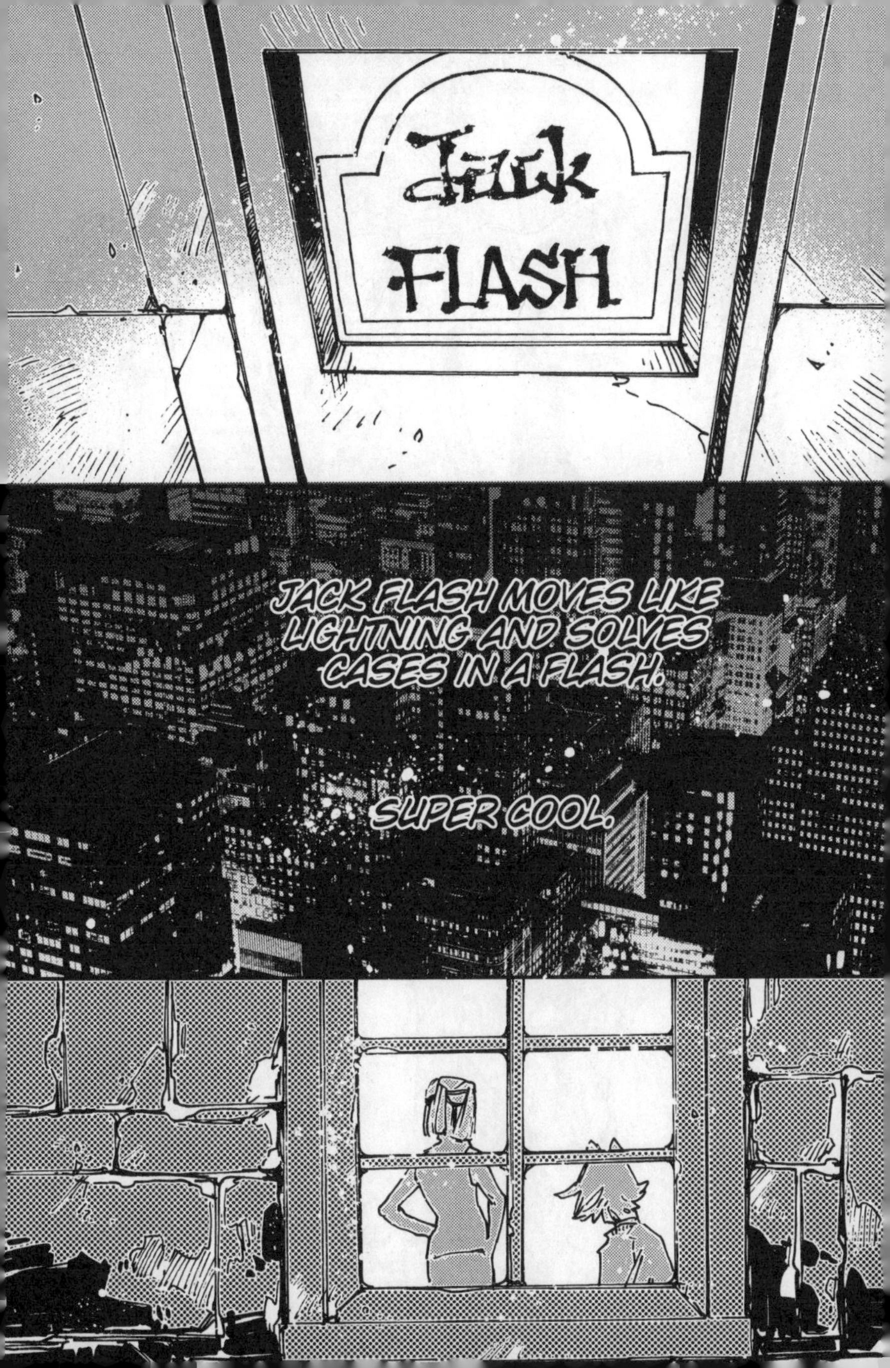
Jack
FLASH
JACK FLASH MOVES LIKE LIGHTNING AND SOLVES CASES IN A FLASH.
SUPER COOL.

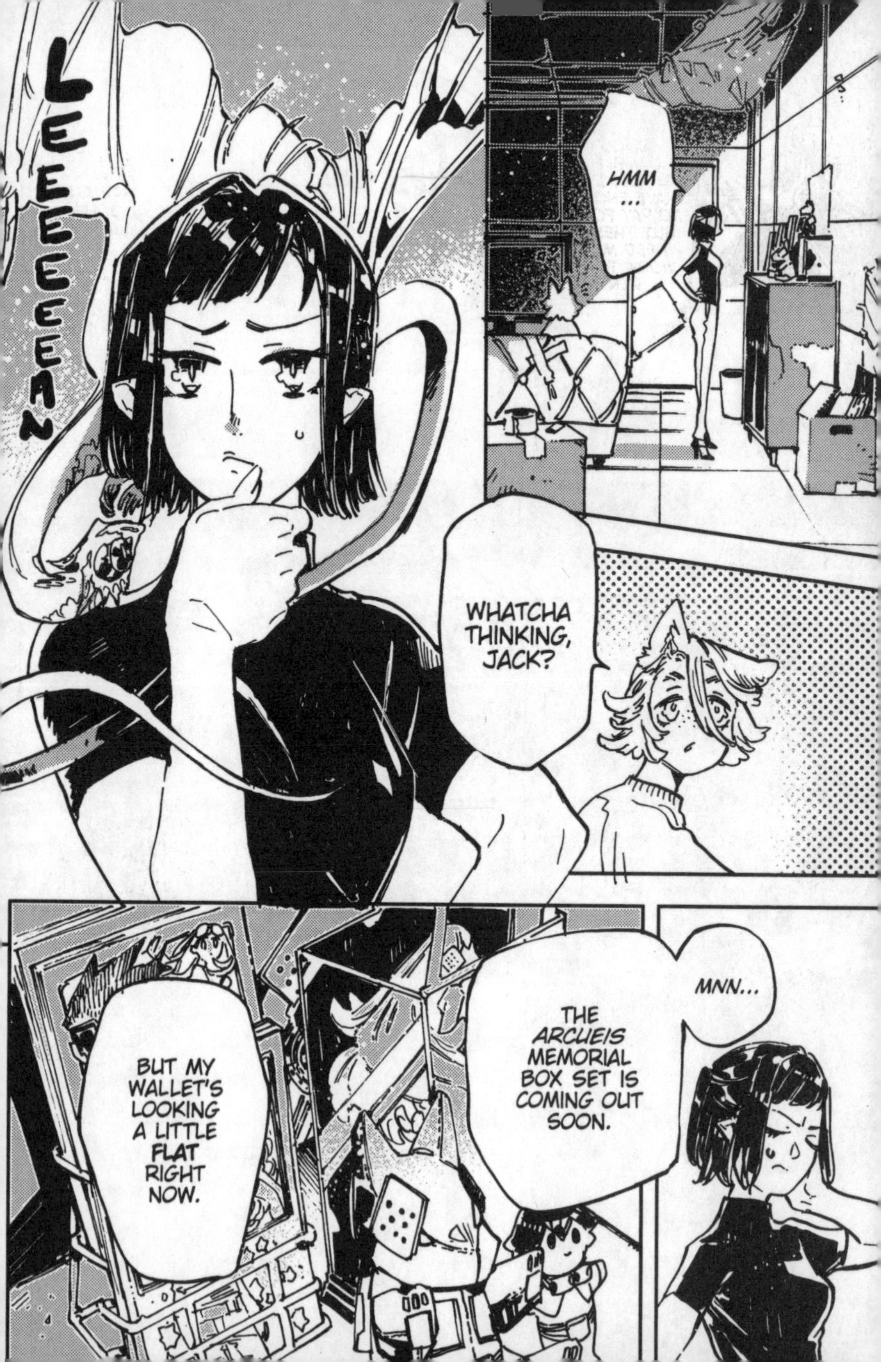
HMM ...
WHATCHA THINKING, JACK?
LEEEEEEEAN
MNN...
THE ARCUEIS MEMORIAL BOX SET IS COMING OUT SOON.
BUT MY WALLET'S LOOKING A LITTLE FLAT RIGHT NOW.

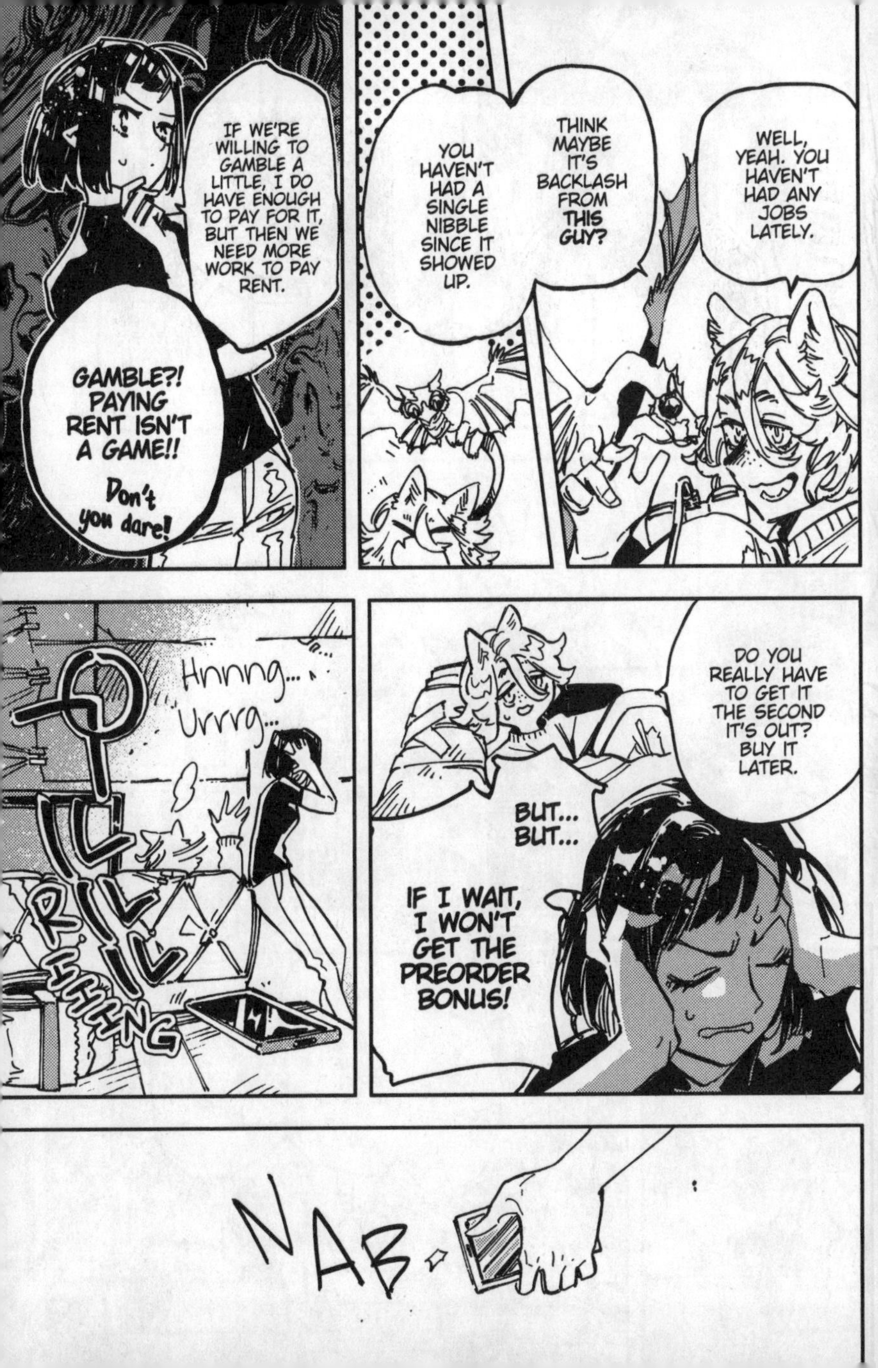
WELL, YEAH. YOU HAVEN'T HAD ANY JOBS LATELY.
THINK MAYBE IT'S BACKLASH FROM THIS GUY?
YOU HAVEN'T HAD A SINGLE NIBBLE SINCE IT SHOWED UP.
IF WE'RE WILLING TO GAMBLE A LITTLE, I DO HAVE ENOUGH TO PAY FOR IT, BUT THEN WE NEED MORE WORK TO PAY RENT.
GAMBLE?! PAYING RENT ISN'T A GAME!!
Don't you dare!
DO YOU REALLY HAVE TO GET IT THE SECOND IT'S OUT? BUY IT LATER.
BUT... BUT...
IF I WAIT, I WON'T GET THE PREORDER BONUS!
Hnnng...
Urrrg...
NAB

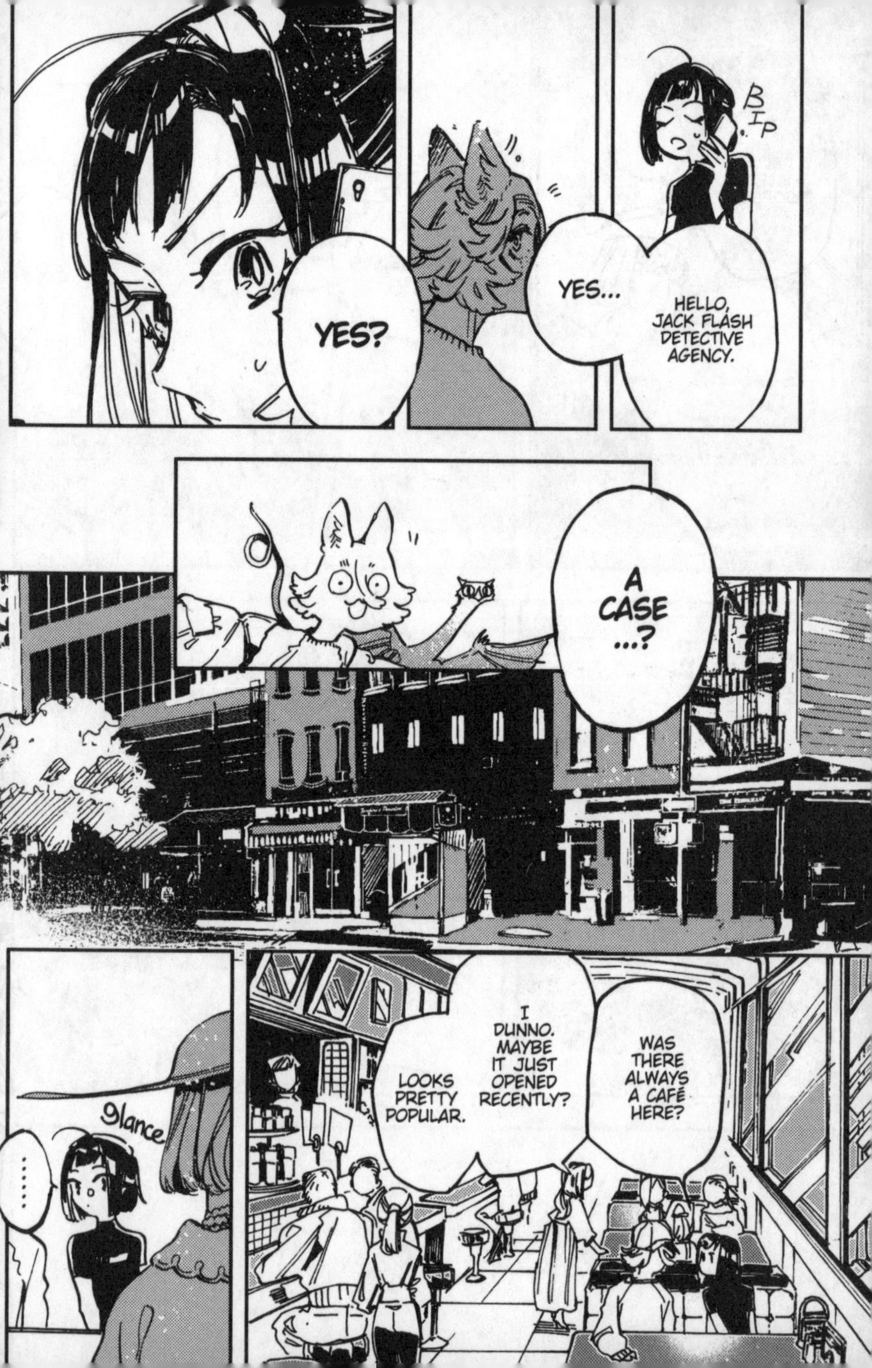
BIP
HELLO, JACK FLASH DETECTIVE AGENCY.
YES...
YES?
A CASE ...?
WAS THERE ALWAYS A CAFÉ HERE?
I DUNNO. MAYBE IT JUST OPENED RECENTLY?
LOOKS PRETTY POPULAR.
glance
......

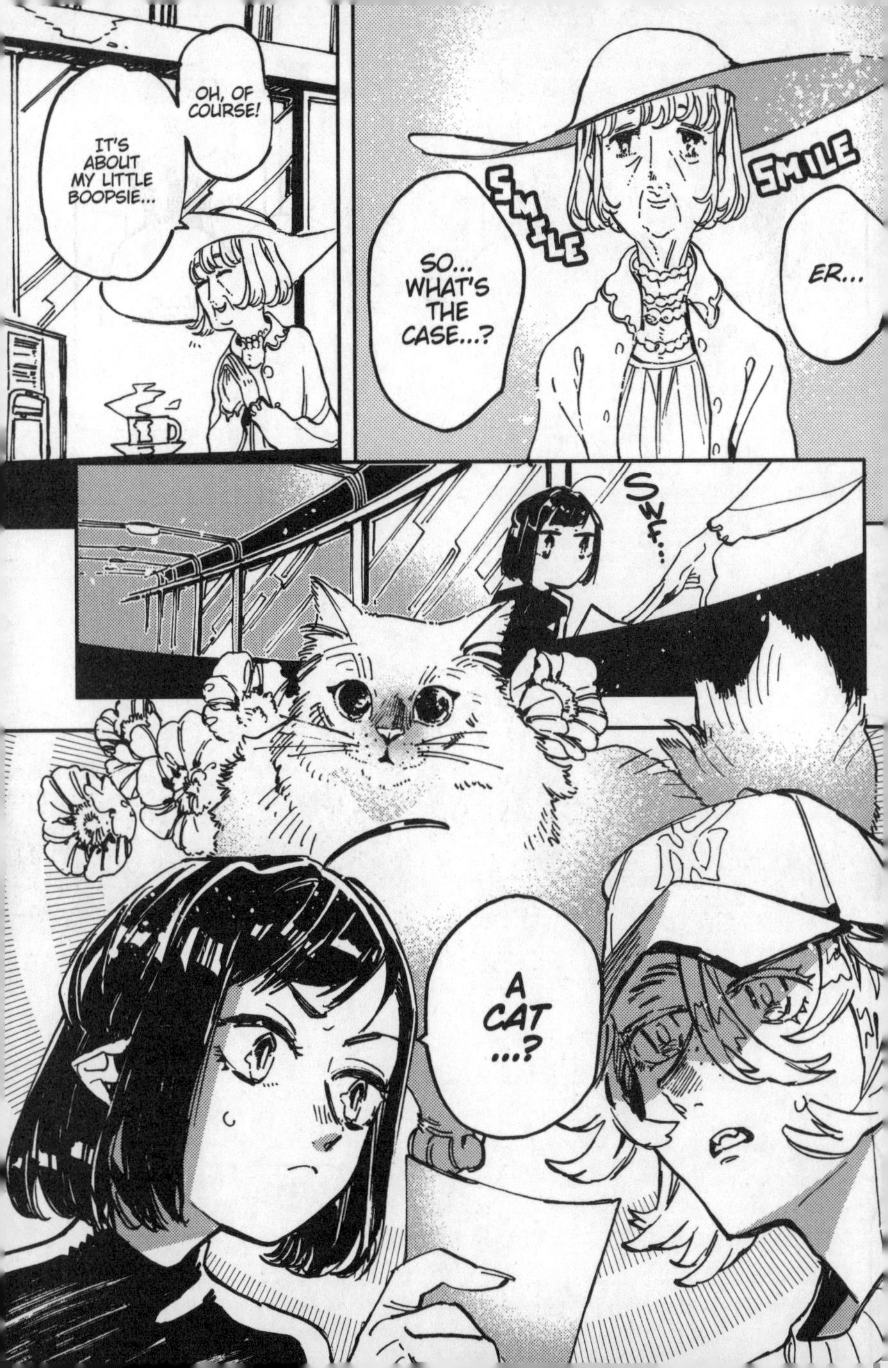
SMILE
ER...
SMILE
SO... WHAT'S THE CASE...?
OH, OF COURSE!
IT'S ABOUT MY LITTLE BOOPSIE...
SWF...
A CAT ...?

The Ancient
Magus' Bride

JACK FLASH AND THE FAERIE CASE FILES

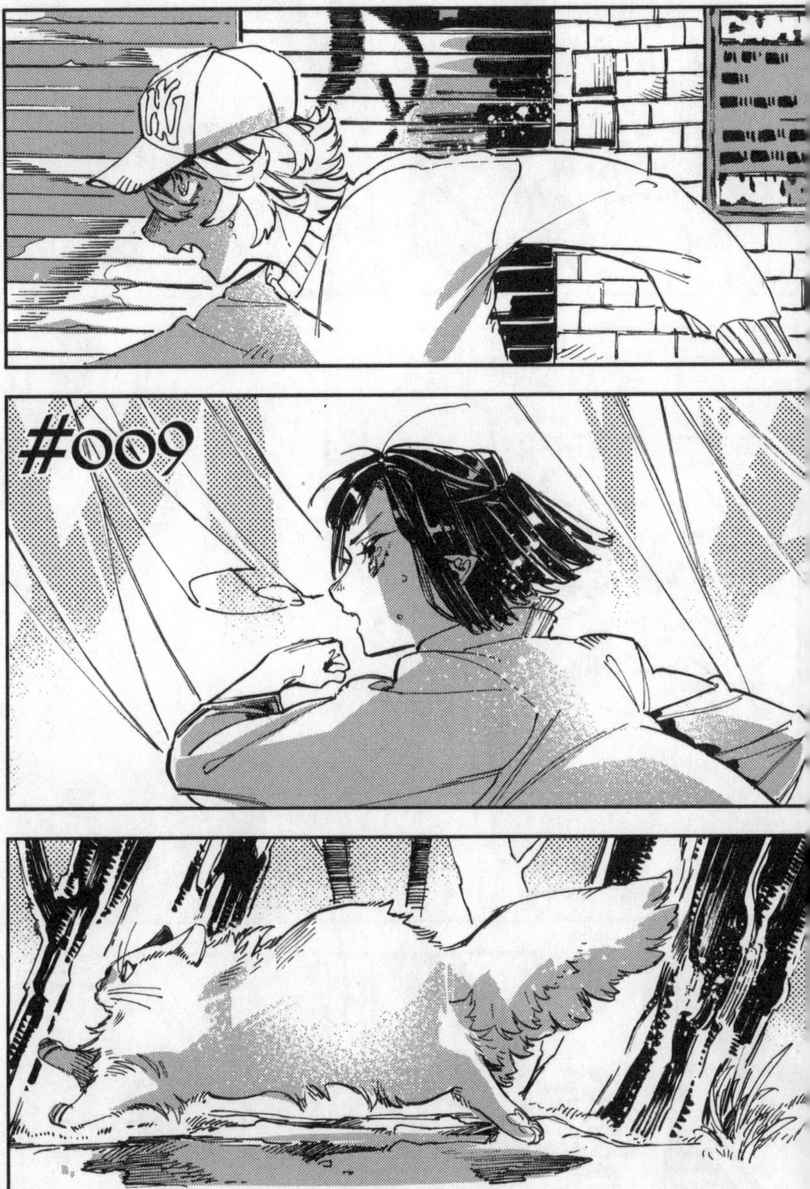
#009

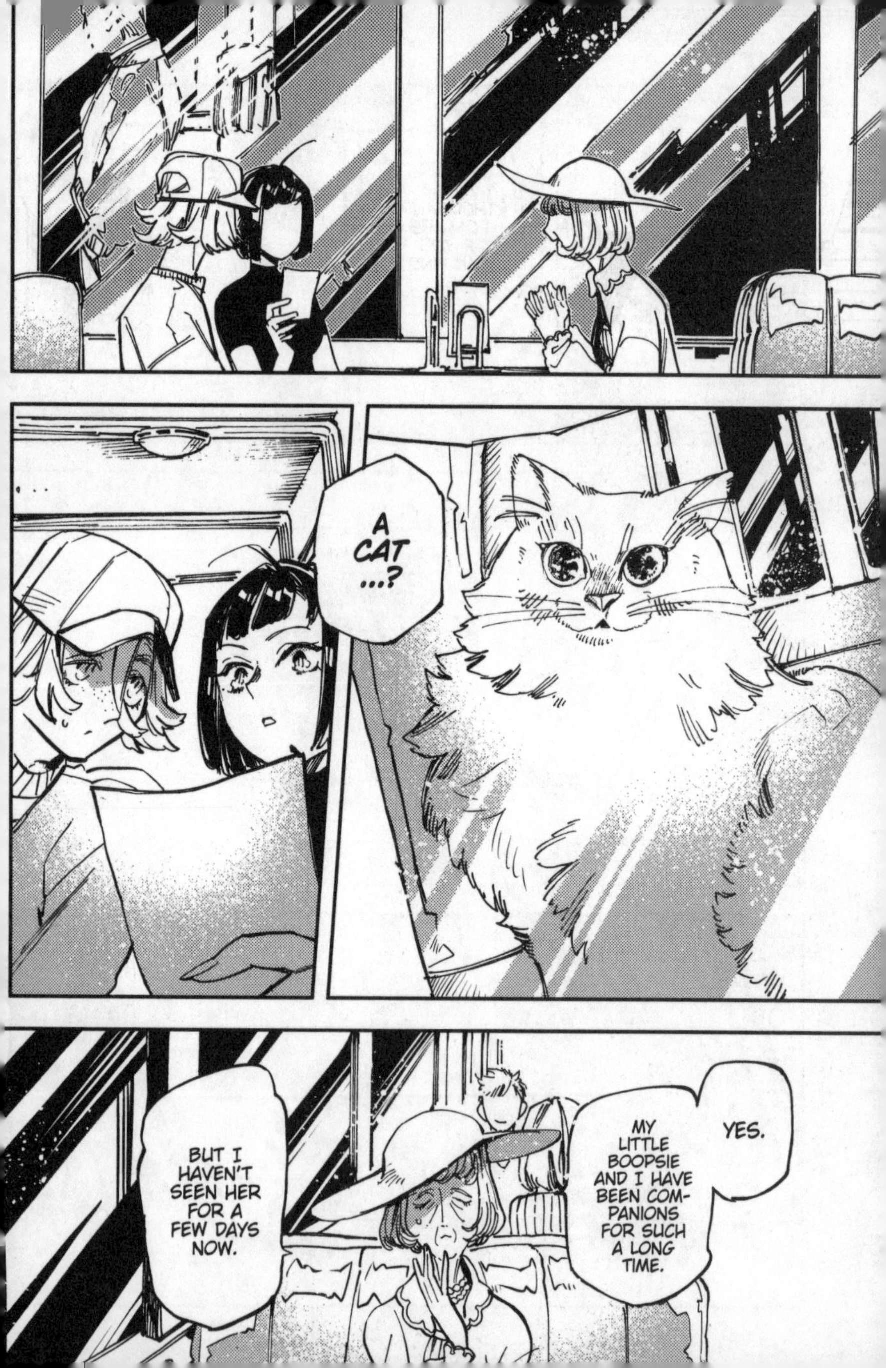
A CAT ...?
...
YES.
MY LITTLE BOOPSIE AND I HAVE BEEN COMPANIONS FOR SUCH A LONG TIME.
BUT I HAVEN'T SEEN HER FOR A FEW DAYS NOW.

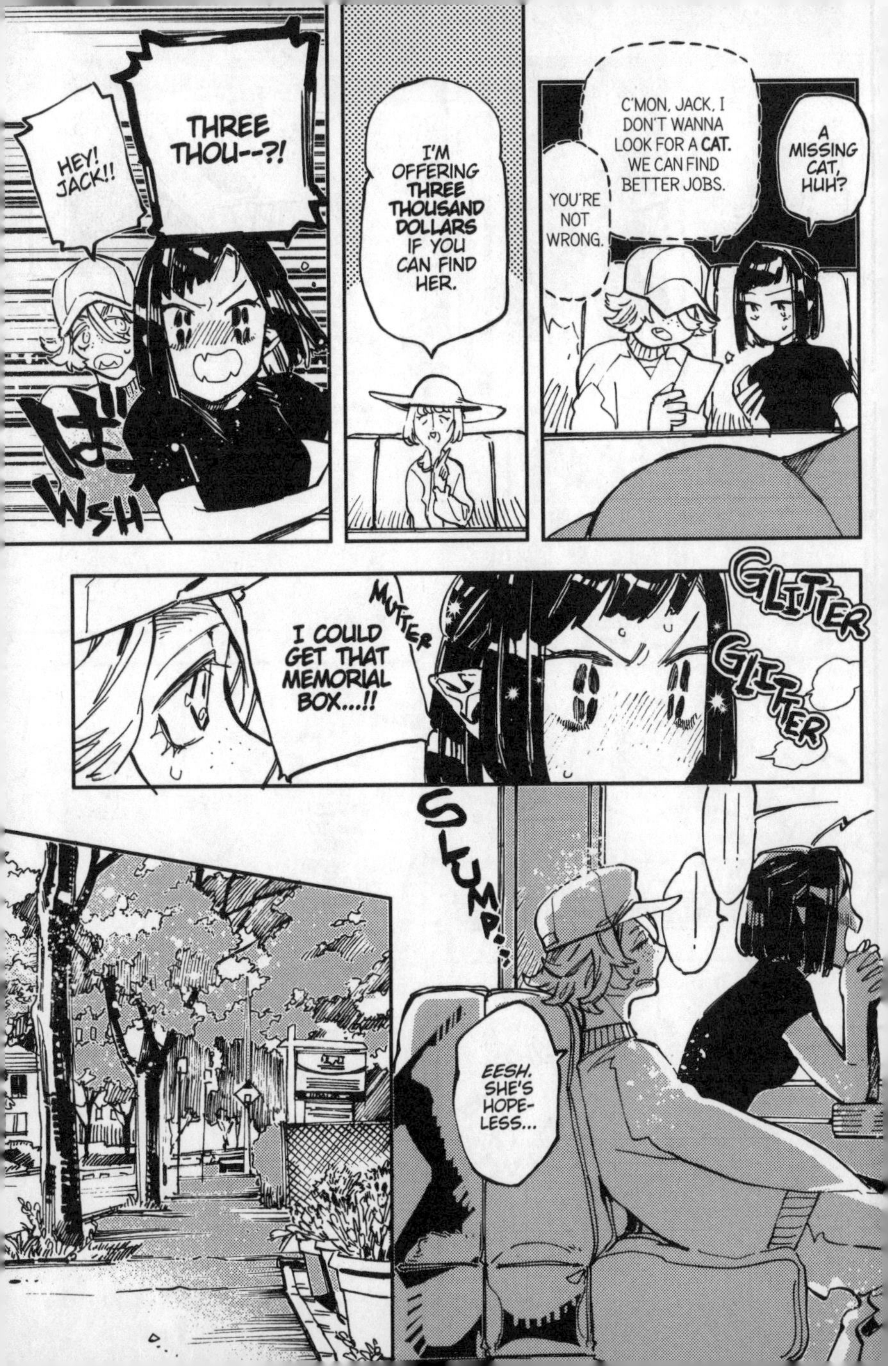
A MISSING CAT, HUH?
C'MON, JACK, I DON'T WANNA LOOK FOR A CAT. WE CAN FIND BETTER JOBS.
YOU'RE NOT WRONG.
I'M OFFERING THREE THOUSAND DOLLARS IF YOU CAN FIND HER.
THREE THOU--?!
HEY! JACK!!
WSH
GLITTER
GLITTER
MUTTER
I COULD GET THAT MEMORIAL BOX...!!
SLUMP...
EESH. SHE'S HOPELESS...

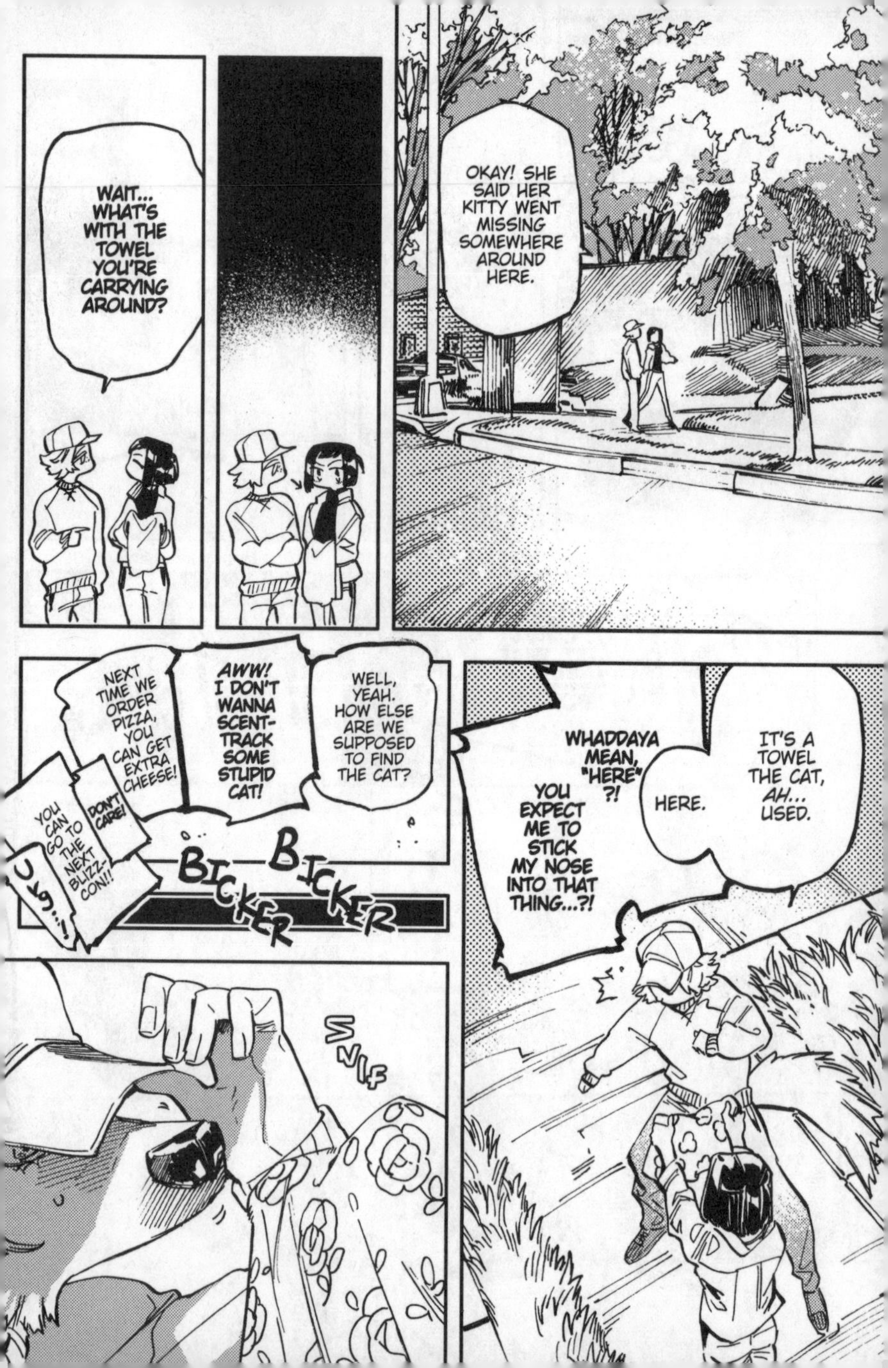
OKAY! SHE SAID HER KITTY WENT MISSING SOMEWHERE AROUND HERE.
WAIT... WHAT'S WITH THE TOWEL YOU'RE CARRYING AROUND?
IT'S A TOWEL THE CAT, AH... USED.
HERE.
WHADDAYA MEAN, "HERE"?!
YOU EXPECT ME TO STICK MY NOSE INTO THAT THING...?!
WELL, YEAH. HOW ELSE ARE WE SUPPOSED TO FIND THE CAT?
AWW! I DON'T WANNA SCENT-TRACK SOME STUPID CAT!
NEXT TIME WE ORDER PIZZA, YOU CAN GET EXTRA CHEESE!
DON'T CARE!
YOU CAN GO TO THE NEXT BLIZZ-CON!!
Ug...!
BICKER
BICKER
SNIF

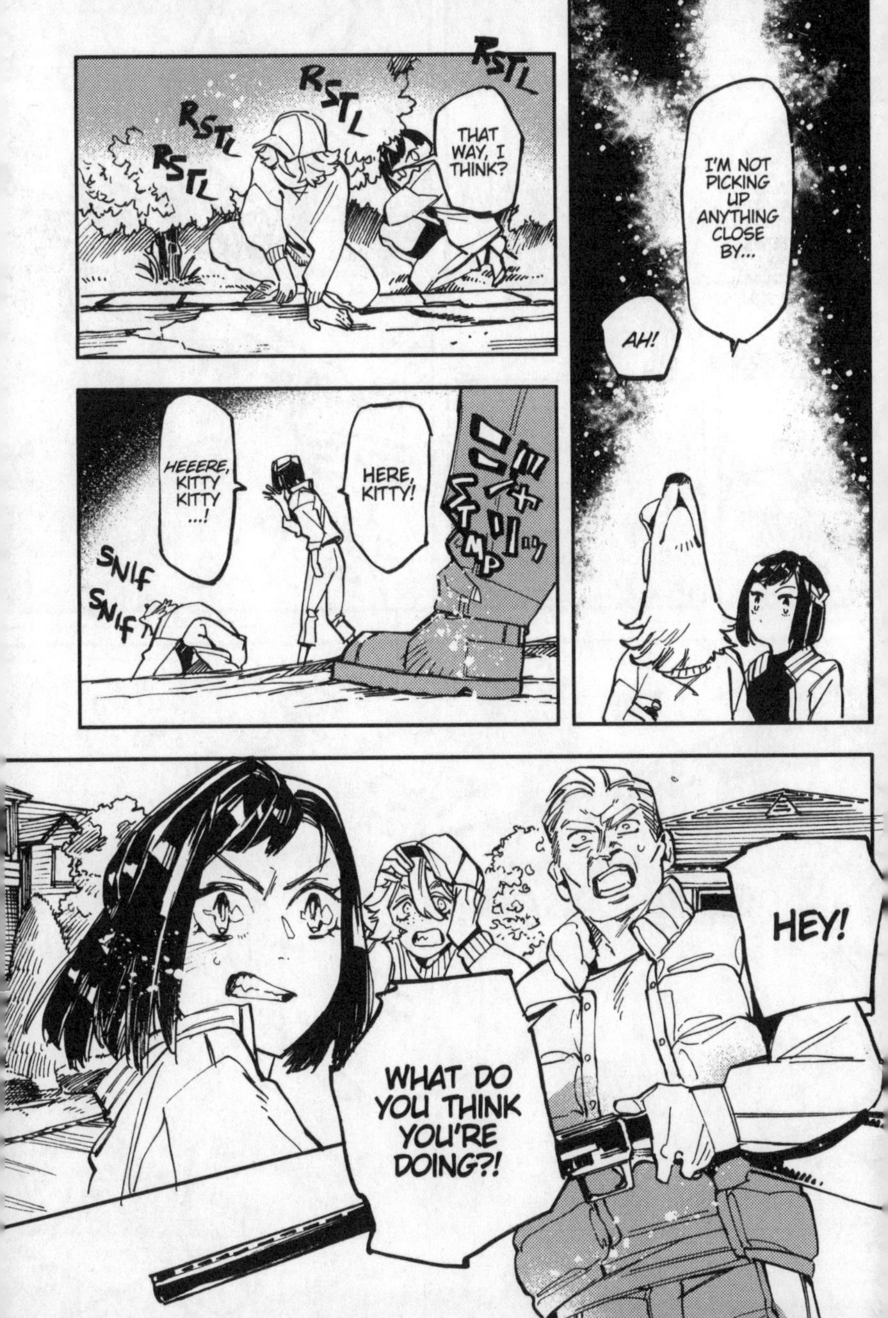
I'M NOT PICKING UP ANYTHING CLOSE BY...
AH!
RSTL
RSTL
RSTL
RSTL
THAT WAY, I THINK?
HERE, KITTY!
HEEERE, KITTY KITTY ...!
STMP
SNIF SNIF
HEY!
WHAT DO YOU THINK YOU'RE DOING?!

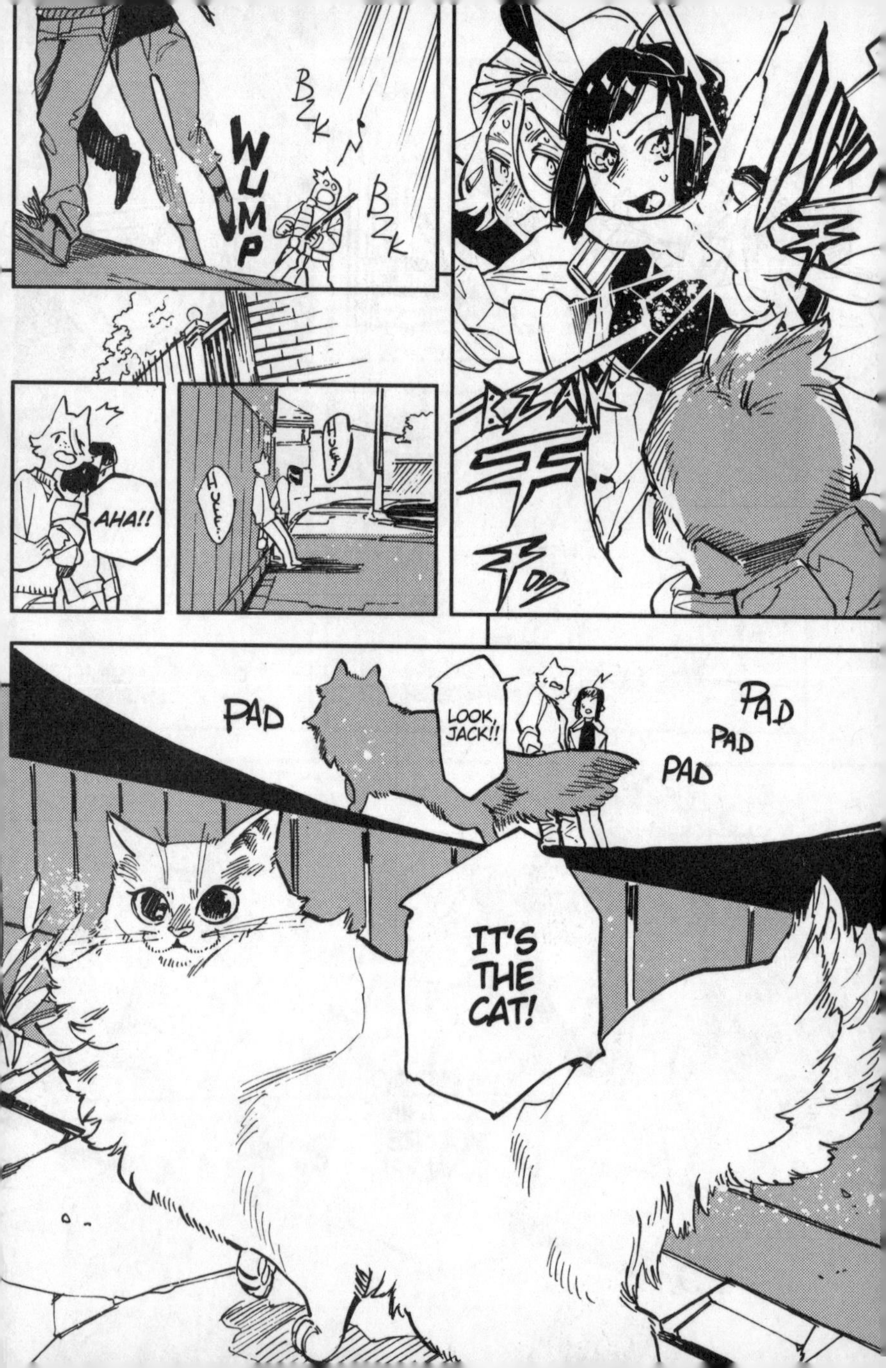
BZK
WUMP
BZK
HUFF...
HUFF...
AHA!!
PAD
PAD
PAD
LOOK, JACK!!
PAD
IT'S THE CAT!

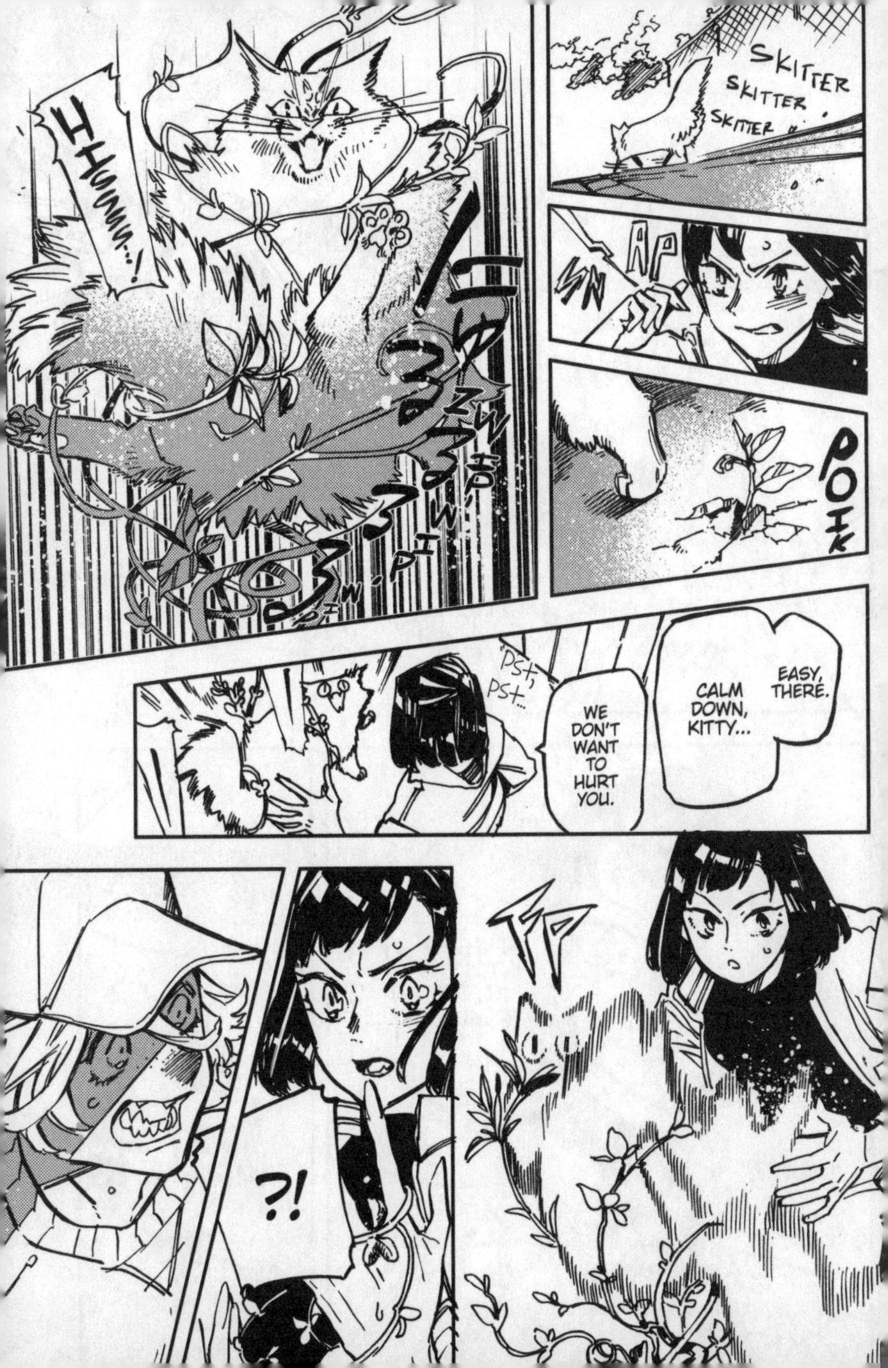
SKITTER
SKITTER
SKITTER
SNAP
POIK
HISSSS...!
EASY, THERE.
CALM DOWN, KITTY...
WE DON'T WANT TO HURT YOU.
PST, PST...
TAP
?!

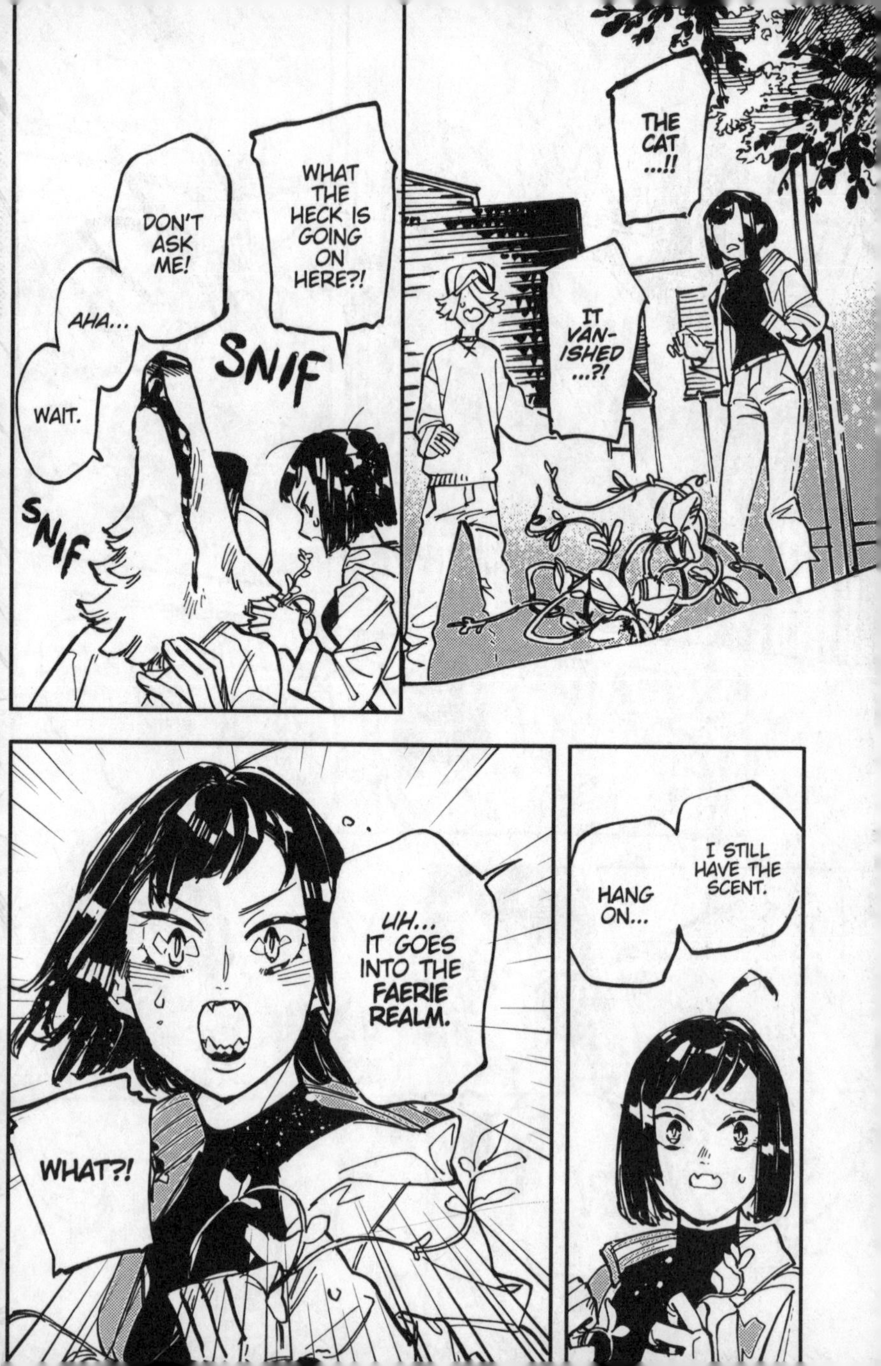
THE CAT ...!!
IT VAN-ISHED ...?!
WHAT THE HECK IS GOING ON HERE?!
DON'T ASK ME!
SNIF
AHA...
WAIT.
SNIF
I STILL HAVE THE SCENT.
HANG ON...
UH... IT GOES INTO THE FAERIE REALM.
WHAT?!

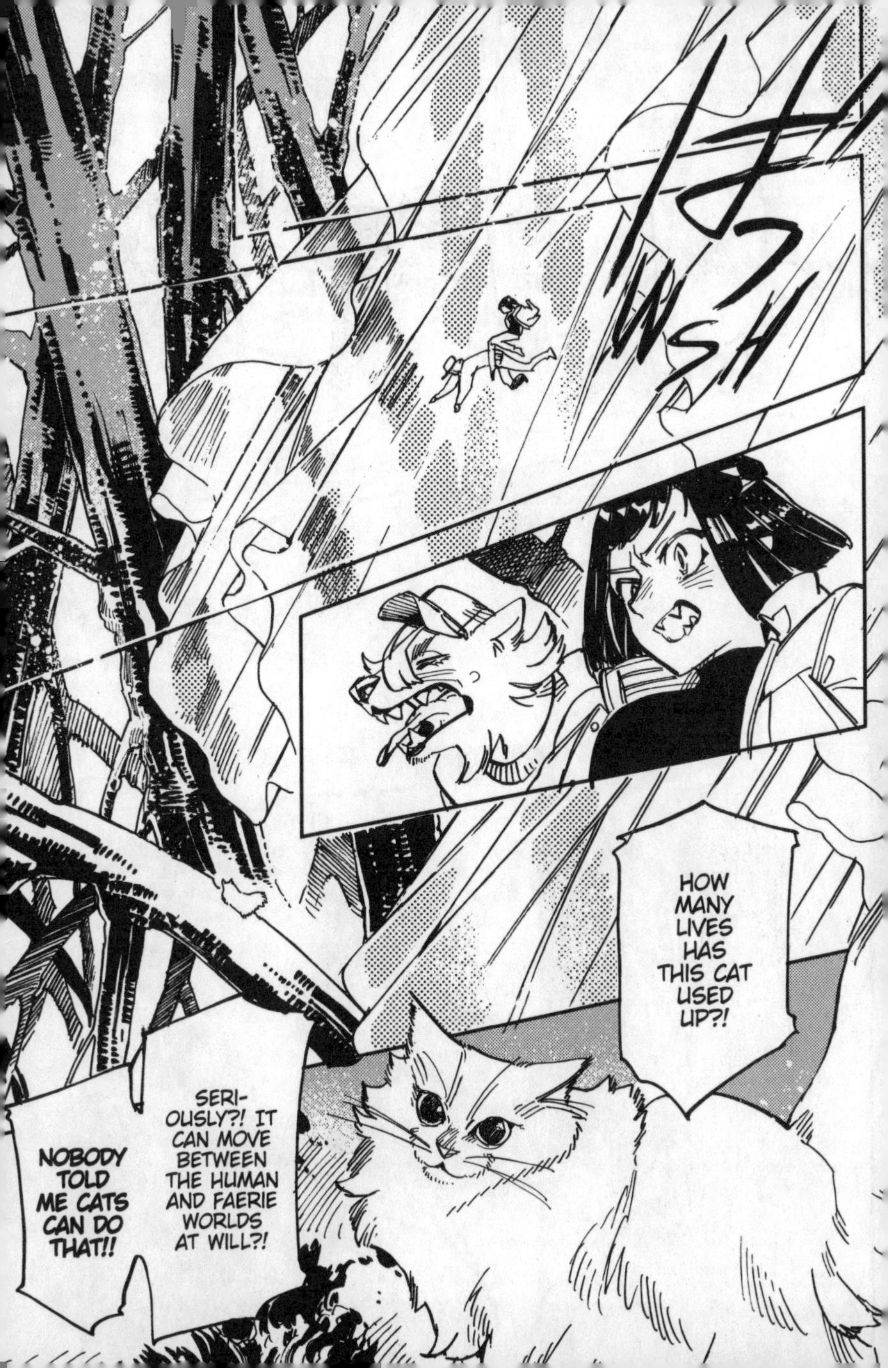
WSH
HOW MANY LIVES HAS THIS CAT USED UP?!
SERI-OUSLY?! IT CAN MOVE BETWEEN THE HUMAN AND FAERIE WORLDS AT WILL?!
NOBODY TOLD ME CATS CAN DO THAT!!

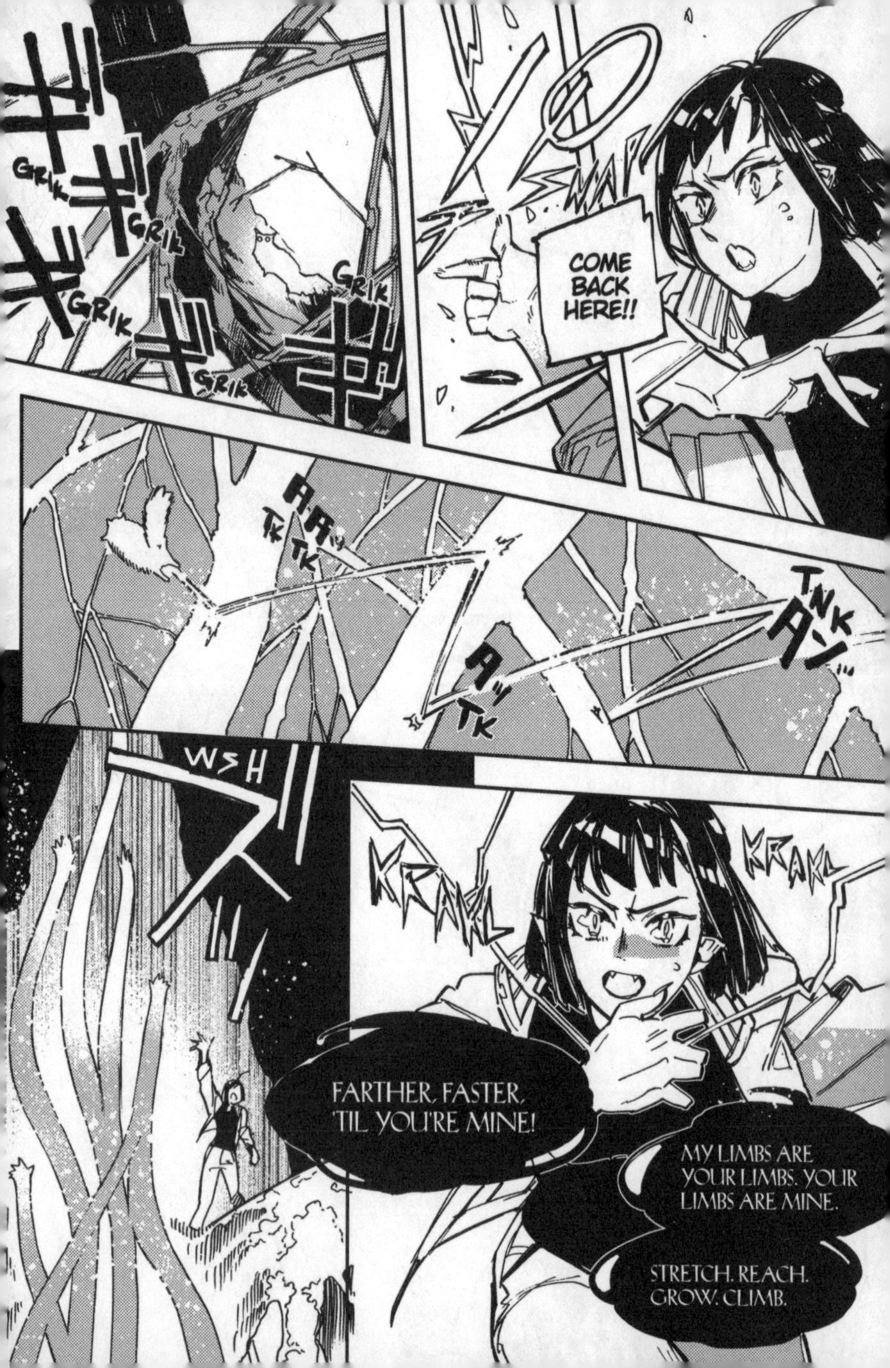
SNAP
COME BACK HERE!!
GRIK
GRIK
GRIK
GRIK
GRIK
GRIK
TNK
TK
AA
TK
TK
KRAKL
KRAKL
FARTHER, FASTER, 'TIL YOU'RE MINE!
MY LIMBS ARE YOUR LIMBS. YOUR LIMBS ARE MINE.
STRETCH. REACH. GROW. CLIMB.
WSH

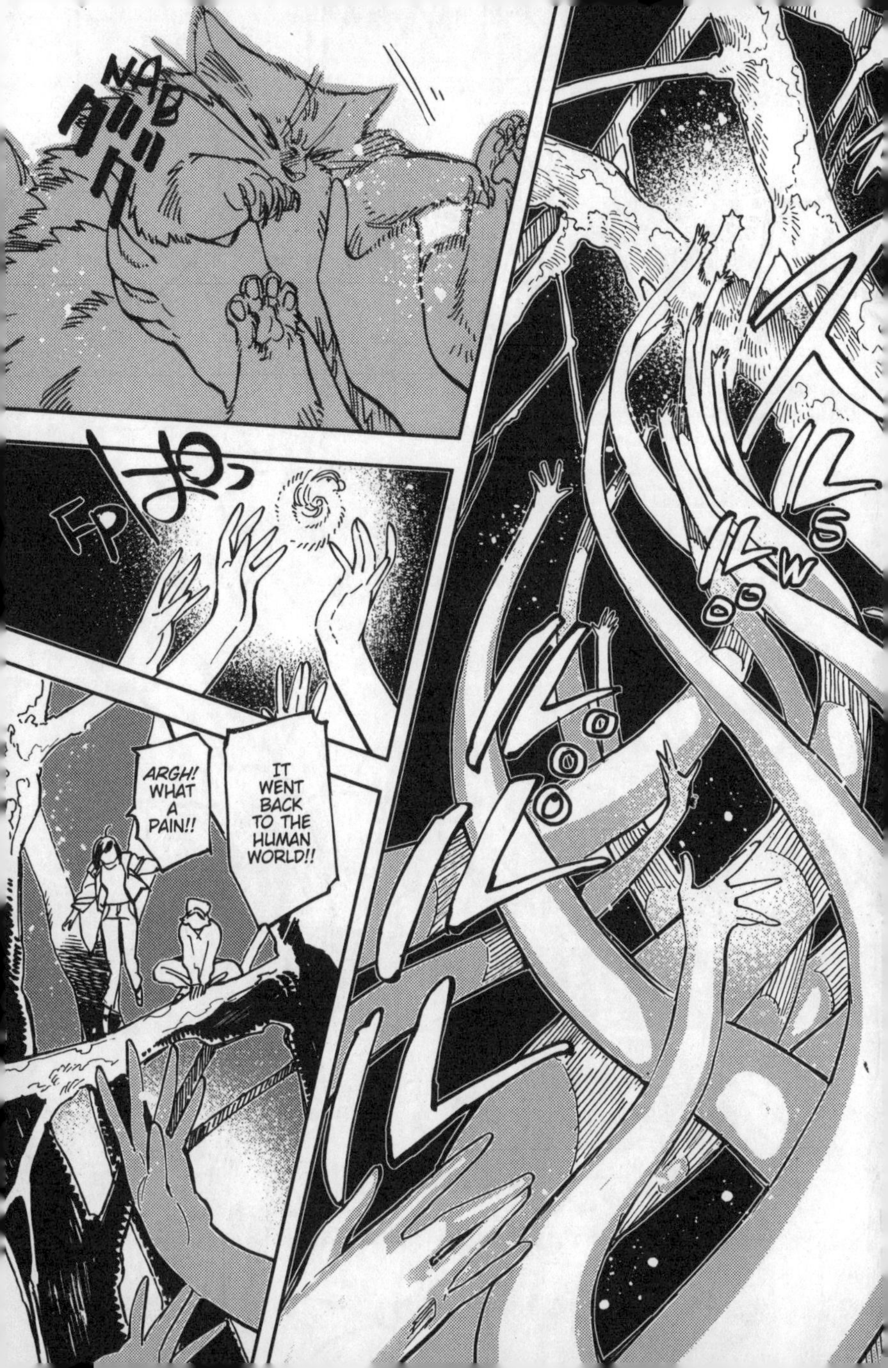
SWOOOOO
NAB
FP
IT WENT BACK TO THE HUMAN WORLD!!
ARGH! WHAT A PAIN!!

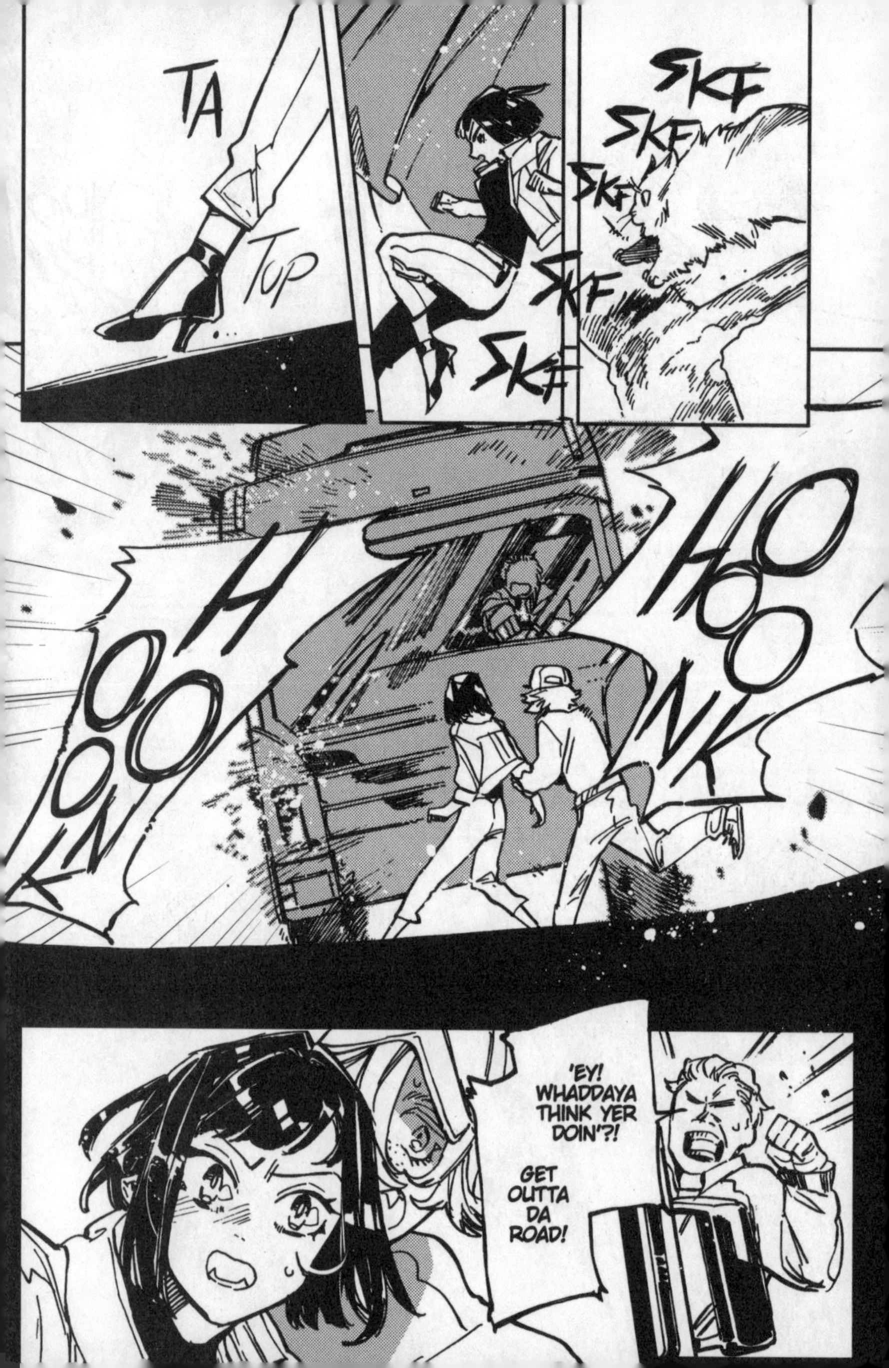
SKF
SKF
SKF
SKF
SKF
TA
TUP
...
HOOONK
HOOOONK
'EY! WHADDAYA THINK YER DOIN'?!
GET OUTTA DA ROAD!

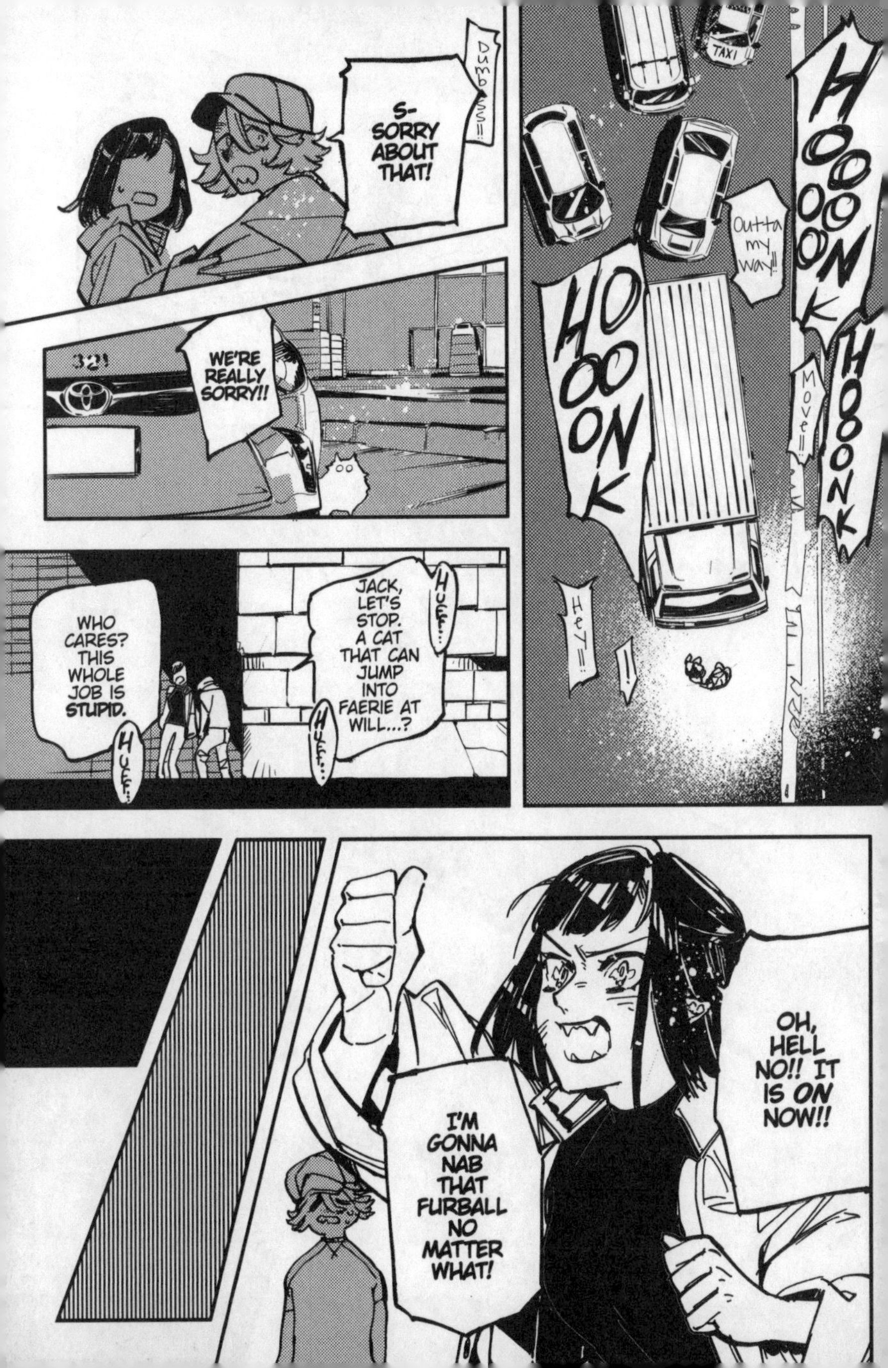
HOOOOONK
Outta my way!!
HOOOONK
Move!!
HOOOONK
Hey!!
!
Dumbass!!
S-SORRY ABOUT THAT!
WE'RE REALLY SORRY!!
HUFF...
JACK, LET'S STOP. A CAT THAT CAN JUMP INTO FAERIE AT WILL...?
HUFF...
WHO CARES? THIS WHOLE JOB IS STUPID.
HUFF...
OH, HELL NO!! IT IS ON NOW!!
I'M GONNA NAB THAT FURBALL NO MATTER WHAT!

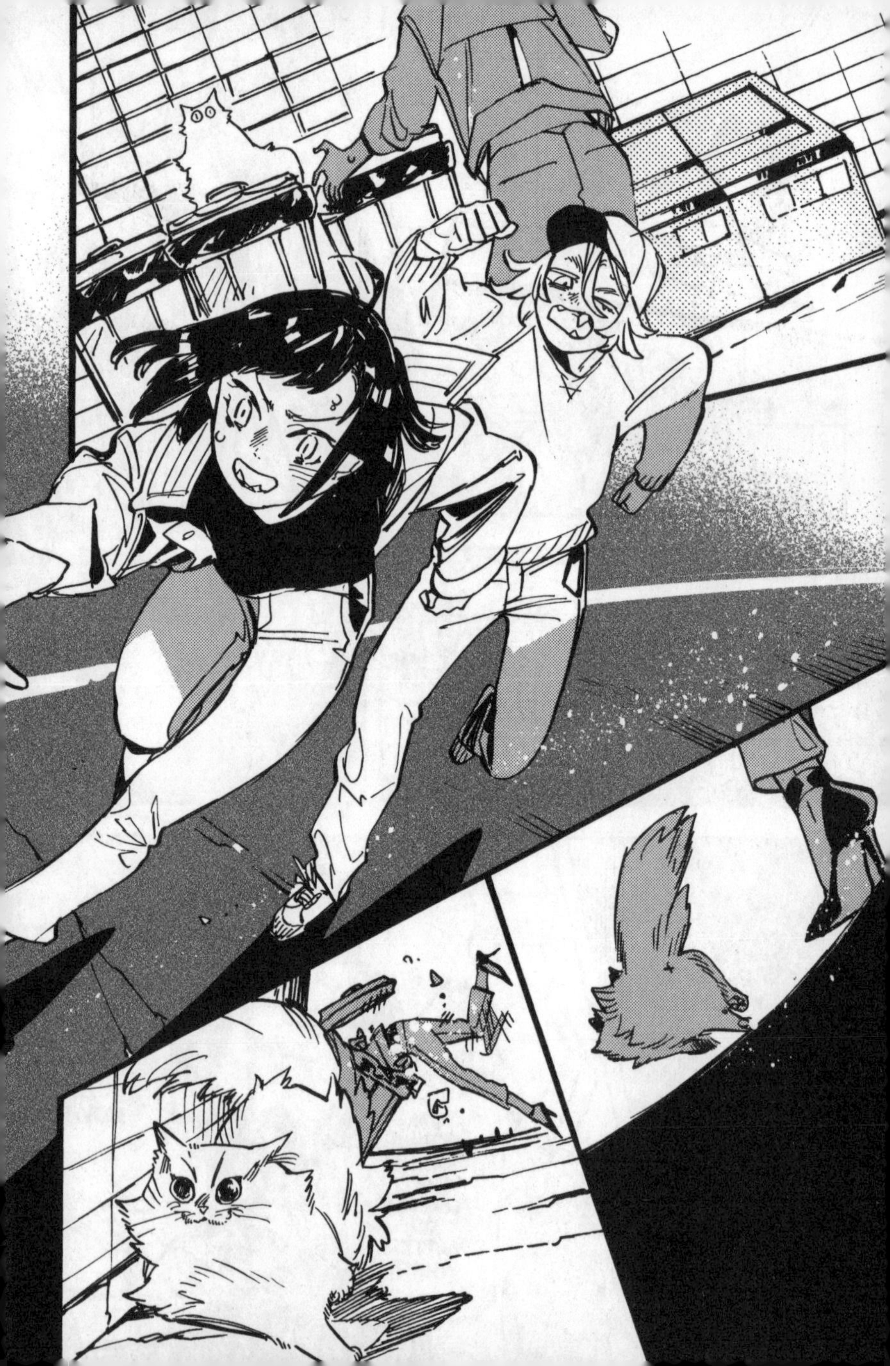

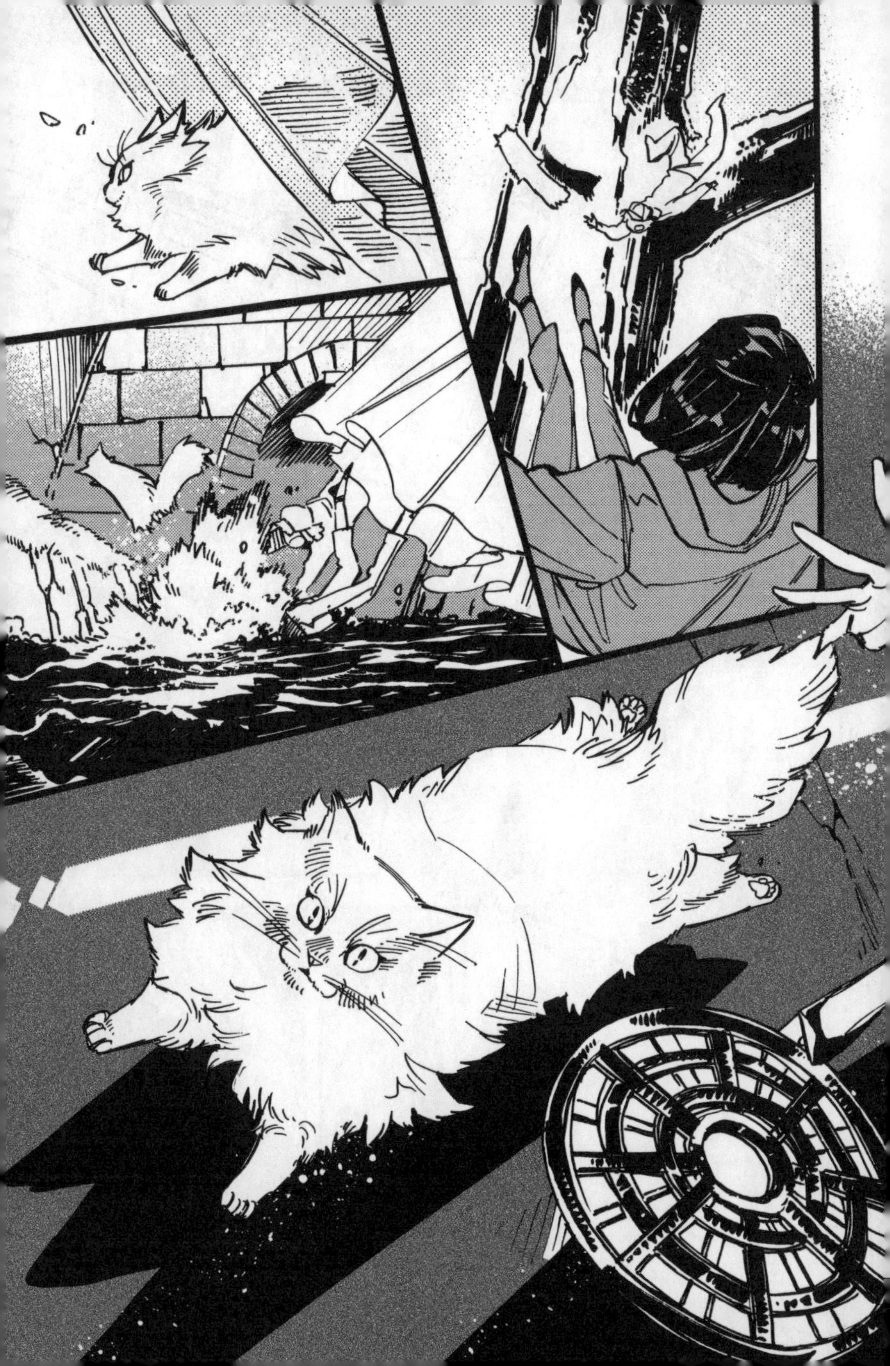

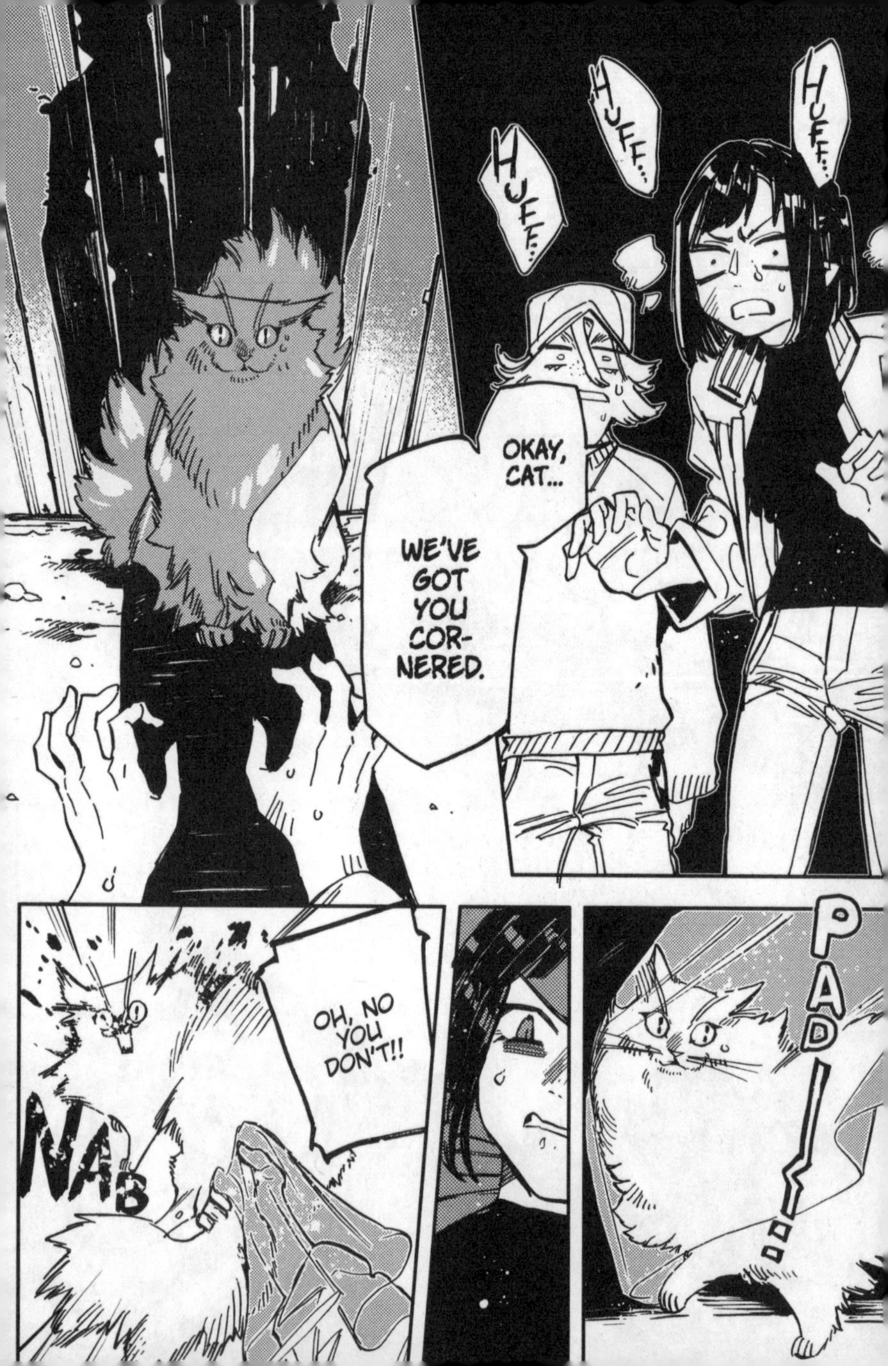
HUFF...
HUFF...
HUFF...
OKAY, CAT...
WE'VE GOT YOU COR-NERED.
PAD!!
OH, NO YOU DON'T!!
NAB

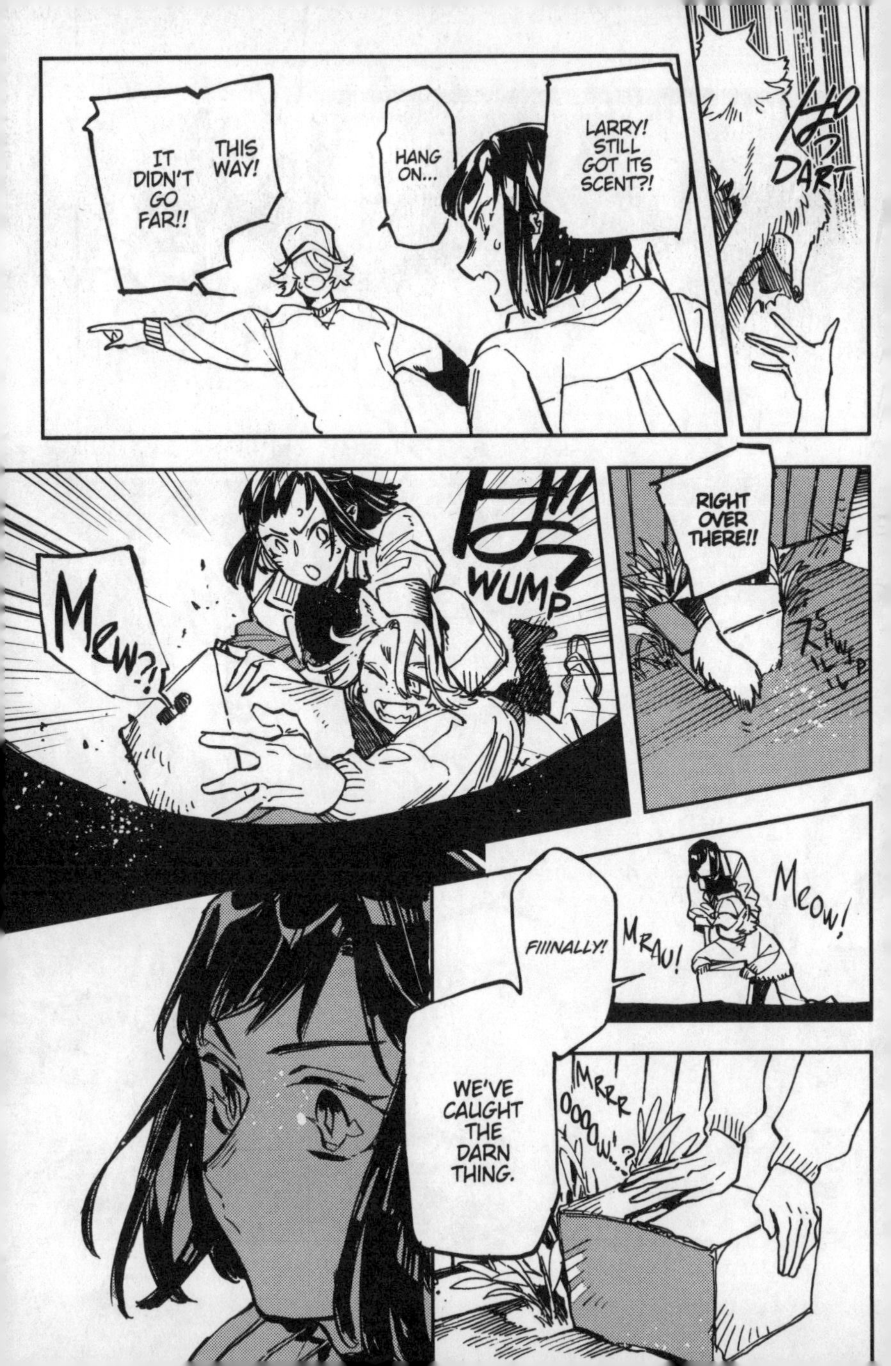

DART
LARRY! STILL GOT ITS SCENT?!
HANG ON...
THIS WAY!
IT DIDN'T GO FAR!!
RIGHT OVER THERE!!
SHWIP
WUMP
Mew?!
Meow!
MRAU!
FIIINALLY!
MRRR OOOOW...?
WE'VE CAUGHT THE DARN THING.

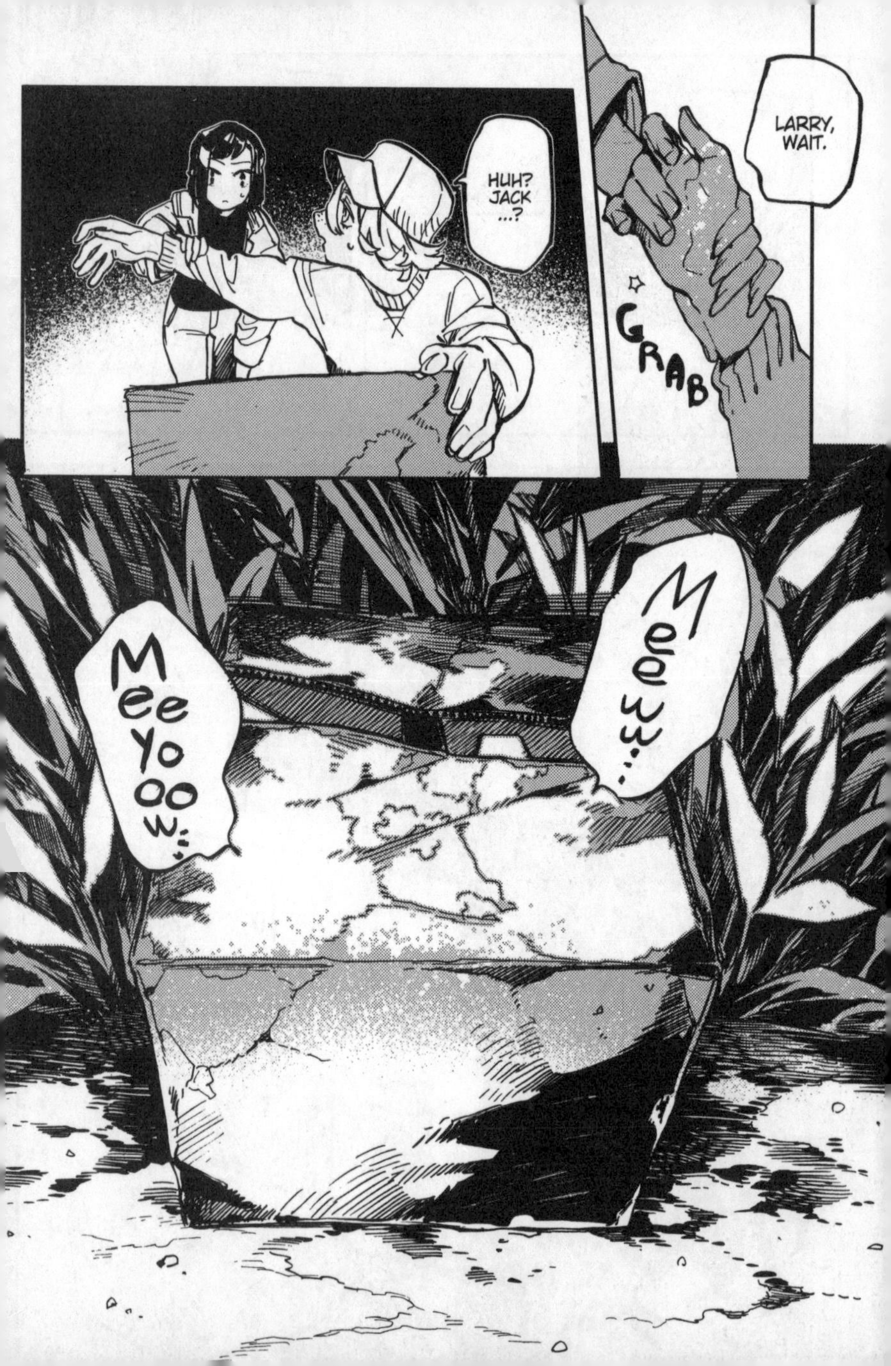
LARRY, WAIT.
GRAB
HUH? JACK ...?
Meeww...
Meeyooow...

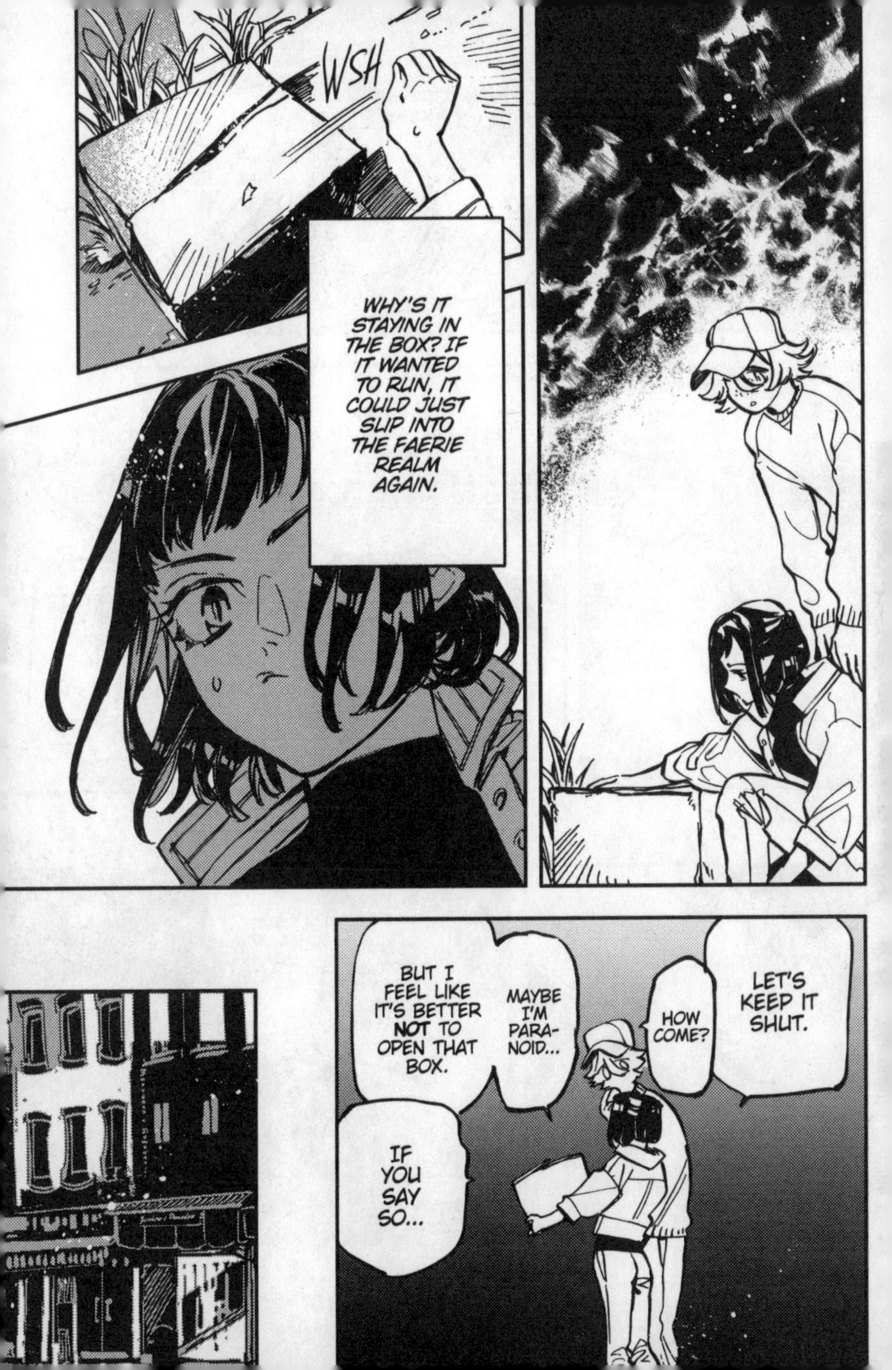
WSH
WHY'S IT STAYING IN THE BOX? IF IT WANTED TO RUN, IT COULD JUST SLIP INTO THE FAERIE REALM AGAIN.
LET'S KEEP IT SHUT.
HOW COME?
MAYBE I'M PARA-NOID...
BUT I FEEL LIKE IT'S BETTER **NOT** TO OPEN THAT BOX.
IF YOU SAY SO...

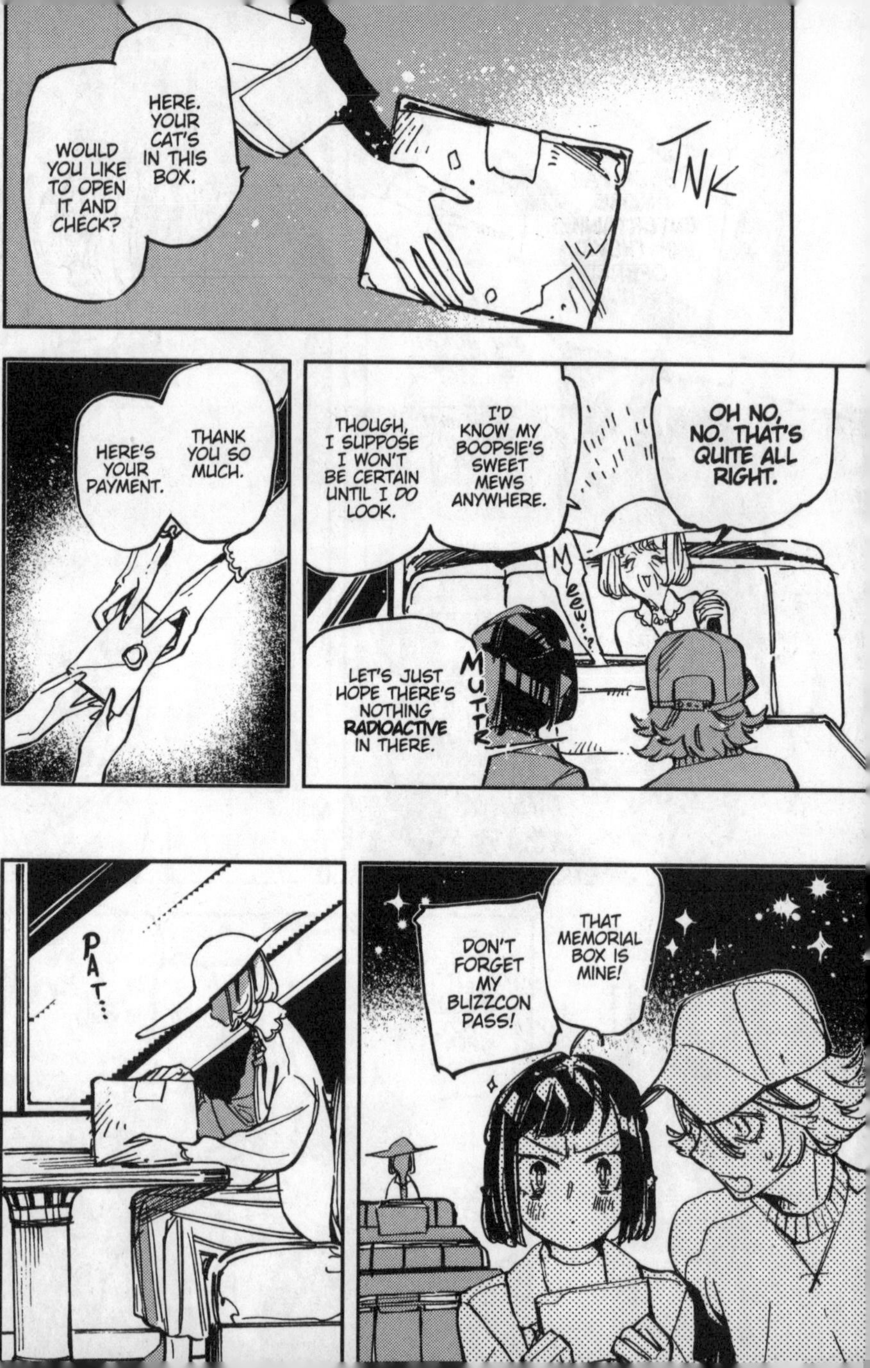
HERE. YOUR CAT'S IN THIS BOX.
WOULD YOU LIKE TO OPEN IT AND CHECK?
TNK
OH NO, NO. THAT'S QUITE ALL RIGHT.
I'D KNOW MY BOOPSIE'S SWEET MEWS ANYWHERE.
THOUGH, I SUPPOSE I WON'T BE CERTAIN UNTIL I DO LOOK.
Myeew...?
MUTTR
LET'S JUST HOPE THERE'S NOTHING RADIOACTIVE IN THERE.
THANK YOU SO MUCH.
HERE'S YOUR PAYMENT.
THAT MEMORIAL BOX IS MINE!
DON'T FORGET MY BLIZZCON PASS!
PAT...

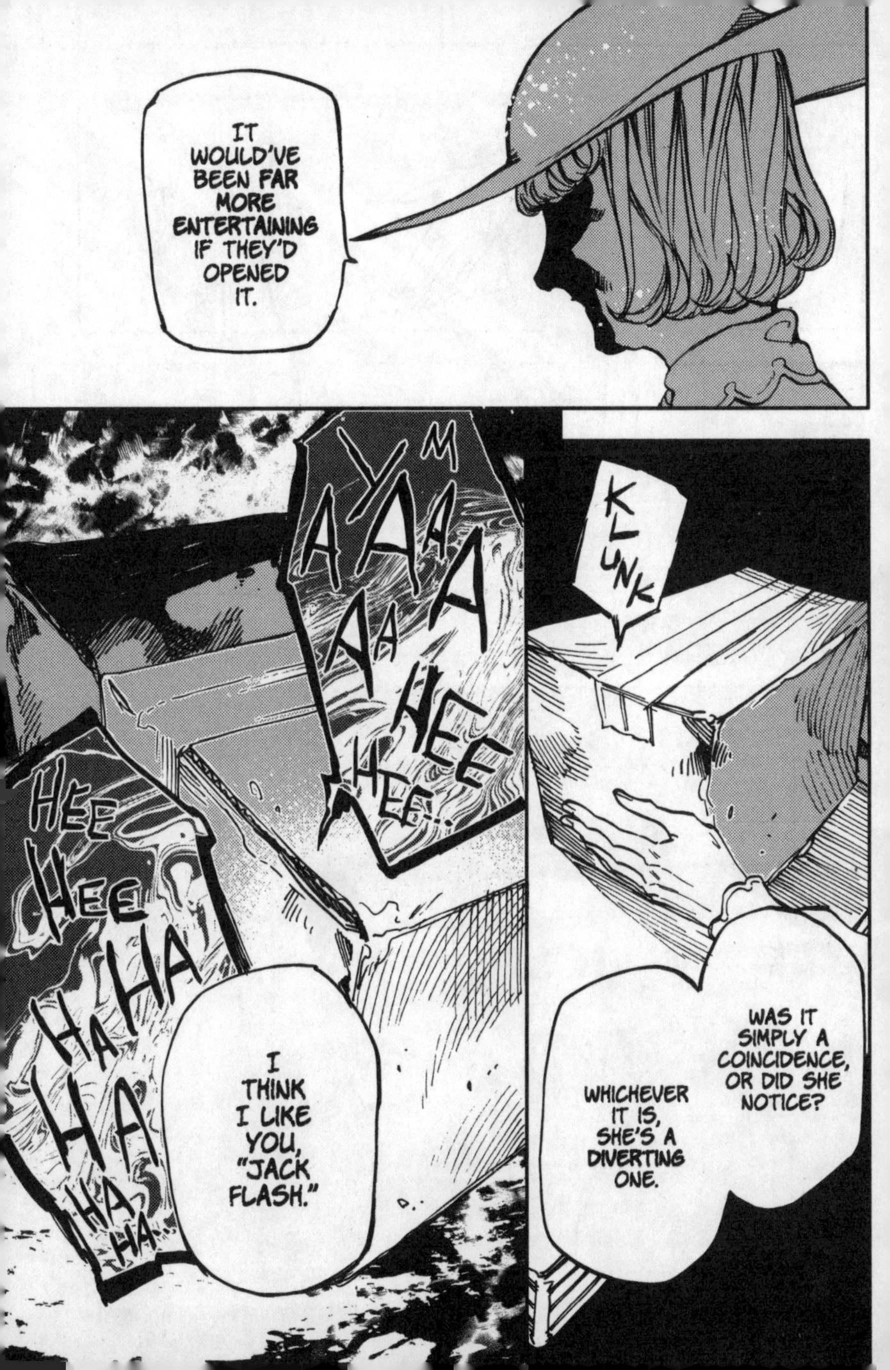
IT WOULD'VE BEEN FAR MORE ENTERTAINING IF THEY'D OPENED IT.
KLUNK
WAS IT SIMPLY A COINCIDENCE, OR DID SHE NOTICE?
WHICHEVER IT IS, SHE'S A DIVERTING ONE.
MYAAAAAA HEE HEE...
HEE HEE HAHA HA HA HA HA...
I THINK I LIKE YOU, "JACK FLASH."

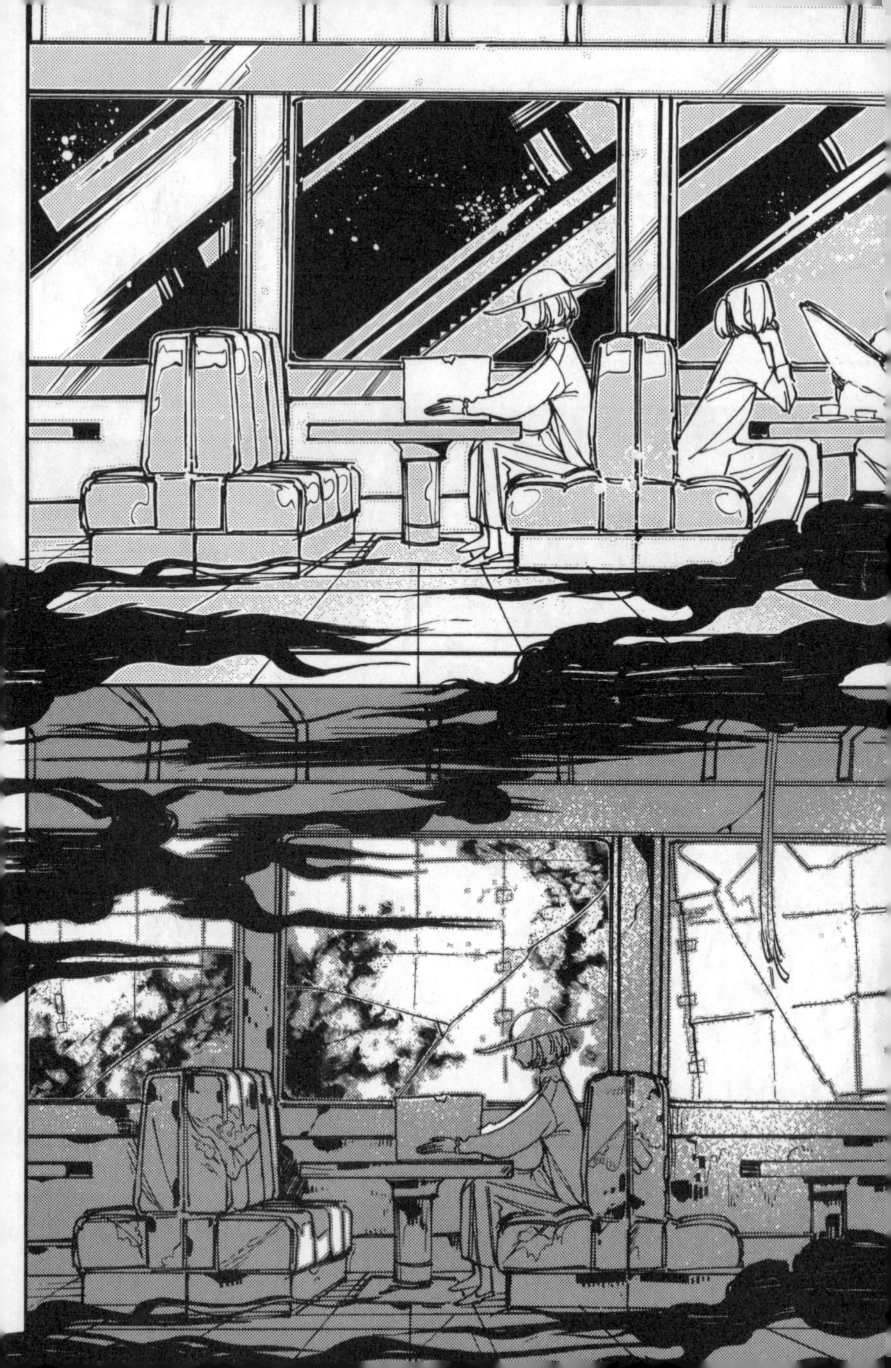

SEVEN SEAS ENTERTAINMENT PRESENTS

The Ancient Magus' Bride
JACK FLASH AND THE FAERIE CASE FILES
VOLUME 2

story: **YU GODAI**   art: **MAKO OIKAWA**   script supervisor: **KORE YAMAZAKI**

TRANSLATION
Adrienne Beck

ADAPTATION
Ysabet Reinhardt MacFarlane

LETTERING AND RETOUCH
Carolina Hernández Mendoza

COVER DESIGN
(LOGO) **Kris Aubin**   **Nicky Lim**

PROOFREADER
Dawn Davis
Janet Houck

EDITOR
Shanti Whitesides

PREPRESS TECHNICIAN
Rhiannon Rasmussen-Silverstein

PRODUCTION MANAGER
Lissa Pattillo

MANAGING EDITOR
Julie Davis

ASSOCIATE PUBLISHER
Adam Arnold

PUBLISHER
Jason DeAngelis

THE ANCIENT MAGUS' BRIDE PSA.75
JACK "THE FLASH" AND FAIRY INCIDENT VOL.2
©Kore Yamazaki @Mako Oikawa @Yu Godai 2020
Originally published in Japan in 2020 by MAG Garden Corporation, TOKYO.
English translation rights arranged through TOHAN CORPORATION, Tokyo.

Seven Seas press and purchase enquiries can be sent to Marketing Manager
Lianne Sentar at press@gomanga.com. Information regarding the distribution
and purchase of digital editions is available from Digital Manager CK Russell
at digital@gomanga.com.

Seven Seas and the Seven Seas logo are trademarks of
Seven Seas Entertainment. All rights reserved.

ISBN: 978-1-64505-961-5

Printed in Canada

First Printing: January 2021

10 9 8 7 6 5 4 3 2 1

FOLLOW US ONLINE: www.sevenseasentertainment.com

READING DIRECTIONS

This book reads from *right to left*, Japanese style.
If this is your first time reading manga, you start
reading from the top right panel on each page and
take it from there. If you get lost, just follow the
numbered diagram here. It may seem backwards at
first, but you'll get the hang of it! Have fun!!

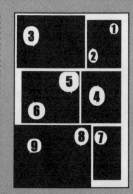

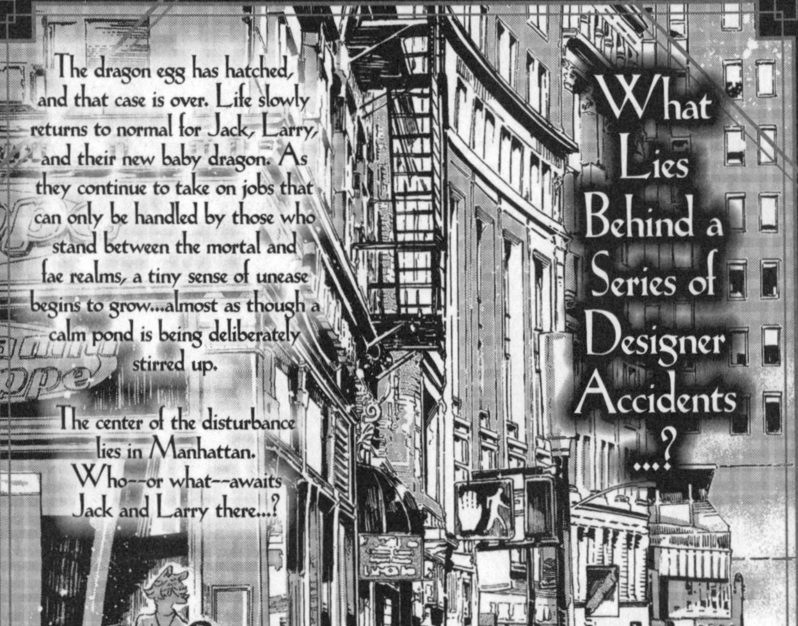
The dragon egg has hatched, and that case is over. Life slowly returns to normal for Jack, Larry, and their new baby dragon. As they continue to take on jobs that can only be handled by those who stand between the mortal and fae realms, a tiny sense of unease begins to grow...almost as though a calm pond is being deliberately stirred up.
The center of the disturbance lies in Manhattan. Who--or what--awaits Jack and Larry there...?
What Lies Behind a Series of Designer Accidents ...?

Delve deeper into *The Ancient Magus' Bride* universe with *Jack Flash*'s fresh take on the relationships between the human and the inhuman!

VOLUME 3 COMING SOON

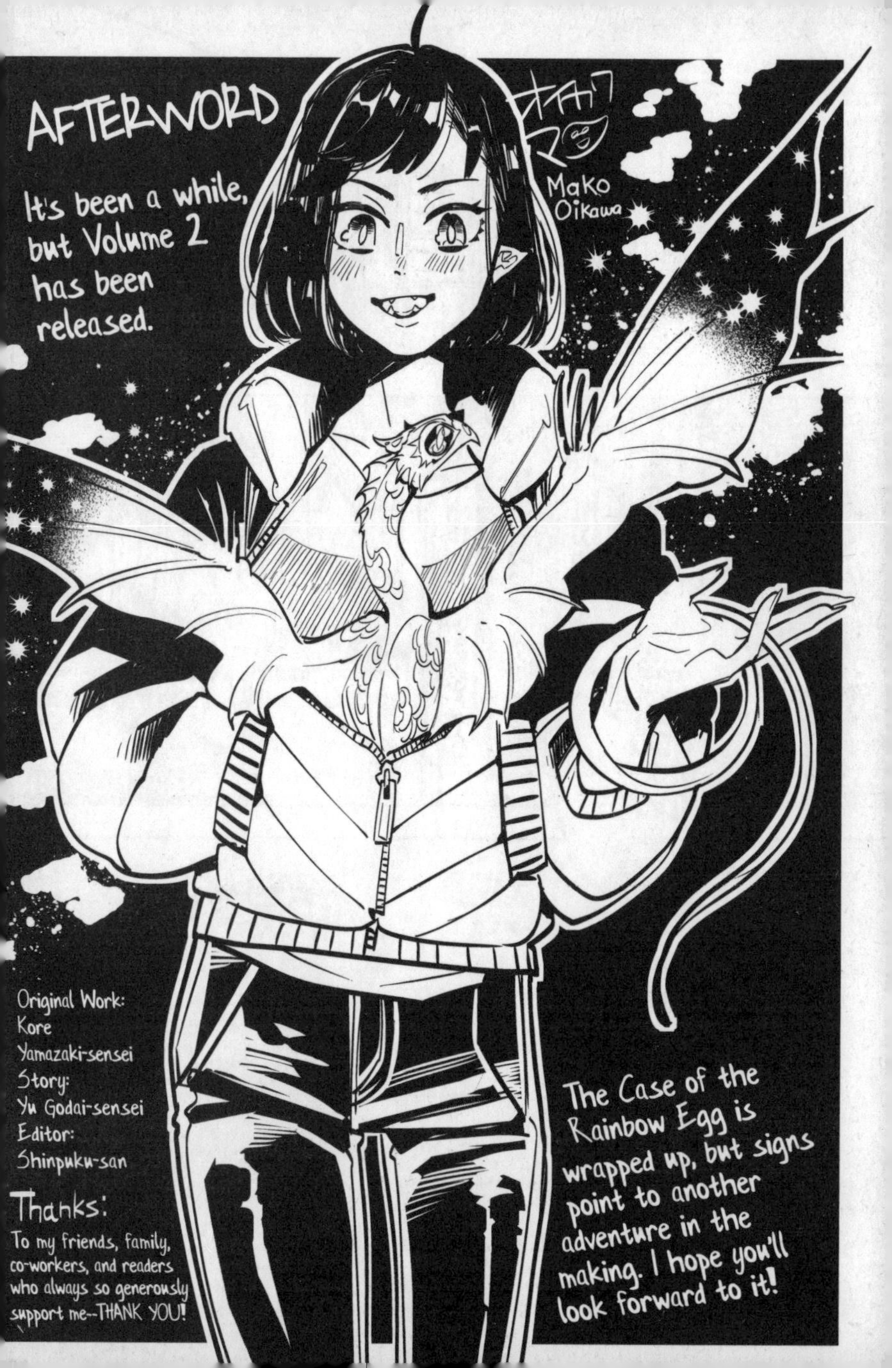
AFTERWORD
Mako Oikawa
It's been a while, but Volume 2 has been released.
The Case of the Rainbow Egg is wrapped up, but signs point to another adventure in the making. I hope you'll look forward to it!
Original Work: Kore Yamazaki-sensei
Story: Yu Godai-sensei
Editor: Shinpuku-san
Thanks:
To my friends, family, co-workers, and readers who always so generously support me--THANK YOU!

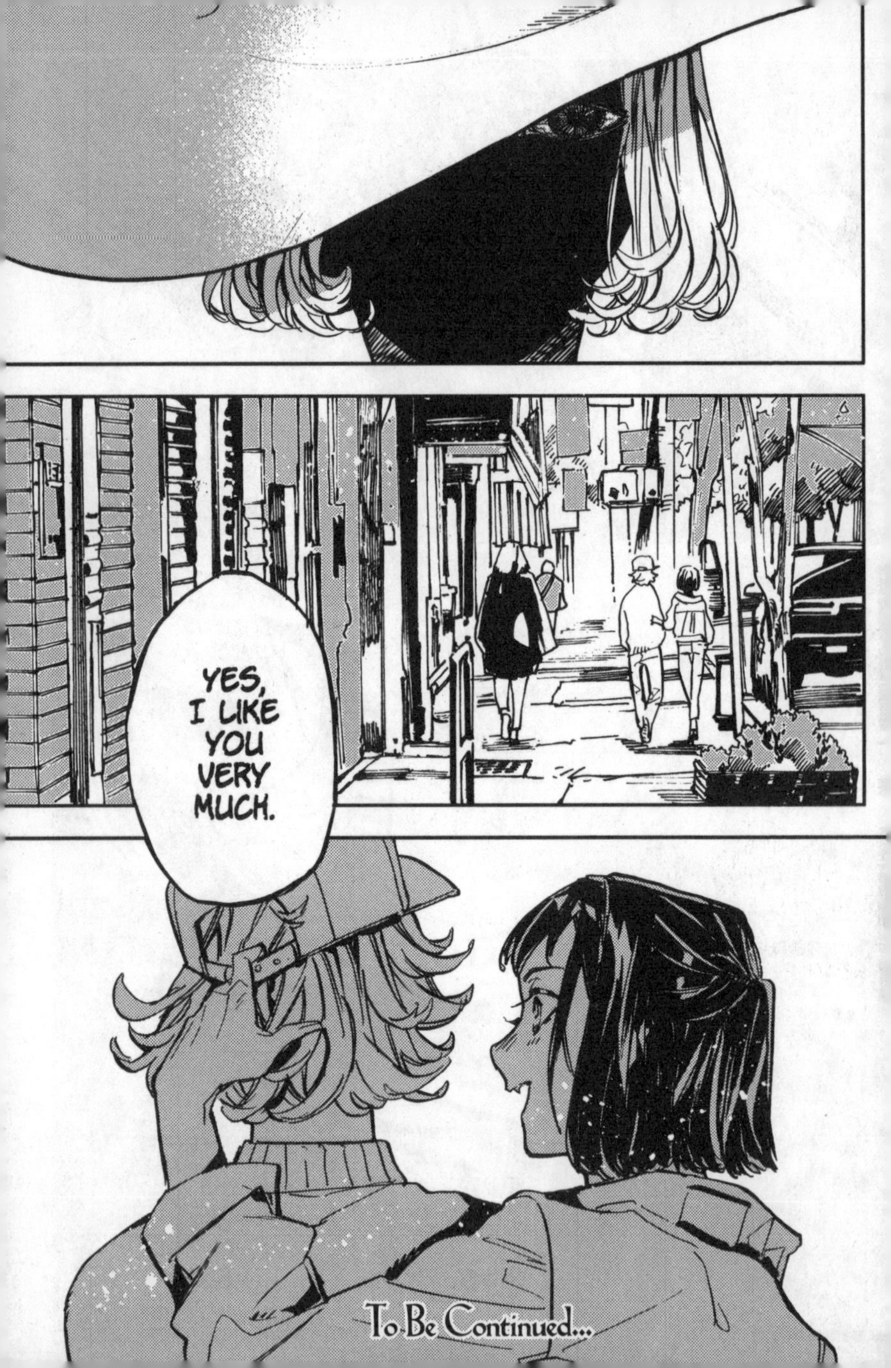
YES, I LIKE YOU VERY MUCH.
To Be Continued...

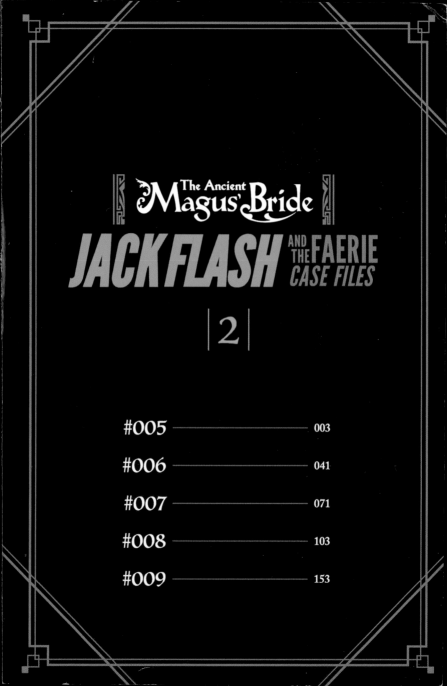

The Ancient Magus' Bride

JACK FLASH AND THE FAERIE CASE FILES

|2|

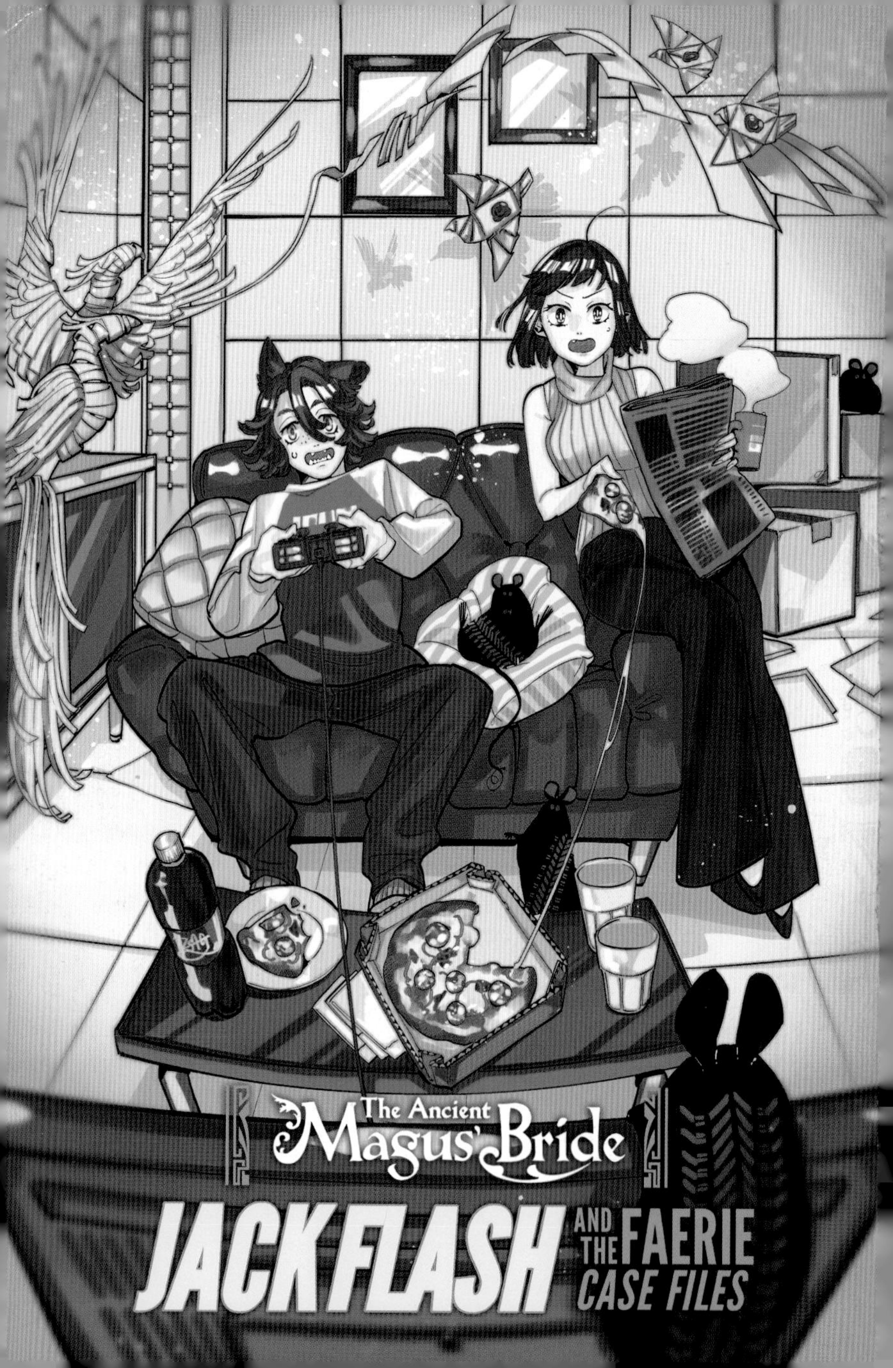
The Ancient
Magus' Bride
JACK FLASH
AND THE FAERIE
CASE FILES